BRITISH SHIPPING AND AUSTRALIA

1920–1939

BRITISH SHIPPING AND AUSTRALIA

1920-1939

BY

KEVIN BURLEY

Professor
Department of Economics
University of Western Ontario

CAMBRIDGE
AT THE UNIVERSITY PRESS
1968

Published by the Syndics of the Cambridge University Press
Bentley House, 200 Euston Road, London, N.W.1
American Branch: 32 East 57th Street, New York, N.Y. 10022

Library of Congress Catalogue Card Number: 68—10328

Printed in Great Britain
at the University Printing House, Cambridge
(Brooke Crutchley, University Printer)

CONTENTS

PREFACE

The study presented here concentrates upon the economic performance of a single sector of the British shipping industry and its relationship with Australia's oversea shipping needs during the inter-war years. The revival of international trade after the First World War was accompanied by a sharp expansion in the tonnage of the world's merchant fleet. As the twenties drew to a close and world trade declined, the excess tonnage on offer created severe problems. The thirties were years of difficulty, often acute, for British shipping as well as for the world's fleet as a whole. They were also critical years in Australian economic growth; the first half of the thirties especially being a period of crisis. For British shipping, links with Australia during the 'great depression' gave stability in employment, absent elsewhere in the world at this time.

My interest in shipping was first aroused by my late father's infectious enthusiasm for the sea. Although never in any way linked professionally with the sea it fascinated him throughout his life. On his retirement he talked of making a grain voyage from Australia in a windjammer. The idea of a study which traced the association between British shipping and Australia was the product of a three-year stay at the Australian National University in Canberra. The nature of Australia's shipping problems was vividly brought home to me during the lengthy return sea voyage on a cargo-liner.

I am indebted to all those who have helped in the collection and supply of material upon which this book is based—persons and institutions; private and official; in Britain and in Australia: I gratefully acknowledge their kindness, hospitality and assistance. I was fortunate in Canberra to work with N. G. Butlin, whose pioneer studies on Australian economic growth are indispensable to any study of the Australian economy. I am delighted to acknowledge the help he has given me in so many ways and for reading the manuscript. The encouragement given by Sir Keith Hancock, also of the Australian National University was of great value to me: his acquaintance with leading personalities in the British shipping industry unlocked many doors. To the companies and institutions which gave access to their records and helped with information generally I am particularly indebted. If I have not always felt able to applaud their past actions and decisions, I trust they will agree that my discussion has been objective. The manuscript was read by my colleagues W. H. B. Court and D. R. Wightman—both made fruitful suggestions. It was also read by S. G. Sturmey, author of the important work on British shipping mentioned in footnotes. Our interpretation of developments in shipping may not always coincide: this does not lessen my debt to him for his valuable comments. My thanks are due to the University of Birmingham for research assistance and to the staff of the university library. My greatest debt, however, is due to my wife for her unfailing good humour and patience.

K.B.

University of Birmingham, 1966

LIST OF TABLES

(*Except where otherwise stated each table refers to Australia as a whole*)

LIST OF FIGURES

ABBREVIATIONS

Brassey	*Brassey's Naval and Shipping Annual*
Butlin	N. G. Butlin, *Australian Domestic Product, Investment and Foreign Borrowing, 1861–1938/39* (1962)
C of S	Chamber of Shipping of the United Kingdom
C of A	Commonwealth of Australia
C.P.D.	Commonwealth of Australia, *Parliamentary Debates*
C.P.P.	Commonwealth of Australia, *Parliamentary Papers*
I.S.C.	Imperial Shipping Committee
Isserlis	L. Isserlis, 'Tramp shipping, cargoes and freights', *Journal of the Royal Statistical Society*, vol. 101, pp. 53–146
Oversea Trade	Commonwealth of Australia, Bureau of Census and Statistics, *Annual Oversea Trade Bulletin*
Production Bulletin	Commonwealth of Australia, Bureau of Census and Statistics, *Annual Production Bulletin*
Sheep and Wool Handbook	Commonwealth of Australia, Bureau of Agricultural Economics. *Statistical Handbook of the Sheep and Wool Industry* (Canberra, 1949)
S.M.H.	*Sydney Morning Herald*
Sturmey	S. G. Sturmey, *British Shipping and World Competition* (London, 1962)

Svendsen	A. S. Svendsen, *Seeverkehr und schiffahrtswirtschaft* (Bremen, 1958) [Transl.: *Sea Transport and Shipping Economics*]
Tpt. and Communications Bulletin	Commonwealth of Australia, Bureau of Census and Statistics, *Annual Transport and Communications Bulletin*
U.K.P.P.	*U.K. Parliamentary Papers*
U.K. Trade Report	*Reports made by the U.K. Trade Commissioner in Australia* to the Department of Overseas Trade of the Board of Trade. These were made frequently but not regularly. (The 'Brown Book' series; the title varies slightly.)
Year Book	Commonwealth of Australia, *Official Year Book*

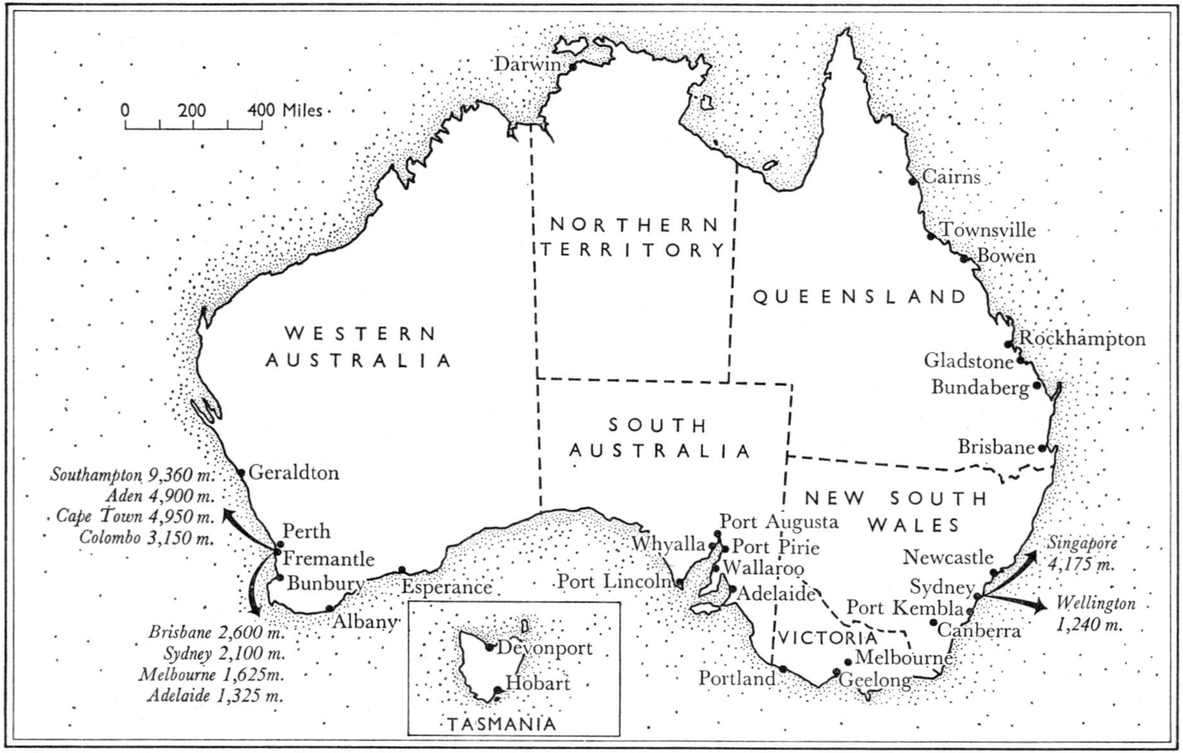
0 200 400 Miles
Darwin
NORTHERN TERRITORY
QUEENSLAND
WESTERN AUSTRALIA
SOUTH AUSTRALIA
NEW SOUTH WALES
VICTORIA
TASMANIA
Cairns
Townsville
Bowen
Rockhampton
Gladstone
Bundaberg
Brisbane
Geraldton
Perth
Fremantle
Bunbury
Albany
Esperance
Port Lincoln
Whyalla
Port Augusta
Port Pirie
Wallaroo
Adelaide
Portland
Geelong
Melbourne
Port Kembla
Canberra
Sydney
Newcastle
Devonport
Hobart
Southampton 9,360 m.
Aden 4,900 m.
Cape Town 4,950 m.
Colombo 3,150 m.
Brisbane 2,600 m.
Sydney 2,100 m.
Melbourne 1,625m.
Adelaide 1,325 m.
Singapore 4,175 m.
Wellington 1,240 m.

INTRODUCTION

Australia is a remote island continent 12,000 miles from the country from which it was first settled. It is geographically isolated. Colombo is 3,200 miles from Fremantle, and Singapore to the north is 4,200 miles from Sydney. Its nearest neighbour of any size, New Zealand, 1,200 miles across the Tasman, like Australia was first settled from Britain and faced similar problems of geographic isolation. From its earliest days of settlement Australia has depended upon ocean shipping for external contact. In part this reflects the persistence of political and cultural association with Britain and the continued influx of British migrants. It was due also to Australia's involvement in international trade from an early date. As oversea-transport costs relative to domestic costs tended to fall, more and more of Australia's products, which have a high bulk-to-value ratio, were brought into intercontinental trade.

The oversea shipping services upon which Australia's external trade has depended have largely been provided by fleets owned overseas. Although some participation by the locally registered fleet took place, as we shall see, it was never very significant. The importance of cheap shipping facilities to the Australian primary producer and the role of the export sector in the servicing of oversea debt commitments have always focussed attention upon Australia's oversea shipping services. Generally, Australian governments and successive generations of Australian primary producers and shippers have been critical of the adequacy, quality and price of the services provided. They have been especially critical of the level of freight rates. Local dislike and suspicion has often been expressed in forthright condemnation. It has also induced the Commonwealth government to adopt policies not always found elsewhere, including, for a time, the operation of a state-owned oversea-merchant fleet.

This study aims at an examination of Australia's oversea-shipping services during the inter-war years, in many ways a crucial period in Australian economic development. The study seeks to test the validity of Australian criticism of the oversea-shipping services upon which Australia relied. Expressed less narrowly it seeks to determine whether the services provided were appropriate, did they promote or obstruct Australian economic growth? It is a complex problem. Factors not always obvious merit notice. The demand for oversea shipping in Australia stemmed primarily from the needs of the export sector of the economy. Demand factors in oversea markets for Australian products exerted considerable influence on the demand for shipping in Australia. Markets elsewhere in the world moreover influenced the world's shipping industry as a whole and thus also that section of the industry which supplied Australia's oversea services. Some consideration of this complex of factors is necessary. The world depression in the trade in primary products, for example, had a profound effect upon demand in Australia for oversea shipping.

The much debated question of freight rates provides another illustration of the interdependence of diverse factors. It did not always have the simple explanation that Australians imagined nor the simple solution they advocated. The overriding importance of exports placed imports in the position of backhaul cargoes and raises the relationship of freight rates to Australian industry. The diversification of the Australian economy which characterises the inter-war years aimed at import replacement. In large measure it relied upon the shelter of tariff protection. But imports carried as backhaul cargoes in lieu of ballast at low rates (in expectation of high outbound rates) reduces the protection of distance. Local infant industry demands greater protection. The export sector, competing in world markets, welcomes high inbound rates if, as a result, outbound rates are low. But high inbound rates apply also to items whose manufacture is not being pursued locally. Here both importer and consumer unite in protest.

Because of the predominant role of British shipping in the Australian oversea-shipping scene this book is also a study in the development of a single sector of the U.K. shipping industry. A theme of obvious importance here is the economics of providing maritime services in the circumstances outlined. Thanks to the cooperation of institutions within the British shipping industry, access to private records has made it possible to add some flesh to the skeletal framework. Although the work is intended primarily as an economic profile it is impossible with any industrial study to divorce economic factors from their political and social environment. The present study, moreover, is concerned with developments and with an industry where non-economic considerations are likely to be particularly important. An industry owned, organised, and controlled in one country and supplying essential services to another is poised on a slender tight-rope; as foreign lines servicing the U.S.A. are at present aware. Many of the developments outlined below were the product of intervention by either the U.K. or by the Australian governments. The economic significance of the shipping industry in the British economy is well known, public interest in the industry as a whole was inevitable. Equally inevitable was intervention by the Australian government. Export earnings were vital in debt servicing. Exports consisted of primary products on which, it is argued in chapter 7, freight rates often formed a significant charge. Official interest was thus to be expected. Discussion in the following chapters which seeks to test economic hypotheses all too often is engulfed by considerations of a non-economic kind.

The choice of period for study has been dictated by a number of factors. The two decades between the wars are bounded at beginning and end by periods of exceptional abnormality. From our viewpoint, a violent upheaval is to be traced in the use of shipping, in shipbuilding and in world trade. Over a wide range of human activity the repercussions of the two wars tend to throw into sharp contrast the years before and the years which followed. Australian experience after each war is similarly sharply differentiated. In the oversea-shipping sector the years before 1914 belong more to the nineteenth century than to the present. The persistence of older types of vessels, for example, characterises the Australian oversea-shipping scene before 1914. For a variety of reasons connected with ocean currents, prevailing winds, Australia's role in world trade, and the pattern of trade developed in the oversea sector, sailing ships were still in common use right down to 1914. Long after sailing ships had virtually disappeared from other major shipping routes, employment continued to be found for them in the Australian trade.

The years since 1945 similarly reveal qualitative as well as quantitative differences as compared with inter-war shipping activity. Any study which attempted to span either or both wars would be compelled to discuss the expedients of wartime control of shipping. In terms of general economic development also, Australia between the wars is qualitatively to be distinguished from the pre-1914 or post-1945 years. There is, in addition, the prosaic but more compelling restriction imposed by the availability of source material. This in fact confined the choice of period to the inter-war years. Few of the private shipping institutions which generously gave access to their records seem still to be in possession of material relating to the years before 1914. Few are entirely happy about granting access to records of the immediate past. In part making virtue of necessity, in part because the inter-war years have an interest and unity of their own, the emphasis throughout the work is thus upon the years 1920 to 1939. Where both relevant and possible, however, comparisons are made with developments before and after our period.

The present study concentrates upon the oversea sector but in the local scene also shipping has always played a significant role. Although the continent of Australia is almost as large as Europe minus the U.S.S.R., the bulk of Australia's small population has always hugged the coast, spread out thinly along the south and east of the 12,000 miles of coastline. Urban growth has occurred at widely separated points on the mainland or across the Bass Strait. Sydney in the east is about 2,100 sea miles from Fremantle in the west. The distance is almost the same as the return journey from Southampton to Gibraltar; it is only 900 miles less than that separating Southampton and New York. In eastern Australia distances between mainland state capitals are at least 500 miles, Hobart is 470 miles from Melbourne.

Apart from the maintenance of communications with Tasmania, the use of the sea was induced along the mainland coast by the physical configuration of the interior. Distance, the nature of the terrain, which itself encouraged coastbound settlement, and the absence of any developed internal communication system, in the past has often restricted the means of access to sea transport. The introduction of railways brought no immediate change. The artificial separation created by variations in rail gauges, the continued sparseness of inland settlement, and the competitive nature of coastwise-freight rates checked any sudden decline of the coasting trade. Today, internal air services, road haulage, and better integrated rail systems provide more efficient competition. Some traffic has indeed been lost to the newer forms of transport. But the continued expansion of domestic trade; the use of modern, purpose-designed ships; improved port equipment and advances in cargo-handling techniques; have sustained demand for coastwise-shipping facilities. The quantity of inter-state cargo moved by sea in 1955 was about 40% greater than the immediate pre-war figure. The trend is still upwards. The 1960 total was 10% higher than that of 1955 and the 1964 total 20% up on 1960. In the oversea sector, ocean transport continues to be as vital as before. Although not without setbacks, the expansion of trade has not only been maintained but considerably increased. The total of inbound and outbound oversea cargo of 12 million tons in 1939 has today soared to 46 million. For most of it the sea remains the only practicable outlet. Even with passenger traffic, despite the encroachment of international air services, the sea journey is still preferred by many and about 70% continues to be seaborne.

For the period chosen for examination, the following discussion distinguishes between the oversea and coastal sectors, the first being served mainly by fleets owned overseas, the second by the locally registered fleet. Before the introduction of the cabotage restrictions of the Navigation Act on 1 July 1921 all vessels, wherever owned, were free to engage in the coastal trade of Australia. It was not uncommon for deep-sea-going vessels to carry passengers and cargo between the east and west, and between Tasmania and mainland states. It is thus impossible to draw any precise boundary between the shipping employed respectively in the oversea and coastal sectors at this time. Nevertheless, even before 1921, the bulk of the seaborne intra- and inter-state trade was probably always carried by locally registered fleets. After 1 July 1921 local fleets were formally given exclusive rights to the coastal trade of Australia including the Territories of Papua and New Guinea (the latter acquired under League of Nations mandate). Originally, we need not doubt, local registration of a vessel was automatically and completely synonymous with local ownership. This is to suggest that in contrast with the oversea sector, local enterprise and resources were always in the past conspicuous in the provision of shipping for the coastal services. By the 1920s, however, it would seem that oversea capital was being injected into the locally registered coastal shipping services. In 1924 it was asserted in the First Report of the Royal Commission on the Navigation Act that Australian coastal services had become an offshoot of the U.K. shipping industry: 'in order not to waste ships and money in competing with the Australian [*sc.* coastal shipping] companies, the English combine [*sc.* the 'Inchcape' Group] has...acquired controlling interests in almost every Australian company'.[1] In federal parliament the reply to a question seeking to determine the ownership of coasting companies alleged that no official source was available to provide the information. The chairman of the Adelaide Steamship Company Ltd, roundly denied that *his* company was owned by expatriate shipping interests. Only 14 of the 2,507 shareholders were resident in England he announced at a meeting in 1924. They had all been domiciled in Australia at one time and between them owned a mere 1 % of share capital.[2]

Nevertheless, it seems certain that by the beginning of our period a large measure of control of the Australian coastal-shipping industry had indeed passed to British companies. This suggestion is supported indirectly by the indifference to the coastal trade shown later by the British shipping industry. Subsequent amendments of the Navigation Act opened the coastal trade once more to British shipping, especially between Tasmania and the mainland. Little use seems to have been made of this concession. Important although it is in the total shipping scene, the coastwise movement of cargo may thus safely be excluded from present discussion. Except in so far as the coastal trade affected port development and thus impinged upon the oversea sector, we are here concerned only with Australia's

[1] *C.P.P.* 1923/4, II, 1,048, 1,116.
[2] *C.P.D.* vol. 117, p. 2,939. *Fairplay* vol. 93, pp. 320–2, 421.

oversea-shipping services. In passing it is perhaps worth noting that the quantity of inter-state cargo shipped and discharged in Australian ports exceeded the tonnage of oversea cargo in all but five of the inter-war years. The somewhat lower totals recorded in these years largely reflects the reduction of coal cargoes during the N.S.W. coal strike. Between 1920/1 and 1938/9, moreover, inter-state cargo increased by 80 % to 18 million tons. Oversea cargo, as discussed more fully below, rose much more modestly by one third to about $12\frac{1}{2}$ million tons a year.

The provision of shipping services in the oversea sector presents a sharp contrast. Australia has always depended heavily, more obviously, and more directly upon the merchant fleets of other nations, above all on the British merchant fleet. Dependence upon the U.K. was in origin the product of historical connections. Continued dependence upon the fleets of others largely reflects the inadequacy of local resources to finance an oversea-shipping industry of appropriate size. Some locally owned vessels moved into the oversea sector from time to time and local companies, with the aid of mail subsidies, maintained a regular service with the island territories. But the size and composition of the privately owned Australian merchant fleet was never such as to provide any serious competition in the external sector to oversea fleets owned overseas.

Shipping was, and is, a vital factor in the country's economy. It was, and is, a factor attracting government notice. Illustrations are given below of the preoccupation of successive Australian governments with the problem and of their uneasiness at dependence upon fleets owned overseas. In contrast with some other countries the Australian government was unable, or unwilling, to offer building and operating subsidies high enough to encourage local effort. But with the intention of checking or controlling oversea fleets the Commonwealth Government Shipping Line, a war-time creation of Prime Minister Hughes, was retained during the early years of our period. For a few brief years the combination of Australian private- and government-owned shipping began to make an impression in the oversea sector. With the sale to oversea buyers of the state-owned line, however, the oversea-owned fleets regained their virtual monopoly.

Before 1900 foreign competition was negligible. Cultural and political affinity, the concentration of Australia's oversea trade on Britain, and British predominance in ocean carrying, ensured that the oversea-shipping services were overwhelmingly provided by the British shipping industry. Since 1900, with the growth of competing European fleets and the diversification of Australia's oversea trade, the lead enjoyed by the U.K. has been steadily reduced. Nevertheless, even in 1965, it still by far outranked its nearest rivals although its share of the total is now only some 35 %. Between the wars 'British' vessels regularly supplied more than one-half of the shipping tonnage entering Australian ports from overseas. The term 'British' in this context is somewhat misleading, however. It is the term commonly used both in imperial and in Commonwealth records to identify shipping registered in *any* British Commonwealth country. If, therefore, we exclude ships registered in Australia and New Zealand (which tended to restrict their activities to Australasian waters) and those registered in other 'British' countries, the significance of the U.K. merchant service for Australia is better illustrated. Omitting such tonnage it is to be noted that the proportion of the total provided by the British shipping industry was never less than about 60 % throughout the inter-war years; in some years it amounted to more than 65 % and on occasions to as much as 70 %. From the slightly different viewpoint of cargo carried, rather than the tonnage of shipping used, a similar pattern is to be traced. Excluding cargo carried by ships registered in Australia and New Zealand, in most of the inter-war years 55 % to 65 % of oversea cargo was carried by ships registered in the U.K. During the depression years, when imports were restricted, the U.K. share of the reduced total fell to only 50 %. Taking the period as a whole, almost two-thirds of oversea cargo discharged and shipped was carried in British ships.[1] From the Australian point of view, until very recently in fact, the most important item of invisible trade between Australia and the U.K. has been the payments to Britain for shipping

[1] To prevent confusion the U.K. shipping industry is referred to either in this form or, more simply, as the British shipping industry. Where it is necessary to refer collectively to vessels registered in *any* British Commonwealth country inverted commas are used to differentiate, thus: 'British'.

charges. As late as the 1950s it accounted for more than one third of all Australia's invisible payments to Britain.[1]

Foreign shipping became more conspicuous in the Australian carrying trade after 1900. In the years before the First World War, Messageries Maritimes introduced regular sailings between France and the French Pacific via Australian ports. Norddeutscher Lloyd and the German-Australian Steamship Company ships also became regular visitors to Australian ports with a total tonnage close to a half million on the eve of the war. The increasingly international composition of Australia's oversea services after 1900 reflects two trends. First, the diversification within, and widening of, the country's oversea trade. Secondly, national self-sufficiency in carrying aimed at by certain European governments. Voyages made by such ships, when the direction of Australia's oversea trade itself was widening, tended to be between the country of registration (or its oversea dependencies) and Australia. In 1929/30, for example, well over a half of the total Dutch tonnage entered at Australian ports arrived from and returned to the Netherlands East Indies. In the same year, more than 90% of U.S. ships calling at Australia came from, or left for, ports in the U.S.A. The conspicuous exception in the pattern of foreign shipping is the Norwegian fleet which developed more noticeably as a general carrier in Australia's oversea trade. In 1929/30, for example, of some 300,000 tons of Norwegian shipping which visited Australia, only 9,000 tons was entered as arriving from Norway and only 58,000 tons left for the mother country.

Judged on the criterion of tonnage employed, the Australian sector at first sight would appear to have been relatively insignificant for British shipping as a whole. U.K. Board of Trade records, which group arrivals and departures into thirteen trade routes, show that British arrivals and clearances with cargo on the Australasian route represented a mere 5% to 7% of all British tonnage. But this is misleading. The Australian sector had an importance for British shipping which the statistics tend to conceal. Shipping movements of the British fleet were overwhelmingly dominated by four major trade routes: Europe, the

[1] J. O. N. Perkins, *Britain and Australia: Economic Relationships in the 1950s* (Melbourne, 1962), p. 16.

Mediterranean, and the Atlantic coast of North and South America. In aggregate they employed about 70 % of British shipping in each of the inter-war years. The remaining nine routes between them account for 30 %. Not one of the nine employed as much as 10 % of the shipping in any of the years under discussion. But the four dominant routes mentioned were not the exclusive preserve of British shipping; considerable foreign competition was encountered. No less than 80 % of the foreign shipping entering or clearing the U.K. was to be found on these four routes. On the trade route between the U.K. and Australasia, in contrast, foreign shipping was quite insignificant, never reaching 1 % of tonnage cleared in any one of the inter-war years nor more than 5 % of tonnage entered.

Australia's oversea services had an importance also for British shipping in other ways which a statistical ranking of entries to British ports fails to illustrate. As well as holding a virtual monopoly of the direct trade between the U.K. and Australia, British shipping was active on other Australian services. Perhaps more than in other parts of the world which rely extensively upon expatriate shipping services, Australia's oversea shipping is not a single product, single market industry. The services are required not only for the more obvious link between Europe and Australia, but also for the carrying trade between Australia and Asia and the Americas. For the British shipping industry the provision of Australia's overseas services did not begin and end with direct routes between Australia and the U.K. The total tonnage of British-vessel arrivals in Australia always exceeded by far the amount arriving direct from the U.K. The discrepancy between the two figures, moreover, tended to widen during the inter-war years, reflecting the expansion of activity by the British merchant fleet in Australia's oversea trade. In the immediate post-war years the total tonnage of U.K. registered vessels entering Australian ports was about 2·7 million of which 1·5 million was entered direct from Britain. On the eve of the Second World War the total had risen to about 3·5 million, but the tonnage entered direct from the U.K. remained about the same as twenty years earlier.

The expansion of demand in Australia for oversea tonnage and the increased supply of British shipping in response is a noteworthy feature of the Australian inter-war scene. It was especially important for British shipping in offering an expanded area of employment at a time when a number of developments were tending to diminish British supremacy. In 1900 the British mercantile fleet accounted for about 45 % of world tonnage. By 1913 the proportion had fallen to 39 %. The growth of national fleets before the First World War inevitably narrowed the gap, but it was the war which accelerated the relative decline of British shipping. The repercussions of war on shipping were more direct and more lasting than elsewhere in the British economy.[1] In 1920, although war losses had been made good, the British fleet amounted to only 32 % of world tonnage. Ten years later its share was down to 30 % and by 1939 was down to about 26 %.

In Australia's oversea services, in contrast, the British lead was sustained throughout the period. British shipping was relatively as important in 1939 as in 1920, notwithstanding the increase in the total tonnage in use. As a carrier in the Australian trade, moreover, to anticipate a point made in a subsequent chapter, the British fleet was more, not less, important in 1939 than it had been in the early 1920s. On the eve of the Second World War British shipping was carrying an increased proportion of both inbound and outbound cargo.

During the years of depressed trade in the early 1930s the supply of services for the Australian trade offered sustained employment for British shipping. When British ships were being laid up in large numbers in home ports, the tonnage needs of the Australian trade were actually increasing. During the trade recession much tonnage in the world was broken up or taken out of commission and laid up. An allusive, rather than conclusive, illustration of the importance of the Australian sector in maintaining employment for British shipping in the slump is to be had from the details of British tonnage in commission. By comparing annual variations in the commissioned tonnage with annual variations in British tonnage entering Australian ports some indication is to be gained of the contrast in experience. In 1938/9 U.K. tonnage entering Australia was 15 % higher than in 1929/30, the peak year of the 1920s. But the total U.K. ton-

[1] C. E. Fayle, *The War and the Shipping Industry* (1927), p. xii.

nage in commission in 1938/9 was still about 11 % less than it had been in 1929/30.

	Percentage change over previous year in	
	British tonnage entering Australia	Total British tonnage in commission
1930/1	−5	−6
1931/2	+2	−7
1932/3	+2½	−4
1933/4	−13	−1
1934/5	+12	+1

British shipping with some marginal competition from other fleets supplied three main classes of shipping tonnage. First were the joint products comprising passenger accommodation and mail services together with cargo space. The tonnage supplied consisted of passenger liners, on which cargo carrying was an important consideration, and cargo liners. As discussed more fully in a subsequent chapter, the cargo-carrying function of passenger liners made a significant contribution to total revenue. Cargo liners normally also carried a few passengers. The number was restricted to twelve and the revenue thus obtained was only marginal. Secondly, the industry provided tramp tonnage, mainly to service the Australian grain trade, the third most-significant in the world's deep-sea trade. Thirdly, and of growing importance during our period, the industry provided some special-purpose cargo space in the shape of oil tankers.

The respective importance of liners and tramps in the provision of cargo services is examined in chapter 2. Here we need anticipate our discussion only to note that liners dominated the Australian trade throughout the inter-war period and that their hold on the trade tended to strengthen. This in turn facilitated the organisation and control of the carrying trade by means of the shipping conference system. The U.K. remained Australia's predominant trading partner between 1920 and 1939 and the chief supplier of shipping. It is not surprising therefore that British ships, more especially British liner companies, dominated the two conferences which controlled the liner services on the highly important trade between Europe and Australia.

At a time when economic nationalism was tending to develop, moreover, the special links between Australia and Britain proved an advantage to the British shipping industry. Economic nationalism, especially in the 1930s, had its counterpart in the assistance given to national fleets. During the contraction in world trade part of the response by the British empire was to aim at increasing imperial trade behind a revived system of trading preference. The British shipping industry, elsewhere beset by smaller cargoes and increased, subsidised, competition found in the supply of shipping for Australia's oversea services a relatively sheltered and expanding market.

Ocean shipping services everywhere are influenced by both economic and natural phenomena. For Australia the major oversea-trade problem during the inter-war years, as it is today, is the nature of her exports and the country's geographical position *vis-à-vis* her principal markets. Long sea distances to be traversed meant the sacrifice of cargo space to bunker needs. They also involved long-term planning of shipping services, months ahead of requirements, and often the programming of voyages long before export items have been 'harvested', long before a season's shipping requirements can accurately be known. It is not uncommon for a vessel to arrive in Australia after market variations elsewhere in the world have radically altered the demand for shipping. Exports, moreover, are seasonal in character; quantities may vary from year to year as climate or disease transforms the pastoral or agrarian scene. Imports, in contrast, which tend to be compact items, are not limited in this way and depend upon frequent, regular shipping services. Mail services in the inter-war years also depended upon regular despatches to and from the country. This suggests that Australia required a regular schedule of oversea service throughout the year supplemented by heavy additional supplies of shipping in times of peak seasonal demand.

The nature of export cargoes and the influence upon them both of market considerations and of weather affects the demand for oversea shipping in other ways. Price variations in oversea markets, even fractional differences, encourage or check the flow of exports. A rise in the London price sends shippers scrambling for space on a mail ship. Stagnant or declining prices will hold exports back, or will encourage their consignment on slower vessels. An expected drought will check shipment; its failure to develop stimulates pressure for urgent despatch. In the domestic scene the geographic dispersal of population and the distances between urban centres along the coastline also create additional demand factors for shipping. Vessels are required to call at a large number of small ports as well as at a few large ports. Between the wars, moreover, with the spread of economic development to remote areas, more and more ports clamoured for direct oversea services.

Australian demand for oversea shipping has witnessed over time a number of changes in emphasis and in requirements on particular sectors. In part the changes reflect developments in trade. In part also they reflect the changing operational needs of the shipping industry itself. A feature of most shipping services is the extreme difficulty of exactly balancing tonnage requirements in both directions on any single shipping route. Either more ships will arrive than can profitably be employed for available backhaul cargoes, or conversely, less ships will arrive from an area than will adequately meet demand for return tonnage; hence the familiar triangular pattern of trade and the familiar pattern of tramping operations. Before 1900 cargo for Europe was not always sufficient to employ all ships arriving in Australia. Many found employment in the N.S.W. export trade in coal. In the twentieth century the growing involvement of Australia in the world trade in wheat together with other developments in the local economy increased the demand for shipping space to Europe. Ships arriving on other trade routes were also pressed into this service. By the end of the 1920s shipping tonnage cleared to Europe from Australian ports exceeded tonnage arriving from Europe by rather more than 600,000 tons a year, equal to about 20–25% of outbound tonnage to Europe; in the following decade the figure went up to 750,000 tons. Overlapping the second phase, and receiving complete expression only in more recent years, is a comparable development on the Asian route. Here also an earlier surplus of arrival tonnage has given way to a deficit. Generally speaking, the additional tonnage for the increased traffic flow from Australia to Europe and later to Asian countries as well, has been drawn from the North and Central America routes. From 1920 until the mid-1930s between 80 % and 90 % of the tonnage required was provided by excess arrival tonnage from the U.S.A.

A study of Australia's oversea-shipping services which confined itself to the operations and economic development of the shipping industry although interesting in itself would have but a limited value. Ocean-shipping services, the product of external trade, derive ultimately from the domestic economic context. A major aim of this work therefore is to outline the importance of Australia's shipping services in the economic development of the country. In the pages that follow, attempts are made at a number of points to relate the demand for shipping to developments in various branches of domestic economic activity. But this fails to provide adequate perspective for the overall picture. It may be convenient therefore to introduce our main discussion with a brief outline of the major characteristics of Australian economic development in the inter-war years. One point that may be made, obvious enough but often overlooked, is that the period divides itself almost exactly into the two decades by the manifestation locally in Australia of the world-wide depression of 1929 and the early 1930s. Some comment is more appropriately linked with one or with the other of the decades and is not always applicable to the whole of the period. For the limited objectives of the present brief discussion, however, the period is treated as a unity in succeeding paragraphs; it is hoped that violence to the sources has been avoided.

Taking the period as a whole, and ignoring the downturn in the depression years, it is readily possible to trace a rise in gross domestic product, whether measured by current market prices or by deflating to measure in constant prices. In real terms, gross domestic product went up by about 25 % between 1921/2 and 1938/9.[1] In terms of *per capita* real income, however, a quite different picture emerges from the sources. Taking into account population increase (a rise of about 28 %, from below 5·5 million

[1] All who write on Australian economic growth are heavily indebted to N. G. Butlin for his monumental work: *Australian Domestic Product, Investment and Foreign Borrowing, 1861–1938/9* (1962) (Subsequently abbreviated to *Butlin*).

in 1921 to almost 7 million in 1939), it is sobering to find that real income per head was about the same in 1939 as it had been twenty years earlier. The figure for 1921/2 is considerably above that for preceding years, however. The year was chosen to avoid abnormality due to war. In taking the year as a starting point the slight but just perceptible rise in income per head between the end of the war and 1939 has thus been obscured. The increase achieved in the 1920s moreover was regained. Notwithstanding the depression when gross domestic product fell by 8% in terms of constant prices and by about 25 % in current market prices, pre-depression levels were maintained. Despite the ineptness of large areas of public policy during and after the depression, and taking population increases into consideration, Australians were no worse off in 1939 than in 1921/2, and slightly better off than in the immediate post-war years.[1] Although not always susceptible to cost-benefit analysis, other gains deriving from the investment of social capital ought not to be ignored: in this sense the level of *per capita* real income may be an incomplete measure. The decline in interest payments in respect of loans raised overseas also meant that a smaller percentage of gross domestic product was being channelled off. Expressed in yet another way, despite widespread distress during the depression years with heavy unemployment in many sectors, despite drastic reductions in imports, and the fall in export earnings between 1929 and 1933, and the persistence of short-time in employment to the end of the thirties, Australia had regained its pre-depression level of prosperity on the eve of the Second World War.

Although, as outlined below, economic diversification is a distinctive feature of Australian development between the wars, the overwhelming importance of the primary sector (other than mining) was never seriously challenged. In this respect Australia faithfully mirrors accepted 'imperial' beliefs of the time. The 'imperialism' of the 1920s and 1930s, a continuation and extension of wartime cooperation, to a large extent was based upon

[1] For discussions of many aspects of the depression and government policy see: E. R. Walker, *Australia in the World Depression* (1933); D. B. Copland, *Australia in the World Crisis, 1929–33* (1934) and C. B. Schedvin, 'Economic Policy in Depression and Recovery in Australia, 1927–1935' (Unpublished Sydney Ph.D. thesis, 1963).

the view that a more tightly knit, self-contained 'empire' was both feasible and attainable. It was accepted as axiomatic that certain of the Commonwealth countries would continue to expand their role as producers of food and raw materials. The belief received expression in the variety of institutional devices brought into existence after the First World War, the Imperial Economic Conference, the Empire Marketing Boards and the like. The theme of close imperial collaboration is reiterated in successive reports of the Imperial Conference and of the Imperial Economic Conference. Above all it was conceived as a way of finding employment for the inhabitants of the mother country. The basis underlying the Empire Settlement Act (and one of the reasons for the failure of inter-war imperial migration) was the transfer of people from Britain to swell the rural population of 'bush and backwoods' of the Empire in order to increase the production of the food and raw materials required in the U.K.

Settlement under the Act itself made no lasting contribution to the development of rural Australia. Output of primary products nevertheless rose, if at a greatly reduced rate in comparison with the years from 1900 to 1914. Between 1920 and 1939 the average acreage under wheat rose from a little under 10 to a little over 12 million. The average annual production of wheat rose from 135 million to about 160 million bushels.[1] A similar sharp rise took place in wool production, from about 600 million to about 985 million pounds in 1938/9. Primary products retained their importance in the export sector. Despite the coming into being during the inter-war years of a more broadly based economy, wool and foodstuffs continued as before (and as they do today) to predominate in exports. It was to prove a mixed blessing during the depression years when the decline in world prices began with such commodities.

Much of the interest of the inter-war years in Australia, however, and more especially of the 1920s, centres upon the mechanism of, and the results derived from, the transfer of resources to the manufacturing sector. Developments in manufacturing

[1] C of A, Bureau of Agricultural Economics, *The Australian Wheat Growing Industry, 1959–60 to 1961–62* (Canberra, 1964). The extension of the area under cultivation into marginal lands forced down the average yield per acre.

industry, indeed periods of rapid growth in such developments, were not in themselves unknown in Australia. But the economic diversification of the 1920s was new in so far as it represented 'the adoption by the Commonwealth government of a deliberate policy of industrialisation and included the calculated use of the tariff instrument to encourage industrial activity'.[1] Even so, much of the effect of the structural change in the economy has been felt only since 1945. Ignoring the depression years, a number of indicators testify to the interest in, and the achievements of, manufacturing during our period. Data on investment and value of output in manufacturing point unmistakably to increases in values. They point also to a quickening in the rate of growth and to the rising percentage share contributed by manufacturing to domestic product and capital formation. As an employer, manufacturing industry steeply increased its demand upon the labour market. Using the unsophisticated records available, we find that notwithstanding the rise in population, in 1939 factories employed 8·2 % as compared with 7·2 % of the population in 1921/2. In absolute terms the numbers employed by factories rose by 170,000 representing a rise of more than 40 %.[2]

Much of the growth in manufacturing was facilitated by the striking investment concurrently being made in urban development. Urban expansion, another characteristic of Australia in the 1920s and 1930s, meant above all increasing concentration of population in the six state capitals. Although at the end of our period the proportion of population classed as urban was only very slightly up on the 1921 figure, the metropolitan proportion had gone up from 43 % to 47·5 % of total population. The bulk of the increased urban concentration, moreover, took place in eastern capitals wherein industry also tended to be concentrated. Urban development was made possible with the help of large oversea loans raised by public authorities. Servicing the mounting oversea debt absorbed an ever-rising proportion of export income. The excess of debits in the balance of payment on current account shows a marked, though not continuous, rise in the 1920s and a much lower range of debits in the 1930s.[3] A fall

[1] C. Forster, *Industrial Development in Australia, 1920–1930* (Canberra, 1964), pp. 4, 5.
[2] C of A, *Year Books* and *Production Bulletins*.
[3] *Butlin*, chapter XXI, table 265.

in export incomes accompanying the depression led, among other repercussions, to a severe cut-back in imports. Exports, on the other hand, still drawn extensively from the primary sector, while recording a very severe fall in value, do not diminish and in fact increase in volume. This uneven demand presented serious problems for the shipping industry for a number of years.

The population changes already mentioned failed, in one important respect, to affect population distribution. At the end, as at the beginning of our period, about 80 % of the total population of Australia was concentrated into the three eastern states of N.S.W., Victoria and Queensland; only some 15 % were in South and Western Australia. The imbalance in population distribution had its reflection in the distribution of oversea trade between states, more especially in the tonnage of imports. The bulk of import cargoes reaching Australia were destined for the eastern states. Cargoes for export tended to be drawn more widely throughout Australia and marked tonnage discrepancies between east and west are less obvious. The growth of export cargoes in Western Australia was still comparatively recent when our period begins in 1920, however. It is largely associated with the expansion of the Australian wheat industry. Before the First World War complaints were made in Western Australia that exports were inadequate to provide back-haul cargoes for ships visiting the state. Giving evidence in 1906 before the federal royal commission on ocean shipping services the Secretary of the Fremantle Harbour Trust stated: 'there is little or no export freight from this port; ships coming here full of cargo have to leave in many cases empty, or practically empty'.[1]

A dependent island economy with an extensive oversea trade such as Australia not surprisingly develops a keen official interest in the oversea-shipping services upon which it relies. Its very vulnerability provides continuing stimulus for official

[1] *C.P.P.* 1906, paper 36, report of the royal commission on Ocean Shipping Service, Q 7305, 7318, etc. A year earlier the Secretary gave similar evidence to a state royal commission. The chairman of the Harbour Trust, a master mariner and a M.L.C. expressed identical views. Possibly because the commissioners were anxious to prove collusion over freight-rate determination, their Report denies that back-loadings were insufficient. (*Western Australia P.P.*, 1905, paper 8, report of the royal commission on Ocean Freights etc. Q 2710 ff. and 3130 ff., p. 7.)

enquiry. With federation, the Commonwealth government assumed powers which included the right to legislate in respect of trade and commerce with other countries and among the Australian states; and also in respect of navigation and shipping. Before and during our period, intervention by the Commonwealth government is to be seen at many points. In succeeding chapters the nature and effect of such intervention is examined in the appropriate context. But the separate discussion of different manifestations of Australian maritime policy fails to bring out its unitary nature. Nor did all areas of official intervention necessarily impinge upon the oversea sector; they may thus be omitted from discussion. Hence a brief introductory outline here of Australian maritime policy is useful both to set the scene and for the sake of completeness.

The basis of policy since federation simply put, has been the creation of an Australian mercantile marine. The policy sprang from two aims. In origin, and in large part, it reflects the needs of imperial defence in that it was aimed at creating a reserve of trained Australian seamen for war service. It also stemmed from Australia's preoccupation with her role in international trade and her concentration on securing low ocean-freight rates for her exports. All users, everywhere, of all forms of transport, seek low rates of freight. As discussed in chapter 7, it is the primary producer engaged in international trade who is particularly conscious of the implications of ocean rates. The evidence for our period abundantly attests to the interest in rates shown in Australia by both private and official bodies. The underlying attitude was voiced in Commonwealth parliament many times. At the beginning of the 1920s it was pointed out that: 'there can be no future for the primary producer unless he is given an opportunity of placing his products on the markets of the world at reasonable freights'.[1] It was a sentiment which is repeated throughout the inter-war years.

Three major instruments were employed in an attempt to achieve the desired end. Primarily designed with the coastal trade in mind was the Navigation Act of which the main provisions were the cabotage restrictions already mentioned in passing. With the oversea trade chiefly in mind the Common-

[1] *C.P.D.* vol. 103, p. 810.

wealth government entered into the ownership and operation of an ocean-going shipping line. As an auxiliary to both sectors of shipping, official policy also aimed at the creation of a viable shipbuilding and ship-repair industry within Australia.

The policy on shipbuilding was least successful and may briefly be dismissed. Before the First World War commercial shipbuilding scarcely existed in Australia. After the end of the war the attempt was made to create an effective branch of the industry in Australia at three separate dockyards of which the best known is that on Cockatoo Island in Sydney Harbour. The best work of the industry during its brief heyday was in building vessels for the Commonwealth government oversea shipping line. In all, 21 ships were built with a total net registered tonnage of about 50,000 tons. Thereafter, little of consequence was built in Australia during the remainder of the inter-war period notwithstanding tariff-board interest in the industry in the late 1920s and early 1930s. Between 1924 and the Second World War only naval craft and vessels under 500 tons gross were built in Australian dockyards.

The passing of the Navigation Act in Australia followed from the 1907 conference in London on merchant shipping. It was recommended that Australia's coastal trade should be reserved for ships on the Australian register. After considerable delay and a number of false starts a Navigation Act received royal assent after war had broken out. At the request of the U.K. government the implementation of the Act was shelved for the duration. From the beginning of July 1921 the various sections of the Act were gradually introduced, the lead being taken with the coasting provisions. The royal commission appointed to enquire into the Act noted in its first report, in 1924:

> that the main reason which actuated the Parliament in placing the Act upon the statute-book, and which lifted the subject to a plane of great national importance above the ordinary considerations of party politics, was the desire to build up an Australian Mercantile Marine.
>
> To build up an Australian Mercantile Marine it was necessary to extend the protective policy of Australia to its merchant shipping. To protect the Australian ship-owner from unfair competition from subsidized foreign ships or poorly paid crews from other countries,

it was necessary to prevent other vessels competing against him unless such vessels complied with Australian rates of wages, provided the same accommodation for their seamen, and had the same manning scale.

Parliament recognized that, as an island continent, we are largely dependent upon the strength of our merchant service for our existence. The Australian coastal trade was to be reserved for Australian-owned ships, which were to be the source of a supply of skilled and trained Australian seamen in time of war...

Originally the restrictions were applicable also to the Territories of Papua and New Guinea. A vessel was judged to be engaging in coastal trade if a visit to the Territories was included in the course of a voyage to or from Australia and cargo was carried between one and the other. One of the recommendations of the royal commission on the Act (subsequently adopted) was to give greater maritime freedom in the Territories trade.

The Navigation Act was not universally acclaimed in Australia. The two chief criticisms concerned excessive freight rates and inadequate services. The most embittered and vociferous critics were in Tasmania. Few debates on shipping or meetings of the Commonwealth and state conference are without some reference to the disability suffered by Tasmania as a result of the Act. The sharp division of opinion in Australia was brought out also in the deliberations of the royal commission which investigated the working of the Act. Although there were only seven members of the commission three separate reports were submitted, each (according to the *Sydney Morning Herald—S.M.H.*) containing the opinions held by each conflicting group of members before they were appointed. Another objection to the reservation of the coasting trade was voiced by the same newspaper: the virtual monopoly it conferred upon the inter-state shipping 'combine'. The inter-state shipowners association was set up long before the Act was passed but 'its most tyrannical behaviour on the coast towards smaller shipping ventures, small ports, and struggling young industries behind those ports, as well as its general unchallenged dictation in the matter of all freights, have been only too clearly buttressed by the support to the combine which the Act affords'.[1] *The Times* went so far in

[1] *S.M.H.* 10 September 1924.

1926 to assert that the Act had produced an effect opposite to that intended with passenger ships on the coast actually decreasing in number. Since 1919 about 80,000 tons of shipping had been withdrawn from the coasting trade and had not been replaced.[1] Six years later in the House of Representatives a member moved the adjournment to discuss the 'necessity for immediate action in connection with the Navigation Act, in view of its baneful effect upon Australian trade and commerce...'. He reminded the House that the purpose of the act 'was to build up an Australian mercantile marine, but since it has been in force the mercantile marine of Australia has decreased by one-half. The accommodation provided for passengers and goods is less than it was before and all the States are paying in higher charges for any privilege the Navigation Act may give'.[2]

To speak more precisely, the Act did not ban from the coastal trade vessels not registered in Australia. But the same real effect was achieved in licensing for the coastal trade only those ships which complied with Australian pay and manning conditions. In an attempt to moderate complaint, British vessels in 1926 were allowed to participate unlicensed with special permission in certain circumstances. In 1935 after a further wave of complaint the Act was formally amended to place the 'permit' system on a statutory basis. During the 1930s also, the government of Australia raised with New Zealand and Britain the possibility of extending the Australian Navigation Act to include trade between Australia and New Zealand in order to exclude an American shipping line. In the event this attempt (which is discussed more fully below) was abandoned.

Dissatisfaction with the Act stemmed from the difficulty of providing low inter-state rates of freight for a relatively high cost economy where comparable cost structures inevitably were carried over into the merchant marine. Pay, manning and accommodation on what other maritime nations regarded as a lavish scale meant relatively high freight rates whether or not oligopolistic practices were pursued by the shipowners. The militancy and strength of the unions involved in the coastwise movement of trade, moreover, tended to raise the crew charge

[1] *The Times* 27 November 1926. [2] *C.P.D.* vol. 137, p. 2,772 ff.

element in voyage disbursements. To a large extent the failure of the Australian government line in the oversea sector derived from identical causes.

The nature and extent of the short-lived contribution of the government line to Australia's oversea carrying needs and the role of the line as an instrument to curb the shipping conference is discussed in other chapters. Here our aim is to outline the policy considerations which led to its creation and to describe the sharp division of opinion within Australia concerning its retention and ultimate sale in 1927. A federal government line had been advocated as far back as 1906 by the royal commission appointed to continue a select committee enquiring 'as to the carriage of mails, passengers and cargo between Australia and the United Kingdom'. The commission's report recommends federal ownership and operation of a deep-sea fleet. 'The prestige and the welfare of the Commonwealth demand that it should no longer remain dependent upon private individuals for the carriage of its mails. The isolated position of Australia, and the many leagues of ocean which separate us from other countries, render the carriage of mails and perishable produce to distant markets a question of paramount importance.' The Commissioners concluded also that the existence of a government line would 'check any exorbitant charges which might be made by private carrying companies.'

No further action was taken, or seems to have been actively considered, between 1906 and the return to power of a Labour government under Fisher in September 1914. It was no coincidence that the vision of a state line should have been revived by a Labour ministry. As our subsequent discussion shows, the retention of the line after the First World War owed much to the socialist programme of the Labour party with its policy of public ownership. State socialism was not new in 1914, it had been a major policy aim of the Labour party for many years. Hughes, later to become Labour prime minister (and to split the party over conscription), had for many years been educating the public. His contributions to the Australian press entitled the 'Case for Labor' included much on the inevitability of public ownership.[1]

[1] See L. F. Fitzharding, *William Morris Hughes* (1964), chapter 12.

In 1914 when the new parliament reassembled, the speech from the throne outlined the government's intention to establish a state shipping-line as soon as possible. But eighteen months were to pass before the line was established. When it was founded moreover, other, more urgent considerations prevailed than the attainment of doctrinaire ends. The First World War revealed to the full the 'isolated position of Australia'. Relying as she did upon oversea shipping owned overseas for the conduct of her external trade, Australia was especially vulnerable to any interruption in the supply of shipping. The outbreak of war in Europe was almost immediately followed by a decline in oversea-shipping arrivals in Australia. Compared with the total for 1913, the tonnage of oversea shipping entered at Australian ports was down by 20 % during 1914/15, by 30 % during 1916/17 and by more than 50 % during 1917/18.

In the U.K. the dislocation of war, the concentration of the shipbuilding industry on naval vessels, port congestion, and mounting losses of merchant shipping led Britain into a series of expedients to offset the serious lack of shipping. To economise in the use of tonnage, ordinary commercial considerations were pushed temporarily to one side. The length of haul became of overriding importance. The short haul was preferred to the long. The needs of Britain's 'siege economy' dominated Admiralty planning. The supply of shipping for Australia's oversea trade was an early casualty; long maritime distances were involved. In addition the curiously uneven incidence and effect of tonnage control before general requisitioning was introduced in Britain in 1917 further reduced the supply of shipping to Australia. British shipowners found it more profitable to concentrate on the indirect trade; it became 'a game of skill to keep ships out of British ports as much as possible.'[1] Since the oversea trade of Australia was heavily concentrated on Britain the repercussions were thus severe. The tonnage of shipping cleared from Australia to Europe between 1909 and 1913 averaged annually about 2 million; in 1917/18 it was down to only some 880,000 tons.

The consequences in Australia were grave, a rude shock was administered to local opinion. Exports, especially perishable

[1] *Sturmey*, p. 47.

foodstuffs, began to pile up. The interruption of shipment represented a sharp set-back to the primary sector. Since 1900 it had been active in widening the range of exports and reducing dependence upon wool and gold. In 1901 two-thirds of the total value of exports were contributed by these two items. On the eve of the First World War they accounted for only 45 % of a total export figure 50 % higher than in 1901. The items of growing importance after 1901 were foodstuffs, 28 % of the total value in 1913 as compared with only 14 % in 1901. Perishable foodstuffs requiring refrigerated space amounted to 15 % as against the 6 % or 7 % of 14 years earlier. The quantity of frozen beef and mutton shipped trebled over the 14 years. The lack of shipping thus caused anxiety as the back-log of unshipped exports increased.

The termination of coal exports and the taking into service of the 12 German vessels interned in Australian ports on the outbreak of war helped a little to ease the acute shortage. But, as Hughes was many years later to recall in his reminiscences, in 1916 Australia's need for shipping was desperately urgent: 'every inch of storage space was crammed to bursting point; wheat silos were overflowing; there were mountainous stacks of wheat bags on the wharves and at the railway sidings throughout the country'.[1]

It was against this background that in 1916, Hughes, Labour prime minister from October 1915, whilst in London sought Asquith's assistance in obtaining a bigger allocation of the available shipping. He failed. His failure meant that 'there was a risk that Australia might be commercially isolated unless we had craft of our own to rely upon'.[2] Acting in secrecy and with speed Hughes therefore turned to a ship broker and without obtaining prior Commonwealth parliamentary authorisation, bought fifteen ships: the Commonwealth Government Line of Steamers was in business.[3] For the remainder of the war the line was operated outside Admiralty control.[4]

[1] W. M. Hughes, *Policies and Potentates* (1950), p. 186.

[2] *S.M.H.* 18 November 1921.

[3] For criticisms of Hughes' 'extra-Parliamentary' activities see for example, *C.P.D.* 6 and 7 December 1916, pp. 9,451 and 9,579.

[4] Hughes, in his autobiographical memoirs, *Policies and Potentates* (pp. 186–91), states that Runciman, then President of the Board of Trade, threatened to

Whether or not the Commonwealth line significantly contributed to the needs of the Australian economy during the remaining war or immediate post-war years is hard to determine. In 1917/18 the oversea entry and clearance at Australian ports of Australian shipping tonnage registered an increase of almost 20 % over the average annual figure for the years 1908–13. In 1919/20, however, the total was actually lower. Complaints were made, and the accuracy of the complaints was officially admitted in Commonwealth parliament, that some at least of the line's vessels were being used during the war for indirect trade (where the freights obtainable were higher) and not for the purpose 'originally intended' namely, for the Australia-U.K. trade.[1]

With the return to peace the question of retaining the line was quickly raised. The public debate which took place during the subsequent nine years revealed to the full the extreme division of opinion within the country. A brief explanatory digression is therefore justified for the light it throws on the working out of public maritime policy.[2] The post-war debate on the fate of the line began on 25 June 1919 when ministerial statement announced the government's policy of continuing to operate the line in peacetime. From then on, doubt and disillusionment within the country among all sectors other than Labour supporters began to grow. The Labour party, in office when the line was created, had been split a few months later over the conscription issue. Hughes left the Labour party with a number of followers and fused with Liberals in the House to form a National War government; it survived until 1923. It was led by Hughes and included, after December 1921, S. M. Bruce, within fifteen months to become prime minister in the Bruce–Page administration.

In opposition was the re-formed Labour party, implacably hostile to Hughes. The newly formed Country party led by

requisition each of the 15 ships as it entered a British port. He also states that Asquith adopted a more conciliatory tone on receiving an assurance from Hughes that no further ship purchases would be made without prior sanction. No references illustrating the British point of view of the transaction have been traced.

[1] *C.P.D.* 21 September 1917, p. 2,488; 30 July 1919, pp. 11,095–7.

[2] Published volumes of the *C.P.D.* form the basic source for the present discussion. They include far too many individual references to permit separate citation.

Earle Page occupied a midway position. It was strongly protectionist, represented primary producing interests, was bitterly opposed to the socialist policies of the Labour party, and disliked Hughes. Over the question of the government shipping line in the early 1920s both Labour and Country parties favoured its peacetime retention; the former because of its socialist policy, the latter because of the importance of low freights to primary producers. An important additional motive for keeping the line was the check it offered to the monopoly of the shipping conference. Different sectors, often with conflicting motives, combined in attacking the oversea lines owned overseas. Mutual dislike, rather than common policy aims, explains much of the alignment. Many outside, as well as inside parliament, subscribed to the view, expressed by Jowett of the Country party, on the value of state subsidized shipping. It was better, he argued, to operate even at heavy loss if by so doing it compelled the conference lines to keep down rates of freight. Tasmania's representatives supported the keeping of the line because of the island's complete dependence upon marine transport. Any measure likely to increase the supply of shipping locally thus had their backing, just as any measure likely to have the reverse effect (such as the cabotage sections of the Navigation Act) was resisted. Supporters of the National government were not always wholeheartedly behind the line. People who disliked seeing the government involved in commercial undertakings and who, like Bruce, represented importers rather than exporters, spoke very critically. Even Hughes, one-time ardent socialist and founder of the line, had been willing to sell it in 1921. But, he reminded the House in 1925, members then had decided otherwise. Hughes was ousted from government in 1923 when the Bruce–Page government replaced the National government led by Hughes. The coalition government linked the Country party with the National party after deliberately excluding Hughes from office.[1]

In the full-scale debate on Commonwealth shipping activities in 1923 the new government announced its intention to persevere with the line. Labour members of both houses taunted

[1] See Earle Page *Truant Surgeon* (1963), p. 86 ff. for the manoeuvering which followed the election results.

Bruce. Mr Mahony found it gratifying that Bruce 'who is such an ardent advocate of private enterprise has now become converted to the beauties and truth of State Socialism.'[1] According to the Labour leader a few years later, however, it was a 'rice-bowl conversion'. It reflected Bruce's willingness to reach a compromise with the Country party in order to achieve a composite government. Until that time Bruce 'was entirely opposed to the maintenance of the Australian Commonwealth Line of Steamers, being a strong supporter of private enterprise'. The need to achieve composite government dictated a fresh policy and 'there is no doubt that the retention of the...Line... played an important part'.[2]

Within a few years however, continued losses by the line and its failure to restrain freights encouraged rethinking of policy by both parties to the coalition. Despite the sustained opposition from Labour members, Bruce disposed of the line to the Royal Mail group in 1927.[3] Labour opposition was manifested in a censure motion debated over four days. Opposition speakers made extravagant claims on behalf of the line, they clearly exaggerated. It cannot be shown, as we argue in a subsequent chapter, that the line held down freights except possibly in the immediate post-war years. Once the line adopted uniform rating with the conference, it ceased to be an effective restraint. Even with conference rates, however, it sustained heavy financial operating losses. The line was also a failure in other ways. Its share of carrying in the oversea sector was never impressive. And it failed also as a nursery for Australian seamen. It failed to become the preserve for Australians as envisaged by the Labour party. Endorsing as it did the 'White Australia Policy', the Labour party considered it 'essential to see that only Australians were employed on the Commonwealth Government boats'.[4]

[1] *C.P.D.* vol. 103, p. 805.
[2] *C.P.D.* vol. 116, p. 1,010.

[3] Almost forty years later A. G. Whitlam, Deputy Leader of the Federal Opposition, stated in Canberra that the Commonwealth Government Line had been sold by 'the Conservative Government of that day in return for contributions to party funds'. (*C.P.D.* 23 March 1966, p. 508.) He cited as evidence the study of Viscount Bruce by C. Edwards. No trace has been found in the biography. In a personal letter to the present author Viscount Bruce described Mr Whitlam's statement as completely inaccurate.

[4] Mr Charlton, Labour Leader, during the 1923 debate on government shipping activities. (*C.P.D.* vol. 103, pp. 804–5.)

On the eve of the line's disposal to an oversea buyer less than one half of its total seagoing staff were domiciled in Australia, the remainder were resident in the U.K.[1]

As with shipbuilding, so also with federal shipping, the outbreak of the Second World War led to a revival. But the present-day successor to the Commonwealth Government Line has ventured less into the oversea sector. The Australian National Line in 1964 consisted of 41 ships and totalled 178,000 gross tons, all recent fleet additions being locally built by the revivified shipbuilding industry. Nevertheless, the Australian registered fleet, both state-owned and private, remains grossly inadequate to meet the demand in Australia for oversea shipping. In 1963/4 the net tonnage of shipping entered from oversea ports reached 20 million tons, almost treble the 1939 total. Less than $\frac{1}{2}$% of the tonnage entered in 1963/4 was made up of Australian shipping; most had arrived from New Zealand and the Pacific Islands. The local fleet plays only an insignificant part outside coastal waters. Australian registered vessels carried a mere $\frac{1}{2}$% of oversea cargo in the year mentioned. The quantity of oversea cargo carried today by Australian ships is actually considerably less than that carried by nationally owned lines in emerging nations. Ships of the Israeli fleet, for example, in the mid-1950s provided for about one quarter of the nation's oversea carrying.[2]

It is unfortunate, if understandable, that an economy heavily involved in oversea trade but lacking an appropriate fleet should persist in seeking participation in oversea carrying. The advocacy of a national fleet may be politically expedient, its possession politically desirable. But the gains may be illusory.[3] As a weapon of control against expatriate shipping rings the mere existence of a national fleet may be insufficient. In Australia's oversea sector, for example, a very large local fleet would be required if it is to make more than a marginal contribution. It is unlikely that the shipbuilding industry in Australia at present could possibly supply the vessels. Between 1941 and

[1] *C.P.P.* 1926/8, IV, 22.

[2] B. Boxer, *Israeli Shipping and Foreign Trade* (Chicago, 1957).

[3] We rely here upon the interesting discussion on this topic by R. O. Goss 'Investment in shipping and the Balance of Payments', *Journal of Industrial Economics*, vol. 13, pp. 103–13.

1964 about 200,000 net tons of merchant shipping had been built locally. On 31 January 1965 current shipbuilding orders in Australian yards totalled about 100,000 net tons. Compared with the 20,000,000 net tons of oversea shipping entered in Australian ports in 1963/4 local building capacity is insignificant. The oversea purchase of a fleet with the aid of a loan merely increases oversea-debt commitments. The Israeli fleet was largely brought into being on the basis of West German reparations. The Indian fleet, in 1965 almost $1\frac{1}{2}$ million gross tons, has been created with the help of 'aid finance'.

The import replacement contribution of a nationally owned fleet providing oversea services may be exaggerated. The oversea operation of a fleet inevitably involves expenditure overseas, especially heavy in the indirect trade, less in the direct trade where a home port serves as a terminal. Apart from such expenditures, there is also to be considered the loss of foreign currency hitherto spent in home ports by oversea-owned ships ousted from the trade by the national fleet.

In competition with established lines, moreover, a newcomer must be able to offer comparably priced products. Given the importance of crew charges as a voyage cost element in international cost comparisons, the level of wages is often critical. A relatively low-cost economy, such as India or Israel is less handicapped than a high-wage-cost economy. Fleets owned in countries where wages are high, and pay and manning scales 'lavish', survive only with protection or a direct subsidy or both. Australian experience in recent years does not inspire confidence that the factors outlined would be avoided.

The failure of the Commonwealth government in the inter-war years to maintain a shipping line as an effective instrument of rate control diminished neither its interest nor participation in this branch of maritime policy. As subsequent discussion shows, from 1929 onwards the government played an active and ever increasing part in rate determination. It engaged in the promotion of oversea trade by touring trade missions; it encouraged and set up produce marketing boards whose activities included an examination of freight rates; and more important, it engaged directly in rate determination with the shipping lines.

Pursuit of other policy considerations involved cross alignments with maritime policy. It witnessed also a complete reversal of official attitude to the oversea-shipping lines. Trade-treaty negotiations during the difficult years of the depression were responsible, it would seem, for state intervention and even Labour party support for oversea shipping in ways not clearly identifiable with the country's basic maritime policy. Australian reaction to the competition experienced by U.K. lines from the U.S.A. and Japanese merchant marine, for example, witnessed massive official support for British shipping companies. Even more surprising perhaps, is the extent to which in the later 1930s official hostility towards the conference lines was replaced by open support for, and indeed confirmation of, the oversea-lines' monopoly. Taken as a whole, Australian maritime policy would seem to have achieved some of its basic aims during our period. Although the state oversea line disappeared, the coastal trade became the entrenched preserve of local fleets. In the oversea sphere the underlying intention of the government in connection with freights was realised. Liner rate-determination became a shared responsibility involving shippers and government. To argue, as some did, that Australian freight rates in 1939 might have been forced lower is to look myopically and in isolation at a single sector of the world's shipping industry.

Chapter 1

THE PATTERN OF SHIPPING SERVICES

Since the time when Australia first became drawn into international contact its oversea-shipping services have witnessed a number of functional changes. Originally a ship sailed from London direct to and from Sydney. By the later nineteenth century, however, it had become appropriate to regard Australia not only as a terminal for the U.K.–Australia trade but also as a useful intermediate point for shipping otherwise unemployed in Australia and the Orient. Ships in the far east bound for Europe which had failed to secure a direct return cargo found it profitable to come in ballast to Australia. There, if direct return cargoes to Europe were not to be had, it was always possible to load N.S.W. coal for San Francisco, later for Chile, where grain or nitrates for European ports could be obtained. It enabled a longer voyage in ballast to be avoided. It is a branch of trade characterised by the continued use of sailing ships long after they had vanished from routes in other parts of the world.[1] The trade persisted into the twentieth century and after the end of the First World War it revived for a brief late summer, but soon declined. After 1900, especially after 1920, cargoes for Europe increased in volume; shipping found more profitable employment in this sector. Cargoes from, and more especially to, Europe increasingly dominated Australia's external trade. Ships from Europe part loaded on the continent, completed loading in Britain and sailed not for Sydney alone but for every major port on the Australian mainland, often with a diversion to Hobart and to minor ports. Once the Australian mainland has been reached it takes almost as long to sail to ports on the further coast as it does to cross the Atlantic. The demands on the shipping industry during the inter-war years

[1] See this author's article on British shipping and the N.S.W. export coal trade in *Economic Record*, vols. 36 (393–413) and 37 (371–81).

were rising and were also becoming more complex as new oversea markets were developed. The growing importance of trade with far eastern countries for example, in the early 1930s brought additional services into existence.

The increase in the supply of shipping services required by developments in Australia's oversea trade may be illustrated initially from the simple tonnage aggregate of vessels entering the Commonwealth from oversea ports. Details are given in Table 1 of all tonnage entered and cleared and also the tonnage recorded as in ballast.[1] Minor discrepancies between the entered and cleared totals are unimportant. Apart from the likelihood of compilation error, two factors probably explain the variations. End of year arrivals included in the following year's clearances and secondly, part of the explanation may stem from the occasional diversion of locally registered vessels from the oversea to the coastal sector. Two obvious features in the table merit notice, the increased tonnage entered and the record of movement in ballast. Between the first and last quinquennial periods a one-third rise in entered tonnage took place, from about 5 to about $6\frac{1}{2}$ million net registered tons a year. Differences in methods of recording make precise international comparison difficult. In the U.K. with which some comparison is possible, the tonnage of shipping entered *with cargo* registers an increase of only 5 % during the period. If from the Australian totals the tonnage in ballast is excluded, the recorded increase in entry tonnage is of the order of some 45 %.

The distribution between tonnage in ballast and tonnage with cargo is arbitrary and undoubtedly distorts the statistics. A 10,000 ton vessel arriving in ballast, for example, is more significant from the shipping point of view than a 2,000 ton vessel arriving with 5 tons of cargo and thus entered as an arrival with cargo. Over the whole period ballast arrivals almost doubled ballast clearances, a reflection of the difference in bulk between inbound and outbound cargoes. Nevertheless ballast clearances were many times higher in 1939 than in 1920, a movement explicable in terms of the growth of oil imports and,

[1] Except where otherwise stated, all tables in chapters 1 and 2 have been constructed from data published in the *Year Book* and in the *Tpt. and Communications Bulletin*.

as shown in chapter 2, in the use of special-purpose vessels. Largely, tonnage entered in ballast was drawn from the British fleet, an overall reflection of the provision of British tramp-ship tonnage for outbound wheat cargoes. The contribution by foreign fleets was uneven. The Norwegian fleet contributed most, especially in ballast clearances, in part because of the Norwegian fleet's role in oil carrying; in the 1930s Norway's fleet included 16% or 17% of world tanker tonnage. In contrast, certain other foreign fleets rarely entered or cleared a completely empty ship. In only 4 of the 13 years for which foreign nationality details are available was an Italian ship, and for only 7 of the 13 years was a German ship, entered or cleared in ballast. The conspicuous increase in ballast tonnage entered in the early 1930s illustrates the effect of import restrictions discussed in chapter 3.

The increase in the total tonnage of oversea shipping entered at Australian ports was accompanied by increases in the size of the individual vessels normally and regularly used. That is to say larger vessels with bigger cargo space and more passenger accommodation were brought into customary use. On the whole the number of vessel entries was about the same at the end as at the beginning of the period. In part, growth in vessel size was in response to the development in trade outlined below. In part, it was because changing marine technology made for operating economies in vessels of certain size ranges. In part also growth in vessel size was an inescapable accompaniment of the quest for speed which characterises the Australian trade between the wars and which, along with size and technology, is considered in chapter 2.

Australian oversea trade is a terminal, rather than an 'omnibus' trade. That is to say that the shipment or discharge of cargo at ports on the routes between Australia and her major oversea markets is relatively unimportant. The pattern is far from rigid. On the Suez route to Europe, for example, items may be carried to Colombo, or to ports in Egypt. In the 1920s indeed a large part of the wheat and flour shipped to Egypt was carried on vessels the bulk of whose cargo was bound for Europe. But the economics of ship management tend to limit such carrying. Full, rather than part, cargoes are preferred.

Table 1. *Oversea shipping entered and cleared, 1920/1–1938/9 ('000 net tons)*

	Entered			Cleared		
	Total	In ballast	% in ballast	Total	In ballast	% in ballast
1920/1	4,759	1,523	32·0	4,744	123	2·6
1921/2	4,560	1,452	31·8	4,521	88	2·0
1922/3	4,738	649	13·7	4,503	220	4·9
1923/4	4,911	652	13·3	5,012	357	7·1
1924/5	5,596	1,159	20·7	5,604	368	6·6
1925/6	5,304	575	10·8	5,365	518	9·6
1926/7	5,559	660	11·8	5,605	577	10·3
1927/8	5,419	426	7·9	5,506	721	13·1
1928/9	5,552	624	11·2	5,546	638	11·5
1929/30	5,444	369	6·8	5,500	955	17·4
1930/1	5,582	1,454	26·0	5,669	452	8·0
1931/2	5,687	1,740	30·6	5,709	453	7·9
1932/3	5,933	1,655	27·9	5,908	695	11·8
1933/4	5,353	871	16·3	5,411	641	11·8
1934/5	5,994	1,148	19·2	5,895	555	9·4
1935/6	6,238	947	15·2	6,307	709	11·2
1936/7	6,274	833	13·3	6,338	726	11·4
1937/8	7,128	1,217	17·1	7,093	1,015	14·3
1938/9	6,711	746	11·1	6,835	845	12·4

A single destination is preferred to a multiplicity of discharge ports. A programme involving a number of discharge ports in the area wherein the voyage terminates is preferred to one which involves frequent discharge of cargo at transit ports *en route*. On completion of loading in Australia considerable time is spent immediately before sailing in securing cargo, hatches, etc. Shipowners are reluctant to incur the expense involved in 'breaking cargo' *en route* in order to discharge relatively small quantities. In the absence of cargo which lends itself to storage in separate cargo spaces, owners sometimes prefer to restrict such carrying to the occasional berth parcel or to deck cargo. A cargo liner with full holds of wool and meat for Europe via Suez is invariably programmed for Aden bunkering. It will carry there small consignments, citrus fruit, for example, especially if it can be deck stowed. Vessels employed outward from Europe to Australia find it even more difficult to take cargo for ports *en route*. Other shipping services provide regular scheduled voyages to ports visited in passing by ships bound for Australia. With the shipping conference organisation of the time (overlapping membership by companies being usual) it is unreasonable to suppose that Australian-bound ships would carry significant quantities of cargo from Europe to intermediate ports. The on-trade from most of these ports to Australia, tea from Ceylon for example, was never large.

The method adopted in Australia to record oversea-shipping movement exaggerates the terminal nature of the country's oversea trade. A ship is recorded as entering from the country at which its voyage was begun and is cleared to the country at which the voyage is planned to terminate. No account is taken of calls made at ports between the two terminals. The Commonwealth Statistician has long recognised the methodological defects. To eliminate some of the imperfections the published data on shipping group countries together in six geographical divisions, Tables 2*a*, *b* and *c*. They bring more realism to the picture. Many ships whose voyages ended at British ports also discharged cargo at Dunkirk and other foreign European ports. The 'Asia' label is similarly a more comprehensive description. Even with these aggregations, however, no account is taken of voyages to and from Europe on which cargo is carried between Africa and Australia or of shipments to New Zealand on vessels bound for North America.

Analysis by geographical area also illustrates quantitatively the well-known triangular pattern of shipping required as a result of differences between export and import tonnages in a trading area. The implications for the shipping industry are better illustrated by tabulating the excess or deficiency of available tonnage, see Table 3, for the five most significant areas. The most important market for Australian exports and chief source of her imports throughout the inter-war years was Europe. But it was a trade which required differing amounts of shipping in each direction. Inbound cargo from Europe tended to consist of relatively compact items with a low stowage factor, outbound cargo from Australia had a high stowage factor and

Table 2a. *Inbound shipping tonnage, source by geographical area, 1920/1–1938/9 ('000 net tons)*

	U.K. and Europe	New Zealand	Asia and Pacific islands	Africa	North and Central America	South America
1920/1	1,372	869	1,468	257	757	35
1921/2	1,538	634	1,481	252	646	9
1922/3	2,000	560	1,100	155	914	10
1923/4	1,793	902	1,082	49	1,064	20
1924/5	1,983	853	1,393	172	1,155	39
1925/6	1,836	763	1,300	90	1,283	31
1926/7	1,866	687	1,506	108	1,381	11
1927/8	1,943	624	1,378	90	1,372	11
1928/9	1,795	625	1,726	133	1,266	6
1929/30	2,063	625	1,452	94	1,203	8
1930/1	1,881	558	1,962	296	874	10
1931/2	2,029	525	2,078	234	803	19
1932/3	2,496	559	1,732	164	979	3
1933/4	2,130	562	1,462	157	1,041	—
1934/5	2,075	647	1,998	166	1,106	3
1935/6	2,093	691	2,075	207	1,168	3
1936/7	1,912	901	2,064	253	1,141	3
1937/8	2,154	978	2,332	346	1,289	29
1938/9	1,997	1,010	2,461	169	1,059	15

hence required more shipping space.[1] Whereas only one-third of shipping tonnage arriving in Australia was entered from Europe, the outbound proportion on this route was considerably higher. Generally 40–45 % of the tonnage cleared was to European ports. During the period there was a slight tendency for this area to become less dominant; it nevertheless continued to outstrip other areas in tonnage cleared. It was a trade route on which ballast entries always exceeded ballast clearances. A close second in order of importance was the Asian and Pacific islands route. Entries by 1938/9 were beginning to exceed those from Europe. Heavy ballast clearances, unlike the Europe route, were made to this area. They reflect the large volume of tanker tonnage employed. In 1938/9, for example, 80 % of the tonnage

[1] See Appendix 1 for a description of the various 'tons' in marine usage and for stowage factors.

Table 2*b*. *Outbound shipping tonnage, destination by geographical area, 1920/1–1938/9 ('000 net tons)*

	U.K. and Europe	New Zealand	Asia and Pacific islands	Africa	North and Central America	South America
1920/1	1,879	813	1,175	396	317	163
1921/2	1,833	586	1,144	581	349	27
1922/3	2,206	568	1,023	121	472	114
1923/4	2,142	855	1,261	109	519	127
1924/5	2,794	828	1,258	189	467	68
1925/6	2,362	737	1,393	157	654	62
1926/7	2,558	669	1,480	171	645	81
1927/8	2,417	625	1,557	162	712	32
1928/9	2,314	544	1,834	123	700	29
1929/30	2,253	589	1,653	49	940	12
1930/1	2,457	489	1,964	57	571	19
1931/2	2,680	452	1,898	42	618	20
1932/3	2,508	554	2,098	36	689	23
1933/4	2,504	553	1,641	25	684	5
1934/5	2,537	542	2,076	36	699	5
1935/6	2,736	611	2,221	50	679	9
1936/7	2,739	872	2,062	46	611	8
1937/8	3,031	956	2,362	162	579	2
1938/9	2,791	938	2,429	178	486	12

cleared in ballast on the Asian routes was cleared to the Netherlands East Indies (N.E.I.) the major supplier of oil to Australia. The source above all whence tonnage was obtained for use on other trade routes was North America whose munificence is brought out in the table. The persistence of surplus tonnage in this sector and the tendency in the late 1930s for the amount to increase, reflects the one-sided nature of Australia's commercial exchanges with North America. Some of the ships arriving from there were tankers which cleared from Australia in ballast. By 1938/9 the U.S.A. no longer dominated the Australian market in crude oil and petrol. It continued, nevertheless, to supply some 300,000 tons a year, about one fifth of the total. Some arrivals with timber and motor vehicles found return cargoes of sugar to Canada. But most ships were compelled to seek engagements on other shipping routes. Many ships from

Table 2c. *Inbound (E) and outbound (C) shipping tonnage in ballast by geographical area, 1920/1–1938/9 (annual average in '000 net tons)*

		1920/1 to 1924/5	1925/6 to 1929/30	1930/1 to 1934/5	1935/6 to 1938/9
Europe	E	151	22	512	249
	C	13	8	9	15
New Zealand	E	305	191	113	188
	C	47	39	50	47
Asia	E	457	233	555	280
Pacific	C	120	413	373	669
Africa	E	149	69	184	195
	C	5	5	1	15
North and Central	E	10	11	5	17
America	C	39	214	126	77

North America cleared from Australia with ore or wheat for Japan, or wheat for China, cleared thence in ballast to North America and returned with timber to Australia.[1]

Changing trade needs probably explain the alteration of pattern in the African sector. Exports to South Africa were considerably lower in the 1930s than in the 1920s. A much smaller quantity of tonnage was involved in the New Zealand services. The persistence of an arrival surplus doubtless reflects the willingness of shipowners to undertake the short journey across the Tasman in ballast.

The geographical areas represent trade routes rather than shipping routes with the exception of the trans-Tasman trade. Most trade routes included a number of different services or differently combined services. Europe is linked to Australia by routes via Suez, Panama, and the two Capes although only a few sailing ships remained in our period to make use of the 'roaring forties' via the Horn. The Suez route cut about 1,000 sea miles off the journey from Britain to Sydney. The actual time saved was probably very little, however, when Mediterranean diversions for mail and passengers and the Suez transit were taken into account. The Panama route was not much different in total mileage but was used chiefly by those ships whose

[1] I.S.C. *38th Report* 'British Shipping in the Orient', p. 45.

Table 3. *Imbalance in outbound and inbound shipping tonnage by geographical area 1920/1–1938/9 ('000 tons)*

	Europe	Asia	North America	Africa	New Zealand
1920/1	507	−293	−440	139	−56
1921/2	324	−337	−296	329	−48
1922/3	206	−67	−442	−34	8
1923/4	349	179	−545	60	−47
1924/5	811	−134	−687	17	−125
1925/6	526	93	−629	67	−26
1926/7	692	75	−736	62	−19
1927/8	473	178	−661	72	2
1928/9	518	108	−567	−1	−81
1929/30	191	204	−262	−45	−36
1930/1	576	2	−312	−127	−69
1931/2	651	−180	−185	−192	−73
1932/3	12	366	−289	−127	−6
1933/4	373	179	−357	−131	−9
1934/5	462	78	−405	−131	−105
1935/6	644	147	−489	−157	−80
1936/7	827	−3	−530	−207	−29
1937/8	877	32	−710	−184	−22
1938/9	794	−33	−573	9	−72

Note: the absence of a sign indicates tonnage obtained *from* other routes; a minus sign indicates the supply of tonnage *to* other routes.

services to or from Australia were via New Zealand. In the depression year of 1931 when under-employment of shipping was common, vessels whose service was normally via the canals went by the Horn and Good Hope routes to avoid paying canal dues.[1] Trade with North America was carried on via Panama to the eastern seaboard, to New York and Montreal, and direct across the Pacific to San Francisco or Vancouver. Three major routes served the trade with Asia and the Pacific islands. One went northwards from Sydney to China and Japan with extensions to the Pacific islands. Another was via Western Australia to India, Ceylon, and Burma. The third was to the Netherlands East Indies and Singapore either north from Sydney or from Western Australia. The less important African trade was served

[1] *S.M.H.* 31 December 1931.

by Australian-bound shipping via the Cape route, a direct service, and by occasional charterings.

It is the aim of this and the following chapter to examine a number of aspects in the supply of shipping. The present chapter provides an outline of oversea services supplied by all fleets involved and discusses certain features of the organisation of the industry. In chapter 2 attention is directed to changes over time in ship size and marine technology, and to the type of ship employed. The role of the British fleet has been referred to above: its importance is illustrated in tables 4*a*, *b* and *c* which show also the aggregate contribution of foreign tonnage and its composition.

At once obvious is the overwhelming predominance of British shipping. However measured, in terms of the number of ships, the tonnage entered, range of services provided, or its role as a cargo carrier, the British shipping industry outstripped its competitors. Equally obvious is the smallness of the Australian contribution to oversea services. The locally owned merchant fleet has never formed a high proportion of the tonnage entered from overseas. Only during the lifetime of the Commonwealth Government Line did the indigenous contribution to oversea carrying begin to look significant. At its peak, in 1922/3, the locally registered fleet contributed about 13 % of inbound oversea tonnage. By 1938/9 the proportion had sagged to a mere 5 %.

The amount of shipping tonnage supplied by foreign fleets in the long-term tended not only to increase absolutely but also to gain slightly on the British share of the total. During the 1930s foreign tonnage entered was about one third higher than in the previous decade. The long-term growth in foreign tonnage was accompanied, but not equalled, by an expansion of British tonnage. As a result, the foreign share of the total tended to be very slightly higher during the 1930s than in the 1920s. The peak activity for foreign fleets in terms of proportions took place in the early 1930s when a rise in foreign tonnage coincided with a slight decline of British shipping activity. Thereafter the British total revived and except for 1933/4, went on to exceed the performance of the 1920s. The rise in foreign tonnage was contributed by three fleets. Initially Japanese tonnage enjoyed a brief expansionist phase before declining equally sharply. The slower but more sustained growth of Dutch and Norwegian

Table 4*a*. *Nationality of oversea shipping entered 1920/1–1938/9 ('000 tons)*

	Tonnage registered in					'British' % of total	U.K. % of total	U.K. % of total less Australasia
	Australia	U.K.	New Zealand	All 'British'	All foreign			
1920/1	551	2,541	150	3,316	1,443	69·7	53·4	62·6
1921/2	589	2,803	103	3,638	922	79·8	61·5	72·4
1922/3	646	2,754	67	3,649	1,087	77·0	58·1	68·4
1923/4	486	2,939	308	3,884	1,027	79·1	59·8	71·4
1924/5	425	3,210	488	4,256	1,341	76·1	57·4	68·5
1925/6	381	2,967	492	3,985	1,319	75·1	55·9	67·0
1926/7	406	3,098	459	4,152	1,407	74·7	55·7	66·0
1927/8	396	3,011	403	3,977	1,442	73·4	55·6	65·2
1928/9	206	3,286	416	4,107	1,445	74·0	59·2	66·7
1929/30	212	3,245	399	3,988	1,447	73·4	59·6	67·1
1930/1	228	3,087	321	3,736	1,846	66·9	55·3	61·3
1931/2	231	3,138	261	3,732	1,955	65·6	55·2	60·4
1932/3	265	3,218	291	3,944	1,989	66·5	54·2	59·8
1933/4	289	2,789	336	3,714	1,639	69·4	52·1	59·0
1934/5	310	3,137	322	4,060	1,934	67·7	52·3	58·5
1935/6	314	3,334	322	4,343	1,895	69·6	53·4	59·5
1936/7	327	3,447	523	4,582	1,692	73·0	54·9	63·4
1937/8	363	4,021	506	5,158	1,970	72·4	56·4	64·2
1938/9	331	3,744	563	4,887	1,824	72·8	55·8	64·4

shipping entering Australian ports largely accounts for the enhanced foreign total at the close of the inter-war years. The share of individual foreign fleets remained small throughout the period. Only the Japanese fleet accounted for as much as one tenth of the total of all tonnage entered. Even this occurred in only four of the inter-war years. Japanese predominance represents the one major variation from the pre-1914 pattern when it was the German fleet which led the field. In marked contrast with British vessels employed in the Australian sector most foreign fleets contented themselves with the provision of shipping limited to the servicing of the trade of their mother country or its oversea dependencies with Australia.

Cargo carrier nationality although indirectly illustrated by shipping activity is better attested by the amount of cargo actually carried by each fleet. Tables 5*a* and *b* contain this

Table 4*b*. *Nationality of foreign shipping entered 1920/1–1938/9* ('*000 net tons*)

	Total foreign	Tonnage registered in								
		Denmark	France	Germany	Italy	Japan	Netherlands	Norway	Sweden	U.S.A.
1920/1	1,443	25	108	—	129	506	134	133	85	274
1921/2	922	28	69	—	105	219	135	123	66	140
1922/3	1,087	39	114	45	51	244	141	149	82	194
1923/4	1,027	54	85	44	61	144	139	173	91	192
1924/5	1,341	43	104	81	116	298	162	219	87	186
1925/6	1,319	85	109	77	62	246	125	264	96	205
1926/7	1,407	61	100	141	62	211	115	303	112	232
1927/8	1,442	61	98	157	77	168	131	284	106	341
1928/9	1,445	34	119	138	55	287	148	255	92	289
1929/30	1,447	72	107	105	64	208	154	308	87	268
1930/1	1,846	45	103	115	68	672	147	340	114	187
1931/2	1,955	46	91	116	68	689	157	395	111	206
1932/3	1,989	107	108	117	77	546	185	395	136	246
1933/4	1,639	76	115	122	83	331	165	336	111	248
1934/5	1,934	49	137	134	62	461	176	427	141	241
1935/6	1,895	55	102	127	40	464	150	463	135	233
1936/7	1,692	53	83	153	43	344	173	440	104	200
1937/8	1,970	56	103	180	71	319	200	483	116	216
1938/9	1,824	55	108	141	68	330	291	325	124	175

Table 4*c*. *Foreign shipping tonnage entered 1922/3–1938/9 (sample years) (% of all tonnage entered)*

	1922/3	1928/9	1931/2	1938/9
Danish	0·82	0·61	0·81	0·82
French	2·40	2·14	1·60	1·61
German	0·95	2·49	2·04	2·10
Italian	1·08	0·99	1·20	1·01
Japanese	5·15	5·17	12·12	4·92
Netherlands	2·97	2·66	2·76	4·33
Norwegian	3·14	4·59	6·95	4·84
Swedish	1·73	1·66	1·95	1·85
U.S.A.	3·88	5·21	3·62	2·61
Other foreign	0·61	0·50	1·35	3·08

detail for the principal carriers from 1924/5 onwards. Before 1914 and again in the early 1920s foreign fleets carried about one quarter of all cargo shipped and discharged. This is a less precise record than for the years shown in the tables. There can be no doubting the overall tendency for foreign fleets as a whole to increase their share of the total after 1924/5 and especially during the early 1930s. These were years of particular difficulty for the British shipping industry. As we have already shown, the volume of inbound cargoes declined in the early depression years and undoubtedly affected the British shipping industry severely. The British fleet nevertheless remained the largest single carrier in Australia's oversea trade throughout the inter-war years. In every recorded year but one it carried more than one half of all inbound and outbound cargo. In ten of the years its share exceeded 55 %. The Australian fleet, which is omitted from the tables, carried some 6 % or 7 % of inbound and outbound cargo between 1924/5 and 1927/8. Shorn of the Commonwealth Government Line in that year, however, the locally registered fleet diminished in significance. During the remaining years its share of carrying rarely exceeded 2 % of inbound and $3\frac{1}{2}$ % of outbound cargo.

The rise in the proportion carried by foreign fleets as a whole was not at the expense of the U.K. fleet. Generally they drew from 'British' fleets other than that of the U.K. in the outbound direction and also for most of the recorded years in the

Table 5*a*. *Nationality of principal inbound carriers 1924/5–1938/9* (%)

	% of total cargo carried by ships registered in							
	U.K.	Germany	Italy	Japan	Netherlands	Norway	Sweden	U.S.A.
1920/1, 1921/2, 1922/3, 1923/4	Not available							
1924/5	61·8	2·6	1·3	4·4	2·2	5·7	2·8	3·8
1925/6	59·8	2·6	1·3	4·4	2·3	5·6	2·4	3·6
1926/7	60·7	2·8	1·0	2·2	1·4	8·0	4·1	4·7
1927/8	59·4	2·7	0·9	2·3	2·0	8·1	3·6	6·9
1928/9	65·0	2·7	0·5	2·4	2·0	7·2	2·9	6·7
1929/30	63·7	1·7	0·6	2·9	1·6	9·9	3·4	5·5
1930/1	Not available							
1931/2	54·4	1·2	0·5	1·6	2·8	17·8	5·3	5·2
1932/3	51·8	1·6	0·6	5·5	2·9	13·5	6·4	4·8
1933/4	48·8	1·4	0·4	5·0	3·0	14·1	4·5	4·9
1934/5	51·2	1·8	0·6	5·5	3·3	14·1	5·6	3·7
1935/6	52·5	2·0	0·2	5·2	1·5	16·1	4·1	3·0
1936/7	58·9	2·0	0·2	3·1	2·4	15·0	2·9	2·3
1937/8	60·7	2·6	0·6	2·3	2·4	13·6	2·7	2·4
1938/9	64·8	1·8	0·4	1·4	5·3	8·4	3·3	1·3

inbound direction. The limited service provided by most foreign fleets accounts for the smallness, generally speaking, of their individual shares of cargo carrying. Trade between Australia and Germany, for example, accounted for only a small proportion of Australia's total oversea trade. German shipping concentrated upon the direct trade and it is therefore not surprising that the German share of Australian cargo carrying should similarly be small. Only the Norwegian fleet in the inbound, and the Japanese fleet in the outbound direction, for a few years carried more than 10 % of the whole. The Norwegian fleet was more clearly a competitor in general carrying, as we suggest below. The Japanese fleet's increased activity in the years 1930/1 to 1935/6 derives from the greatly expanded export trade to Japan of these years.

The data on cargo tonnages carried by individual fleets also make it possible to determine the relationship of cargo to ship-

Table 5*b*. *Nationality of principal outbound carriers 1924/5–1938/9* (%)

	% of total cargo carried by ships registered in							
	U.K.	Germany	Italy	Japan	Netherlands	Norway	Sweden	U.S.A
1920/1	Not available							
1921/2								
1922/3								
1923/4								
1924/5	55·2	3·1	1·4	4·0	2·4	5·9	2·8	1·1
1925/6	53·9	4·2	1·4	3·3	2·7	4·8	2·7	2·4
1926/7	50·0	3·8	1·7	4·9	3·0	7·3	3·4	1·3
1927/8	54·1	4·6	1·6	3·6	3·0	5·2	3·0	2·7
1928/9	57·5	4·2	1·1	7·3	3·0	4·7	2·9	3·3
1929/30	57·2	3·4	1·4	5·4	3·9	4·8	2·8	3·2
1930/1	Not available							
1931/2	57·1	3·2	0·9	16·7	2·6	5·2	2·4	1·8
1932/3	56·5	3·1	1·3	13·4	3·1	5·5	2·6	0·6
1933/4	56·8	4·4	1·6	8·6	3·2	5·1	2·8	0·9
1934/5	56·1	3·5	0·6	10·8	2·5	5·9	2·4	1·1
1935/6	54·1	3·9	0·4	10·3	2·4	5·3	2·7	2·2
1936/7	58·4	4·6	0·8	6·1	3·0	5·1	2·4	2·2
1937/8	58·6	4·2	0·9	3·2	2·7	4·6	1·9	1·4
1938/9	57·3	4·0	0·8	2·7	3·8	4·7	2·2	1·2

ping in order to make some assessment of the relative efficiency of carrier utilisation. The relationship may be expressed in two ways (Table 6). First, the tonnage of cargo carried may be related to the tonnage of shipping actually employed in cargo carrying. Secondly, it may be related to the total tonnage of all shipping used, both with cargo and in ballast. The second provides a rough yardstick of excess shipping tonnage on offer. Both results must be used with caution. Outbound tonnage in ballast included empty oil tankers for which no outbound cargoes were available. Over the period oil imports increased and hence also the clearance of tankers in ballast. Inevitably the increased tonnage of tanker shipping entered reduced the ratio of cargo carried per ton of all shipping used. We would be justified therefore in expecting to find in those fleets not supplying tankers for the Australian oil trade a consistently higher ratio. In fact quite the opposite is shown in the data. It would similarly be unwise to use cargo shipping tonnage ratios as a precise basis for determining relative profitability of individual fleets. Cargoes vary in their space and other stowage needs and hence partly in the rates of freight they sustained. With all this qualification, however, it is neither difficult nor inappropriate to associate excess shipping capacity with a low cargo tonnage to shipping tonnage ratio.

The cargo ratios are thus useful in conveying the impression, which other evidence confirms, that relatively rather more shipping was being used at the end of the inter-war years than twenty years earlier. The effect on shipping of trade contraction in the early 1930s is unmistakable. In 1932/3, taking all fleets as a whole, the amount of cargo carried per ton of all shipping used had fallen from about 18½ cwt. to a mere 11 cwt. Thereafter the ratio improved. But for the combined fleets, British and foreign together, the quantity of cargo carried per ton of shipping with cargo was lower than it had been twenty years earlier. Largely, it will be noticed, it was in the foreign component where revival is least conspicuous, a reflection possibly of the ability of subsidised foreign fleets to maintain relatively uneconomic services. The British fleet, in contrast, was carrying a little more per ton of shipping in 1938/9 than in the later 1920s. For the British fleet as a whole, it is of interest to note, the Australian trade offered relatively more employment than did other sectors of international sea-borne trade. In 1937 British ships entering and leaving Australian ports with cargo carried about 15 % more cargo per ton of shipping than did British shipping entering and leaving British ports.[1]

Taking all foreign fleets together, it will be seen that their aggregate carrying performance exceeded that of the British fleet in the 1920s, but fell short of it by the close of the 1930s. In the 1920s foreign fleets together were carrying about 16 % more cargo per ton of shipping used than the U.K. fleet. When the positions were reversed, the U.K. fleet's lead was about 7 %. Variations between foreign fleets are most clearly to be seen if comparison is made on the basis of all shipping tonnage employed. As a rule, the Italian fleet carried the least, and the Norwegian the most cargo per ton of shipping. This in part

[1] *Sturmey*, p. 68.

Table 6. *Cargo carried, inbound and outbound combined, per net ton of shipping employed, 1920/1–1938/9 (sample years) (tons)*

	Ships registered in							
	U.K. fleet	All foreign fleets	Germany	Italy	Holland	Japan	Norway	U.S.A.
1920/1								
All shipping	0·93*a*	—	—	—	—	—	—	—
Shipping with cargo	1·16*a*	—	—	—	—	—	—	—
1926/7								
All shipping	1·00	1·15	1·31	1·01	1·66	1·06	1·48	0·60
Shipping with cargo	1·13	1·32	1·43	1·18	1·02	1·07	1·79	0·80
1932/3								
All shipping	0·88	0·96	1·01	0·69	0·83	0·99	1·15	0·44
Shipping with cargo	1·15	1·20	1·17	0·73	0·95	1·35	1·54	0·44
1938/9								
All shipping	1·02	0·95	1·26	0·59	1·00	0·38	1·31	0·45
Shipping with cargo	1·15	1·10	1·29	0·59	1·17	0·40	1·69	0·47

a, data relate to *all* fleets employed; —, not available.

probably reflects the Norwegian fleet's role as a general carrier. The performance of the U.S.A. fleet suggests the greatest excess capacity throughout the years recorded with a tendency to worsen towards the end of the period. It is noteworthy that the Japanese fleet alone in the depression year experienced an increase in the ratio for employed shipping. It is the result, as is also the decline in the ratio for *all* Japanese shipping, of the sharp expansion of the bulk trade in iron ore exports to Japan and the heavy arrivals of Japanese vessels in ballast for its carriage. The problem of excess shipping capacity and its effect upon rates of freight was not ignored in Australia. As our discussion in chapter 6 shows, from 1930 onwards attempts were made in Australia to achieve some rationalisation in the supply of shipping. With the object of providing full cargoes for a smaller number of ships, forecasts were prepared on the basis of known or anticipated export quantities.

A final introductory point to make before turning to a discussion of services is the tendency for foreign shipping companies especially those of European countries, to be less specialised to particular trades. Unlike most British-liner companies, foreign European lines engaged simultaneously in a number of quite disparate trades. The large British-liner groups often embraced under single control many separate companies. Usually they retained their identity and their links with a particular trade route. European companies on the other hand when taken over simply disappeared. Only a few individual ships of large foreign shipping companies were committed to the Australian trade. In 1923/4 only 2 ships of the 51-vessel fleet of the Holland-Amerika Lijn called at Fremantle. In 1938/9 only 5 of the 88-vessel fleet of Norddeutscher Lloyd called at the port. In 1923/4 German ships calling at Fremantle included vessels of the Kosmos Deutsche Dampschiffarhts and the Deutsche-Australische Dampschiff lines. Both companies were later taken over by the Hamburg-Amerika, the company names disappeared and their ships joined the fleet of the new owner.

Commonwealth shipping data are compiled in such a way as to prevent duplication of entry. An oversea ship calling at several Australian ports is recorded once only as arriving from overseas and once only as clearing for overseas. A ship entering Fremantle from an oversea port is recorded as an arrival from overseas. All subsequent movements of the ship on the Australian coast are recorded as coastwise arrivals within each state. Otherwise it is statistically ignored until cleared from an Australian port for overseas; it is then shown as a departure from Australia. Commonwealth published sources make no attempt to show the repeated voyages made to Australia by an oversea ship. Each entry from overseas is recorded separately. A vessel making 10 voyages a year to Australia is entered 10 times and its net registered tonnage appears 10 times in the tonnage total. Thus in 1938/9 the 'number' of British vessels entering the Commonwealth was about 1,200, foreign vessels about 670. Although this gives an accurate record of oversea *tonnage* handled, it gives no information about the actual number of individual vessels employed. In fact, as we shall show, the number of ships used was relatively small.

Records compiled by Fremantle Harbour Trust and published in the *Annual Reports*, however, list oversea arrivals individually by name. With their aid it is possible to supply some of the detail hidden in the aggregates published by the Commonwealth Statistician. They are an imperfect guide to oversea shipping activity in Australia. Not all oversea arrivals called at Fremantle. Tramps were often chartered to load at other Australian ports. Detail compiled by the Tramp Shipping Administrative Committee and discussed in chapter 2 shows that this was common. Cargo liners programmed to clear from ports in eastern Australia are unlikely to have called (or similarly to call today) at Fremantle. Trans-Pacific services terminated at Sydney or Melbourne. Nevertheless, the Fremantle records are illustrative of Australian oversea shipping activity. Towards the end of the inter-war years about one-quarter to one-third of all oversea tonnage entering Australia called at Fremantle. Most scheduled liners on the European service would certainly have called at the port. We need not, therefore, doubt the generally representative nature of the shipping data available for this single port.

The systematic record by name of all arrivals at Fremantle along with *Lloyd's Register* makes it possible to identify the various foreign and British companies supplying vessels for Australia's oversea services. Each oversea ship mentioned in the Fremantle Harbour Trust's *Annual Reports* has been identified by nationality and ownership. Summary detail for three sample years is shown below. As well as comparing the end with the beginning of the period, the years chosen include 1930/1 to illustrate shipping activity in a year of depression. Although a year of depressed trade, no hint of this is contained in the number of arrivals. With foreign fleets, indeed, the number of companies, ships used, and visits made were all higher than at the beginning or end of our period. In part this may have been because of the overall rise in foreign-fleet activity in the Commonwealth in 1930/1. In part also it reflects the disappearance of Japanese trading vessels from Fremantle after 1936/7 (but not from the Commonwealth as a whole). In 1937/8 and 1938/9 only Japanese whaling vessels each with its spat of satellite chasers called at Fremantle.

Shipping activity at Fremantle: all fleets

	Foreign shipping			U.K. shipping		
	C	S	V	C	S	V
1923/4	31	54	89	37	155	261
1930/1	35	72	128	55	173	312
1938/9	26	58	115	54	154	312

C, companies; S, ships; V, visits.

THE AUSTRALIAN FLEET

The least important contribution was that of the locally owned fleet. The failure of the Australian merchant fleet to assist significantly in the country's oversea trade has already been mentioned. Nevertheless, the fleet was not exclusively employed in the coastal services nor did it, for the whole of our period, confine its oversea activities to Australasian waters. Although unimportant in the long-term context of trade with Europe, the part played by the fleet in the European services, in the eastern services, and in the Australasian scene cannot be ignored. The nature of the services provided by the local fleet reflects its composition. This in turn reflects local unwillingness or inability to invest in shipping on a scale adequate to Australia's needs. Although at times the net registered tonnage of the fleet sums to a not unimpressive total, it always included a variety of estuarine craft, tugs, dredges, hulks, and the like. Deep-sea tonnage formed only a small proportion of the whole. In 1914 the local fleet included 48 ships (with a total of 123,000 tonnage) of 2,000 net tons and over, a size representing 3,200 gross tons and hence approximately the lower limit of oversea entries in Australia at this time. In 1925, with 3 ships less, the aggregate tonnage had increased to about 165,000. But by the end of 1938 the number had fallen to 28 and total tonnage to about 100,000.

During the First World War, as already noted, the privately owned Australian fleet was augmented by the creation of the Commonwealth Government Line designed primarily for oversea services.[1] State ownership of shipping in Australia in itself was

[1] Details of the line and its sorry history are to be found in *C.P.P.* 1926/8, IV, 5 ff.

not new. Apart from the estuarine craft used in harbour-navigation services, certain states also operated merchant shipping for the carrying of cargo. Usually it was found in those states wherein the operation of coastal services was uneconomic unless subsidised. In addition to or instead of subsidies, Tasmania and Western Australia operated publicly owned merchant shipping. (The Western Australian government in fact still operates a fleet of six 2,000–3,000 gross ton vessels.) What was new about the federal government's intervention (other than being federal rather than state) was the decision to operate in the deep sea as distinct from the Australasian trade. For a few years the combination of private effort and public funds, profit on the latter not necessarily being the main criteria, made oversea carrying by the indigenous fleet of more significance.

The original fleet of 15 ships bought by Hughes in 1916 was enlarged. At one time or another 62 vessels with a total net tonnage of 185,000 were owned by the line. Peace did not witness a speedy disposal of the line. It was retained among other reasons to act as a scourge and goad for the conference lines; this is discussed in chapter 6. The profits of war-time disappeared with the return of peace. Many vessels in the line were too small, too slow, and too old to combat the double disability of world excess shipping capacity and hence low freights, coupled with pay and manning on the Australian scale. Many of the ships were inadequately fitted. In 1921 the line had only a half million cubic feet of refrigerated space, compared with more than 24 million on the oversea lines owned overseas.[1] When the system of fleet management and control was changed in 1923 as many as 27 ships had been laid up for lengthy periods. Only 24 of the 51 ships in the fleet were less than 11 years old and of this number 18 were no bigger than 1,900 net registered tons, 5 were each about 8,500 tons. Two-thirds of the line were sold in 1923. By 1926 only the 5 *Bay* class and the 2 *Dales* (built in 1924) remained in effective service. But these were modern vessels and for a time it seemed that the line might survive. It failed partly because of the heavy financial losses from which it suffered, partly from Australian unwillingness to provide a direct operating subsidy.

[1] *S.M.H.* 6 April 1921.

During the lifetime of the government line three main services were undertaken by the Australian registered fleet as a whole: the Australasian service (including the Pacific islands), the eastern service, and the European service. The last was maintained solely by the Commonwealth Government Line. The eastern service involved Burns, Philp & Co. (better known for their Territories services mentioned below) who had operated from Sydney to Singapore for many years. The Commonwealth line also began a three-weekly Sydney-Java-Singapore service in 1921 using some of the Commonwealth line vessels in the 1,900 net tons class. It proved to be unprofitable and was surrendered in 1924 to a British line, Ellerman and Bucknall Co. Ltd, on their undertaking to continue the service.[1] In the 1930s the government line of Western Australia operated a Fremantle-Java-Singapore service from which it withdrew in the 1930s handing over the service to the Blue Funnel Line.[2]

The main service for which the Commonwealth line was retained, however, and of major interest here, was on the Suez route with Britain. It was a regular service based upon the 5 *Bay* ships and the 2 *Dales*. The *Bay* class, vessels of 8,500 net tons, carried 750 passengers, had a deadweight capacity of about 12,600 tons, and were each equipped with 350,000 cubic feet of insulated space. The two *Dales* were dry cargo carriers, 5,800 net tons, a deadweight capacity of almost 13,000 and with a smaller refrigerated hold space of 180,000 cubic feet. Together the 7 ships totalled about 63,000 net tons with about 6 million cubic feet of refrigerated space, the latter equal to about one sixth of the volume available on the British lines regularly employed on the service.[3] They were all turbined oil-burning steamers with a service speed of about 15 knots.

The *Bay* and *Dale* ships maintained a monthly service between London and Sydney. The *Dales* in addition were used to open up a direct trade with east-coast ports, with the west of England and with Glasgow. This was to foreshadow the policy later adopted by the various Australian marketing boards in the 1930s to divert Australian exports away from London to other

[1] *C.P.D.* vol. 106, p. 1,348. See also vol. 115, p. 407 for proposals to establish eastern services. *S.M.H.* 29 April 1924. I.S.C. *38th Report*, pp. 43–4.

[2] *U.K. Trade Report*, 1938, p. 190.

[3] *C.P.D.* vol. 117, p. 2,484.

British ports. During the years of maximum activity by the government line, Australian-registered vessels as a whole carried about 7% of inbound and outbound cargo. Voyages by the government line alone in 1925 in the U.K. service amounted to about 10% of total tonnage employed. As discussed in another chapter, however, industrial disputes and a high cost structure ultimately led to the disposal of the seven remaining ships of the line in 1928. Ill chance dogged the line even after its sale; the buyers went into liquidation with £750,000 of the purchase price unpaid. It had proved to be a costly venture for the Australian taxpayer. Some of the capital invested literally 'went up in smoke'. In 1928 the remaining two wooden vessels in the fleet were burnt in Sydney harbour; perhaps the pyrotechnics gave some compensation to the onlookers. These were the last of the wooden ships bought in the U.S. in the line's early days. Many were defective from the outset because built of unseasoned timber; some had scarcely been used.[1]

With the sale of the Commonwealth line the local fleet reverted to its earlier, more restricted role. Thereafter, with only minor variations, local ships concentrated on the coastal and Australasian trades. A large number of shipping companies were involved. In 1927 no fewer than 34 companies were at work around the Australian coast. Except for the ships of the Union Steam Ship Company of New Zealand all vessels employed were registered in Australia. The Union Steam Ship Company presents a slight complication to the simple pattern. To prevent confusion it may here be described briefly. It was a company registered in New Zealand and had been acquired by the P & O in 1917. Its ships were registered in New Zealand but were based on Sydney where repairs were normally carried out and where crews were obtained. The ships were manned on the Australian scale (and hence were free to operate in the Australian coastal trade without special license) and the crews were mainly Australian. Certain of its vessels operated outside Australasia and were engaged on trans-Pacific mail, passenger and cargo services, one to San Francisco and a second to

[1] *C.P.D.* vol. 138, p. 303; vol. 155, pp. 1,432, 1,455. *C.P.P.* 1926/8, v, 441. See also *S.M.H.* 24 February, 1 May, 5 June 1925; November 1927 *passim*; and April 1928 *passim*. *Fairplay* vol. 117, p. 273.

Vancouver. In 1931, for reasons connected with competition discussed in chapter 6, two of the company's ships were sold to a newly created subsidiary, the Canadian-Australasian Line Ltd. The new company was owned jointly by the Union Steam Ship Company and the Canadian Pacific Company and was registered as a company in Canada. The two ships, the *Aorangi* and the *Niagara* at the same time were re-registered, this time at London. The terminals of the new line were Vancouver and Sydney via Hawaii, Fiji and Auckland. A few years later the service between Sydney and San Francisco was abandoned by the Union Steam Ship Company. During the remainder of our period the ships of the company concentrated on the Trans-Tasman and Australian coastal services.

Many of the purely Australian companies were small. Some were single-ship companies. One such company, J. S. Lee and Sons of Melbourne, in 1939 owned one sailing vessel (with auxiliary power) of 145 gross tons. Not all were companies specialising in shipping; for some, ship ownership was an offshoot of, or derived from, other activities. Timber millers owned ships. The Newcastle coal mining firm of J. and A. Brown became ship owners. Broken Hill Proprietary Ltd, after moving into iron and steel not only acquired coal mines, it also created a merchant fleet for the transport of ore. In 1939 it owned 8 ships totalling about 32,000 gross tons. In the reverse direction some shipping companies moved into coal-mine ownership.

Not all the shipping companies owning fleets registered in Australia were themselves owned locally. Many were wholly or partly owned subsidiaries of U.K. shipping companies. The P & O Line and its chief subsidiary the British India held substantial or controlling interests in the A.U.S.N., in Huddart Parker Ltd, and in Burns, Philp and Company of Sydney, the famous island traders. It was often argued that division of function between local subsidiary companies and their oversea owners prevented local companies from extending their operations. This seems unlikely in the light of what is known about their development. That there was no insuperable scarcity of investible funds locally is abundantly suggested by the evidence assembled on capital formation by Professor Butlin. Nevertheless, few of the Australian shipping companies could have competed in the oversea sector and it is this factor rather than the subordination of local companies to oversea interests which limited the services provided by local shipping.

Only a few local companies offered regular services beyond coastal waters. A number of ships, of the A.U.S.N. and Huddart Parker fleets joined the Union Steam Ship Company in serving the trans-Tasman trade with additional outside charterings as occasion required. Apart from the New Zealand trade the principal area of interest was in the Territories and islands. The best-known company supplying services in this trade is Burns, Philp of Sydney.

Burns, Philp was founded in the 1880s and from the outset developed connections with the Pacific islands and the Territories. After the First World War, when control of German New Guinea was vested in Australia, Burns, Philp received the mail contract and subsidy and following the implementation of the Navigation Act in 1921 strengthened its hold on the Territories and islands trade. One effect of the Navigation Act was to reduce the volume of shipping entering the Territories. It would seem clear that the bulk if not all the 'British' shipping entering the Territories was Australian-registered and certainly most of the Australian tonnage was owned by Burns, Philp.[1]

After the cabotage restrictions of the Navigation Act were relaxed in favour of the Territories the tonnage of shipping visiting them increased significantly. In addition there took place a return to the pre-1914 practice of making direct copra shipments to Europe. It was indeed a logical method of handling the copra exported from the Territories. Australia offered neither a market for copra nor facilities for its processing prior to re-export. Transhipment at Sydney merely increased handling charges. But in the absence, generally speaking, of other cargoes either to or from the Territories, local shipping companies disliked the intrusion of oversea shipping which cleared the one bulk cargo on offer. The development had been discussed in the local press and in *The Times* as early as 1922. Complaint increased after the exemption of the Territories from the Navigation Act. In 1934 a lengthy protest from Sydney ship-

[1] *C.P.P.* 1923/4, II and 1925, II for first and second reports of the royal commission on the Navigation Act. For annual shipping data see *Year Book*.

ping interests appeared in the *S.M.H.* following a further 'intrusion' by oversea companies into the copra trade. An adjournment motion at Canberra was devoted to the theme.[1]

Competition from oversea-owned vessels prompted local owners themselves to undertake direct carrying between the Territories and Europe. In 1934 W. R. Carpenter and Company of Sydney, one of the four signatories of the complaint mentioned above, instituted a direct service between the Territories and Europe, 'the first purely Australian company to provide such a service'.[2] The company's chairman was later to complain acidly of the lack of government support. His was the only all-Australian company trading to Europe. Not only was it not paid a public subsidy, he said, but it was actually being boycotted by the government. Large munition import cargoes were being carried solely by expatriate companies.[3] W. R. Carpenter & Co., like Burns, Philp had been active in the Territories trade for a number of years. The two companies had many links. The first Carpenter, whose name was used for the firm's original title, had captained the first Burns, Philp ship. His son, W. R. Carpenter from whom the present title derives, was also a one-time employee of Burns, Philp whose service he left in 1908 to found the family firm.

One further manifestation of Australian participation in the oversea-shipping scene which merits brief mention was the venture into ship management in the 1930s. Two separate and unrelated groups took part: Australian Tramp Steamers Ltd, during 1932, and the 'Westfarmers Line' in the following year. Australian Tramp Steamers Ltd, was formed in April 1932 to operate the first Australian tramp service between Australia and ports in the east. One ship was in fact bought (a vessel hitherto employed on the coast) and it was intended to charter other vessels to operate on a management basis.[4] The company made no perceptible impact. The absence of further information about the company probably indicates its early dissolution. The one

[1] *The Times* 15 November 1922 and 13 November 1934. *S.M.H. passim*, March and April 1922 and 1 November 1934. *C.P.D.* vol. 149, p. 296 ff.

[2] *Fairplay* vol. 131, p. 310. See also *C.P.D.* vol. 144, p. 815.

[3] *S.M.H.* 17 November 1938.

[4] *U.K. Trade Report*, 1932, p. 138. *S.M.H. Financial and Commercial Supplement*, 9 February 1933. *C.P.D.* vol. 135, p. 373.

ship that it owned, the *Tarcoola*, was in fact registered at Hong Kong, and hence not Australian-owned within the restrictions of our definitions. It was sold within a year to the North China Steam Ship Company, renamed and re-registered. The one vessel known to have been chartered, the *Barunga*, was sold to a Japanese fleet in 1935 and also renamed and re-registered.

The second group through its conflict with the federal government attracted more interest and made a greater impact on the oversea-shipping scene. Believing that freight rates were excessive, 'growers' organisations approached the Western Australian cooperative Westralian Farmers Ltd. 'to enter into the shipping business'. This they did (and still do) using a number of vessels chartered on a time basis. The irritation caused by the 'West Farmers Line' to the Australian government in connection with freight rates, where the major effect was felt, is discussed in chapters below. Inasmuch as the vessels were chartered and managed rather than owned, and were chartered from oversea companies which would in any case have supplied shipping to Australia, the overall effect of the local venture is more properly discussed in the context of the shipping conference monopoly.

FOREIGN FLEETS

The principal foreign fleets represented in Australia's oversea services are shown in the tables on pp. 44–8. A few ships of fleets not separately recorded have also been identified from Fremantle records; the occasional Spanish vessel as in 1923/4, one from Esthonia in 1930/1, and, in 1938/9, a ship owned in New York but sailing under the Panama flag of convenience. The one foreign fleet of any importance not separately recorded in Commonwealth records (but included today) was that of Greece; it was unimportant until the closing years of our period.

For a number of reasons it is convenient to group the foreign European fleets together for discussion. The major lines involved were all members of the homeward shipping conference organisation, most concentrated on the Suez route. For the fleets of France, Germany, Italy, and the Netherlands there is an additional common factor which justifies their examination separately from the fleets of Greece, Norway, and Sweden. All four

Shipping activity at Fremantle: Foreign European fleets (a)

	1923/4			1930/1			1938/9		
	C	S	V	C	S	V	C	S	V
France	2	4	9	1	4	4	2	3	3
Germany	3	4	5	2	8	12	2	11	16
Italy	4	10	20	2	5	23	1	4	24
Netherlands	7	13	24	3	11	14	7	13	20

C, companies; S, ships; V, visits.

fleets, whose activity at Fremantle is shown above, primarily concerned themselves with the direct trade between their mother country and Australia. The French and Dutch fleets were engaged also in the trade between their eastern or Pacific territories and Australia.

Links with Germany in pre-war years involved the use of Australia as a point of call for ships *en route* to and from German New Guinea. Prior to the war the German fleet had been the most conspicuous foreign fleet in Australian waters; between 1908 and 1913 about 10 % of all tonnage entered at Australian ports was German. The outbreak of war and the Australian occupation of New Guinea was accompanied by a disruption of the services. Direct trade with Germany was not resumed until 1 August 1922 and then only in the face of local opposition. Just as the renewal of trade with Japan after the Second World War was accompanied by outbursts of protest and by demonstrations during official Japanese visits, so also was the restoration of normal commercial relations with Germany disliked in the early 1920s. The anticipated re-appearance of German lines gave rise to hostile comment. It was suggested that they would not be admitted to the shipping conference. The Australian correspondent of *Fairplay* quoted a Sydney shipping representative who sought at one and the same time to augment local port revenues and penalise erstwhile enemies. He urged that 'the German companies should be made to suffer a penalty by increased harbour dues, which would benefit the Commonwealth'.[1]

[1] *Fairplay* vol. 83, p. 592.

'British and continental lines were not slow in stepping in with new services to cope with the expected traffic.' But the two German lines active before the war promptly reappeared on the scene and with A. Holt and Co. Ltd, established a joint service to Australia. The return of native lines quickly ousted other companies from the German trade. Although direct wool exports to Germany rose sharply, very little was shipped in British vessels.[1] The connection between the German lines and former German Pacific territory survived the war, the loss of the colonies, and the exclusion of foreign lines during the currency of the Navigation Act. Subsequently, when the Act was amended in order to free the Territories trade, Norddeutscher-Lloyd vessels quickly reappeared in the islands.

At no time during the inter-war years, however, did Germany's share of entry tonnage approach the pre-war figure. The smaller fleet visiting Australia in the inter-war years initially consisted of up-to-date tonnage as modern vessels were brought into service. On the eve of the war the Hamburg-Amerika Line planned to introduce into the Australian service three new diesel-electric vessels (similar to the company's M.V. *Wuppertal* built for the trade in 1936). As well as the main services between Germany and Australia, Norddeutscher-Lloyd, in the early 1930s introduced a far-eastern service between Hong Kong and Australia via New Guinea fed by an inter-island Pacific service. Local hostility in Australia may well have influenced the company in 1934 to sell to Burns, Philp & Co. the two 6,000 ton motor vessels employed.[2]

The French fleet similarly conducted a Suez service to Australia and beyond to the French Pacific. Messageries Maritimes resumed the combined passenger and cargo service in 1922 with three new vessels operating a monthly service from Marseilles. The first vessel left the port in early June. Between 1920/1 and 1926/7 about 700,000 net registered tons of French shipping were entered. More than 80% arrived from or subsequently cleared for France and New Caledonia. During the 1930s the activity of the French merchant fleet in Australia tended to decline. Of the increased foreign tonnage in 1938/9 the French

[1] *S.M.H.* 1 January 1923.

[2] *S.M.H.* 1 November 1934; 12 February 1935.

share had sagged to below 2 %. In that year only three ships made three visits to Fremantle.

The Dutch fleet conversely was of increasing importance during the inter-war years, largely as a result of the growth in the trade in oil from the N.E.I. to Australia. The tonnage of shipping doubled and the Dutch share of the total rose to more than 4 %. In 1938/9 as many as 9 of the 13 Dutch ships visiting Fremantle were oil tankers. Three major lines maintained the Suez service, the Royal Packet Co. (K.P.M.), the Holland-Australia, and the Holland-East Asia Lines. The Royal Packet Co. was chiefly active in eastern Australia and operated also a far-eastern service from Melbourne (later from Adelaide) via Sydney to Singapore and Java. The Holland-Australia Line's vessels visiting Australia were replaced in the later 1930s by new, fast diesel cargo-passenger liners.[1]

Italian ships entering Australian ports in the early 1920s were augmented by a new passenger service introduced by Lloyd Sabaudo Line, later called Lloyd Triestino. The process of company concentration and amalgamation is particularly conspicuous in the Italian fleet. At Fremantle, for example, the four companies of the early 1920s had, by the end of our period, been reduced to a single company, Lloyd Triestino. The Italian fleet was not significant as a cargo carrier; in the 1930s its share of inbound and outbound cargo was consistently less than 1 %, in the inbound direction the share rarely exceeded ½ %. It was not involved with other conference lines in the annual sugar contract and its share of wool-carrying to Europe was usually only 3–4 %. It was nevertheless important because of its role in the Italian migrant trade. Italians were the next most numerous component after the British in the migration flow throughout the inter-war years. They exceeded by far any other foreign national group. Measures for the control of migrant traffic adopted by the Italian government at times restricted the carrying rights of foreign vessels in favour of domestic lines. In 1925, for example, the Italian emigration department reduced the number of foreign ships licensed to carry migrants from three to two. As a consequence the Orient Line's *Orama* was denied access to the trade. As the migrant traffic increased in the 1920s

[1] *U.K. Trade Reports*, 1935, p. 129; 1938, p. 189.

the Navigazione Generale Italia entered the trade with new motor vessels.[1] Compared with British migrants in the lean years of the depression fewer Italians permanently repatriated themselves. Nevertheless, in 1931 some passenger space on Italian vessels was taken up by Italians unable to find employment in Australia. More significant as a demand factor to Italian shipping than returning migrants was the effect of restrictions on inward migration to Australia imposed in early 1931. Reinforced by agreement with the Italian government, only relatives of Italians living in Australia were henceforth permitted to enter the country.[2]

Unlike the European fleets discussed above, the ships of Greece, Sweden and above all Norway were engaged in general carrying, mostly between other European countries and Australia. Trade between Australia and Greece was never large enough to justify a separate entry in the Commonwealth *Year Book*. Nor indeed were Greek ship-arrivals sufficiently numerous during the 1920s and early 1930s to merit mention in the *Transport and Communication Bulletins*. By the later 1930s, however, Greek tonnage in the world's fleet had risen from less than 1 % to almost 3 % of the total. Greek tonnage has been traced in the Fremantle harbour records. All the ships seem to have been engaged on tramping. The Swedish services provided were similarly only little connected with trade between Sweden and Australia.

Of the foreign European fleets, however, it was that of Norway which predominated in the Australian shipping scene. It most closely resembled that part of the British fleet which provided oversea services not directly connected with trade between Australia and Britain. Few of the voyages made by Norwegian ships in Australia's services were to Norway. In 1927/8, for example, only 12 % of Norwegian tonnage was entered from Norway, less than 10 % of it is recorded as cleared for home. Calculations made of Norwegian liner tonnage employment in 1930 show that 40 % was employed solely between foreign countries.[3] Today, 90 % of the Norwegian tanker fleet and 80 %

[1] *Fairplay* vol. 94, p. 209; *S.M.H.* 9 July 1926.
[2] *Fairplay* vol. 119, pp. 155, 612.
[3] *Fairplay* vol. 118, p. 128.

Shipping activity at Fremantle: Foreign European fleets (*b*)

	1923/4			1930/1			1938/9		
	C	S	V	C	S	V	C	S	V
Greece	—	—	—	2	2	2	8	10	11
Norway	4	10	16	5	14	33	6	17	41
Sweden	1	8	8	1	7	8	1	7	12

C, companies; S, ships; V, visits.

of its merchant fleet as a whole operates the year round away from Norway.

A single company, Wilhelm Wilhelmsen of Oslo outstripped the rest. Often called by its earlier original name, the Norwegian-Australia Line, it had a fleet of fifty-two ships including forty-eight modern motor vessels. One quarter of the latter regularly visited Australia. Three main services were provided, outward via South Africa, homeward via Suez, and a third on the Sydney to Singapore-Java route where it competed with the Dutch K.P.M. and the Sydney firm of Burns, Philp. Towards the end of the 1930s a Norwegian company whose ships appear not to have visited Fremantle established a new trans-Pacific cargo and passenger service between San Francisco and eastern Australia via New Guinea. For those Norwegian ships visiting Fremantle, as well as Greek and Swedish vessels, entry details are shown above.

The most significant foreign fleet in Australia's oversea services was that of Japan. In 1931/2, its year of peak importance, it contributed about 12% of all oversea tonnage entered in Australia, equal to about one fifth of British tonnage. As with most of the foreign ships engaged in Australia's oversea-shipping services, the Japanese fleet concentrated on the direct trade between Australia and Japan. As a consequence, Japanese shipping activity in the Australian sector ebbed and flowed with the current volume of trade. The dramatic expansion of services in the early 1930s especially may be linked precisely with the expansion of Australian exports to Japan, especially iron ore and wheat.

Japan was not only the most important eastern market for Australian produce it was also the one eastern country at that time able and determined to develop a merchant fleet. Official Japanese policy for many years was directed towards creating and expanding a powerful merchant marine. As well as the more obvious measures, cabotage legislation, subsidies and the like there were also, as in Germany, the restrictions attached to the financing of trade. As we show, the very success of the Japanese fleet created friction with the one British line at work on the route to Japan.

The expansion of the Japanese fleet was so successfully achieved as to alarm British shipping interests generally; a brief digression is thus necessary to explain the background to the acrimonious negotiations in the Japan-Australia conference outlined in chapter 6. During the inter-war years the tonnage of the Japanese fleet almost doubled and rose from 5% to 8% of the world's fleet. The 'scrap and build' schemes of 1932, 1935, and 1936 moreover had the effect of transforming the age structure of the fleet. In 1938/9 more than one third of all Japanese tonnage was less than ten years old as compared with one quarter in the world's fleet. More striking is that almost one quarter of Japanese tonnage was under ten years old and in the size range 6,000 to 20,000 gross tons; in the world's fleet the comparable proportion was only 13%.

Much of the new Japanese tonnage consisted of fast liners. It was this aspect particularly which induced British shipping companies to pressure the government for an enquiry. The investigation made by the Imperial Shipping Committee in 1937 into *British Shipping in the Orient* concluded that British shipping would not have 'relatively failed, where it has failed, had it not been faced by the peculiar competitive strength of Japan'.[1] On the eve of the Second World War British shipping was pressing for the creation of a liner-defence fund. The Joint Liner Committee of the Chamber of Shipping in its memorandum on the subject showed that Japanese shipping had been ousting the British from a number of sectors. In the three main trades affected, between Japan and Australia, India, and the

[1] I.S.C. *38th Report*, p. 97. For an interesting survey of factors accounting for the success of Japanese shipping during the inter-war years see *Sturmey*, p. 120 ff.

Persian Gulf, the Japanese share had risen from negligible proportions to between 70 % and 90 % of all tonnage employed.[1]

The Australian sector gave employment in 1924 to about 5 % of Japanese deep-sea tramp tonnage; 15 years later, with a much greater tonnage at work, the proportion was much the same. In May 1936 about 11 % of all Japanese tonnage was at work in Australian and Indian waters.[2] Japanese ships first appeared on the Japan-Australia route in 1895 when the Nippon Yusen Kaisha (N.Y.K.) introduced a monthly service between Japan and Australia. In the early 1920s with the expansion of trade an additional monthly service was begun by the Osaka Shosen Kaisha (O.S.K.) and by a composite line, the 'Japan-Australia' made up of the Kawasaki, Kokusai, and Yamashita steam ship companies (slight variations in the formal title of these companies are unimportant). Based originally upon the direct route between the two countries the services were extended to include Hong Kong, China and, in the 1930s, to New Zealand. On the whole the companies named above concentrated on eastern Australian services, especially in the wool trade. But many other Japanese lines, mostly tramp companies, were also at work. In 1930/1, for example, no fewer than 16 companies are represented at Fremantle; they used 24 ships which between them made 36 visits to the port. At Fremantle the trade items chiefly shipped were wheat and flour. As well, the rapidly expanded if short-lived trade in iron ore also offered extensive employment to Japanese tramps as the tonnage figures of shipping indicate.

For a short time during 1925 it seemed as if the Japanese fleet would extend its activities into the homeward route to Europe from Australia. The three companies in the 'Japan-Australia' line announced their inauguration of a monthly service from Australia to the U.K. and Continent. Secret rate rebates were rumoured to the obvious disliking of the lines in homeward conference. Observers in Australia noted the imminence of a freight war if not actually a freight-rate war.[3] Nothing further is

[1] Various files, notes, and memoranda on Japanese competition and liner 'defence' at the C of S. The press contained many references to both aspects, on the latter see, for example, *The Times* 4, 11 and 12 January 1939.

[2] *Fairplay* vol. 94, p. 142; vol. 150, p. 121. C of S 'Japanese Competition' file.

[3] *Fairplay* vol. 94, p. 126; *S.M.H.* 21 August, 19 and 22 September 1924.

heard of the alleged intrusion. It may be, as shipowners claimed, that shippers 'remained loyal' to the established lines.

The impact of Japanese competition on the British line at work on the Japan-Australia route is appropriately examined in the context of conference organisation and the long-term effects of the conference system. Here we may note, however, that towards the close of the inter-war years the Japan-Australia route was heavily over-tonnaged. The tendency for trade with Japan to contract after 1935/6 was not accompanied by an immediate adjustment in the supply of shipping. As a consequence, by 1938/9 Japanese ships on the Australia route were carrying only 8 cwts. of cargo per net registered ton of shipping in contrast with 27 cwts. in 1932/3.

Among the less important foreign fleets both as a cargo carrier and in terms of tonnage entered was the U.S. fleet. Its share of the total moreover tended to decline. During the 1920s on average about 230,000 and in the 1930s about 218,000 net tons of U.S. shipping entered Australian ports, mostly in eastern Australia with services terminating at Melbourne. At Fremantle, only three U.S. ships were entered in one of the sample years analysed. Paradoxically the U.S. merchant fleet became an irritant to the British shipping industry only during the 1930s when its share of entry tonnage was actually lower than in the 1920s. The source of irritation lay in the subsidized competition of the U.S. Matson Line and its marginal role in cargo carrying on the trans-Tasman route. In the 1920s although the actual tonnage entered and the proportion of the whole which it represented were both higher, the activities of the U.S. fleet pass almost unnoticed. Generally speaking, friction was absent.

Largely the unremarked activity of U.S. shipping in the 1920s stems from the nature of the traffic and the relative success of the British lines in maintaining their share.[1] The friction and clamour of the 1930s signifies the erosion of the earlier British dominance. The trans-Pacific trade consisted of cargo and passenger traffic. The passenger trade was not one involving migrants, it was chiefly a tourist trade which demanded high

[1] In the absence of readily available information Commonwealth shipping records have been supplemented by the incidental references contained in the I.S.C. *35th Report* [on a passenger service between Canada and Australia].

Tonnage of shipping from North America

	(a) Entered from North America ('000 tons)	(b) Entered by U.S.A. ships ('000 tons)
1925/6	1,281	205
1929/30	1,186	267
1931/2	802	205
1934/5	1,072	240
1938/9	1,021	175

standards of personal service and ship accommodation. As we show in chapter 6, these criteria worked to the advantage of the U.S. Matson Line and to the disadvantage of the British line. Cargo on the whole tended to be one-way. Many of the vessels bringing motor-vehicles, lumber, and so on were British, Japanese and Norwegian. The smallness of the share enjoyed by the U.S.A. fleet is suggested above for representative years. During the 1930s the Matson Line's three vessels *Lurline*, *Mariposa*, and *Monterey*, each of some 10,000 net tons, were employed on a monthly service between San Francisco and Australia. A monthly entry of 10,000 net tons over a year in aggregate accounted for between 50 % and 70 % of all U.S.A. arrivals in Australian ports during the decade. In the later 1920s the Roosevelt Steam Ship Co. introduced a cargo service from the eastern seaboard via Panama. The occasional entry of a freighter from the eastern U.S. together with the Matson tonnage accounts for almost the whole of the U.S. fleet at this time. Interest in the U.S. fleet lies in its success within the shipping conference organisation which is discussed in chapter 6.

'BRITISH' FLEETS

Our discussion in the following pages on the organisation of the industry and on the services provided by ships of the British Commonwealth is in fact an examination of the British shipping industry. Apart from the Australian fleet, whose activities have already been described, only a handful of 'British' ships registered outside the U.K. are to be traced in the Australian trade. Their importance was slight; they may be dismissed in a few sentences. They consisted of Canadian and South African ships plus vessels registered in Hong Kong. Development of the Canadian-Australasian Line from the Union Steam Ship Co. of New Zealand has already been mentioned. Interest in the line revolves around the competition it experienced from the U.S. Matson Line; discussed in chapter 6. Another line with Canadian connections was the Canadian government line, the Canadian National Steamship Co., with monthly sailings via Panama to eastern Australia. As with the Australian government line, it too was a creation of the First World War. Unlike the Australian line it began as the product of indigenous shipbuilding yards. Like the Australian line, however, it too was unable to compete successfully because of its high cost structure. In 1936 the ships employed on the service with Australia were sold to a composite British line.[1] In addition there are the occasional entries of ships registered in South Africa and Hong Kong. From the latter were provided the tankers of the seventeen vessel Standard Transportation Co. fleet, mentioned in the Fremantle records. Taken as a whole, however, the total tonnage entered at Australian ports by 'British' ships registered outside Australia or the U.K. was always small. At the beginning of the period such ships accounted for about 1 % of tonnage entered and as late as 1938/9 for no more than 5 %.

The British shipping industry predominated in Australia's oversea shipping scene on all counts—frequency of sailings, type and quantity of shipping used, and tonnage of cargo carried. British ships were to be found on all the shipping routes listed above: between Australia and Asia, South Africa, Europe and in the trans-Pacific trade. Some British ships were also used in the trans-Tasman trade, the Shaw Savill group and the Port Line usually making a few despatches each year to Britain via New Zealand. In 1938/9, for example, sixteen homeward sailings called in passing at New Zealand ports. But with these exceptions, and the arrivals in Australia of British tramps from New Zealand, usually in ballast, we may safely conclude that

[1] *Brassey* 1921/2, p. 305 ff. *U.K. Trade Reports*, 1932, p. 139; 1936, p. 157; 1938, p. 189. *Fairplay* vol. 139, pp. 223–4. *S.M.H.* 21 May 1936.

British shipping clearances from Australian ports

	Number of British vessel clearances	Number of vessel clearances to Britain	Tonnage of vessel clearances to Britain as % of all British tonnage clearances
1925/6	687	344	60
1926/7	703	355	61
1927/8	698	331	60
1928/9	754	321	55
1929/30	730	323	55
1930/1	NA	NA	NA
1931/2	703	460	69
1932/3	715	385	61
1933/4	586	404	73
1934/5	675	409	68
1935/6	714	452	67
1936/7	740	460	65
1937/8	860	543	65
1938/9	803	448	63

trade between Australia and New Zealand was primarily carried by shipping registered in Australasia.

The most important Australian oversea market was Europe, especially the U.K. It was upon this trade that British shipping concentrated, as the actual services provided between Australia and Britain abundantly attest. It is not, unfortunately, possible from Commonwealth records to establish quantitatively by carrier nationality the destinations to which vessels were cleared. Carrier nationality and carrier destination are both shown, but separately; it is not possible to link the two. As for clearances to the U.K. from Australia, we are able to give some measure of the concentration of interest by the British shipping industry from British records. U.K. Board of Trade statistics indicate that 95 % or more of the tonnage entered from Australasia was British. If we make the not unreasonable assumption therefore that all clearances from Australia to the U.K. represent British vessels, the relative importance of the U.K. routes are at once obvious. Detail above shows that about one half of British clearances from Australia were to the U.K. In terms of shipping tonnage the proportion was even greater. The number of *ships* actually employed in the services to Britain was of course much higher than that required for services to nearer Australian oversea markets when voyage length and service frequency are taken into account.

Although less important than the U.K. sector (and with it the related route to South Africa), a brief glance is necessary at the shipping serving the two remaining markets, North America and Asia. In the former we are concerned primarily with the trade to the Pacific coast of North America. In the latter 1930s a line was created by three British companies, Ellerman & Bucknall, the Port Line, and the New Zealand Shipping Co. called the Montreal-Australia-New Zealand line to buy out, as noted above, eight ships of the Canadian National Steam Ships. It maintained the infrequent service hitherto provided by the vendor from Montreal and was used for the despatch of sugar to eastern Canada. But the major trans-Pacific route terminated on the west, or Pacific north-west coast. The services upon this route need not, however, detain us; passenger traffic and an essentially one-way flow of cargo made up the trade. Tramps bringing timber from North America often cleared Australia with wheat for Europe or with wheat and flour to China and Japan. If cleared to eastern ports they often reappeared later in Australia with fresh timber cargoes from Canada or the U.S.A. In the liner traffic in the trans-Pacific service only two ships were at work by the end of the 1930s. Developments on this route are discussed in chapter 6 in the context of conference and competition.

British maritime services between Australia and Asian ports never represented a large area of employment for the British shipping industry as a whole. In 1936 the gross earnings of British ships employed throughout Asia amounted to about one quarter of the total receipts of the U.K. shipping industry. Earnings of British shipping engaged in the carrying trade between Asian countries and Australasia (that is including both Australia and New Zealand) amounted to less than 1 % of the total.[1] From the purely local point of view, however, the role of the British shipping industry transcends the overall picture suggested by detail on earnings. The three main shipping routes

[1] I.S.C. *38th Report*, p. 10.

serving the Asian trade have already been mentioned; Japan and China; India and Malaya; and the N.E.I.

The most important eastern market was Japan, with which should also be associated Australian exports to China. Much of the interest on the shipping route between China, Japan and Australia derives from conflict and competition between the British and Japanese shipping industry; it is similarly reserved along with the trans-Pacific route for discussion in chapter 6. Apart from British tramps, only one British line, the Eastern and Australian Steam Ship Company Ltd, (E & A Line), was involved in the direct trade between Australia and Japan via China, returning by way of the Pacific islands. The company was a subsidiary of the P & O group, it inherited obsolescent vessels from the P & O or British India Steam Navigation Co. (B.I.), and with its three aged vessels maintained a monthly service from ports in eastern Australia.

Trade with the remaining eastern markets provided between 10 % and 15 % of Australia's imports; they rarely took more than 7 % or 8 % of her exports. Imports achieved their relatively high figure towards the end of the 1930s as a result of the expansion of oil imports from the N.E.I. It was an increase at the expense of the oil trade with the U.S.A. which became relatively less important during the inter-war years. Services to Malaya were operated from both eastern and Western Australia. The service from the west was provided by three ships of the Blue Funnel Line (the combined Holt Co. fleets of the China Mutual Steam Navigation Co. and the Ocean Steam Ship Co.). The service from Sydney was undertaken by the Australian company of Burns, Philp. The growing oil trade from the N.E.I. was served by British tanker companies competing with Dutch, Norwegian and Panamanian vessels. The two British tanker companies chiefly engaged were the Anglo-Saxon Petroleum Co., (which owned the Shell Co. of Australia Ltd) and the British Tanker Co. In 1938/9 about one half of the oil discharged at Fremantle was from British tankers. Shipping links between Australia and India were maintained by a regular monthly cargo service operated by the B.I. Assistance was given by the normal P & O service to Australia which called at Bombay and by the occasional chartering of a tramp.

It was in the provision of services between the U.K. and Australia, however, where the British shipping industry truly predominated. Of the four possible routes between the two countries we need concern ourselves with only the Suez and Cape of Good Hope routes. A few despatches to Britain were made each year via New Zealand and Panama but their contribution to the total trade was small. A few sailing ships persisted in the wheat trade via the Horn. The glamour of sail made it possible to attract 'gentlemen' sailors at low rates of pay. During the worst years of depression sailing vessels were frequently used. In November 1932 it was announced that fourteen sailing ships were to engage in the annual grain 'race'. The depression was also responsible for the somewhat unusual step taken a year earlier to divert steamers from Panama to the Horn routes. In 1931 the Commonwealth and Dominion Line routed a number of its vessels via the Horn.[1]

Of the two principal routes to Europe, via Suez and the Cape, the former was throughout our period the more significant.[2] Most of the despatches made by the conference lines, British and foreign, were via Suez; only some 4 % of all despatches made between 1929 and 1939 were via the Cape. The bulk of all wool shipments and other fine cargo to Europe were made via Suez. In large part, more especially in the 1920s, the Cape service provided by British liner shipping derived from Australia's trade with South Africa. For the much smaller number and tonnage of British homeward bound tramps, it is possible that most would have preferred the Cape route since the longer steaming time of a day or two was still cheaper than the Canal dues.

Trade between South Africa and Australia was never very important during our period in terms either of value or of ship-

[1] *S.M.H.* 9 November 1931, 29 November 1932.

[2] For a discussion on the Suez Canal and its importance to Australia see: W. Woodruff and L. McGregor, *The Suez Canal and the Australian Economy* (Melbourne 1957). The authors do not, unfortunately, attempt to establish the proportion of Australia's trade with Europe which went via Suez. Their 'approximations' of the proportions of Australasian wool shipped through Suez are, presumably, grossly distorted by the inclusion of New Zealand figures. So far as the 1930s are concerned, conference line wool-despatches from Australia to Europe (amounting to about three-quarters of all wool exports) were primarily via Suez, a mere 5 % of the total shipped went via the Cape. The greatest discrepancy is in the authors' figures for the years 1935 to 1939.

ping requirements. Imports into Australia of South African origin rarely amounted to 1 % of all imports in the 1920s and were usually less than ½ % in the 1930s. Exports to South Africa usually topped 1 % of the total in the first decade but were well below ½ % in the depression decade.[1] Nor was the trade between the two countries one which required a large amount of hold-space. The two bulky exports to South Africa were wheat and timber; both items ceased to be exported in significant quantities after 1930. In the 1920s wheat averaged 150,000 tons a year. This quantity if consigned entirely by tramp (and not in berth parcels by liner) would not have required more than 20 of the 'handy' sized tramps normally used in the Australian trade. Timber shipments in the same decade sometimes reached 80,000 measured tons a year. Imports from South Africa consisted principally of diamonds, often representing two thirds or more of the total import bill. The two items of bulk were maize and asbestos. The former averaged about 17,000 tons a year in the 1920s, the trade in both declining during the 1930s. It is therefore not unexpected that shipping services between the two countries were incidental to the main U.K.-Australia services. The frequency of Cape sailings, moreover, makes it clear that British ships took the Cape route often for reasons not connected with the trade between South Africa and Australia. In the mid-1920s, for example, trade seasonality encouraged the Aberdeen, Blue Funnel, and White Star lines to provide a joint cargo-passenger service to Australia via the Cape.[2]

Services via the Cape were provided by the P & O, White Star and Blue Funnel lines. Just as trade between South Africa and Australia was more significant during the 1920s so the services provided were more plentiful in the first than in the second decade of our period. The most regular service in the twenties was the three-weekly schedule maintained by the P & O branch service (the rechristened Blue Anchor Line acquired by the P & O in 1910). The branch fleet numbered nine vessels with a total gross tonnage of 110,000. Each ship made two round

[1] For an interesting discussion on conflicting statistics of Australia's trade with South Africa during the inter-war years see: A. G. B. Fisher, 'The Balance of Trade between South Africa and Australia', *South African Journal of Economics* v, 1–10.

[2] *S.M.H.* 3 January 1927.

voyages a year to Australia via the Cape. In certain years of the 1920s the branch service was augmented by additions from the main line service. In 1923/4 for example, five additional outward despatches were made to Australia via the Cape, each vessel returning homeward via Suez. Cargo shipped to Australia in that year on P & O vessels was approximately equally shared between the two routes, Suez and Cape. By the end of the 1920s, however, the service pattern had changed considerably. The branch service had proved to be uneconomic. In 1928 the service was changed, sailings being made alternately via Suez and the Cape. In the following year the five remaining branch-service vessels were converted to oil and switched to the Suez route. In 1930/1 only one outward P & O despatch was made via the Cape and thereafter all P & O sailings were via Suez. The Cape services provided by the White Star and Blue Funnel lines although drastically reduced were maintained throughout the 1930s, however. During the worst phase of the depression, services via the Cape were completely suspended. Between May and October of 1931 mails and passengers from Australia to South Africa were routed via Colombo, to await an on-despatch to the Cape.[1] For most of the decade the two lines between them made only twelve despatches a year from Australia to the U.K. via the Cape.

British shipping engaged in Australia's oversea services consisted, as already mentioned, of passenger and cargo liners on the one hand and dry-cargo carriers and tankers on the other; liners predominated. The division of trade between the two groups is discussed more fully in the following chapter. It is necessary to refer to the two groups here, however, as an introduction to our examination of the chief lines engaged in the trade and their association with larger British shipping groups. During the 1930s, vessels of as many as 50–60 separate British shipping companies called at Fremantle. Between 40 and 50 were tramp companies; the remaining handful were the liner companies whose names are familiar to every Australian resident of the state capitals.

The respective importance of the two groups from the point of view of industrial organisation may be illustrated by reference

[1] *U.K. Trade Report*, 1932, p. 137.

to a single year's experience at the port of Fremantle. In 1938/9 ships of 37 British tramp companies called at Fremantle. On the whole they were small companies with small fleets of small ships. As many as 20 of the companies owned fewer than 5 ships, 12 were single-ship or two-ship companies (sometimes part of a larger group, however) and only 6 companies had fleets numbering 9 ships or more. Of the larger companies one or two were especially conspicuous. The Hain Steam Ship Co., for example, at the end of the period owned 27 ships with a total gross tonnage of 139,000. It had been acquired by the P & O in 1917. The Bank Line with 49 ships totalling 277,000 gross tons was part of a larger organisation of bulk liquid and dry-cargo carriers managed by Weir & Co. Another was the Pool Shipping Co. also part of a larger dry-cargo carrying organisation managed by Sir R. Ropner & Co., a well-known name in the tramp industry.

Large tramp companies notwithstanding, the tramp ships visiting Fremantle made only a slender contribution to the total carrying scene. Of the 312 entries at Fremantle in 1938/9 only 80 or so were made by tramps. The liner companies, in contrast, were larger, had bigger ships, and were frequent, regular visitors. They formed, moreover, a tight-knit group associated together (with certain foreign European lines) in the outward and homeward shipping conference, the characteristic feature of the liner section of the shipping industry, then as now. Throughout the inter-war years 14 or 15 British liner companies were conspicuous in the Australian trade for a number of reasons, above all for the scale of service they provided and for the provision of a fleet appropriate to the needs of the trade. In terms of 'despatches' or vessel clearances, conference line sailings from Australia amounted to about one half of all clearances to the U.K. throughout the 1930s. See table opposite. Despatch or vessel clearance is nevertheless a misleading indicator unless qualified in terms of tonnage employed; ships of 3,000 or 23,000 gross tons are recorded alike as a single unit cleared. When tonnage is taken into account the preponderance of conference vessels becomes even clearer. In 1938/9 80 conference ships visited Fremantle. Their aggregate gross tonnage was about one million. The 74 British non-conference ships aggre-

British homeward conference-line despatches

	1929/30	1930/1	1938/9
Mail vessels	49	45	47
Others:			
via Cape	16	12	14
via Suez	141	117	114

gated less than a half million. Even this approach fails to bring the subject into precise focus. The point made in chapter 2 concerning the relative carrying potential of tramps and liners may be strikingly illustrated here. The 80 conference vessels, each larger than the 74 non-conference ships, made 224 visits to Fremantle out of the total of 312 made by all British ships in that year.

Most of the British shipping lines in the conference in our period, as today, were members of a few large predominant shipping groups—the P & O, Cunard, Ellermans and so on. The groups and those of their lines which belonged to the Australian conference are shown below together with fleet details for 1938/9. The size of an individual group does not necessarily reflect its relative ranking in the U.K.-Australian trade. Of the lines listed only the Orient Line concentrated exclusively on the provision of services between the U.K. and Australia. For many of the remainder the Australian sector formed part of a large canvas of shipping operations. The P & O initially extended its activities from the Iberian 'Peninsular' to the middle and far east and tended to be more heavily committed to the far-east service than to Australia during our period. The Cunard is a name not normally associated with the Australian trade, it acquired the Commonwealth and Dominion Line (later renamed the Port Line) in 1916. The Royal Mail group for a time was also active through its acquisition of the Commonwealth Government Line. On the unfortunate retirement from the shipping world of Lord Kylsant the line was acquired by the Furness group through Shaw Savill.

A better indication of the relative importance of individual lines in the Australian trade is the number of their homeward

British shipping groups with lines engaged in the Australian trade 1938/9

	Ships	Gross tons ('000)
Australind (Trinder Anderson)	2	10
Blue Star group (Vestey):		
Blue Star Line	25	232
F. Leyland & Co.	10	89
Clan group:		
Clan Line	46	294
Scottish Shire Line	4	32
Cunard:		
Port Line (originally Commonwealth and Dominion Line)	28	230
Ellerman:		
Ellerman Line	26	78
Ellerman Bucknall	13	83
Ellerman City	16	137
Ellerman Hall	49	309
Ellerman Wilson	39	86
Blue Funnel (A. Holt & Co.):		
China Mutual Steam Navigation Co.	24	197
Ocean Steam Ship Co.	46	358
P & O–Orient:		
P & O (including branch line)	39	476
B.I.	111	665
Federal	14	142
Orient	8	162
Furness:		
Shaw Savill	19	203
Norfolk & North American Steam Shipping Co.	6	51
Aberdeen & Commonwealth (jointly managed)	4	57

Lloyd's Register. The *formal* association of the Orient with the P & O took place after 1945.

sailings and the allotted share of the conference trade. Both reflect the acquisition and jealously cherished carrying-rights built up over time. The P & O clung to the separate title of the branch service and the rights obtained with the old Anchor Line. Hence also the similarity in despatches between lines of vastly differing size. The Ellerman group, for example, was 20 times larger than the Aberdeen and Commonwealth Line in

1930/1 but in fact provided exactly the same number of sailings. Although Ellerman sailings expanded in the 1930s the group's lines made only 2½ times more despatches than the Aberdeen and Commonwealth as late as 1938/9.

The services provided by the conference lines included a mail service, scheduled sailings via the Cape and Suez and non-scheduled sailings via Suez. The difference between scheduled and non-scheduled despatches reflects the slightly less rigid time-tabling of the latter. The mail service was operated by the P & O and Orient Lines with nine and eight ships respectively to achieve a weekly service. The P & O held the outward mail contract from Britain, part of a bigger subsidy bearing contract. The Orient Line held the Commonwealth government homeward mail contract. The first separate mail contract arranged by the Australian government was in 1905 when it was awarded to the Orient Line.[1] Prior to the First World War the ocean leg of the mail service to Australia was begun at Italian ports and went via Suez, and so on, to Fremantle. When the contract and service were resumed after the war, the European sea-terminals were switched to French Mediterranean ports. The subsidy paid to the Orient Line by the Commonwealth government amounted to £120,000 prior to the war and between £130,000 and £140,000 during the inter-war years.[2]

Subsidies for mail services had wider implications than mail transits. At the 1906 royal commission on Ocean Shipping Services, Sir Kenneth Anderson of the Orient Line sought to dispel the general impression 'that a mail contract is a mere make-weight...that the line would be run in any case... nothing could be further from the truth. The mail contract is the originating cause of the mail line and the determining factor in the cost. It determines the speed and therefore the type of ship; it determines the route, and it determines their sailings

[1] Originally a two-way Australian mail contract was arranged by the U.K. government, the Australian government made a financial contribution. The two were separated in 1905 for reasons connected with the insertion of certain clauses relating to the carriage of Australian mails.

[2] In 1931 at the height of the financial crisis in Australia the company made an unusual contribution to the resolution of Australia's economic difficulties. It voluntarily abated the contract sum by £20,000 a year although its own profits had fallen and its annual dividend had been reduced. (*Fairplay* vol. 120, p. 193; *The Times* 17 July 1931.)

and their regularity, and all without regard to economic or commercial considerations'.[1] The main feature other than mails underlying the Australian mail-subsidy was the provision of refrigerated space written into the mail contract. Estimates made in the later 1920s (in pleading a special case) went so far as to suggest that about 60 % of the mail subsidy was designed for refrigerated hold space.[2]

Other liner companies without the benefit of a mail subsidy also equipped their vessels with refrigeration plant, initially for fruit, dairy products and frozen meat, later also for chilled beef. A measure of the installation of marine refrigeration plant is to be had from the fleet details of liner companies at work. But this would give a misleading figure in its inclusion as well of vessels not normally engaged in the Australian sector. Instead we concentrate on those conference-line ships calling at Fremantle at the beginning and end of our period. In 1923/4 about 15½ million cubic feet of refrigerated space was available, by 1938/9 this had almost doubled at 28·9 million. In terms of cubic feet per registered ton of shipping, the period witnessed a rise from about 25 to about 28 cubic feet. As we show in subsequent discussion, annual shipments of refrigerated cargo in the last quinquennium averaged about 52 million cubic feet compared with about 23 million in the first five years of the period. Ships were completing the journey between Australia and the U.K. in a shorter time and hence their annual carrying capacity was higher.

The services required between the U.K. and Australia tended during our period to become less concentrated on one or two British ports and more and more to include direct shipments to British outports away from London. A superficially comparable development in Australia is discussed in chapter 5 within the context of Australian port-charges. In Australia, however, vessels were required to make multiple port calls because no single port was able to provide or to accept a full liner cargo from or to an oversea port. On arrival on the Australian coast, most British liners called at every mainland capital port and often, in the fruit season, added a visit to Hobart.

[1] *C.P.P.* 1906, Paper no. 36, Q. 1,454.
[2] *C.P.D.* vol. 117, p. 2,485.

Developments in Britain on the other hand stemmed from different reasons. Demand in Britain was always sufficiently concentrated to make it possible for a relatively small number of ports to handle the bulk of the deep-sea trade. Traditionally London has always been the major British port handling the Australasian trade. For many years indeed it was virtually the only port thus engaged. We need not doubt that the outports were always willing to promote their own expansion. But the initiative in widening Australian trade in our period was primarily taken by the various Australian produce-boards seeking to exploit the British food market more efficiently. It meant for British shipping a considerable widening of the services provided for the Australian trade.

The long-established and unique position of London in the Australasian trade not surprisingly has been accompanied by close links between Australia and the Port of London Authority (P.L.A.). From an early date the P.L.A. found it useful to maintain a representative in Sydney for liaison purposes with shippers and to advise the Authority.[1] Originally a local man was appointed on a part-time basis. In the 1920s the representative divided his energies between journalism and representing the P.L.A. During the inter-war years however, as more and more direct shipments from Australia were being made to the outports, the P.L.A. found it necessary to pay greater attention to liaison in Australia. In the later 1930s a London official was seconded to Sydney on a less casual basis. 'London was feeling the stress of competition from other U.K. ports, and felt the necessity of doing everything possible to maintain its position'.[2] During the period, apparently in the 1930s, the port of Liverpool also found it expedient to appoint a representative in Sydney.[3] Here it was a response to the challenge of expansion, rather than a measure taken to defend a threatened trade. As direct shipment to Liverpool increased, so the port found that a 'traffic' representative in Sydney was desirable to act in an advisory capacity and as a two-way channel for information.

[1] Port of London Authority *Annual Report* 1938, p. 9 and letter from P.L.A. Director of Finance, dated 22 December 1965.

[2] Director's letter cited above.

[3] S. Mountfield, *Western Gateway* (Liverpool, 1965), p. 118 and letter from Docks and Commercial Manager dated 4 March 1966.

The policy of extending direct shipment of Australian exports to British outports was one of the measures adopted by the Australian produce marketing-boards, especially in the 1930s, to expand the consumption in Britain of Australian foodstuffs. The Dairy Produce Board, for example, whose special difficulties in this context are mentioned below, regarded the extension of butter shipments to the outports as of particular importance.[1] The widening of shipments involved the outports, as well as London, in attention to cargo-handling facilities especially for refrigerated items. But it is not always easy to associate specific dock-improvements or developments with specific areas of trade or services. Changes in the Royal Docks group in London at this time however, clearly had their origin in the expansion of the Australian trade, especially in refrigerated products. On the Clyde, the largest single extension between the wars was the King George V dock opened about 1930. The first section of the dock to be completed was to give accommodation to Holt and Co.'s Blue Funnel service with Australia.[2]

More relevant to the present argument is that the widening of the Australian market in Britain meant an extension of services for the British shipping industry. The best quantitative indicator of trade diffusion and at the same time of the implications for the shipping industry, is the changing volume of Australian trade handled by the outports. The trade records of British ports are not always detailed, or have not always survived the war or changes in administration. The records of a few ports, however, together with data assembled by the Australian marketing boards for canned fruits, meat and dairy produce give an adequate picture of change. The trade in canned fruits multiplied four times between 1928 and 1939. During the ten years the proportion of the total shipped to outports rose to more than 40 %. The meat trade experienced a similar proportionate change. The trade in butter, paradoxically, despite the efforts of the Dairy Produce Board witnessed not a dispersion but growing concentration of shipping on London. In 1939 however, changes in the methods of marketing and the introduction

[1] *C.P.P.* 1937/40 II, 525.

[2] *S.M.H.* 28 September 1922. P.L.A. letter dated 22 December 1965. Clyde Navigation Trust, Harbour Master's letter dated 5 November 1965.

of a price equalisation scheme seemed likely to reverse the process. Today, in the 1960s, only one half of Australia's butter imported into Britain comes to London. But the dispersal of the refrigerated meat trade has been reduced; nowadays as much as three-quarters of the total is handled in London.[1]

Of the outports, Liverpool was the most important. It is unfortunate that the records of the Mersey Harbour Board do not include for the inter-war years details of the origin of imports. The annual reports of the produce boards show that to the port by 1938/9 was consigned 10% of Australian canned fruit and 15% of refrigerated meat. No other outport came within striking distance. At Southampton imports of Australian origin went up from about 2,000 tons a year in the early 1920s to more than 30,000 tons in 1938, from less than ½% of total imports to about 4%. On the Tyne the major change to be noticed is the greater diversity of imports of Australian origin. Diversification at Bristol accompanied a three-fold increase in the quantity imported. On the Clyde a four-fold increase in import quantity took place between 1928 and 1939. The tonnage of shipping entered from Australasia increased from about 300,000 tons in 1928 to more than 1 million in 1935, a considerably sharper rise than the overall expansion of shipping activity on the Clyde between the wars.[2]

Our final point concerns the adequacy of the various services provided for the Australian export trade. Our discussion shows that an increased tonnage of shipping accompanied the long-term upward trend in export cargo-tonnage. The tonnage of exports, on average, increased by about 15% between the first and last quinquennium. But the rise in shipping tonnage was of the order of one-third. Even making an appropriate deduction for the specialised oil-tanker tonnage in use, the rise was about 20%, proportionately more than the increase in cargo would seem to have required. Earlier analysis has shown that a con-

[1] *P.L.A. Monthly*, February 1963.

[2] I have to acknowledge with thanks information received from the Clyde Navigation Trust (5 November 1965); Port of Bristol Authority (25 October 1965); British Transport Docks Board, Southampton (29 October 1965); Mersey Docks and Harbour Board (30 November 1965); Tyne Improvement Commission (2 November 1965). See also *Fairplay* vol. 137, p. 496. *U.K. Ministry of War Transport* 'Report of the Clyde Estuary Committee' (1945).

sequence of this disproportionate increase was the decline in the ratio of cargo carried per ton of shipping with cargo. Individual fleets, it will be recalled, often ran counter to aggregate experience. The British fleet, for example, increased its load ratio. The tendency for excess capacity to appear (or to increase) does not, however, tell us much about service adequacy.

The true test is not the experience of one year compared with another, but the long-term availability of an appropriate type and amount of shipping when required by the shipper. A common enough casual denunciation is that shipping companies all too often failed to cater effectively for needs. Serious, specific complaint, however, is limited to two major aspects, mail and chilled beef services. With these two exceptions only minor short-lived complaints have been traced in contemporary sources. The relative silence of an uninhibited local press concerning short-run phenomena would seem to support a belief in the adequacy of services. Complaint where traced has been directed chiefly against the liner section. Tramp ships respond to effective changes in the volume of demand as reflected in freight rates; they provide a differently organised service. Criticism of the liner trade on the whole was of a short-run nature. An unusually heavy demand for an additional quantity of shipping often led to irritation, on both sides. A large apple crop in 1933, for example, disrupted the normal commodity flow. The chartering of outside vessels to supplement normal programmed carriers upset discharge schedules in British docks. The simultaneous arrival of a number of ships with Tasmanian apples led to dock congestion and depressed market prices. In reverse, the variation by shippers of export consignment programmes was equally disturbing to owners. In 1925, for example, the cancellation of the May and June wool-sales without warning withheld from shipping already programmed (some already *en route* to Australia) more than 200,000 bales of wool, enough to provide thirty vessels with the average quantity consigned per vessel in the 1930s.[1] On the whole, however, the local press is free from complaint. With the two exceptions to be discussed, shippers complaints about *services* (not freights) were infrequent.

[1] *Fairplay* vol. 109, p. 217; vol. 118, p. 53; vol. 126, p. 391. *S.M.H.* 9 May 1925.

The Australian chilled beef trade was a development of the 1930s; it depended upon vessel speed and the adaptation of refrigerated-hold space. The storage of meat under refrigeration may be by freezing or by chilling. The one freezes the meat hard, which will then store almost indefinitely. The second merely 'chills' it at a temperature only just below freezing point. Chilled meat has a short safe life. Mutton and lamb appear not to be adversely affected by freezing. The freezing of beef, on the other hand, destroys certain qualities and reduces its value. The technical problem involved in the shipment of chilled beef from Australia was the provision of separate 'chilled' hold space and the completion of the loading, the voyage and the discharge to market within the safe life period.

The first trial shipments of chilled beef from Australia were made in 1925. A year earlier, a report from a leading refrigerated meat export company in Australia gave publicity to the new trade in chilled, as distinct from frozen beef. The report illustrates its point by reference to the rapid rate at which Argentine meat exports to the U.K. were switching from frozen to chilled beef. Further trial shipments were made from Australia in 1926. But the Argentine trade involved a much shorter journey, well within the three or four weeks at that time assumed to be the safe life period. Except on a few mail vessels the journey from Australia usually took longer.[1]

It was not until the mid-1930s that Australia was able to develop a chilled beef trade. It was made possible by new chilling methods which preserved chilled beef for slightly longer periods and by the introduction of faster ships. It was a trade which developed significantly after the appearance in Australia of the U.K. firm of Vestey Ltd, long active in the Argentine trade. For almost two years prior to the arrival in Australia of the Vestey group in 1933, British shipping had provided some space for chilled beef 'but it had been on the whole of an incidental nature'. The contribution of Vestey Ltd, was to introduce with its Blue Star Line, purpose-designed vessels of which the *Imperial Star* was the first. Other shipping lines followed

[1] *S.M.H.* 16 May 1925, various dates in July and December 1926. *Fairplay* vol. 90, p. 609. *Brassey* 1925, p. 285.

Chilled-beef voyage time, shipments made in

Percentage of total shipments made in:	1937 April to July	1938 April to July	1938 April to June	1939 April to June
Under 45 days	24·5	24·7	24·6	13·1
45–50 days	25·8	36·0	29·1	20·6
51 days and over	49·7	39·3	46·3	66·3

suit.[1] For the shipping industry the new trade involved the provision of separate compartments and faster journeys. Conversion of existing vessels incurred an expenditure estimated in 1935 to be about £50 per ton apart from the loss of revenue-earning space which conversion involved. New buildings in the 1930s show the service speed of cargo liners for the Australian food trade being pushed up to 16 knots.[2] In 1939 nine ships of the Blue Star fleet, representing 70% of its total tonnage, were capable of 15 knots or more, two ships had a service speed of 17½ knots.

The trade in chilled beef expanded dramatically, from 100 to 36,000 tons a year by 1938/9. The Australian Meat Board (which controlled marketing) nevertheless remained dissatisfied with the services provided. Although the use of carbon dioxide in refrigeration chambers preserved chilled beef for longer periods than was possible in the 1920s, the optimum voyage time was still relatively short. The length of voyage was the factor of greatest importance in marketing if loss of 'bloom' and mould growth were to be avoided. The Meat Board aimed at a journey of 45 days with a margin of up to 5 days longer. In fact, as the above table shows, most ships were at sea for longer times. The problem was a fine one of balance. The Meat Board conceded that the total space available for chilled beef 'was more than adequate'. But the ships were of varying capacity and speed. If the vessels of appropriate speed were used exclusively they 'would probably provide a service approaching the

[1] *S.M.H.* 30 December 1933, 12 October 1934. See also *Brassey* 1935, p. 132. In the older Orient Line 20,000 tonners, for example, holds were reconstructed. The new launchings of the 1930s included appropriate chambers for chilled beef installed during building.

[2] *Fairplay* vol. 135, p. 408; *Motorship* March 1934, p. 425.

service stipulated by the Board as being essential for the satisfactory development of the Australian chilled beef industry'. The trade itself was of a limited nature, shipments were spread over many months to avoid overloading the country's freezing-plant capacity, and to avoid saturating the British food market. The Board sought to limit supply to about 1,000 tons a week. Shipowners were unable 'because of the needs of other cargoes, to provide with existing vessels, the specialised service that chilled beef requires'. The requirements were impossible to meet, argued the British shipowners, who investigated the problem at the request of the Board, without the aid of a fleet of small, fast carriers. Such fleets would require higher rates of freight and a ten-year contract. Understandably, in the late 1930s, the Meat Board dropped the matter. The trade in chilled beef was halted by the war. It enjoyed a brief post-war revival but in recent years has declined to about 1,000 tons a year. Today the emphasis is on the export of frozen boned beef.[1]

The second major complaint, concerning mail services, chronologically preceded the chilled-beef problem. It attracted attention in the 1920s and represented a preoccupation of the Australian business community and governments for more than a generation in their efforts to obtain a speedy mail service between Britain and Australia. The Dominions royal commission devoted considerable time to the whole question of Empire mail services and the 'all-red route'. The mail service between the two countries was considered inadequate even before the First World War when the mail contract required a service speed of about 15 knots. In 1911 the Australian government expressed its willingness to give a 'very large subsidy' to obtain an 18-knot service. Acting on this statement the Dominions royal commission invited both the P & O and Orient lines to estimate the additional subsidy they would require to provide a 17- and a 20-knot service. Neither company felt able to give an estimate.[2]

With the resumption of the regular mail service after the war, the European terminals were switched from Italian to French

[1] *C.P.P.* 1937/40, II, Australian Meat Board, Third and Fourth Annual Reports, 593, 688/9. For earlier reports see *C.P.P.* 1934/7, III, 297; 1937, V, 2,289.

[2] *U.K.P.P.* Cd. 7120, 7173, 8460, 8462.

Mediterranean ports. The effect was to lengthen mail-transit times. Criticism in the Australian press was widespread in the early 1920s. The U.K. Board of Trade drew attention in its weekly *Journal* to the complaints of Australian importers that goods often arrived in advance of the relevant documents.[1] In 1922 Prime Minister Hughes invited the I.S.C. to report on the economic size and speed of vessels required for the trade between the U.K. and Australia. The Committee was asked to devote particular attention to mail service, 'bearing in mind the importance of the curtailment as much as possible of the time occupied in the conveyance of mails between the two countries'.[2] In its discussion on mail services the committee was strongly influenced by two considerations: the high marginal cost of extra speed in the light of existing marine technology and the possible development of air services (they actually envisaged air-ships). Accordingly they opposed the introduction of an 18- or 20-knot service. Instead they urged, as an initial and possibly interim measure, the speeding up of the mail service by re-arranging existing facilities.

Public debate continued during the remainder of the 1920s. Commenting upon the I.S.C. report in 1923 the editor of *Fairplay* reminded his readers that the whole question of mail services to Australia had been prominently before the public for many years. In the same year Sir John Biles, whose views on speeds had been included in the Dominions royal commission evidence, re-entered the arena advocating a 20-knot service. Three years later Biles, together with Sir Charles Parsons and Sir James Connolly, formerly Agent-General in London for Western Australia, urged the feasibility and creation of a 7-vessel fleet of 24,000 tonners to give a 22-knot service. They claimed that entirely without subsidy they could provide an 18-day schedule between Genoa and Fremantle.

The scheme received wide publicity, and was strongly condemned in shipping circles. At the annual meeting of the Orient Line in December 1926 the chairman rejected the idea that the suggested service was possible without a 'most formidable subsidy'. He argued, correctly as events were to prove, that the

[1] Board of Trade *Journal*, July–December 1922, pp. 146–7.
[2] *U.K.P.P.* Cmd. 1917, p. 25.

fast mail transit required by only small amounts of mail was much more likely to be provided by an air-mail service. In 1926, it is worth recalling, mail transit times were substantially unchanged since 1900. The speeding-up achieved between 1923 and 1926 merely restored the times common before 1914.[1]

After the end of the 1920s little further is heard of sea-mail services; interest switched to the air. Today air-mail services are taken for granted. In the later 1920s the public had to be warned that no spectacular increases in sea speeds were possible on the Australasian routes, given the technological context, depth of waterways, volume of trade and passenger traffic and so forth. In fact, as we now know, the Orient Line mail-carriers built in the later 1930s had a mere 1 knot or 1½ knot advantage over their launchings of the early 1920s. But by the early 1930s oversea air-mail services were well established. A weekly air service between England and Karachi was inaugurated in 1929 and by 1931 had been extended to Singapore. Imperial Airways made its first flight from London to Darwin in April and May 1931 and within a year a regular service was in operation.[2]

[1] *Fairplay* vol. 89, p. 292; vol. 92, p. 636; vol. 101, pp. 160, 216. *The Times* 22, 23 and 30 October 1926. *Economist* 27 November and 18 December 1926. *S.M.H.* 22, 26 October, 17 November 1926.

[2] A. J. Quin-Harkin, 'Imperial Airways, 1924–40', *Journal of Transport History*, vol. 1, 197–215. See also *Year Book* 1932 and 1933.

Chapter 2

TECHNOLOGY, SIZE, AND TYPE OF VESSEL

Australia's oversea trade was dependent upon the supply of shipping of an appropriate quantity and, as important, of an appropriate type. Vessels of two main groups were employed: liners and tramps. A third was to become increasingly important during the period, the special-purpose oil tanker. Vessels of all three groups during the inter-war years underwent change, in varying degrees, in size, speed and propulsive power. In many ways the technical changes which took place among the oversea fleet in the Australian sector reflect no more than trends generally at work in the world's shipping industry as a whole. But there are also certain features unique to the Australian scene. Vessel size, for example, was constrained by factors often absent on other sectors. Other features also are related to the character of the services or to the needs of the trade. It is the object of the present chapter to focus attention on three main areas of change which occurred in the shipping employed in Australia's oversea services: vessel size, vessel type, and technological innovation. For much of our information we rely upon the records of the single port of Fremantle which, despite their limitations (outlined in the previous chapter) serve as a valuable complement to the more embracing but less detailed records compiled by the Commonwealth government.

VESSEL SIZE

Tables illustrating entries at Fremantle are contained in an appendix. Here it is enough to summarise their main points on voyage frequency and ship size. The data suggest a decline in the relative importance of ships making only a single voyage to Fremantle. In 1923/4 ships entering the port only once in the year accounted for one third of the total tonnage entered.

Fifteen years later their share had fallen to one fifth. Instead, ships making 2, 3 or 4 voyages annually to Fremantle increased in number. The development, which is exclusive of, and ignores the repeated voyages of the large passenger and mail-carrier, provides tenuous support for the point made in the following pages that tramps in the Australian sector were tending to become less important during our period.

The detail on ship size shows that almost all ships arriving from overseas were larger than 3,000 gross tons. Few ships below this size are mentioned in the Fremantle records. In aggregate they contributed less than ½ % to the total entered in any single year from 1920 to 1939. This is not unexpected. Australia lies many miles from her principal markets. Small ships would not be appropriate. Information about U.K. tramp shipping in 1935, moreover, shows that although the freight earnings of ships smaller than 3,000 gross tons remained important, such vessels were used almost exclusively in European waters.[1]

Among the groupings of vessels above 3,000 gross tons, changes occurred in the relative contribution made by each group to the total entered. In 1923/4 about 60 % of all entered tonnage was contributed by vessels of between 3,000 and 10,000 tons; by 1938/9 their share had declined to 40 %. The major change took place in the smallest and largest size range. The smaller ships tended more and more to be overshadowed by the very large ships. In the 1920s the smallest size group, 3,000 to 7,500 gross tons contributed 40 % and the largest (16,000 tons and over) only 13 % to the total. In 1938/9 the share of the former had sagged to 20 % while that of the latter had grown to 33 %.

It is clear that the pattern in the tables is affected by the inclusion of the repeated voyages of the large passenger liners. Between the wars they tended to become larger and faster, and hence more frequent visitors. The effect of such entries on the statistics is amply shown in the records of Fremantle. In 1938/9 17 large passenger liners made no fewer than 84 entries at Fremantle. Their aggregate tonnage, as mentioned above, represented 33 % of the total entered. The next most important

[1] *Isserlis*, p. 80 ff.

group were the cargo liners with a tonnage ranging between 8,000 and 14,000 gross tons depending upon the year of build. They were of especial importance in the refrigerated trade and are discussed more fully in the section on vessel type. After the passenger- and cargo-liner group were the tramps. These tended to be smaller than liners. Calculations for 1938/9 based on a *single entry per ship* show that vessels between 3,000 and 10,000 gross tons represent 60 % of entry tonnage. Most *tramp* ships were in fact even smaller, about 6,000 gross tons being the normal upper limit. Tramp employment may vary from voyage to voyage, the area of employment may vary much more. The point made below concerning the adaptation of vessels to the dimensions of waterways and harbours on any given route applies even more forcibly to tramps. Hence the 'handy' tramp ship rarely exceeded about 6,000 gross tons, about 10,000 deadweight tons. Records of British tramp movements in 1935 and 1936 were compiled by the Tramp Shipping Administrative Committee. Details for the Australian sector show that 95 % of the total tonnage of British tramps entered in Australia in these two years was contributed by vessels of between 3,000 and 6,000 gross tons.

TECHNOLOGICAL INNOVATION

Growth in vessel size was made possible by technical change. In part, indeed, technical change in marine propulsion made increases in vessel size inescapable. Two aspects claim attention: increases of sea speeds and the use of oil as a marine fuel. The basic substitution of power for sail may here be ignored. Although Australia, as sea sagas rightly claim, was one of 'the last strongholds of sail' the strength of the hold was dissipated by the First World War. A few sailing ships survived into the 1920s and windjammers added brightness and nostalgia if not economic significance to the Australian grain trade in the 1930s. Large vessels and increases in speed tended to be inseparable companions during our period. In the quest for speed in the Australian sector there were two objectives. The more arresting concerned the large passenger liner. Important, if for different reasons, was the speeding up of cargo liners for the growing trade in chilled beef. Speed for passenger liners stemmed from their second function, mail-carrying on contract schedules. The preoccupation of governments with sea-borne mail services as recently as thirty years ago may strike an archaic note to a generation accustomed to air-mail services. But the evidence referred to in chapter 1 abundantly shows that it constituted a theme of compelling importance.

Increases in speed, in the absence of technical innovation, tend to be at increasing marginal cost. They are uneconomic if not accompanied by increases in vessel dimension. As speed is raised more fuel is consumed and either more frequent bunkering or larger bunker space is necessary. Where repeated bunkering is not possible, larger bunkers means less cargo space. Calculations made in the early 1920s of the earning capacity of a vessel of about 7,000 tons deadweight capacity vividly show the 'cost of speed'. On a voyage of about 3,000 miles the vessel's performance was as follows:

Speed, knots	18	19	20	21
Cargo carried (tons)	3,740	2,800	1,625	0

Brassey 1921/2, 270.

The effect of speed increases on size may be illustrated for the Australian sector by the changes which took place in the Orient fleet. In the early 1900s the *Omrah* and *Orontes* were each about 8,000 gross tons and less than 500 feet in length. If fuel was somewhat extravagantly used, they were capable of 16 knots. The dimensions of fleet additions during the inter-war years are shown below. To point the continued growth, in 1960 the *Oriana* was launched; almost 42,000 gross tons, with a draught of 32 ft. 6 in., and a length of over 800 ft., the vessel's speed is 27 knots.

Growth in the size of the large passenger liners, however, was subject to other limitations. Factors unrelated to optimum speeds or to trade requirements, or to investment decisions acted as constraints to size. Ships for use on specific routes are designed to conform to the available depth of the shallowest waterway or harbour on the intended route. Where alternative routes are possible the minimum available becomes the designed maxi-

Orient Line flagships

	Approx. g.r.t. ('000 tons)	Length feet	Speed knots	Draught feet
1910s	12	530	18	?
1920s	20	630	19	30 ft. 6 in.
1930s	23·6	640	20	30 ft. 2 in.

mum. At the existing level of marine technology in the inter-war years the depth of the Suez Canal was the crucial limitation in the Australian trade. Successive works programmes on the Canal designed to accommodate larger vessels had succeeded by 1924 in making transit possible for vessels drawing up to 33 ft. of water. The new programme adopted in 1921 provided for further deepening. It was expected as a result that vessels with a draught of 35 or 36 ft. would be able to transit the Canal.

The Orient Line detail given above shows that the draught limit was a long way from being reached even in the 1930s. But the simultaneous growth in vessel size and deepening of the Suez Canal in the early 1920s alarmed the ports of both Colombo and Singapore. Both were important staging points, both had waterways restricted to vessels with draughts of up to 33 ft. Both invited the Imperial Shipping Committee to investigate their need for further harbour works. The Committee's report on Colombo Harbour 'on the prospective size of vessels in the Eastern and Australian trades via Suez...' noted that further deepening to shelter vessels drawing 35 ft. would involve costly rock removal.[1] The opinion of 'shipowners engaged in those trades' was opposed to costly improvements because vessels drawing more than 33 ft. were unlikely to be built in the ensuing ten years. With hindsight we see that the forecast was extremely conservative. Further technological innovation made possible the design of even bigger ships without the same proportionate increase in draught. Today, the largest vessel employed on the Australian route is the 818 ft., 45,000 ton

[1] *U.K.P.P.* Cmd. 2250; for Singapore see Cmd. 3328.

Canberra with a draught of 32 ft. 8 in. This is within the draught limit achieved in the Suez Canal as long ago as 1924.

Apart from the application of technological innovation to vessel-speed and size, technical change in the 1920s and 1930s above all was centred on the adoption of oil as a marine fuel. As early as 1922 oil-bunkering facilities were provided by the Anglo-Iranian Oil Company at Fremantle, Melbourne and Sydney. They were quickly put to use by the P & O and Orient and by the Norwegian-Australia Lines.[1] The subsequent decline of coal as a marine fuel is shown in the fall in the quantity of bunker coal supplied. About $1\frac{1}{2}$ million tons of coal annually in the early 1920s were supplied to oversea ships; by the late 1930s the total was down to about 600,000 tons although the tonnage of shipping had increased by one-third.

Oil at sea is used as a fuel in two ways: as a substitute for coal in steam-raising, especially with the turbined engine, and for the new type of motor vessel powered by diesel engine. The cost advantages of the motor vessel are three: fuel economy making for smaller bunkering space; lower charges for bunkering; and lower engine-room charges. In 1921, long before the full potential of diesels or turbined oil-burners was appreciated, comparisons were made of costs and revenue for a round trip London–Brisbane–London via Suez by steamers, both old and new, and by a motor ship. The figure for earnings per round trip converted to an index number for each type is as follows:

Steamships			Motor vessel
Reciprocating engine		Turbine	
Coal	Oil	Oil	
100	150	164	198

Source: *C.P.D.* 2 November 1921, p. 12,289.

Oil-burning steamers are discussed below. Concentrating attention initially on diesel vessels and the older coal-burners, a series of comparisons are available. In 1924 costs were compared of a coal-burner of about 8,000 tons deadweight and a motor vessel of similar size making a 105-day voyage carrying coal out-

[1] *U.K. Trade Report*, 1922, p. 14; 1923, p. 10. Melbourne Harbor Trust, *Annual Report* 1922, p. 19.

wards and returning with grain. On the motor vessel actual space available for outward cargo was 20 % greater and for the homeward 8 % greater than on the coal-burner. Higher earnings capacity plus lower operating charges resulted in an 11 % advantage on total earnings. The significant elements in the voyage accounts are as follows:

	Steamer (Coal-burning) £	Motor vessel £
Fuel costs	2,418	1,562
Wages	1,530	1,365
Victuals	498	406
All charges	11,804	11,429
Freight earned	13,083	14,823

Fairplay vol. 90, p. 48, *S.M.H.* 13 May 1924.

Some years later, in the early 1930s comparisons for two similar vessels for engine-room costs alone show a 40 % advantage for the motor vessel. In 1937 the I.S.C.'s report on *British Shipping in the Orient* makes extensive comparisons for coal-burners and a motor vessel making passage of 6,300 miles; details, converted to index numbers, are shown in the table opposite. All the vessels of the Norwegian-Australian Line visiting Australia in the later 1920s were motor vessels. In 1933 each of the eleven new cargo liners built in Britain for the Australian trade was diesel engined.[1]

The diesel engine was not the most efficient form of propulsion for all sizes of craft during the inter-war years, however. For high speeds the diesel was inappropriate. It was costly to run at speed, breakdowns were frequent, and it caused excessive hull vibration. Between 1920 and 1939 vessels designed for a performance in excess of 16 knots tended not to adopt the diesel engine. From the point of view of vibration the diesel engine was unsuitable for passenger-carrying and for certain classes of cargo. Despite the many claims made on behalf of the diesel in the 1920s and 1930s the limitations referred to above are only now being overcome. In 1939 only one-quarter of the world's tonnage was diesel-engined; as recently as 1965 the proportion

[1] *S.M.H.* 13 May 1924, 3 January 1927, 14 February and 31 December 1928, 14 February 1929. *Motorship* November 1934, p. 425. *C.P.D.* 2 November 1921, pp. 12,286 ff.

Estimated earning power of 5,000 gross ton cargo vessels

	Coal burners			
	Pre-1914	Average modern	Outstanding modern	Modern diesel
Fuel consumption	100	85	65	22
Cargo capacity	100	107	116	120
Charges for fuel	100	78	62	43
Net earnings per passage	100	111	124	132
Potential annual earnings	100	121	129	133

Ships launched in the world 1945–64

	Over 10,000 tons		Over 15,000 tons	
	S	M	S	M
1945–54	3,412	6,448	219	78
1955–64	1,891	17,114	869	597
1960			102	37
1961			62	78
1962			77	83
1963			67	127
1964			61	149

S, steamers; M, motor vessels. *Lloyd's Register.*

was still only one half. It has become possible to exploit the full potential of this form of propulsion only during the last few years when its application to the larger vessels has increased.[1] Recent change may be illustrated as shown in the table above. During the inter-war years steam-propulsion continued to predominate, especially in the larger vessels. Its continued use was

[1] The technical problems have been resolved only very recently. In 1910 marine-engine builders forecast for a reliable marine diesel an upper limit of 200 b.h.p. By the early 1930s about 12,000 b.h.p. had become more usual. In the post-war years the figure had risen to about 20,000 and in 1959 an upper limit of 25–27,000 b.h.p. was suggested. Forecasts now being made claim the feasibility of diesel propulsion for vessels of 500,000 tons d.w., larger than anything yet built. (*Motorship* March 1934, p. 425. *Fairplay* 14 January 1965. *Shipbuilding and Ships* (1947) (Papers read at Worshipful Company of Shipwrights Exhibition), E. G. Warne 'The Large Marine Diesel Engine'.)

assisted by technical innovation also taking place in this branch of marine engineering. The resulting economies meant that the steam engine was made much more competitive with the motor vessel. Operating efficiencies achieved in steam-propulsion in the inter-war years ensured the survival of the steamer. Considerations of service speed required, load to be propelled and so on, meant that for certain functions steam-propulsion continued to be more appropriate. Generally speaking, the diesel engine was rarely used in the Australian services on ships larger than about 10,000 gross tons. The distinguishing features of change in steam-propulsion were three: the introduction of the turbine; high-pressure steam; and the use of oil in place of coal for steam raising.

The turbine-engine developed by Parsons in the late nineteenth century was not used commercially on a wide scale until after the First World War. It quickly replaced the less efficient reciprocating engine, especially in the large liner craft used for the Australian mail-services. The first all turbine-engined steamer to be built for the Australian service was the *Ormonde* in 1917. She was converted to oil in 1923. Mail vessels and many others in the Australian trade were converted in 1929/30. A number of variants were tried, the turbo-electric engines, for example, of the P & O *Strathnaver* built in 1931 or the *Strathaird* the year after. But for all practical purposes the developments in propulsion machinery of significance were the diesel-engine and the geared steam-turbine. Associated with the introduction of the turbine in the inter-war years are the improvements concurrently taking place in steam-raising. Improved boiler design and construction and the use of superheated steam produced more power from less fuel. The use of oil, moreover, meant that oil bunkers could now be fitted in areas hitherto inappropriate for coal (because inaccessible) with a consequent increase in cargo-carrying capacity. The use of oil also produced significant economies in bunkering time and thus greatly accelerated vessel turnround. In the later 1920s a large Atlantic liner took as long as 3 days to replenish coal bunkers; if oil were used bunkering time was cut to 5 or 6 hours.[1]

[1] See *Brassey* 1921/2, pp. 267 ff.; 1930, pp. 185 ff. *Fairplay* vol. 127, pp. 58–9. C of S *Annual Report*, 1928/9, p. 62.

The switch to oil as a substitute for coal in steamers and the introduction of the motor vessel in Australia's shipping services reflects the change taking place in the world's shipping industry during the inter-war years. It also reflects the disadvantages of coal in both the Australian coastal and oversea sector. The rising price of bunker coal in Australia and the distance between ports *en route* encouraged the change from coal to oil in the oversea services. In the coastal services, where more frequent coal-bunkering was possible the switch was to motor vessel rather than to oil-burning steamers. The advantage here lay in the economy achieved in engine-room labour charges. A smaller labour force also helped to minimise industrial friction in a sector of the Australian economy where militancy was all too frequently displayed, especially during the 1920s.

No published source for the Commonwealth is available to illustrate the decline in the use of coal beyond the recorded fall in the quantity supplied for bunkers. But for the two principal Australian ports, Sydney and Melbourne, details of the shipping entered testify to the pace and extent of the change both from coal to oil and to the diesel engine. Motor vessels are first mentioned in Sydney harbour records in 1926 when they amounted to 4 % of total tonnage. In Melbourne in 1927 oversea motor-vessels represented about 7 % of total oversea tonnage entered. For representative years of the 1930s detail in tabular form below shows the rapid introduction of oil both for motor vessels and as a substitute for coal. In the coastal services the motor vessel with its smaller labour requirements was more popular than the oil-burning steamer. Today with 55 % of its registered tonnage diesel-propelled, the Australian fleet has an above-average proportion of motor tonnage.

In Australia's oversea services the motor vessel seems to have been especially appropriate in comparison with other parts of the world. In 1939 less than one-quarter of world tonnage was equipped with diesel engines. Yet in 1938, in both Sydney and Melbourne, about one third of all oversea tonnage entered was diesel-propelled. The records of Melbourne include propulsion details by nationality. These too show that for certain fleets visiting Australia motor vessels were increasingly replacing steamers. In 1938 28 % of British tonnage entering Melbourne

Propulsion employed by vessels entering Sydney and Melbourne

	% of total tonnage entered					
	1930		1934		1938	
	S	M	S	M	S	M
Oversea						
Coal	50	83	38	33	30	30
Oil	34		42	44	36	36
Motor	16	17	20	22	34	34
Inter-state						
Coal	81	87	73	84	59	76
Oil	9		13		10	
Motor	10	13	14	16	31	24

S, Sydney; M, Melbourne. (*Annual Reports* of the respective harbour trusts.)

was diesel engined; in Britain's whole fleet the proportion represented by diesels at this time was less than one-quarter. In foreign fleets, especially those of countries deficient in indigenous coal and where vessels below 10,000 tons were normal, the switch to the motor vessel was more impressive. About 45 % of all foreign-owned tonnage entered at Melbourne in 1938 was diesel-propelled.

VESSEL TYPE

The object of the concluding section is to discuss the relative importance of liners and tramps in dry-cargo carrying. In passing we mention also the growing use of oil-tankers and the effect of this on the statistics of shipping tonnage in ballast. The use of tankers increased sharply between the early 1920s and the later 1930s. In 1924/5 the tonnage of oil-tankers in the world's fleet amounted to about 8 % of the total; by 1939 it had increased to about 16 % (in 1965 the proportion was about one-third). In the Australian trade the spread of oil-tanker usage was rapid. In the early inter-war years oil was imported in barrels on dry-cargo carriers, as elsewhere in the world. In 1920/1, for example, all inbound vessels with oil cargoes arriving at Fremantle, (including those owned by the Anglo-Saxon Petroleum Company Ltd, a subsidiary of the Royal Dutch Shell Group and later to become a notable tanker shipping-company) are registered at Lloyd's as dry-cargo carriers. Increasingly in the 1920s and 1930s, however, as the records for Fremantle illustrate, there is a switch first to 'part tankers' and later to fully specialised tanker-craft. The royal commission appointed in 1933 to investigate the oil and petrol industry in Australia discusses the conveyance of oil to Australia solely in terms of tanker carriage.[1] Although as late as 1938/9, some oil still arrived in dry-cargo carriers it formed only a minute proportion of the total. By 1938/9 petrol and oil imports had reached 1½ million tons requiring between 600,000 and 700,000 net tons of shipping.

Lacking an appropriate outbound cargo, oil tankers between the wars were never cleared with cargo but in ballast. They were, as we have described them above, special-purpose vessels. Not until war-time shipping-scarcity became acute was much thought given to tanker-cleaning in order to permit the carriage by tanker of a bulk dry cargo in lieu of ballast.[2] The effect on the statistics of ballast clearances of oil-tankers from Australian ports is at once clear from the data already set out in Table 1. As the import of oil and petrol into Australia increased so too did the total tonnage of shipping cleared in ballast. In 1938/9 for example, a total of about 850,000 tons of shipping in ballast was cleared. In 1920/1, when a much lower quantity of fuel-oils was imported, ballast clearances totalled about 123,000 tons.

Little justification is needed for the inclusion of a lengthy discussion on the respective contribution made to shipping services by liners and tramps. The adequacy of shipping services may be measured in terms of tonnage provided, of service regularity, and of the rates of freight charged. All three aspects are closely connected with the type of carrier used. Secondly, as discussed in chapter 6, an integral part of the organisation of Australia's oversea-shipping services during our period was the liner con-

[1] *C.P.P.* 1934/7, III, 695 ff.

[2] Tanker-cleaning both for dry-docking and for change of cargo initially was a dirty, difficult, and uneconomic affair. Today the use of special chemical detergents and the practice of cleaning at sea between ports of oil-discharge and of dry cargo loading have transformed the economics of tanker use for dry cargo (See G. A. B. King, *Tanker Practice* (1965), p. 100; *Lloyd's List* 13 October 1965.) I have to acknowledge with thanks information supplied by Dasic Chemicals Ltd, of Hampshire, a pioneer firm specialising in world-wide tanker-cleaning.

ference system. The strength of the conference was largely a function of its monopoly in carrying. And finally, organisational differences within the shipping industry derive in part from carrier difference. Contemporary interest in the carriers employed in the oversea services was never entirely absent in Australia. In its angry rumbling it rarely reached in vain for an epithet to hurl at the handful of U.K. liner-companies said to have a 'stranglehold' on Australia's export trade. Colourful emotive language to describe these companies was commonly used. In federal parliament on one occasion the companies were anathematized as 'this gang of British capitalists'.[1] The shipowners' attitude is aptly summarised in the comment of *Fairplay*'s 'Look-out Man' that: 'the shippers in Australia... demand Atlantic liners, but want their cargoes carried at tramp rates'.[2]

Liners may concentrate either on cargo or on passengers. Cargo liners maintain regular services but operate to a less rigid time-table than the passenger liner. They often carry up to twelve passengers beyond which number a Board of Trade passenger certificate is necessary. Passenger liners are more specialised to passenger carrying. But they all have some cargo space. Passenger liners employed on the Australian service it is important to note, made a significant contribution to cargo-carrying between the wars. Lack of detail makes precise comparison difficult over the whole range of cargo carried by liners. For wool consignments to Europe, however, it is possible from conference data to establish that about 8 % of all wool consigned on British vessels was shipped on the mail services alone. For refrigerated products and other fine cargo, passenger liners as a whole similarly were active in the homeward trade. From the point of view of ship earnings, the revenue provided by cargo carrying was also important. One line employed in the Australian passenger service, whose accounts are analysed in chapter 8, on average throughout the period obtained about one third of its gross earnings from cargo freights. The cargo liner carrying up to twelve passengers had an entirely different economic basis. The revenue such vessels obtained from passenger traffic is often, by rule of thumb, reckoned as paying for all victuals con-

[1] *C.P.D.* vol. 94, p. 5,681.

[2] *Fairplay* vol. 100, p. 700.

sumed on a voyage—equal perhaps to 4% or 5% of total disbursements.

The role of passenger liners as cargo-carriers in the Australian service between the wars (and on certain other sectors also) is reflected in the internal design of the ship. It is only since the Second World War that the completely specialised passenger-ship has made its appearance in the Australian service with the sharp expansion in the migrant trade since 1945.[1] During the inter-war years the Australian service passenger-liners were so constructed as to provide large cargo capacity, much larger than on the trans-Atlantic Cunarders. The *Queen Elizabeth* has a cargo-carrying capacity of not much more than a quarter of a million cubic feet. The ship is almost four times the size of the Orient Line's *Orion* built five years earlier. Yet the *Orion* has 40% more cargo space, including a large insulated area, which is absent from the Cunarder. In terms of measured tons of 100 cubic feet, the *Queen Elizabeth* has cargo space equal to only 6% of its net registered tonnage, that is to say, its internal capacity less non-revenue earning space. The *Orion*, in contrast, had a cargo capacity equal to about 30% of its net tonnage.

A dry-cargo carrier, of course, has a much higher ratio of cargo space. A 'handy' sized tramp of about 6,000 gross tons, as normally used in the Australian trade, had bale space equal to a little more than $1\frac{1}{2}$ times its net tonnage.[2] But in absolute terms the passenger liner normally used between Britain and Australia had a greater capacity than the 'handy' sized tramp. The Orient Line ships of the 1920s had a capacity of about 9,000 tons of cargo. The *Orion* and *Orcades* built in the 1930s had slightly more at 10,000 tons. The 6,000 gross tons tramp had a total dead-weight capacity of about 9,000 tons or 8,000 tons after deducting permanent bunker space. The passenger liner of about 23,000 gross tons, that is to say, had a carrying capacity for both general and refrigerated cargo in excess of that of the tramp ship normally used in Australian services. The cargo capacity of the

[1] The best known service is that provided by the Italian 'Sitmar' Line which bought 2 ex-U.S.A. lend-lease ships previously used as troop carriers.

[2] Cargo space is conventionally measured in terms of grain space or bale space. The former is the cubic capacity of a hold into which a bulk cargo is free to flow to fill all space. Bale space, 5–10% less, is the same area into which bales, crates, etc. can be packed.

passenger liner is more adequately attested when differences in speed are taken into account. Operating to a fixed schedule and travelling at about 20 knots to the tramp's 10, the passenger liner clearly was *capable* of lifting considerably more cargo in a year than the tramp. In terms of carrying capacity multiplied by speed it would be possible, if laborious, to estimate the annual potential carrying-capacity of the passenger liners. The calculation would not, however, testify to the quantity actually carried. As we know, liners often sail with unfilled space. As vessels increased in size, moreover, their increased carrying capacity brought new problems. Before 1914 the P & O fleet on the Australian mail service, for example, numbered ten ships of 108,000 tons; by 1925 the new fleet, still ten ships, totalled 166,000 tons. The P & O agent in Sydney complained in 1923 of the difficulties of finding adequate cargo for mail vessels in the early post-war years. In pre-war days the small mail ships could nearly always be filled with wool and other fine cargo on offer. The large post-war ships, with little or no flexibility to offer in the range of discharge ports, initially created problems of unused capacity. The diffusion of the wool-trade meant also that ships able to offer discharge at continental ports or Hull were more sought after. A partial solution was to consign wheat on mail ships, hitherto only rarely done. Growth in the size of cargo liners also tended to encourage the diversion of wheat from tramps to liners; with a consequent diminution of the tramp's role in the Australian trade.

Europe for many years has been the principal receiving area in the world trade in bulk cargoes. Equally familiar is the original preponderance of the U.K. shipping industry in the supply of tramp ships for the carriage to Europe of these primary products. As every schoolboy knows, the U.K. tramp shipping industry was assisted by the export trade in British coal. The British coal industry provided outbound bulk-cargoes for the more distant parts of the world and thus helped to restrain the level of freights on return cargoes to Europe. By the 1920s and 1930s this pre-1914 or even pre-1900 pattern was fast disappearing.[1] In the Australian sector this simple pattern was excluded from the first by the availability of N.S.W. coal. Inbound coal-

[1] For an interesting discussion on tramp shipping see: *Isserlis.*

cargoes into Australia thus were rare except during strikes in the local coal-fields. In miniature the N.S.W. coal industry before 1914 in fact served the British tramp much as did the British coal industry. In default of direct cargoes for Europe, British ships carried N.S.W. coal at low rates of freight to the east or to the Pacific where homeward cargoes for Europe were to be found. Tramp arrivals in Australia enjoyed the dual possibility of coal or grain cargoes. Interrupted by the First World War, the N.S.W. coal export trade never fully revived and virtually disappeared in the early 1920s. Although an export trade in other minerals later developed, it never completely replaced the lost coal-cargoes in quantity or in direction.

The growth of foreign shipping after the First World War was accompanied by an increase in foreign tramp tonnage, especially in the Greek, Japanese, and Scandinavian fleets. Nevertheless, the British tramp continued to predominate. In the three representative ocean-going tramp activities, the grain trade of the River Plate, of the St Lawrence and of Australia, British tramps contributed the largest single amount of tonnage. Between 1931 and 1937 British tramps chartered for the River Plate represented 42 % of the total. During the years 1935, 1936 and 1937 they formed 80 % of tramp tonnage chartered for the St Lawrence, and 84 % of that chartered for the Australian trade.[1]

The appearance of foreign tramps was not in response to a rising world demand for tramp tonnage nor does it reflect any tendency to extend tramp activity. In fact, the inter-war years witnessed a decline of the importance of the tramp which tended to carry relatively less of the world's seaborne trade. Several factors were responsible. As trading routes and commodity patterns became well established over time, regularly scheduled shipping services were increasingly more appropriate. Trades requiring specialised shipping increased. Refrigerated cargo increased and required more insulated space. World trade in oil expanded and the development of bulk transport led to a doubling of tanker tonnage between the early 1920s and the Second World War. As shown below for the U.K. fleet, the effect of changing demand patterns was to reduce the tonnage of ship-

[1] *U.K.P.P.* Cmd. 5750, p. 9.

ping employed as tramps. There is the additional factor that marine innovations widened the speed gap between liner and tramp. In terms of speed multiplied by cargo space, the carrying capacity of liners was thus increased.

In 1916 the Booth Committee, appointed to consider the post-war U.K. shipping scene, estimated on the basis of vessel speed that in 1914 tramps represented 60 % and liners 40 % of a total U.K. tonnage of about 11½ million net tons. It also commented on the absorption of tramp tonnage by liner companies and warned that: 'after the war, trades which were formerly the recognised domain of the British tramp owner, may, as a result, be carried on by the lines, or more probably by foreigners'.[1] The prognosis was borne out by changes during our period. Although estimates of tramp tonnage are difficult to make because of mobility in function, enough data are available to indicate the magnitude of the decline. Fact-finding committees of the U.K. Chamber of Shipping reported that by 1933 U.K. tramp tonnage had fallen 50 % and that it had fallen a further 13 % by 1938. In quantitative terms the decline was from about 6½–7 million net tons in 1914 (the Booth Committee estimates) to about 3 million in 1935. For foreign-going U.K. tramps, persistent decline by 1938 had taken the figure down to about 2¼ million net tons.[2] In following pages it is argued that tramp ships in the Australian sector register a sharp decline, matching, if not exceeding the experience of the U.K. tramp industry as a whole.

The distinction between liners and tramps is usually based upon service regularity, rather than upon constructional differences. 'The main features of the "tramp" system are that, unlike the liners, the tramp has no fixed itinerary and only sails if she has a cargo to carry or in prospect. The shipper, or shippers, charter a vessel which will go from any port of the world to any other port as required, but she does not normally take cargo in parcels, as the liners do, but deals almost entirely with full cargoes.'[3] Mobility between tramping and cargo-liner

[1] *U.K.P.P.* Cd. 9092, p. 86.

[2] C of S: 'Report of Special Committee on Tramp Shipping' (1933), and 'Report of Deep Sea Tramp Committee' (1938). See also *Isserlis*, pp. 58–82, 96–103.

[3] Committee on Industry and Trade, *Further Factors in Industrial and Commercial Efficiency* (Balfour Committee) (1928), p. 218.

services generally speaking makes difficult any clear-cut distinctions between the two in discussing the shipping industry as a whole. Seasonal variations in cargo availability might encourage a cargo liner to switch to tramping. Tramps on time charter carrying regularly between fixed points become converted to cargo liners. During the depression, moreover, when the trade in bulk cargoes tended to decline sharply, the larger tramp vessels found themselves loading part cargoes for several shippers and loading and discharging at two or three ports. Partly as a consequence some larger tramp companies abandoned tramping and moved into the liner section of the industry.

For the Australian sector between the wars, distinctions based solely upon service characteristics and which ignore ship design are somewhat artificial. A feature of both the cargo and passenger liners normally used in the Australian services was their extensive refrigerated hold space. Vessels thus equipped were not suitable for the carriage of cargoes in bulk and would, moreover, have been uneconomically used for such purposes. Dry-cargo carriers other than cargo liners to be found in the Australian sector at this time were not, on the whole, fitted with refrigerated holds. Fleet details of the Hain S.S. Company illustrate the point. Ships of this leading tramp company frequently called at Australian ports. In 1939 the fleet numbered 24 ships totalling 123,000 gross tons. Only 4 (which may never or only rarely have visited Australia) were fitted with refrigerating machinery, they totalled about 24,000 gross tons and had between them only some 40,000 cubic feet of refrigerated capacity. In contrast, the cargo liner *Australia Star* of only 11,000 gross tons had more than a half million cubic feet of refrigerated space.

The distinction more appropriate in the present context is between the different classes of cargo normally carried by each type of ship. Broadly speaking liners carry a vast heterogeneous range of relatively compact items usually described as berth parcel items or case goods. Outbound liners from Australia also carried items for which specialised or fast shipping was required. Tramps, inbound or outbound, concentrate on the carriage in bulk of relatively low value bulky commodities. Tramp-type cargoes are few in number. In 1935 twenty item headings accounted for 94 % of U.K. tramp voyages, for 95 % of the total weight of tramp cargoes carried and for 92 % of tramp freight earnings.[1] Apart from considerations of bulk and value there are also institutional factors which restricted the carriage of liner cargoes to liners. Wool-carrying provides a good example of one type of restriction. Wool could be carried by the newer faster tramps. On occasions, as in 1921, market considerations might even prefer the slower transit possible on sailing vessels.[2] But generally speaking it was a cargo carried by liners for reasons connected with the wool trade itself. Asked why tramps were so rarely used for wool consignments a spokesman for wool-exporting interests replied that wool buyers:

> will not purchase unless assured that tonnage will be available to lift their wool, and enable them to obtain bills of lading so that they may negotiate documents immediately after purchase. Without security of prompt suitable tonnage buyers at auctions would not operate...the only method...which can give wool buyers the service which the trade demands is the regular liner berth tonnage. [Wool carriers have other functions, he continued.] Vessels which cater for the wool sales have also their programme outlined for refrigerated cargo and other products, most of which require specialised tonnage. If it were possible...to cater for wool shipment by means of tramp charter tonnage then refrigerated and general cargo ...right from Cairns to Fremantle...would have to pay vastly increased rates of freights.[3]

Details available for the years 1924–8 and information kindly supplied by the Australian Tonnage Committee for the years 1936–8 make it clear that virtually all the wool and refrigerated items shipped to Europe in these years were carried by liners. The second institutional feature stems from the shipping industry itself. In the 1930s it worked to exclude tramps from even occasional excursions into the carriage of liner cargoes. As discussed in another chapter, developments in the liner conference organisation of trade from Australia after 1930 was based upon the agreement system. This involved the payment of freight rebates to 'loyal' shippers who shipped in conference liners. It made it even less probable that tramps would poach liner cargoes.

[1] *Isserlis*, p. 82. [2] *Fairplay* vol. 82, p. 96. [3] *S.M.H.* 27 October 1931.

In terms of value, cargoes carried by liners dominated both the inbound and outbound trade. Wool, together with refrigerated cargo and other items normally shipped by liner, accounted throughout the inter-war years for 70–80 % of export values. Towards the close of the period, moreover, the proportion of the total represented by liner cargoes was tending to rise. But, contemporaries complained, liner companies sought to extend their carrying and were increasingly loading cargoes traditionally carried by tramps. It is the accuracy of this complaint which is here examined. The supply of tramp shipping is a function of demand for inbound as well as for outbound shipping space. Tramps may arrive with cargo and thus automatically be available for outbound cargoes. In default of inbound tramp cargoes they may arrive in ballast in response to demand for outbound tramp shipping. If it is possible to trace a high volume of demand for inbound tramps it is reasonable to postulate a lower, more competitive outbound tramp freight rate. If tramps arrive in ballast the outbound freight rate necessarily is higher and thus more easily undercut by liners. Few inbound tramp cargoes existed in Australia's oversea trade. Most imports were berth parcel items carried by liners. Generally, only three tramp commodities regularly and one item spasmodically were imported into Australia. From time to time, during Australian coal strikes, coal and coke were imported. The coal strike in the Maitland district of N.S.W. in 1923 was accompanied by shipments of South African and Tyneside coal. During the catastrophic N.S.W. coal strike of 1929/30, for example, almost a half million tons of coal were imported from the U.K. in the calendar year 1929 and about 400,000 tons in the following year. (The additional employment for U.K. tramps proved to be a mixed blessing for the shipowner. An already low outbound spot charter rate for wheat was forced even lower.)[1] In 1938, N.S.W. strikes similarly led to heavy imports of coal.

But the principal regular inbound bulk cargoes were three: oil, carried by tanker and thus here ignored; timber; and above all, phosphates. Inbound timber cargoes tended as a rule to exceed timber exports. But at its peak, surplus tramp shipping

[1] *Fairplay* vol. 114, pp. 155–6. *S.M.H.* 25 July, 2 August, 1923.

space from this source available for the carriage of exports amounted to a mere 200,000 measured tons. The amount of timber carried beyond Australasian waters by vessels registered outside Australasia moreover was probably always relatively small. It is noticeable that Angier's annual freight surveys, published in *Fairplay*, only twice refer to timber charters from Australia during the whole of our period. Neither refers to voyages to New Zealand, a major market at this time for Australian timber.

The largest single item of inbound bulk cargo were the rock phosphates from which fertilisers are made. Imports grew steadily between the wars. By 1939 they had reached 600,000 tons a year. It was not, nevertheless, a trade which created much surplus shipping space in Australia available for outbound deep-sea cargoes. First, the main area supplying Australia was in the nearby Pacific islands, sufficiently close to encourage the direct use of Australasian-registered shipping. During the periods when Australian shipping engaged in voyages to the far east they often returned via the phosphate islands when other direct return cargoes were hard to get.[1] Secondly, only very limited cargoes were available for transport to the phosphate islands and hence the carriage of phosphates on a spot charter by oversea shipping was relatively unlikely. Almost all the rock phosphates imported into Australia were obtained from the Nauru and Ocean islands in the Pacific, only some 2,800 miles from Victoria, and 4,400 from Western Australia, the chief import-states. The trade in phosphates from the islands was controlled by the British Phosphate Commission, set up in 1919 by the governments of Australia, New Zealand and the U.K., most exports being shipped to Australia and to New Zealand. The Commission itself owned shipping.[2] In 1939 it owned four vessels with a total gross tonnage of about 23,000. In normal circumstances the speed and capacity of these vessels would have enabled them to transport about one-third of the phos-

[1] *U.K. Trade Reports*: 1921, p. 10; 1932, p. 138; 1938, p. 188. *C.P.D.* vol. 135, p. 373.

[2] For incidental references to the shipping aspect of the phosphates trade see the annual reports made by the British Phosphates Commission and published in *C.P.P.* The importance of the Nauru and Ocean islands is also discussed in 'Report on the superphosphate industry...' *C.P.P.* 1932/4, IV, 1,965 ff.

phates exported from Nauru and Ocean. On a *pro rata* basis they could carry about one-third of the quantity shipped to Australia. For the remaining tonnage required, oversea vessels were likely, for the reasons outlined, to be chartered on a time or consecutive voyage basis. A comment by Angier in his annual freights survey for 1927 suggests that already spot charters had become relatively rare. Confirmation that time charter had become common is to be had from the records of the Tramp Shipping Advisory Committee covering the calendar years 1935 and 1936.[1] The records relate only to U.K. tramps engaged on voyages eligible for the tramp-shipping subsidy. They include details of eighty-seven voyages from Nauru to Australia made in these two years; the ships carried about 670,000 tons of phosphate, or almost one-half of the total imported. Some of the ships arriving with phosphate later cleared from Australia with grain for the U.K. Many of the ships employed made repeated voyages between Nauru and Australia, however. One company in 1935 used 16 ships for 25 voyages, in 1936 the same 16 ships made 28 voyages. Ships of other lines also made repeated voyages.

In the absence of large quantities of inbound bulk cargo, tramps arrived in ballast. The records show that ballast arrivals were a common feature of the Australian shipping scene. In the 1920s it is probable that almost all the ballast entries were indeed tramps. Official records at this time describe such entries as 'vessels seeking coal or wheat' or more simply as 'vessels seeking freights'. It is possible also to infer the use of tramp shipping in the heavy Japanese ballast arrivals between 1929 and 1935 when large quantities of iron ore were being exported to Japan. But for the 1930s as a whole the much higher proportion of tonnage arriving in ballast is unlikely to have been tramp ships only. It seems likely that during the depression many cargo liners whose major employment always lay in the outbound direction arrived in ballast.

The long-term factor most likely to restrict the supply of tramp shipping, however, was the reduction in the quantity of available cargo. Both locally and in the international scene cargoes were tending to decline during the 1930s. The contrac-

[1] C of S 'T.S.A.C.' volumes.

tion of world trade during the depression years is abundantly documented. League of Nations estimates illustrate the dimensions:

	Volume of World trade	Volume of Seaborne trade
	1913 = 100	
1929	130	135
1932	96	101
1935	106	115
1936	111	120

Initially the tonnage of Australian grain exports show no comparable pattern of decline. Between 1930 and 1933 Australian exports in fact rose; only later is a decline to be traced. Nevertheless the reduction of cargoes elsewhere in the world led to wholesale laying up of tramps. In Britain, Chamber of Shipping figures show that more than 2 million net tons of British shipping was laid up in July 1932. Thereafter demand for shipping improved. By October 1933 laid-up British tonnage in U.K. ports had fallen to about 1½ million net tons, half being foreign-going U.K. tramps. Ultimately 'assistance to British shipping' was introduced and laid-up shipping recommissioned. By July in 1937 only 56,000 net tons of U.K. shipping was still laid-up.

Of more significance in the long run was the tendency for liners to carry tramp cargoes at cut rates. After the introduction of the tramp-shipping subsidy in Britain, the rates fixed by the Tramp Shipping Administrative Committee were observed by liners also. But long before this, tramp cargoes were being lost to liners. Only three tramp bulk cargoes were involved; certain minerals, sugar and, above all, wheat. Only those minerals in compact, part-processed form were normally carried by liner, concentrates and ores seldom if ever. Tramp charter quotations in *Fairplay* often include rates for the latter, never for the former. Conversely Australian official statistical summaries quote liner rates for zinc blocks, copper ingots and the like, never for ores in bulk. But the total tonnage involved was never high enough to cause concern to tramp owners.

Sugar exports were similarly small during the 1920s when annual shipments averaged less than 100,000 tons. In the following decade three times as much was exported on average; by the late 1930s the total had reached 400,000 tons. In the early 1920s isolated references to tramp spot charters are mentioned but these disappear from the records before 1930. The explanation lies in the new organisation of the sugar export trade from 1928 onwards. From that year an annual contract was concluded between the Colonial Sugar Refining Co. Ltd (C.S.R.), and the homeward conference lines. The C.S.R. carries out most of the marketing of sugar produced in the South Pacific including the oversea export of raw sugar. The shipping arrangements made by the C.S.R. thus cover virtually all the sugar exported from Australia. The annual contract provided for the carriage by the conference lines of all sugar exported to Britain and eastern Canada, the two principal oversea markets (often the sole markets) for Australian sugar. Details of sugar carrying under contract are summarised below. They show a tendency for sugar to be increasingly carried in full cargoes rather than in berth parcels. Except during the last four years of the period, however, the greater proportion of sugar in full cargoes as well as in parcels was carried by conference line regular vessels. To supplement the conference vessels, outside vessels were occasionally chartered on conference lines account to carry full cargoes. During the closing years both the quantity carried by chartered ships and the proportion which this represented of the whole began to look significant. But even at the eve-of-war peak, the amount of employment offered to tramps chartered by the conference lines was not very impressive.[1]

The commodity above all where friction was greatest and liner activity most noticeable was in the wheat trade. The failure in Australian wheat ports as a whole to proceed far or fast with mechanised bulk grain loading undoubtedly facilitated the shipment of bagged grain on liners in berth parcel quantities. Grain for 'stiffening', to give weight to a vessel taking bulky but light cargo, wool, for example, had doubtless been carried for many years. But the systematic and sustained increase in

[1] Letter from General Manager of the C.S.R. Ltd, dated 30 December 1965 and information kindly supplied by the Australian Tonnage Committee. See also: Lowndes (ed.) *South Pacific Enterprise* (1956) for information on marketing and *Fairplay* vol. 118, p. 379 for ships engaged in 1931.

Sugar exports to U.K. and Canada 1928/9–1938/9

	% carried		
	(*a*) In full cargoes	(*b*) By outside chartered ships	Tonnage carried by outside chartered ships ('000 tons)
1928/9	32	10	19
1929/30	20	9	14
1930/1	30	27	52
1931/2	52	20	56
1932/3	54	24	24
1933/4	64	19	59
1934/5	64	6	17
1935/6	65	38	111
1936/7	77	33	134
1937/8	65	45	190
1938/9	68	54	233

liner carriage of grain during the 1920s was acutely disliked by tramp owners. Not surprisingly, given that homewards grain offered the major area of employment for U.K. tramps in Australia, tramp owners' resentment found expression. In 1929, for example, the chairman of the Nitrate Producers Steamship Company in the course of his address at the company's annual meeting remarked that:

Royal Commissions have decided that conference rings are not inimical to the public interest. If, however, liner companies arbitrarily use privileges so procured to the detriment of tramp owners, an abuse...arises. This frequently occurs...For example: during the present season from Australia, unprotected freights were precipitately reduced...simply because a particular liner was short of a small balance of cargo. Two months later, with equal callousness, a further reduction...was announced. In each case these reductions were 5*s*. per ton under the obtaining tramp rate. It is apparent that the liner companies on the strength of their privileged outward and partly protected homeward freights at profitable rates, are adopting yet another method of overcoming those who provide importers and exporters with...a safeguard.[1]

[1] *Fairplay* vol. 111, p. 505.

The quantity of wheat carried by liners is known with certainty for only a few of the inter-war years. In 1927 liners in the homeward conference lifted 50 % of the wheat exported to Egypt and Europe, equal to 36 % of total wheat exports in that year. In the 5 years 1924–8 conference lines carried 40 % of all wheat and flour shipped to Europe.[1] Details available for the two calendar years 1935 and 1936 show that excluding shipments to Japan, the quantities of wheat and flour carried by British tramps represented only 30 % and 40 % respectively of the total in the two years. It seems likely that the bulk of the remainder was carried by liners in line with the pattern for 1932, 1933 and 1934.[2]

In concluding our brief survey of tramp shipping at work in Australia's oversea services we turn to the evidence for the calendar years 1935 and 1936 contained in the records of the Tramp Shipping Administrative Committee. The evidence enables us to assess with some exactness the relative importance of tramp ships in the supply of British shipping in Australia's oversea services. The evidence derives from records assembled in the course of administering the tramp-shipping subsidy. It includes all British vessels making tramp voyages eligible for and claiming the subsidy. In 1935 and 1936 the number of British tramps entered at Australian ports was 143 and 170 respectively. The higher number represents about one quarter of the annual number of all British ships arriving in Australian ports between 1934/5 and 1936/7. In terms of tonnage, the detail shows that in each of the two years, 1935, and 1936, British tramp tonnage amounted to only 13 % of all oversea tonnage cleared from Australian ports. It amounted to less than one-quarter of *British* tonnage similarly cleared. When we recall, moreover, that 80 % to 85 % of all tramps chartered for Australian grain-carrying were British, it is clear that tramp shipping as a whole by the close of the 1930s was relatively less important in Australia's oversea-shipping services.

The evidence also provides a measure of the financial importance to the British tramp industry of the Australian sector. In 1935 and 1936 between 400 and 450 separate British tramp

[1] *C.P.D.* vol. 118, p. 4,673.

[2] C of S 'T.S.A.C.' volumes; Government Questionnaire, vol. 4.

owners shared the tramp-shipping subsidy. Only 50 of them had engaged in the Australian trade. In these two years, moreover, less than 10 % of the voyages made by ships of upwards of 3,000 gross tons were to or from Australia. Not surprisingly therefore, the contribution made by the Australian sector to British tramp freight earnings was small; in 1935 it represented only 5 % or 6 % of the total.

Chapter 3

OVERSEA TRADE AND COMMERCIAL POLICY

The supply and type of shipping described in the two preceding chapters marks the response of fleets owned overseas to the demand for shipping in Australia. It is the object of this and the following chapter to relate the shipping needs of the economy to the supply of shipping services. The present chapter is concerned with the total tonnage of oversea cargo, with the geographic distribution of Australia's oversea trade, and with changes in distribution stemming from the changing aims and ends of commercial policy.

During the inter-war years Australia's oversea trade consisted, in essence, of the exchange of primary products, more especially wool and foodstuffs, for the sophisticated manufactured goods of Europe and the U.S.A. The period witnessed, on the whole, an expansion of the export trade in foodstuffs, especially refrigerated items, and a significant increase in the import of motor vehicles and motor fuel. To-day the composition, if not the direction, of the export trade is little changed. The continued diversification of the Australian economy referred to above, however, has significantly altered the import profile. The most important variation in the make-up of imports is in the reduced volume of final goods imported. The encouragement of local industry has involved an increase in the import of semi-finished products and some change in the finished items range. During our period, however, import substitution had made little headway and, as we shall see, had little effect upon the composition of trade.

Most useful as a point at which to begin would be a comprehensive record of cargo carried, differentiating bulk and berth parcel cargo, dry cargo and bulk liquid, and so forth. Such refinements are wanting. Instead we have from official sources a simple record of annual tonnage totals of oversea cargo shipped and discharged. Details first appear in the Commonwealth

Year Book for 1922 (three years later in the *Transport and Communication Bulletin*) with the record taken back to 1913 (Table 7*a*). How accurate and useful are the official figures? So far as inward cargoes are concerned it is impossible to say. With a few exceptions imports consisted of 'general cargo' that is to say manufactured goods and the tendency was to record such items in official trade statistics by value rather than by quantity. It is extremely unlikely that the aggregate import tonnage figures shown in official published sources represent much more than informed guesses made by customs officials. This is not to suggest they are incorrect, but that it would be difficult, if indeed possible at all, to check these figures.

Exports, on the other hand, are more homogeneous, fewer in number, and as a rule are recorded by quantity as well as by value. In the following chapter eight major export groups are identified and have been analysed in some detail in order to reconstruct their space requirements, their destination and so on. In aggregate these eight groups (representing 80 % to 90 % of the total value of exports) provide a yardstick against which to compare official published totals. In Tables 7*a* and *b* below the official tonnage figures are shown together with the tonnage totals calculated for the eight selected export groups.

The tonnage data are somewhat contrived in that they represent the combination of two different standards of measurement; these are more fully described in Appendix 1. They include first, the normal ton of 2,240 pounds weight in customary use and secondly, a volume ton measured in cubic feet. Many items of cargo have a high bulk-to-weight ratio. A consignment of cigars requires about 180 cubic feet of stowage space in which to load 2,240 pounds: coal requires about 40 cubic feet for the same weight. Differences in density have given rise to the convention that cargo measuring more than about 40 cubic feet per ton of 2,240 pounds weight is treated as 'measurement cargo' in contrast to 'deadweight cargo'. Volume or measurement cargo is converted into measurement tons at the rate of 40 cubic feet to the ton. The tonnage data in Tables 7*a* and *b* combines tons weight together with tons measured. Before 1925/6 official published records give a combined total; after 1925/6 the two are shown separately. Nevertheless, in the following tables the two different tons are aggregated for the whole of the period to facilitate comparison.

Table 7*b* at first sight would appear to suggest that official sources understate the quantities of cargoes shipped, by about 300,000 to 400,000 tons annually in the 1920s and by 600,000 to 700,000 tons in the 1930s, and this, it should be noted, on the basis of calculations for only eight export groups. In fact this is probably misleading. The major discrepancy arises when tons measured are compared, official totals for tons weight in contrast tend to be higher than those here calculated. Explanation is to be sought in differences in the choice of items assessed respectively by weight and by measurement. In official records wool exports are shown in terms of the pound weight. Ocean freights on wool are similarly based on weight. But wool is a bulky commodity, especially in the grease. Weight for weight, the space occupied by a ton of sand or lead is about one sixth of that required by a ton of wool. From the shipping point of view, adopted throughout this study, it is more appropriate to assess the space needed for wool shipments in measured tons. Official records, however, probably register wool exports in tons weight. In 1926/7, for example, wool shipments required a trifle more than one million measured tons of shipping space. Other items shipped by volume rather than weight increased the total in that year by a further 700,000 measured tons. Yet the official total for that year is less than a million measured tons. If official figures are recalculated to switch wool from the tons weight to the measured tons total, the discrepancy largely disappears. It thus would appear reasonable to accept official totals as providing an adequately accurate yardstick of changing orders of magnitude in the demand for shipping space.

The detail set out in Table 7*a* (and shown in Figure 1) merits brief discussion to emphasise certain features which it illustrates. We begin with the tonnage data. Assuming exactly comparable standards of recording accuracy throughout the period, the data show marked instability in year-to-year totals. Fluctuations were more violent in inbound cargo where the trough figure of 1931/2 is less than one half the tonnage totals achieved in the peak years 1929/30 or 1937/8. Outbound totals vary much less. The lowest recorded figure is only one-third less than the highest recorded figure. There is also to be noticed a cyclical pattern. The aggregate tonnage figure builds to a peak in 1929/30, is then forced back towards the 1920/1 total, and subsequently regains the earlier zenith. Taking the period as a whole, the trend is distinctly upwards, however.

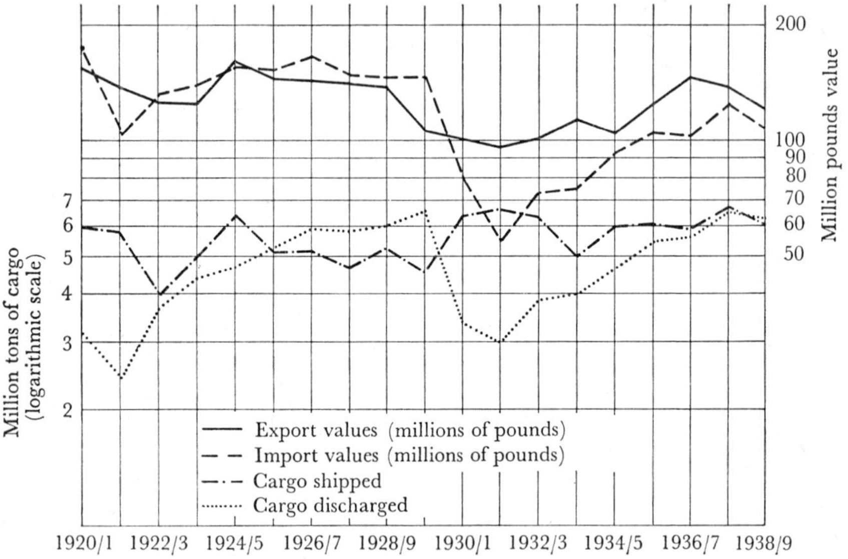

Fig. 1. Australia's oversea trade 1920/1–1938/9.
(Sources as in Table 7*a*.)

Imports, as already noted, tend to be recorded by value rather than by quantity. But for two significant import items, fuel-oil and timber, it is in fact possible to measure the rise in quantity as well as value. Increases in oil imports represent additional cargo space by 1938/9 of about 1·3 million tons, and increases in timber imports about three quarters of a million. Together they represent about a half or more of the total increase in import tonnage during our period. On the whole, import tonnages show less variation from year to year. They do, however, record a much more violent downswing in the early 1930s and testify to the violence of trade contraction and possibly to the efficacy of government measures taken in March

1930. The effects felt in Australia of world-wide depression caused sharp government reaction. Faced with a drain of reserves the government introduced heavy increases in import duties, import embargoes, and the rationing of imports.[1] The measures taken by the government were followed by a sharp drop in import tonnages as illustrated in the table. By 1938/9 the level achieved in 1929/30 had been regained.

When we turn to the relationship between tonnage figures and export and import values the most obvious feature to note is that values were about the same at the end as at the beginning of the inter-war years.[2] That is to say they failed to increase *pro rata* with the tonnage figures. With exports, for example, the tonnage figure for 1938/9 was 7 % higher than in 1921/2, the total value was 11 % less. In 1931/2, tonnages had risen by 15 % whereas values had decreased 30 %. The composition of exports on the whole remained substantially unchanged throughout the inter-war years. Explanation is therefore to be sought in the decline in the price of primary products which characterises the 1930s. Using 1910/11 as our base year the price index of the three principal export groups in 1938/9 registers a fall of about 20 % from the level of the early 1920s.[3] At the bottom of the depression, in 1931/2, with the tonnage of exports still higher, the price index for the three main export groups records a fall of as much as 40 %. For the pastoral sector the fall was even higher at almost 70 %, as the sag in the realised price on a bale of greasy wool amply testifies, from about £34 in 1924/5 to not quite £11 in 1931/2.[4] On the eve of the Second World War the worst of the depression was past but, as noted above, compared with the years immediately after the First World War export prices had not fully recovered.

Far more striking if less easily explained is the record of imports. In 1938/9 the tonnage of imports was 2½ times more than in 1921/2. Increased volume was not matched by a com-

[1] For a discussion on the whole problem see D. B. Copland, *Australia in the World Crisis 1929–1933* (1934).

[2] The abnormal year 1920/1 is here ignored. The cancelling of foreign orders at the end of the war enabled the U.K. to meet immediately a large proportion of outstanding Australian orders. (*Year Book*, 1923, p. 224.)

[3] *Butlin*, table 267.

[4] *Sheep and Wool Handbook*, p. 45.

parable increase in value, however, where the gain was a mere 5%. Official Australian compilations on oversea trade, as already noted, on the whole do not include quantities when recording imports and content themselves with *values*. Hence it is difficult to make valid comparisons over time. So far as the composition of imports is concerned, the impression given by the records is that no significant changes took place. In line with other evidence of the time we might expect that the price decline of the 1930s would largely account for the failure of values to keep in step with quantities. For the two import commodities referred to already, timber and motor fuels, it is in fact possible to show with some certainty the extent to which falling values accompanied rising volumes. Imports of oil and motor spirit in 1938/9 amounted to more than 470 million gallons as compared with only 64 million in 1921/2. In terms of value, however, this item was recorded as only £8·8 million in 1938/9 or rather less than twice the 1921/2 figure. Timber imports similarly increased more sharply in volume than in value, from 27 to 384 million superficial feet of undressed timber with a money value of £1·8 million in 1938/9 as against less than £0·4 million in 1921/2.

Two further features may be noticed. During the depression years the terms of trade moved sharply against Australia. Tariff restrictions were introduced. The combination of higher import duties and lower export earnings produced a severe fall in both the tonnage and value of imports. In the worst year, 1931/2, both were halved. Secondly it is to be noted that although the value of imports and exports move in the same direction, rising and falling together, the *tonnages* of imports and exports fluctuated inversely. It is only during the years 1922/3 to 1924/5 and 1934/5 to 1938/9 that they move together. For most of the other years and more especially between 1928/9 and 1933/4, their movement was out of phase, as imports fell, exports rose. The imbalance in shipping resulting from the discrepancy in the demand for inward and outward tonnage was not welcomed by the shipping industry. It was seriously to hamper negotiations in the early thirties when attempts were made to hold freight rates steady.

The aggregate tonnage data, however, provide no indication

Table 7*a*. *Oversea trade, 1920/1–1938/9, total values and tonnages*

	Value of		Tonnage of		
	Exports	Imports	Exports	Imports	
	(£m)		('000 tons)		Total
1920/1	154·3	171·7	5,925	3,201	9,126
1921/2	137·7	103·8	5,816	2,420	8,236
1922/3	126·8	132·0	4,064	3,719	7,783
1923/4	127·3	140·2	4,982	4,377	9,359
1924/5	163·8	154·0	6,498	4,696	11,194
1925/6	148·1	151·9	5,169	5,343	10,512
1926/7	146·4	167·3	5,246	5,955	11,201
1927/8	142·3	149·3	4,686	5,889	10,575
1928/9	139·2	147·4	5,289	6,067	11,356
1929/30	104·1	146·8	4,598	6,647	11,245
1930/1	101·6	82·1	6,442	3,413	9,855
1931/2	97·2	57·8	6,678	2,967	9,645
1932/3	100·2	73·5	6,420	3,897	10,317
1933/4	115·8	76·8	4,999	4,001	9,000
1934/5	104·8	93·7	6,079	4,693	10,772
1935/6	126·0	108·2	6,108	5,481	11,589
1936/7	148·2	103·0	5,961	5,680	11,641
1937/8	141·3	127·2	6,820	6,646	13,466
1938/9	122·1	109·4	6,231	6,340	12,631

Source: Values: Butlin, *Australian Domestic Product*, tables 256, 257 and 263*a* and *b*. Tonnages: *Transport and Communication Bulletin*.

of the destination of exports nor of the source of imports. For eight major export groups analysed in chapter 4 shipping requirements by trade routes have been determined. For the remaining exports and for imports as a whole this is not possible because insufficient information is available. In default of data on geographical distribution in tonnages, an impression of the relative importance of individual oversea markets may be gained from the value of Australia's trade with each. Details are given in Table 8 for sample years of the proportion of total merchandise trade with major markets. In every year but one the proportion shared by the markets shown in Table 8 sums to 90 % or more of the total value of Australia's oversea trade. Trade with countries whose individual share is too small to justify separate entry adds 3 % to 4 %. Trade with South Africa and Mauritius

Table 7*b*. *Oversea trade, 1920/1–1938/9, export tonnages* (*'000 tons*)

	Official figures			Calculated		
	Tons measured	Tons weight	Total	Tons measured	Tons weight	Total
1920/1	NA	NA	5,925	1,408·2	4,577·2	5,985·4
1921/2	NA	NA	5,816	1,964·0	4,301·8	6,265·8
1922/3	NA	NA	4,064	1,823·6	2,899·1	4,722·7
1923/4	NA	NA	4,982	1,348·6	3,948·5	5,297·1
1924/5	NA	NA	6,498	1,785·6	4,742·2	6,527·8
1925/6	4,281	888	5,169	2,085·9	3,455·8	5,541·7
1926/7	4,313	933	5,246	1,815·0	3,678·1	5,493·1
1927/8	3,740	947	4,686	1,892·0	3,178·5	5,070·5
1928/9	4,529	760	5,289	1,934·7	3,799·9	5,734·6
1929/30	3,955	643	4,598	1,941·5	3,101·2	5,042·7
1930/1	5,803	639	6,442	2,107·2	4,905·9	7,013·1
1931/2	5,952	726	6,678	2,323·6	5,041·6	7,365·2
1932/3	5,642	779	6,420	2,532·6	4,667·5	7,200·1
1933/4	4,260	739	4,999	2,443·2	3,301·8	5,745·0
1934/5	5,221	858	6,079	2,690·3	4,135·8	6,826·1
1935/6	5,214	894	6,108	2,536·4	4,263·0	6,799·4
1936/7	5,028	933	5,961	2,563·2	4,009·5	6,572·7
1937/8	5,731	1,089	6,820	2,685·6	4,793·1	7,478·7
1938/9	5,139	1,092	6,231	2,771·9	4,082·0	6,853·9

NA, not available.

accounted for less than 1 % and with New Zealand about 2 % of imports and between 3 % and 6 % of exports.

The variations illustrated in Table 8 in the proportions of the total attributable to each trading area stem from a variety of causes. The records of imports from the Netherlands East Indies (N.E.I.), for example, reflect changes in the composition of trade in response to new demands in Australia. The import of oil from the N.E.I. enlarged from 1 % to more than 7 % the share of the total contributed by that market. The changing proportions also illustrate the local effects of world depression. The U.K.'s share of the import total sagged in 1930/1. This had been forecast by the U.K. Trade Commissioner in December 1930: 'U.K. manufacturers must accept the fact that what was their second largest export market will offer a very much

Table 8. *Oversea merchandise trade, 1920/1–1938/9 (selected years), geographical distribution*

	% of total value					
	1920/1	1922/3	1927/8	1930/1	1932/3	1938/9
Imports from:						
U.K.	46·9	51·9	42·7	39·6	42·5	41·6
Europe (incl. U.K.)	55·3	61·0	54·0	51·6	53·3	51·7
Japan	3·2	3·0	2·9	4·1	6·4	4·2
N.E.I.	0·4	3·3	3·9	6·8	5·3	7·3
Other eastern countries	5·8	5·0	6·8	9·3	8·3	5·2
U.S.A. and Canada	24·8	22·7	26·0	21·7	18·8	23·0
Exports to:						
U.K.	51·1	45·4	37·8	44·0	47·8	54·5
Europe (incl. U.K.)	65·6	69·1	70·6	66·7	67·4	71·4
Japan	2·2	7·9	9·0	10·6	11·6	4·0
N.E.I.	1·9	1·6	1·4	1·6	1·2	1·1
Other eastern countries	2·7	3·0	3·7	8·3	9·3	6·9
U.S.A. and Canada	4·1	8·5	5·6	4·3	2·5	4·6

Source: *Year Book* and *Oversea Trade.*

reduced demand for their products over a number of years.'[1] In part also the variations manifest the effect on trade of the commercial policies and restrictions adopted both in Australia and in her markets overseas. In following pages the major characteristics of each market are briefly examined and an attempt is made to relate policy changes to their effects on trade.

The major consideration which gives unity to Australian commercial policy between the wars was the attempt to diversify the economic base of the country. Above all the aim was to create within Australia a sound import-replacement industry. The Commonwealth Bureau of Commerce and Industry, for example, encouraged U.K. firms to set up branch factories in Australia.[2] The principal measure adopted to implement the policy, however, was the protection afforded by tariff barriers and by anti-dumping legislation. The new tariff introduced in 1921, claimed the Minister for Trade and Customs, was specifically designed to give shelter for local industry. He quoted

[1] *U.K. Trade Report,* 1930, p. 12.

[2] *U.K. Trade Reports:* 1922, p. 16; 1923, p. 46; 1925, p. 19.

an extract from a speech made by Prime Minister Hughes that: 'this Tariff will protect industries born during the war, will encourage others that are desirable, and will diversify and extend existing industries'.[1] To permit flexibility an intermediate level was inserted between the British preferential tariff and the general tariff. The intermediate tariff was designed primarily to apply in certain circumstances to imports from foreign countries. Dropped in 1932 because not much used in the 1920s it was reintroduced in 1935 when it played a noteworthy part in the commercial negotiations of the later 1930s.

Tariff protection was not accompanied by any significant oversea retaliation during the 1920s. Until 1929 the general buoyancy in world trade enabled Australia to dispose of her products overseas without difficulty; imports ran at a high level. The onset of the world depression in 1929 radically altered the picture, however. For Australia it meant a sharp fall in export earnings, balance of payments problems, and difficulties in servicing her oversea debts. One of the remedial measures adopted was to cut back imports heavily by means of tariff increases. Economic nationalism was not confined to Australia, however. It was widespread throughout much of the 1930s, and involved retaliatory tariffs or the introduction of other restrictions in Australia's oversea markets. It is the disturbed years of the 1930s which chiefly claim attention in the following pages.

Europe in general and the U.K. in particular predominated in Australia's oversea trade. Never supplying less than one-half of Australia's imports nor taking less than about two-thirds of her exports, Europe's connections with Australia were of overwhelming importance throughout the period. Significant changes nevertheless are to be traced. Although Australia offered preferential entry to goods of U.K. origin, and there existed a strong sentiment in favour of U.K. products and methods of trade, the U.K. tended to become less dominant as a source of Australia's imports. As a market for Australian exports, on the other hand, the U.K. became more, rather than less, important as the period drew to a close. With European countries other than the U.K. the converse happened. In 1938/9

[1] *C.P.D.* vol. 91, p. 700.

they accounted for about 10 % of Australian imports; this represented about 1 % rise on the early 1920s. As a market for Australian exports, however, the change is more conspicuous. At the end of the period only 17 % of Australian exports were consigned to foreign European countries compared with about 24 % in the early 1920s and about one-third in the later 1920s.

The enhanced importance of the United Kingdom as a market for Australian exports reflects two trends. First it resulted from the economic nationalism adopted by foreign countries in Europe during the world depression and the associated contraction of world trade. Secondly it reflects and (in part at least) stems from the attempt at Ottawa to counter foreign economic nationalism by developing closer economic ties within the Empire. The importance of the Ottawa Conference in 1932, following Britain's final abandonment of free trade, lay in the preferential trading position accorded Empire producers in the United Kingdom market. For the first time since Britain went free trade in the nineteenth century, ignoring the minor concessions in the 1920s, the countries within the Empire now had a competitive advantage. As for Australia, the U.K. as a supplier was less important in 1938/9 than in the early 1920s. Ottawa in this sense failed in its purpose.[1] It failed partly because of economic nationalism within Australia itself and the consequent protection of Australian manufacturing industry. Nevertheless, as discussed below, Australian willingness in the immediate post-Ottawa period to assist British exporters where-ever possible led to friction between Australia and her other markets.

It is of course true that not all the commodities apparently shipped from Australia to the U.K. were necessarily retained there for domestic consumption. Many items recorded as cleared for the U.K. may have been diverted *en route*. Ships employed for bulk-wheat cargoes, for example, were chartered for U.K. waters 'for orders'. On, or before, arrival the vessels may well have been diverted to other European ports. In other instances it is known that items shipped to and discharged in the

[1] For an examination of the effects of the Conference see W. K. Hancock, *Survey of British Commonwealth Affairs Vol. II, Problems of Economic Policy 1918–1939 Part I* (1940) chap. III, sect. IV and F. V. Meyer, *Britain's Colonies in World Trade* (1948).

U.K. were subsequently re-exported. But whether shipped to the U.K. or to other European countries via the U.K. the recorded or final destination in this sense does not affect our analysis of shipping-space requirements. It does, nevertheless, concern our point that during the 1930s the U.K. market revived in importance for the Australian producer. For two reasons, however, we may feel confident that the rise in the recorded volume of Australian exports to Britain accurately mirrors the new importance of the U.K. market following the Ottawa Conference. First, it seems extremely unlikely that in the 1930s European countries during a period of international exchange difficulty, of bilateral agreements, and of trade contraction would have increased their consumption of Australian products and obtained them via the U.K. Secondly, and here it is possible to be more precise, the major rise in exports during the 1930s occurred in refrigerated produce. As discussed below, the principal recipient for such commodities was the U.K. and the evidence confirms that virtually none of this produce was re-exported from the U.K.[1] The growing importance to Australia of the U.K. market during the difficult 1930s is well attested in Australian newspapers and in other private and official sources. Australian official publications occasionally reproduced verbatim U.K. parliamentary papers when the British food market was discussed in Westminster. The various official Australian produce marketing boards (some of which were born out of the depression) attached considerable importance to the market and took pains to cater for it. Their annual reports devote much space to its needs and they set up offices in London as two-way channels of information.

In the light of historical record and of more recent testimony illustrating the association between Australia and the U.K. it may appear to be superfluous here to make it the focus of special attention. But the depression and its aftermath in Australia had a shattering effect upon contemporary opinion and actions. It is all too easy to overlook these effects. The 1930s were years

[1] See the annual reports of the various Australian marketing boards. The 13th and 14th Annual Reports of the Australian Dairy Produce Board, for example, or the 3rd and 4th Annual Reports of the Australian Meat Board all of which are contained in *C.P.P.* 1937/40, II.

of economic nationalism when national self-sufficiency was widespread. As a consequence, trade restrictions and a decline in world trade dominated the scene.[1] The attempt by British Commonwealth countries at Ottawa to offset some of the effects of declining world trade is important in the present context for the new, expanded commercial relationship it created between Britain and Australia. The effect is not always obvious. It can indeed be all too easily overlooked if the viewpoint is taken of the U.K. exporter and attention is concentrated upon the reverse side of the coin. As a market for U.K. exports Australia undoubtedly records a decline in importance as the U.K. trade commissioner had forecast in 1930 and as he repeated in reports made throughout the 1930s. The aspect upon which he concentrated was the decline in the U.K.'s share of the 'competitive' trade, that is to say imports excluding those of a kind not manufactured or produced in the U.K. In 1921/2 he calculated that Britain supplied about 64 % of the value of 'competitive' imports into Australia; in 1937/8 the share had fallen to 57 %.[2] Taking imports as a whole it is clear that Britain's share fell throughout the period. In 1938/9 imports of U.K. origin formed about 41 % of the total as contrasted with the 52 % in 1922/3. Exports from Australia to the U.K. on the other hand rose from about 44 % of total exports at the earlier date to 54 % in 1938/9. The changed role of the U.K. as a market for Australian produce during the decade of contracting world markets is a factor of some importance. As discussed below, it exerted considerable influence on Australian attitudes and commercial policies at the time.

As a whole, Europe was more important as a market for Australian produce than as the source of Australian imports. Table 8 suggests that this was especially true of foreign European countries, that is to say Europe excluding the U.K. This impression is confirmed by the absolute figures of the trade balance on merchandise account. Of the four principal Australian foreign trading partners in Europe: Belgium, France, Germany and Italy, only Germany achieved a favourable balance with Australia and this only for the years 1934/5 to

[1] See H. Chalmers, *World Trade Policies* (Berkeley, 1953) for a year-by-year conspectus of trading restrictions.

[2] *U.K. Trade Reports:* 1923, p. 28 and 1938, p. 136.

1938/9. With the other three countries throughout the inter-war years and for all four prior to 1934/5, Australia successfully maintained an export surplus. In aggregate the surplus was considerable, especially in the early 1920s. In 1922/3, for example, it represented about 15 % of total export earnings. Although the surplus declined in the 1930s, in 1938/9 to only 8 %, the favourable balance with Europe played an important part in multilateral settlements. It went far to offset the deficit which annually characterised Australia's commercial relationship with the U.S.A.

The favourable balance of trade with foreign European countries made Australia vulnerable to retaliation. Ultimately it explains certain areas of Australia's commercial negotiations during the 1930s.[1] Correctly or not, the fall in imports into Australia in the early 1930s was attributed to the new tariff restrictions. As Australia's favourable trading balance with some European countries rose, so tariff retaliation, or its threat, led to second thoughts in Australia. Commercial treaties with foreign European countries were not unattractive because of the minimal effect they were likely to have on the U.K.-Australia trade. As suggested also below, Australian willingness initially to observe the Ottawa agreement to the full underlies much of the policy considerations of the time.

Discussions on trade were undertaken with Belgium, Czechoslovakia, France, Germany, Greece, Italy, Norway and Switzerland, treaties being successfully concluded with the first three. All the countries were markets for Australian wool; France for many years ranking second after Britain as a wool buyer. Most were markets also for hides and skins, especially France, and for grain. Some bought Australian fruit, many imported refrigerated meat products, and the first four were buyers also of certain Australian minerals. It was the fear of restrictions on the purchase of foodstuffs which encouraged Australia to initiate negotiations.

The trade discussions had a two-fold objective. They were designed to explore acceptable ways of avoiding tariff retaliation or other restrictions which might hamper the flow of Australian exports. Secondly, wherever possible, in order to formalise entry

[1] For a survey of Australia's oversea trading arrangements see D. F. Nicholson, *Australia's Trade Relations* (Melbourne, 1955).

to markets it was the intention to conclude bilateral trade agreements with the countries concerned. Except with the first round of discussions, ending in 1933 with the first bilateral trading agreement ever concluded by Australia with a foreign country, negotiations were assisted by the reintroduction of the intermediate tariff level in 1935. This was intended 'to provide a convenient avenue for expressing the level of duties which the Government propose should form the basis for trade treaties. The rates proposed...express, in every case, a protective level for Australian industry as well as preserving the margins of preference required under the Ottawa Agreement'.[1]

The first treaty was with Belgium. It had its origins in the Australian embargo on the import of sheet glass the value of which in 1928/9 represented less than ½ % of total imports. The restriction was intended initially to cut import totals, in the long-term to stimulate local production which had in fact begun in 1931 as a protected industry. The Australian embargo on sheet glass was followed by restrictions imposed in Belgium on the import of foodstuffs. The effect was a sharp fall in the value of Australian refrigerated meat exports to Belgium. This and later trade treaties both with Belgium and with other European nations, provided for free trade on a bilateral basis—in this instance glass for foodstuffs.

The treaty with Belgium was followed by trade discussions with other foreign European countries mentioned above. The importance attached in Australia to the discussions was recognised by the appointment of a minister responsible for treaty negotiations. In general terms negotiations hinged upon an attempt to secure liberal import quotas where in force, and 'most favoured nation' treatment in return for concessions in the Australian market via the intermediate tariff. Negotiations were complicated: by exchange difficulties, as with France, where the franc was not devalued until 1936; by attempts to effect straight barter deals as with Germany; and by the assumption in Italy and Germany of full government control of external trade. A catalogue of negotiations and treaties is easier to provide than any conclusive evidence of their usefulness in promoting trade or, at least, arresting decline. As a whole,

[1] *C.P.D.* vol. 149, p. 365.

foreign European countries were buying both absolutely as well as relatively less from Australia at the end of the 1930s than at the end of the 1920s—less wheat, less wool, and less refrigerated produce. Although Australia continued to have a trading surplus with them, it formed a significantly smaller proportion of export earnings than twenty years earlier. Within the total, however, variations in experience between countries are to be traced. Some increased their trade with Australia, others drastically reduced imports from Australia. It is possible to suggest an association between trade treaties and the revival of trade with some countries. Some of the revival doubtless reflects the general improvement in trade which distinguishes the later 1930s. But some developments go further than mere restoration and show a marked increase. For other countries it is possible to show more conclusively the link between declining trade and the failure of trade-treaty negotiations.

The treaty with Belgium illustrates the former. It provided for the division of the Australian market for plate and sheet glass between local producers (who had appeared on the scene beneath the tariff umbrella), and Belgian and U.K. suppliers. It is difficult to reject the treaty as the decisive factor in the development of the glass import trade. The introduction of the tariff was at once followed by a sag in the quantity of Belgian glass imported. The trend was equally sharply reversed after the conclusion of the treaty. With one variety of imported glass, indeed, the closing years of the period saw the Belgian share increased three-fold. The effect of the treaty on Belgium's role in the Australian import trade is more tellingly illustrated by reference to the total value of glass and glassware imports; this includes items not recorded in quantities. In 1928/9 only 4 % of the total was derived from Belgium. By 1938/9, however, the total being approximately the same, Belgian suppliers accounted for no less than 45 %. What had happened, in short, was that other suppliers had been squeezed out, leaving the import market to be shared between the U.K. and Belgium. The cooperation of local manufacturers seems to have been secured, moreover, by U.K. and Belgian suppliers and price agreements concluded between them.[1]

[1] *C.P.P.* 1937/40, II, 2,041 ff.

The trade agreement with France, effective from 1 January 1937, was preceded by some revival of exports. But for the two fiscal years which followed agreement, the rate of trade expansion significantly quickened. Since, moreover, no marked rise in imports from France accompanied export growth, the balance on current account grew noticeably healthier. For these two countries, Belgium and France, the 1930s witnessed a steady return to the 1920s pattern of imports from Australia. The surplus for Australia deriving from trade with them was about 16 % higher in 1938/9 than in 1930/1.

The next two most important foreign European customers in the 1920s were Germany and Italy, taking between them about 10 % of Australia's exports and yielding a large trading surplus. Discussions without success were undertaken with both countries. Much of the failure to reach agreement with Germany stemmed from the trading arrangements dictated after the First World War and from the exchange restrictions later imposed in Nazi Germany. German retaliation after the expiry in 1925 of certain treaty obligations withdrew the 'most favoured nation' entry of Australian goods into Germany. By the end of the 1920s Germany was lost as a market for Australian wheat. The market for certain other items had also disappeared when, in 1932, Australia claimed on the strength of the 1924 Anglo-German Treaty 'most favoured nation' treatment again. But more important as an obstacle to trade were the exchange restrictions introduced in Germany and the attempt there to institute barter arrangements in trade. With the direct state control of external trade after 1933, moreover, and the use of quota methods, the 'most favoured nation' clause became worthless. With Italy, the tapering down of Australian imports similarly followed government intervention when a system of quotas was applied. As noted already, although improved trade following a trade treaty does not necessarily offer proof of its effectiveness, the converse is more easily established. Between 1930/1 and 1938/9 the trading surplus accruing from Australia's trade with Italy and Germany of almost £5 million was converted into a £1¾ million deficit.

After Europe the countries of the east were the next most important outlet for Australian exports although not the next most important source of imports. The record of Australia's trade relations with this area provide some interesting paradoxes. As shown in Table 8, the tendency over time was for the markets in the east to provide a higher proportion of imports and to take more Australian exports. During the early 1930s, at the peak, they accounted for as much as one fifth of Australia's external trade. A number of different markets were involved, the exploitation of which was not always uniform. The principal countries concerned were Japan and the N.E.I., shown separately, and China, Hong Kong, Ceylon, India and Malaya.

The market of greatest simplicity was the N.E.I. It was a major supplier of Australia's oil and petrol and as early as the 1920s outranked its competitors. By 1938/9 it accounted for about 58 % of all oils imported into Australia. For certain fuel-oils its significance was even greater, two-thirds of the petrol and kerosene imported came from the N.E.I. Although the trade in oil with Australia dominated the country's exports (with 70 % of the total value) tea, with 20 % was also important. Tea, from the N.E.I. tended to be cheaper than that of Ceylon and as a consequence accounted for about 60 % of the total imported into Australia. Shipments *to* this market, however, never exceeded 2 % of total exports. Flour and other foodstuffs virtually exhausts the list. The actual values of trade confirm its one-sided nature. After the U.S.A., Australia's trade with the N.E.I. produced the largest adverse trading balance. But the overriding importance to the Australian economy of the fuel-oils obtained from the N.E.I. precluded the friction associated with the U.S.A. market.

Nor was the character of the trade with India, Ceylon and Malaya such as to produce commercial difficulties. Taken as a whole, the trade on balance usually resulted for Australia in a small net gain. India recorded a sizeable surplus, largely offset by Malaya's deficit, the somewhat smaller trade with Ceylon usually being in approximate balance during the 1930s. From India were obtained the bulk of the bags, hessian, and jute required for the bagged exports of ore, wheat and flour. These three sack items dominated imports from India. In the early 1920s they accounted for 55 % to 60 % of the total, by 1938/9 the proportion had risen to 80%. From Malaya was obtained the major part of the crude rubber required in the rapidly expanding tyre and tube industry. From Ceylon was obtained about one quarter of the tea consumed in Australia. Exports from Australia consisted chiefly of foodstuffs, especially flour to Malaya, some wool to India, and silver bullion to both India and Ceylon.

Trade with China and Hong Kong was also free of the complexities and complications of commercial restrictions. Both markets provided Australia with an export surplus, both served as outlets for Australian food exports. China especially along with Japan offered a market for Australian flour during the three lean years of depression between 1929 and 1932. China's purchases of Australian wheat and flour were always severely limited by price considerations. Hence when world prices fell with overproduction, she was able significantly to expand her imports of Australian wheat. The remaining area of trade, with Japan, merits slightly extended discussion for the paradox it reveals. Commercial policy concerning Japan witnessed curious contradictions both of official policy statements and, an onlooker would think, of good sense. To set the scene it is necessary to paint on the backcloth the development of trade policy with eastern markets. During the early 1930s trade with the east as a whole and with China and Japan in particular began to increase. To many in Australia it seemed to offer new and exciting trade possibilities. Optimistic views were taken of the new developments, aptly summed up in 1935 in the foreword to a study of diplomatic and trade relations. The far east, notes the writer, was 'far' to Europe but 'to Australia...it is the Near North'.[1] But even before this work appeared a growing interest in Australia's eastern trade was already to be traced. In 1931, for example, the attention of federal members was drawn to freight increases between Australia and eastern countries with the warning of the probable effects upon trade. 'The importance of our trade with Eastern countries is recognised by all Australians...it is highly desirable that we should develop our export trade [*sc.* to the east] and these freight increases gravely pre-

[1] I. C. Ross, *Australia and the Far East* (Sydney, 1935), p.v. This work was published in conjunction with the Australian Institute of International Affairs.

judice our business in certain lines to the East.'[1] In the following year Australian interest in trade with the east received recognition in a three-month visit to China and Japan made by the then Mr, later, Sir Herbert Gepp, 'consultant on development to the Commonwealth Government'. His report to the respective Ministers for Commerce and Development was presented to parliament and ordered to be printed.[2]

Eighteen months later an official 'Goodwill Mission' left Australia for a two-month tour of the east. This was the first diplomatic mission from Australia ever to visit foreign countries. Although discussion on trade was not the prime object of the tour, the leader of the mission remarked that 'commercial men naturally...took advantage of the visit of the Mission to discuss trade matters'. The bulk of the report is in fact connected with trade. It not only analyses the composition of trade and growth possibilities, it also makes various recommendations on how trade might be expanded—most of these strike a note familiar today, quality control, labelling, packaging and the like.[3] The decision to send an official mission to the east was well received in Australia. The Bank of New South Wales in an issue of its *Circular* discussing 'Australia and Industrial Development in Japan' noted that: 'the proposal of the Commonwealth Government to send a delegation is one that must be commended'. The *Circular* suggests that 'the industrialisation of Japan promises to bring with it great possibilities for the development of markets for Australian foodstuffs and raw materials'.[4] (The same *Circular* also adopted an unpopular view and one initially rejected in government circles, that trade with Japan should be fostered in preference to the doubtful attractions of Empire self-sufficiency.) Official interest in trade with the east was conspicuous between 1930 and the opening months of 1936, perhaps more clearly after the Lyons government took office in 1932. It led, among other developments, to the creation of a special division of the Department of Commerce, under which 'a Committee of business men, whose advice and assistance is

[1] *C.P.D.* vol. 132, pp. 158, 527, 919.

[2] *C.P.P.* 1932/4, IV, 2,343 ff. 'Report on Trade between Australia and the Far East.'

[3] *C.P.P.* 1932/4, IV, 423 ff. 'Australia's Eastern Mission, Report...of Leader.'

[4] *Bank of N.S.W. Circular*, IV (March 1934), 1, 7.

given to the Department, has been formed in the capital city of each State'.[1]

But at this point in time a fatal diversion was introduced. In contrast with Australian attitudes towards other eastern countries, the policy adopted towards Japan after 1935 forms a curious chapter of history. In the early 1930s Australian products became increasingly imported into Japan. As recently as 1928 only 5 % of wheat consumed in Japan came from Australia whence came about 12 % of Japanese wheat imports in that year. By 1931 these figures had catapulted to 30 % of wheat consumption and to 70 % of the wheat imported.[2] The growth of wool exports was even more impressive. Japanese raw-silk exports, like Australian wool shipments in 1929/30, sagged during the depression's early years. To offset the fall in export earnings Japan switched to the export of fully, or semi-manufactured articles and partly in order to do this increased her imports of Australian wool. She quickly became the second largest customer for Australian wool, buying more than France and Germany taken together.

From 1936, however, the trend was reversed. In 1936/7 Japan's share of Australia's merchandise exports fell to 6 % from the 14 % of the previous year, later to only 4 %. The actual values of the trade fully confirm the decline suggested by the proportionate decline. In 1933/4 Australia had recorded a favourable balance of trade with Japan of almost £8 million. By 1937/8 this had been converted into a deficit of about half a million, imports of Japanese origin into Australia having remained virtually unchanged. This unhappy experience derives directly from the 'trade diversion' policy adopted without warning by the Lyons government early in 1936, 'the immediate effect of which was to start a trade war with Japan'.[3]

The new policy, introduced into parliament on 22 May 1936

[1] *C.P.P.* 1934/7, III, 2,139. This comment was made in the introductory section of the 'Report of the Australian Trade Delegation to India, Burma and Ceylon', paper no. 278, 2,127 ff.

[2] *C.P.P.* 1932/4, IV, 'Report on Trade Between Australia and the Far East', appendix 8.

[3] J. Shepherd, *Australia's Interests and Policies in the Far East* (Institute of Pacific Relations, New York, 1940), p. 40. This work provides an invaluable survey of the diplomatic attitudes at the time.

by Sir Henry Gullett, minister directing negotiations for trade treaties, had the three aims of: 'increasing our exports of primary produce, expanding secondary industry, and bringing about a considerable increase of rural and industrial employment'.[1] To achieve these ends 'the Government proposes...to bring about a diversion of carefully selected portions of our overseas trade'. One effect of the new policy, he continued, would be to boost secondary industry by halting certain imports, 'the chief of these...is the motor chassis, which we hope will be manufactured in Australia on a large scale within a very few years'. Another would be to ensure that Australia in the future imports from countries 'which are already great customers of ours, and which we may confidently expect will become greater customers if we increase our purchases from them'.[2] In part also, his speech elsewhere makes clear, the new policy reflects continued adherence to the aims and principles of Ottawa and the attempt to achieve empire self-sufficiency.

The implementation of the policy so far as Japan was concerned, however, suggests a somewhat different motivation. It may be that disquiet over Japan's growing strength and successes in the far east, especially over the Manchurian question, may have encouraged Australia to take the line she did.[3] Australian uneasiness hardened considerably in 1937 on the outbreak of the Sino-Japanese war and was followed, in 1938, by the prohibition of exports of iron-ore to Japan. Of more immediate importance were the respective attractions of Japan and the U.K. as 'great customers' for Australian products. Japan, although a 'good customer' was not as valuable a customer to Australia as Great Britain. 'If we are not to come to a national standstill, primary production must be increased, and the only way it can be increased is by selling more of our rural output in the British market. Putting it plainly, there is room for a substantial increase of Australian exports of primary produce to

[1] *C.P.D.* vol. 150, p. 2,211. [2] *Ibid.*

[3] It was rumoured, and officially denied by the New Zealand prime minister in 1936, that New Zealand had been invited by Australia to join in a united economic front against Japan. 'Except as a recipient of unanticipated gains [i.e from increased wool exports to Japan] New Zealand played no part in the trade war of 1936.' (I. F. G. Milner, *New Zealand's Interests and Policies in the Far East.* (Institute of Pacific Relations, New York, 1940), p. 69.)

Britain provided we are able to give to Britain an increased share in the Australian market.'[1] It was unfortunate that certain Japanese exports to Australia, especially textiles, competed with similar items coming from the U.K.

The Australian trade-diversion policy not surprisingly was well received in some British circles. *The Economist* commenting on the higher Australian tariff announced in 1936 quoted a statement by the President of the Manchester Chamber of Commerce that: 'Australia's action will be very warmly appreciated in Lancashire.'[2] The U.K. trade commissioner in his report of October 1936 noted that the 'action recently taken by the Australian Government in an endeavour to divert trade ...will doubtless have some effect in increasing the United Kingdom share of the total'.[3] To some extent the difficulties which Japan encountered elsewhere, commercial hostility, anti-dumping legislation, import quotas, tariffs and the like, aggravated the problem. Countries still open to Japanese goods found that the pressure of Japanese exports increased. Where-ever Japan appeared to have a strong bargaining advantage, that is to say, in her dealings with countries enjoying a favourable balance of trade with her, the flow of Japanese goods tended to rise. The detailed story of the economic manoeuvres of both Australia and Japan, import licensing, the leap-frogging tariffs in each country, etc.,[4] matter less in the present context than the repercussions.

The new policy had a swift effect upon Japan. Hastily she sought to reduce her dependence upon Australian products. Initially she turned to South Africa for wool. This in itself was thought to be of little consequence to Australia. South African wool diverted to Japan freed other areas of world demand for supply by Australia. Subsequently Japan sought to create alternative sources of supply for wool and wheat in Manchuria; this was more serious. If the coarse varieties of Manchurian wool available were brought up to internationally accepted standards of quality, the total world supply would rise and prices fall. The

[1] *C.P.D.* vol. 150, p. 2,212.

[2] *The Economist* 30 May 1936, p. 482.

[3] *U.K. Trade Report*, 1936, p. 101.

[4] See N. F. Hall, 'Trade Diversion—An Australian Interlude', *Economica* n.s. v (1–11).

disappearance of Japan as a customer for Australian wheat and flour had obvious implications. For Australia, preoccupied as she was with expanding her oversea markets, the outcome can only be described as unfortunate. It is difficult to disagree with the editorial comment of the *Labour Daily* in July 1936: 'even a charitable interpretation of the Government's blundering would be that it is cutting off its economic nose to spite its political face'.[1] As noted above, the effect of the policy was to convert a favourable balance of trade with Japan into a deficit. As the leader of the federal opposition wryly pointed out, the ministerial statement on trade diversion 'could mean only that countries which buy goods from Australia are those from which we shall encourage imports...a good customer nation for Australia's products should find Australia a good customer in return'.[2] Instead of this, Australia quite deliberately sacrificed a market. Before parliament reassembled in September of 1936 commercial repercussions were being felt. A deputation from the Australian Wool Growers' Council complained that: 'during the worst years of the depression and in the recovery of wool values the support accorded by Japan had been an outstanding factor. As soon as the recent legislation brought down by your Government became effective, Japan ceased to buy wool on the Australian market and the result was an immediate drop in wool prices'.[3]

Another less obvious but related repercussion was felt in shipping. One British line and certain Japanese lines were associated together in a shipping conference. Tensions and difficulties about trade were carried over into the maritime scene. During the negotiations leading up to the trade treaty, ultimately arranged with Japan when tensions eased, an attempt was in fact made to link shipping directly with the treaty discussions. This is discussed in chapter 6. The successful conclusion of a trade treaty with Japan which took effect in 1937 and was renewed in 1938 did little to restore the volume of exports to

[1] Reproduced in Copland & Janes, *Australian Trade Policy—A Book of Documents 1932–1937* (Sydney, 1937), p. 318.

[2] *C.P.D.* vol. 152, p. 2,194.

[3] Statement by the vice-chairman of the council leading the deputation to the prime minister on 17 July 1936. (Reproduced in Copland & Janes, *Australian Trade Policy*, p. 295.)

Japan before war intervened, however. What is of interest, of course, is the simple fact of the restoration of friendly commercial relationships with Japan. It reflects new thinking and new policy-making at work and is discussed below.

The trade-diversion policy of 1936 was not aimed solely at Japan. By means of the new import duties and the introduction of the import licensing system the Australian government sought to deal with every sector wherein she had an unfavourable trading balance. Apart from Japan, however, only the U.S.A. was significantly affected. As *The Economist* pointed out, 'the general purpose of the import licence system is to enable Australia to refuse to buy from countries which do not buy to a corresponding extent from her...no attempt is made to disguise the fact that...the United States will be severely affected by these measures'.[1] The U.S.A. with Canada (whose contribution to the total was always modest) was the second-largest source of Australian imports. It never, on the other hand, took a very large proportion of Australia's exports. Except for wool, skins and hides, and iron-ore in certain years, the U.S.A. was not a significant market for Australian exports, which, by and large, were competitive with domestic products in the U.S.A.

The effect of the Australian trade restrictions was designed to fall chiefly upon the import from the U.S.A. of motor-vehicle chassis. The policy reflects also the second aim announced by the government, to expand secondary industry, and manifests 'the determination of the government to give strong, and... decisive encouragement to the establishment of this industry [*sc.* the motor-car industry] in the Commonwealth'.[2] Reaction in the U.S.A. was immediate. The 'most favoured nation' clause extended by the U.S.A. to Australia less than a month earlier was suspended with effect from 1 August 1936. Exports to the U.S.A. fell sharply. The total for 1937/8 was 70% below the high level of the previous year and 40% down on the 1935/6 figure. Within Australia doubts were voiced about the wisdom of carrying the trade war to the U.S.A.[3] Even more doubtful

[1] *The Economist* 30 May 1936, pp. 481–2.

[2] *C.P.D.* vol. 150, p. 2,216.

[3] See, for example, Copland & Janes, *Australian Trade Policy*, pp. 328, 341.

was local opinion concerning the introduction of an indigenous motor-vehicle industry. The U.K. trade commissioner reported that 'objection to the proposal to manufacture complete cars in Australia...has been fairly general in the trade'.[1]

Confirmatory evidence is to be found in the report made by the Tariff Board when, in a belated search for supporting evidence, the minister for Trade and Customs in December 1936 referred to it the task of examining 'the best means of giving effect to the government's policy of establishing in Australia the manufacture of engines and chassis of motor vehicles'.[2] In the light of the testimony presented to the Board it is scarcely surprising that its report should have proved unhelpful to the government. As one member explained: 'usually the Board can make recommendations...by weighing the differing opinions of those engaged in the business. In this case...the Board was unable to obtain any convincing evidence to set against that unfavourable to local production.'[3] The Minister tried again. Criticising the report for its 'absence of balance which lessened its value as a guide to the Government' the minister put additional questions to the Board. This attempt too failed to produce convincing testimony.

Neither policy was completely successful. As Australia emerged from depression and demand began to rise, motor chassis were imported once again in growing numbers. The introduction of restrictions on the import of chassis from the U.S.A. tended to check a resumption of the pre-depression pattern, however, and to slow down the flood. Between 1934/5 and 1938/9 the proportion of the total number of imported chassis supplied by the U.S.A. fell from 45 % to 26 % whereas the U.K.'s share rose from 20 % to 36 % over the same year. The decline in terms of value was from 45 % to about 30 %, suggesting perhaps that the U.S.A. chassis was bigger and more costly than that obtained from the U.K.

The creation of a local motor-car industry was less successful. The revival of demand witnessed the restoration of the indigenous motor body-building industry. But it continued to be

[1] *U.K. Trade Report*, 1936, p. 167.
[2] *C.P.P.* 1937/40, II, Tariff Board, Report on Motor Vehicles (paper no. 67, 1,763 ff.), 1,765.
[3] *Ibid.* 1,791.

based upon the imported motor chassis. The unfavourable report of the Tariff Board mentioned above unequivocally concluded that: 'it would be unwise at present to encourage or enforce the manufacture of the complete motor vehicle in Australia'. Accepting the situation Australia dropped the licensing system in 1938 and regained the U.S.A. concessionary tariff position in February 1939. In the meantime, however, the trade gap had widened and war began before the effects of the new relationships could be felt.

The dramatic reversal of commercial policy with Japan in 1937 which aimed at restoring trade and the slowness in reaching agreement with the U.S.A. reflects two separate but related factors. There was first the growing awareness in Australia that little more could be expected from trade with the U.K. Secondly Australia was disturbed by the opening of trade talks between the U.K. and the U.S.A. with the implication that some modification of the Ottawa agreement might be necessary in favour of U.S.A. agricultural products. Australia was reluctant to agree to any alteration to the trading arrangements which might affect the volume of Australian food products exported to the U.K. She was also reluctant, however, to make any easier the entry of U.K. manufactures into Australia lest this should affect economic diversification within the country.

The Ottawa agreement was on the agenda of the 1937 Imperial Conference. But 1937 was also an election year in Australia and domestic politics undoubtedly exerted a restraining influence on the Lyons government. As early as February 1937, a few months before the Imperial Conference was due to meet, *The Economist* reported a statement on the Conference by Lyons which was indicative, the writer comments, of the 'dilatory attitude of a Government which will soon have to fight for its life at the polls'.[1] The report of the Conference ('brief and platitudinous' according to the same paper) contains no hint of Australian dissatisfaction.[2] Towards the end of 1937, the elections over and won and the Lyons government returned, a statement by the Attorney-General, however, gives a broad

[1] *The Economist* 20 February 1937, p. 405.

[2] *Ibid.* 19 June 1937, p. 667. *U.K.P.P.* Cmd. 5,482.

indication of the new government thinking. Speaking of the 'proposed revision of Ottawa', and of the U.K. as a market, the then Mr Menzies told the House that: 'it is impossible to believe that Great Britain with all her goodwill can go on indefinitely absorbing more and more surplus production from Australia and although preferential agreements must continue they must be elastic enough to seize every opportunity to encourage the nations of the world to...come back into...full commercial life'.[1] In his speech the new keynote was struck: '...as a young country, on the threshold of development, we must look to the whole world for our markets'. But if Australia looked to the whole world for her markets she was also reluctant to agree to alter the Ottawa agreement. In 1938 the governments of Australia and Britain opened trade discussions in London, the Australians seeking a new trade agreement. The discussions ended on a cool inconclusive note. All that was agreed was that the Ottawa agreement should continue. 'Certain immediate difficulties arise when an attempt is made to reconcile the desirability for Australia to expand her secondary industries to the maximum extent economically possible with that of the U.K. to...secure for her exports a stable position in the Australian market.'[2]

It is difficult to resist the conclusion that the 'tough' Australian policy with Japan may well have been more acceptable to the U.K. than a similar policy with the U.S.A. The vexed question of the Matson Shipping Line and maritime competition in the Pacific illustrates the point. The issue dragged on unresolved from the early 1930s until after the outbreak of war, with the U.K. government apparently reluctant to act. Although on the surface, it would seem to have been of more consequence to the U.K. than to Australia (it was after all a U.K. shipping line involved), the impression conveyed by the evidence is that the governments of Australia and New Zealand were more active and more determined in their opposition to U.S.A. shipping policy. Although the contention of the historian of the

[1] *C.P.P.* 1937/40, II, 905 ff. 'Australia's Trade Relations and the Proposed Revision of the Ottawa Agreement' statement by the Attorney-General...7 December 1937.

[2] For full details of the White Paper see Commonwealth *Year Book*, 1938, p. 481 ff.; or *U.K.P.P.* Cmd. 5,805.

Anglo-American trade agreement is probably correct, that 'it would have been far more valuable had an agreement with Australia been concluded at the same time', it is not easy to see where and how the conflict of interests might have been reconciled.[1]

[1] C. Kreider, *The Anglo-American Trade Agreement* (Princeton, 1943), p. 188.

Chapter 4

PASSENGER AND COMMODITY TRAFFIC

The demand for shipping space in the Australian oversea scene was a function of the movement of both cargo and passengers. It is the object of this chapter to examine the volume of space needed and to trace, by destinations, the relationship of passenger traffic and commodity flows to shipping needs. It is tempting to use the data available in official sources on vessel arrival and departure; these have indeed been used in earlier chapters to measure the response of the oversea shipping industry to Australian needs. But they would provide a misleading picture if used to illustrate demand. Above all their use would conceal the excess supply of shipping which characterises the Australian inter-war scene. Factors unrelated to the demand in Australia for oversea shipping space were often more important than domestic factors. Tramp-shipping operations, for example, normally involved speculative, unfixed voyages which brought tramp tonnage to Australia in ballast in anticipation of rising demand. At times the demand failed to materialise. In the liner section, which as we have shown was predominant, excess capacity (that is under-loading) was a normal feature.

Only long-term variations in demand tend to produce alterations to the number of scheduled liners in service. Even longer-term considerations of demand are a necessary preliminary to alterations to vessel *size* in normal use. Non-scheduled despatches offer greater flexibility in vessel programming but here also, once a vessel is committed, it is difficult to abandon a voyage. Generally speaking, it is easier to cater for temporary increases than for occasional short-falls. The chartering of an outside vessel and its programming for an additional voyage is not difficult. Far less easy is the cancellation of programmed voyages, as the operating experience of liner companies at this time testifies. In 1922, for example, when cargo shipped from

Europe to Australia increased in volume, the response of the shipping industry erred on the side of generosity. Many of the additional ships put on berth could obtain only part cargoes. One line in that year achieved only some 30% loadings on voyages from the U.K. to Australia. During 1924 the scarcity of cargo was in the opposite direction. Between March and September outbound cargo averaged only 33% of hold capacity and was as high as this only because a large quantity of wheat was taken in parcels.[1] Efficient ship management usually requires an approximate correspondence between the tonnage of inbound and outbound cargo and in passenger berths. Where an established pattern of shipment and discharge is suddenly interrupted a marked imbalance arises and difficulty may follow. During the depression of the early 1930s migration received a severe set-back and a sharp reduction of imports took place. Export tonnages, however, moved sharply in the opposite direction. During the worst phase of this period an informed observer estimated that ships arriving from the U.K. had two-thirds of their cargo space empty. 'Imports had dwindled almost to vanishing point as a result of new tariff policy and the exigencies of exchange. The number of vessels in actual practice required to bring goods to Australia only represented a fraction of that required to lift exports.'[2]

A more sensitive indicator of the demand for oversea shipping and a more appropriate measure for present purposes is to be constructed from recorded detail of the passengers and cargo actually carried. Cargo data provide a measure of output, both in aggregate and for individual commodities; they focus attention upon the type, as well as on the amount, of cargo space; and they illustrate also variations in the amount required both in total and for individual destinations. Except with tramp ships, where short-run variations in demand can speedily be met, ship owners are reluctant to increase the supply of ships on permanent schedules. The liner company especially prefers to reassure itself on the test of time that a trade has become established before arranging shipping tonnage to serve it. As noted above, in practice, outside *ad hoc* chartering is far from difficult and excess

[1] *S.M.H.* 1 January 1923; *Fairplay* vol. 94, p. 126.
[2] *S.M.H. Financial and Commercial Supplement*, 11 February 1932.

tonnage rather than a scarcity is to be traced in Australia's oversea-shipping services between the wars.

The demand for shipping basically is measurable in terms either of imports or of exports. About 2,000 separate import items are recorded in the official trade statistics. They are grouped in 21 classes for convenience of enumeration. In general terms they include manufactured articles (consumer goods, durable and otherwise), fuel-oils, some raw materials, and a variety of 'producer' goods. With some exceptions imports are recorded by value rather than by quantity, the records are thus unhelpful in estimating hold-space. A notable exception is fuel-oil whose importance as a demand factor for shipping justifies a quantitative assessment. Apart from fuel-oils, however, imports discussed here are treated in qualitative rather than in quantitative terms.

Exports on the other hand are fewer in number, more homogeneous, and are usually recorded by quantity as well as by value. With the exception of tankers for oil-imports, the type of shipping found in Australia's oversea services was, moreover, in direct response to the needs of the commodities exported. Generally speaking, export tonnages exceeded imports; more disengaged ships arrived in, than left from, Australian ports during the inter-war years. Hence in following pages it is the record of exports which claims chief attention.[1]

We cannot ignore the passenger trade, however, for two reasons: the demand which this produced for passenger services was important and secondly, because of the role of passenger liners as cargo-carriers. During the inter-war years the two-way flow of migrants and of visitors to and from oversea countries required the provision of a not inconsiderable volume of passenger services, especially between Australia and Europe. As is well known, in relation to the size of its population Australia is conspicuous for the oversea travel undertaken by its inhabitants partly because of their links with Britain and partly for ordinary tourist purposes. Details published in the *Year Book* from 1924

[1] All tables of exports are constructed from two official sources, the *Year Book* and the detailed *Oversea Trade*; any variation is indicated. All conversions of export quantities into shipping space are based upon stowage factors shown in R. E. Thomas assisted by O. O. Thomas, *Stowage: The Properties and Stowage of Cargoes*. The fourth edition (1957) has been used.

onwards show the number of 'temporary' departures of residents to oversea destinations. Professor Butlin has calculated the oversea expenditure by these 'temporary' departures. It represents, comparatively, a large sum, especially during the 1920s.

In addition to tourism the migration movement was important to the shipping industry. In contrast with the great migratory waves of the nineteenth and early twentieth centuries from Europe to North America or, to a lesser extent, to Australia during the gold-rush decade, the passenger flow to Australia between the wars was less uneven. The traffic tended to be two-way. Nevertheless during the 1920s average net inward migration (that is to say the excess of arrivals over departures) ran at about 31,000 persons a year. This figure is included in the totals shown below of all arrivals and departures combined. The onset of the depression severely reduced passenger movement. In part this reflects the sharp fall in migration with, in the first half of the 1930s, a net *outward* flow of about 2,000 persons a year. The second half of the 1930s, as Australia emerged from the depression, reversed the direction of migration once again and from 1936 to 1939 net inwards movement averaged about 7,400 a year.

The demand for passenger accommodation is indicated below by reference to the annual combined totals of sea arrivals and departures recorded in the *Year Book*. Most of Australia's passenger traffic was with Europe via Suez. The one other route of any significance was the trans-Pacific from Vancouver and San Francisco to eastern Australia. It was a route of increasing popularity with the purely tourist trade. In 1913 the total of southbound and northbound passengers was about 8,000. The annual average in the early 1920s had gone up to about 10,000 and by the late 1920s to about 12,000. During the early depression years the total had fallen to 5,000 but by 1936 was regaining the earlier levels.[1]

The effect of the decline both in the trans-Pacific crossings and in the migrant and tourist trade to and from Europe via Suez is reflected in the figures. The more useful figure to consider is the long-term average. A passenger liner sails on schedule, empty or full. Generally, only long-term alterations, changes recognised to be permanent affect the total supply of liner ship-

[1] I.S.C. *35th Report*, pp. 13–14.

ping. During 1931 and 1932 the number of passengers fell to less than one-half of the 1927 peak. On the Pacific route the total declined to about one-third. Services on this route, however, were increased, not reduced, with the introduction of U.S.A. shipping subsidies which, by unhappy chance, coincided with the slump in trade. Even on the major route to Europe no drastic reduction in services took place. A service between Britain and South Africa was withdrawn and replaced by an Australian service via the Cape. But only two vessels were completely withdrawn. The industry adopted other expedients to deal not only with lower demand but also with the alterations in the nature of the demand for passenger space. The P & O used the trough of the period to undertake a refit of vessels used on the mainline service. Their place was taken by the temporary diversion of two ships from the Cape branch service. Another expedient was the introduction of cruising during times of slack demand for berths to Europe. Summertime cruises were arranged from Australian ports and, in the northern hemisphere, winter cruises from Britain to warmer areas. Another feature of the demand for passenger shipping during the depression years was the pressure for cheaper berths. In 1931 it was estimated that 90 % of departures from Australia left in tourist accommodation. It was not unknown for liners to clear from Australia with more first-class saloon stewards than first-class passengers. To cater for the pressure for less expensive berths the P & O and Orient Lines converted certain vessels into 'one-class' ships.[1]

Oversea passenger traffic 1920 to 1939 ('000 persons)

1921	158	1928	169	1934	105
1922	146	1929	152	1935	111
1923	145	1930	134	1936	118
1924	161	1931	90	1937	134
1925	160	1932	86	1938	146
1926	171	1933	95	1939	136
1927	183				

The failure of passenger traffic to coincide exactly in both directions and the absence of a sufficient volume of passenger traffic in the Australian trade to justify completely specialised

[1] *S.M.H.* 2 March, 31 December 1931; 10 January, 9 February 1933. *Fairplay* vol. 118, p. 52; vol. 119, pp. 112, 156, 611.

passenger ships had two important implications. In the first place, as previously noted, it led to the reliance upon dual-purpose ships. The passenger liners drew heavily upon cargo-carrying as a source of voyage revenue. The operating experience of one passenger line whose accounts are analysed in chapter 8 illustrates the point. In 'normal' years cargo-carrying provided about one-third of total revenue, during the early depression years the proportion rose to about 55%. For another passenger line cargo-carrying in 'normal' years ranged between 45 % and 50 % of total revenue; in 1932/3 it was almost 60 %. In the same year, to point the significance more emphatically, passage receipts of the second line had declined to about three-quarters of the 1923/4 level; but receipts from cargo freights were slightly higher than in the earlier year.

Fixed passenger sailing schedules, moreover, of such dual-purpose vessels were an advantage in another direction. As outlined above, the outbound tonnage of shipping for Europe was consistently higher than the quantity of inbound tonnage from Europe. That is to say that imports into Australia from Europe were carried on fewer ships than were Australian exports to similar European destinations. Australian exports moreover were markedly seasonal in character. As a rule about 15 % by value of Australia's exports are shipped in the three months of July, August and September as contrasted with more than 30 % in the three months of November, December and January. Given that imports could be more evenly distributed throughout the year the regular availability of scheduled inbound cargo-space was a decided advantage to Australia.

Of the 500 items entering into the export trade it is possible to confine analysis to eight main commodity groups: wool; refrigerated cargo; sugar; non-refrigerated fruits; hides; grain; timber; and minerals, ores and concentrates other than precious metals. On the dual criterion of volume and of value these eight groups dominated exports during our period. In value they regularly accounted for between 80 % and 90 % of merchandise exports as is shown in Table 9. Their aggregate space requirement has already been illustrated in Table 7*b* and their individual requirements are examined in the following pages.

The overwhelming importance of wool in the export sector

Table 9. *Composition of merchandise exports, 1920/1–1938/9* (%)

	Wool	Wheat and flour	Refrigerated cargo	Minerals, etc.	Hides	Dried fruits etc., sugar and timber
1920/1	26·7	31·2	14·2	6·6	2·7	1·9
1921/2	38·8	27·3	11·3	4·6	2·5	2·4
1922/3	49·9	11·9	12·2	6·4	5·8	2·2
1923/4	48·7	17·0	7·6	7·2	5·4	1·1
1924/5	39·5	26·1	10·9	5·3	5·1	3·8
1925/6	44·1	17·3	10·5	6·5	5·8	5·9
1926/7	45·2	20·7	8·0	5·6	6·4	3·8
1927/8	47·4	14·6	9·3	5·6	7·1	5·2
1928/9	43·7	19·2	10·2	4·4	6·6	6·4
1929/30	37·6	16·0	15·0	7·0	6·8	6·1
1930/1	35·7	20·0	17·6	5·4	4·1	6·0
1931/2	33·5	24·7	19·6	4·2	2·4	5·9
1932/3	38·2	15·6	18·8	4·2	2·5	5·0
1933/4	50·4	11·1	15·6	4·1	3·9	5·5
1934/5	38·1	16·2	20·2	4·2	3·4	6·5
1935/6	41·4	15·4	16·6	5·2	4·5	5·1
1936/7	42·3	17·6	14·3	5·8	4·9	5·2
1937/8	33·4	19·6	17·8	6·1	4·4	6·5
1938/9	35·1	11·2	22·1	6·4	3·4	7·6

makes the simple fleece an appropriate point at which to begin. Throughout the inter-war years wool regularly contributed at least one-third of export earnings, often the proportion was more than 40 % and in four years it represented about one-half of the total value of exports. As with human population in Australia, so too with the sheep population, uneven distribution of sheep and hence an uneven distribution in the trade in wool characterised the economy between the wars, as it does today. Although sheep are to be found in most parts of Australia and are becoming more evenly dispersed, even today about 75 % of the sheep are to be found in the three mainland eastern states. In the inter-war years the concentration was more marked with perhaps 80 % of the total. Almost all the residue then (as now) is divided fairly equally between South and Western Australia. The production and export of wool reflect the geographical location of the sheep population. Figure 2 and Table 10 below shows in summary form for quinquennial periods wool production in Australia as a whole and separately for the eastern states. Although total output is not completely synonymous with exports, the quantity retained for processing in local mills rarely exceeded 6 or 7 %. The overwhelming importance of wool production in the east is obvious from detail given in the table, in each of the periods chosen a little more than 80 % of the total was contributed by the three states.

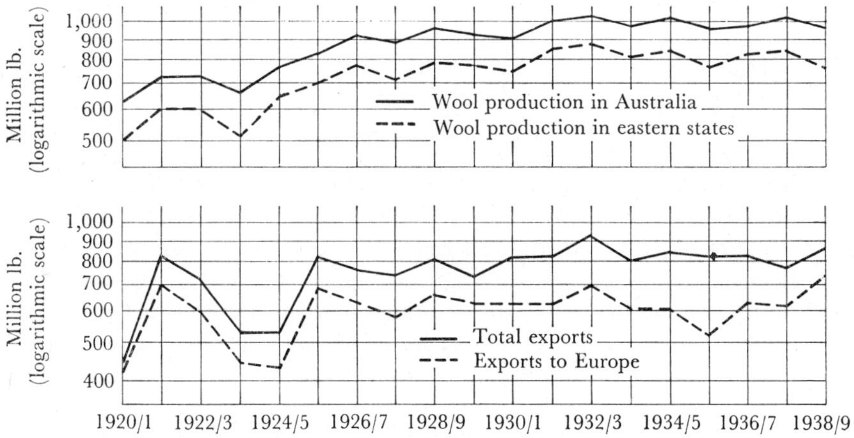

Fig. 2. Production and Export of Wool 1920/1–1938/9.
(Source: *Statistical Handbook of the Sheep and Wool Industry*.)

A factor of some importance in the demand for shipping was the organization of the wool market. In the years before 1914, and more especially before 1900, the bulk of the wool exported was sold in London, being shipped there on consignment. Largely this meant shipment in U.K. vessels. Developments in Australia's commercial and financial institutions stimulated pressure for local wool auctions. Increasingly after 1900 wool was sold in Australia before shipment.[1] Buyers from the U.S.A. and from the continent who hitherto had attended the London wool sales now came to Australia which, with transport innovations, was becoming more readily accessible. Local sales had

[1] By the 1920s and 1930s 90 % or more was sold locally. See *Year Books*.

Table 10. *Production of wool, 1920/1–1938/9 (m. lb.)*

Annual average during period	Australia	N.S.W.	Victoria	Queensland	Total eastern states
1920/1 to 1924/5	702·8	323·6	122·4	139·2	585·3
1925/6 to 1929/30	910·5	457·7	155·9	147·1	760·8
1930/1 to 1934/5	998·8	488·0	159·0	179·3	826·4
1935/6 to 1938/9	990·2	477·0	167·7	162·6	807·6

Source: *Sheep and Wool Handbook*, p. 21.

important repercussions on the economy as a whole. They also affected the shipping industry. Sales direct to foreign buyers encouraged them to make use of their own national merchant fleets then concurrently being developed. Although only one of many relevant factors, these changes in the marketing system affected the demand for U.K. shipping. By 1914 the pattern in wool-carrying characteristic of the inter-war years was already clearly discernible. After the war, long-established services were resumed. The post-war reappearance of the German-Australia Line and of the Norddeutscher Lloyd in Australia, for example, had an immediate effect upon U.K. vessels. Credit facilities granted by German finance institutions were often tied to the use of German ships. During the 1922/3 season out of the six lines maintaining shipping services between Australia and Germany only the two German lines had relatively full loadings. Very little of the wool exported to Germany was shipped in U.K. vessels.[1] Nor did the tendency towards national exclusiveness in wool-carrying diminish. Towards the end of our period heavy Japanese purchases of wool in Australia were heralded with the reported slogan: 'Japanese ships for Japanese goods', together with the pessimistic (and not unfamiliar) forecast of the 'ruin' of British shipping.[2]

[1] *S.M.H.* 3 November 1922; 1 and 8 January, 19 July 1923.
[2] *S.M.H.* 27 January, 17 February and 4 March 1938.

The transfer of the wool market from London to Australia did not, initially, lead to any dispersal of wool shipments. 'Paradoxically...(it) created a new centralisation.'[1] But the claims of regionalism, and the handicap of distance soon led to decentralisation of wool sales and to a corresponding increase in the number of Australian ports making direct oversea shipments. Not all the additional wool-selling centres brought into existence had access to alternative sea outlets. Wool sold at Albury, Ballarat and towards the end of our period at Goulburn, continued to be shipped through Sydney and Melbourne. But the wool auctions at Geelong, Newcastle and Brisbane tended to divert wool away from the older ports. From an insignificant quantity at the turn of the century, the amount of wool auctioned and shipped at these three ports had risen by 1938/9 to almost one-quarter of the total. The increase in the number of ports making direct oversea shipments required oversea vessels to call at more ports. A feature of the inter-war years, discussed below, was the wider range of services provided by oversea vessels and the additional costs which this entailed.

With the ending of the war-time system of control and purchase by 1924, and the disposal by the British Australian Wool Realisation Association of accumulated stocks, pre-war methods of wool sales were largely resumed. The one major alteration in selling was the introduction of shared control of the sales. Before the war, wool brokers alone had controlled sales. After the war responsibility was divided between wool brokers (now organised into a National Council of Wool Selling Brokers) and a newly organised Wool Growers Council. The pre-war method of disposing of the bulk of each year's wool-clip in the year of production was, however, retained, no increased tendency to carry-over was introduced.[2] Shipping requirements were thus known only when the size of the total wool-clip had been estimated.

The export of wool was also tied closely to the periodic wool

[1] A. Barnard, 'A Century and a Half of Wool Marketing', in Barnard, ed. *The Simple Fleece* (Melbourne, 1962), p. 483.

[2] For a survey of wool marketing practices see: 'Report by the Commonwealth Wool Inquiry Committee', October 1932 in *C.P.P.* 1932/4 IV, paper no. 91, p. 769 ff. Between 1920 and 1939 on average only 5 % of the bales on offer in any season were carried over to the next.

sales. For a number of reasons these were (and are) spread over a period of many months. Although the production of wool is seasonal, shearing dates themselves vary slightly and marketing considerations also dictate the spacing out of sales. Once the size of the total clip is known, sales are arranged to apportion available bales over the coming months. To a large extent the organisation of auctions in a series of consecutive sales is of convenience also to the shipping industry; it makes it possible for the regular programmed vessels to lift the bulk of wool auctioned. It reduces unevenness in the demand for shipping, which otherwise would arise if the whole clip were auctioned at a single sale or at a few sales. For an unusually large clip, additional cargo liners were programmed to assist in the wool liftings. Once the dates of wool auctions were announced any subsequent alteration was likely to throw the shipping industry violently out of joint. In 1925, for example, the wool sales arranged for May and June were cancelled without warning when prices began to sag. But ships had already been despatched to cater for the cancelled sales. Early arrivals secured wheat cargoes at good rates (which clearly displeased the tramp owners). But a simultaneous fall in the Plate demand for grain carriers diverted tramps to Australia with a consequent decline in Australian wheat rates.[1] Losses incurred on such abortive voyages in the end were, and are, made good by the consumer in higher freight rates. A major aim of the Shipping Conference convened by the Australian government in 1929 and discussed below was to reduce wasted space by accurate forecasting of shipping requirements.

Wool entering into export takes a number of forms. It may be exported in the grease or as scoured wool; it may be wool shorn from a slaughtered sheep or be attached to the skin; or it may be in the partially processed form of tops and noils. From the shipping point of view, however, only wool in the grease or scoured wool are important. For most purposes indeed attention may be focussed upon greasy wool, in terms of which wool exports are usually recorded. A brief mention of scoured wool is merited because of the freight differentials which apply. Wool in the grease is the wool as shorn. It is matted, dirty, and contains burrs and other impurities. The removal of such unwanted

[1] *S.M.H.* 9 May 1925.

matter results in weight loss. The clean yield from a bale of greasy wool is much less than the original bale weight; it is usually estimated that one pound of clean wool is equivalent to two and one-sixth pounds of greasy wool. But the high waste content of greasy wool is not entirely reflected in the respective rates of freight. The rate for greasy wool was not one-half that for scoured, during the inter-war years at most it was 25 % less. Although the average price realised on scoured wool was higher than on greasy, by about 75 %, the difference does not seem to have been high enough to offset the charges which scouring involved.[1] Buyer preference, moreover, tended to be for wool in the grease. Not surprisingly, therefore, wool in its natural shorn state predominated in the export trade. In the inter-war years scoured wool formed about 15 % of total wool exports although prior to the First World War the proportion seems to have been somewhat higher.[2] If the waste content of greasy wool in fact amounted to one-half or more of the weight, shipping companies understandably had little inducement to widen the freight differential so long as excess shipping capacity existed.

Wool export data are shown in tables below. Table 11*a* contains export figures in terms of weight. But the pound weight although an important statistic for official records and a convenient unit upon which to base freight rates is of less interest to the shipping company than the hold-space needed. For this purpose it is more relevant to measure the volume of hold-space required. Although bale weight and size vary according to wool type, and according to the severity or mildness of burrs and dust in particular seasons and so on,[3] a standardised notional bale is adequate for our purposes. As a standard we assume a bale weight of 320 pounds each measuring eighteen cubic feet.[4] On this basis Table 11*b* shows shipping requirements in measured tons.

[1] This point was made in the 'Report by the Wool Inquiry Committee' *C.P.P* 1932/4, IV, 830.

[2] *Year Books*, 1921, p. 698; 1925, p. 672; and 1939, p. 599.

[3] In N.S.W., for example, between 1925 and 1939 average bale weights of greasy wool ranged from 296 to 320 pounds. Over the same years in Tasmania the range was from 269 to 285 pounds and for Australia as a whole from 299 to 316 pounds. (*Sheep and Wool Handbook*, p. 42.)

[4] This assumed standard was one which also received official recognition in Australia, see *C.P.D.* vol. 132, p. 627.

Table 11*a*. *Exports of wool, 1920/1–1938/9 (m. lb.)*

	U.K.	Europe incl. U.K.	North America	Japan	Total exports
1920/1	326·6	423·8	41·5	13·5	486·0
1921/2	403·5	710·2	50·4	55·8	819·2
1922/3	334·7	596·3	56·8	56·4	711·0
1923/4	187·8	443·8	33·6	50·4	531·3
1924/5	203·1	437·0	40·1	56·4	535·9
1925/6	288·5	693·5	63·3	66·0	825·1
1926/7	241·9	641·8	42·4	83·9	770·0
1927/8	215·3	585·3	28·3	109·5	742·7
1928/9	236·8	665·4	20·9	103·0	810·5
1929/30	229·2	629·1	20·6	84·5	744·3
1930/1	251·9	634·1	21·8	153·5	814·6
1931/2	290·2	627·2	11·4	188·1	833·1
1932/3	278·1	699·4	8·4	201·0	925·7
1933/4	242·7	610·7	9·0	172·3	811·7
1934/5	327·1	613·5	6·9	196·6	852·7
1935/6	278·2	532·8	29·0	236·3	825·7
1936/7	311·9	629·1	77·9	84·5	831·4
1937/8	325·3	622·6	8·8	69·8	783·4
1938/9	369·8	733·1	26·7	74·2	866·6

Source: *Sheep and Wool Handbook.*

The largest single buyer was the U.K. a partial reflection of the continued dependence of Britain's manufacturing sector on the textile industry. Never taking less than an average of 240 million pounds a year, at least 30 % often more than 40 % of the total, the U.K. dominated the market. Her nearest rival, France, accounted for almost one-quarter of the total in the five years 1925/6 to 1929/30 being overtaken by Japan in the following quinquennium. Until the closing years of the period the three trade routes shown in the tables between them took almost the whole of Australia's wool exports. In the last few years before the Second World War the proportion fell to about ninety-five per cent. Throughout the period Europe was the most important trade route along which was consigned three-quarters of total wool exports.

Although the export trade in refrigerated products did not invariably rank next after wool in terms either of value or of

Table 11*b*. *Exports of wool, 1920/1–1938/9 ('000 measured tons)*

	U.K.	Europe incl. U.K.	North America	Japan	All destinations
1920/1	459·3	595·9	58·4	19·0	683·4
1921/2	567·5	998·8	70·8	78·5	1,152·1
1922/3	470·7	838·5	79·9	79·4	999·9
1923/4	264·1	624·2	47·3	70·9	747·1
1924/5	285·6	614·5	56·4	79·4	753·6
1925/6	405·7	975·2	89·1	92·9	1,160·3
1926/7	340·2	902·6	59·6	118·0	1,082·9
1927/8	302·8	823·1	39·8	154·0	1,044·4
1928/9	333·0	935·7	29·4	144·9	1,139·8
1929/30	322·4	884·7	29·0	118·9	1,046·7
1930/1	354·3	891·8	30·7	215·9	1,145·5
1931/2	408·0	882·1	16·0	264·6	1,171·5
1932/3	391·2	983·5	11·8	282·6	1,301·8
1933/4	341·3	858·7	12·6	242·3	1,141·5
1934/5	460·1	862·8	9·8	276·5	1,198·5
1935/6	391·2	749·2	40·8	332·3	1,161·2
1936/7	438·7	884·7	109·6	118·8	1,169·2
1937/8	457·5	931·8	12·4	98·2	1,101·7
1938/9	520·1	1,031·0	37·5	104·4	1,218·7

shipping-space needs, it was a trade closely associated with wool. As a representative of wool-exporting interests pointed out, 'vessels which cater for the wool sales have also their programme outlined for refrigerated cargo'.[1] The more important items of refrigerated cargo shipped from Australia consisted of meat, certain dairy products, and fresh fruit. There were also a number of less important items, de-shelled eggs or the few hundred pounds of fish annually exported. These made only a tiny contribution to total values and are here ignored.

Meat exports were dominated by consignments of beef, lamb and mutton, and later of pork. Less important were the shipments of game, poultry, and rabbits. To simplify discussion, exports of the minor meat products have also been omitted from our calculations. In aggregate value, exports of game, poultry, and rabbits were never very significant. In the early 1920s they rarely account for as much as 2 % of the total value of refriger-

[1] *S.M.H.* 27 October 1931.

ated exports. By the late 1930s the proportion was even lower. The impressive expansion of major components of refrigerated meat exports was not matched by a comparable upturn in exports of the minor items. Their space needs, moreover, were comparatively small and their exclusion from statistical tables made up of only a few significant figures represents no large omission.

For similar reasons of simplification, in calculating the amount of hold-space required for fruit exports, a single fruit stowage factor has been adopted. Fruit exported included apples and pears, citrus fruits and the more exotic pineapple. But apple shipments were always the most important, amounting in the main to about 80 % of the total and often to as much as 90 % during the later 1920s. Although not all the remaining fresh fruits could be stowed, weight for weight, in the space occupied by apples, for simplicity the stowage factor applicable to apples has been used throughout.

Table 12 sets out the main items of refrigerated exports expressed in terms of the volume of refrigerated space each component required. The most noteworthy feature at once obvious from the table is the extent of the expansion in shipments in each individual item and, as a consequence, in the total. From about 20 million cubic feet in 1920/1 the total had soared to more than 55 million by 1938/9, an annual rate of increase of about 4·5 %. This was considerably more than the growth of demand for cargo space by the other two staple Australian exports during our period. In terms of earnings, moreover, refrigerated exports tended to maintain their value during the depression or at least not to suffer falls comparable with those experienced in wool and wheat. Hence, of the lower total export earnings recorded after 1928/9 the proportion contributed by refrigerated exports was higher. In absolute figures also the rise tended to be sustained throughout the 1930s in contrast with the performance recorded for wool and wheat. The concentration in Australia upon the marketing of refrigerated products throughout the 1930s thus would seem to have been justified.

It is not altogether surprising to find that the more dramatic gains in refrigerated items were registered in the newer products. The longer established trade in fruit, butter, and frozen beef, mutton and lamb, shows an annual rate of growth of between 3·5 % and 5 %. The more recently traded items, starting from a smaller base, show more striking increases. Pork exports, for example, went up from 6,000 to more than a million cubic feet during the twenty years under review. Still more striking is the experience of the chilled-beef trade. In 1932/3 a trial shipment was made of a little more than 100 tons of chilled beef, equal to about 13,000 cubic feet of refrigerated space. The technical problems involved in shipping having been overcome, the years which followed witnessed a rise in space needs for this item to more than 3 million cubic feet a year. Nor was the development of the chilled-beef trade at the expense of frozen-beef shipments, where expansion continued with an increase from 6 to about 11 million cubic feet.

Table 12 fails, however, to illustrate either the source within Australia of the refrigerated products entering into the oversea trade or the destinations of such exports. These aspects are illustrated for sample years in appendix tables. As for the direction of the trade in refrigerated products it is sufficient here to note that for every major item, and indeed for almost the whole range of exports in this class, Britain was the major market. During the 1930s, moreover, the proportion of refrigerated cargoes shipped to Britain tended to rise. Among dairy products, for example, cheese and eggs especially found their chief outlet in Britain which regularly took more than 95 % of exports. Butter during the 1920s found its way into a wider market. After Ottawa, however, butter shipments also tended to become concentrated upon the U.K. Except for frozen beef in the 1920s meat exports similarly found their market in Britain as also did fruit exports. Perhaps the most convenient way of illustrating here the importance of the U.K. as a market for Australian refrigerated exports is by abstracting from the appendix tables the amount of refrigerated space required for such consignments to the U.K. In our first sample year about 90 % of the total refrigerated space was required for exports to the U.K. During the 1920s the market tended to widen, hence in our second sample year the proportion required for the U.K. had fallen to about 75 %. During the 1930s, however, this process was reversed and an annual requirement for the U.K. in excess of 90 % became usual. Just as the concentration of interest in Australia upon the refrigerated market was justified, so also was the care taken by the produce marketing boards to cater for the U.K. market. The main marketing boards, for example, set up London offices whose annual reports testify to the attention given to analysing market requirements.

The appendix tables also show for each item analysed the state from which final shipment was made. This is not necessarily the same as the state wherein the item was produced or processed. Our main interest, however, is in port facilities and shipping services available; hence the recorded detail is satisfactory. The point made above concerning wool shipments and the multiplication of loading ports applies even more to refrigerated exports. The expansion of the frozen meat trade and the increase in the number of ports with preserving establishments was accompanied by demands for direct oversea shipments. We show in chapter 5 below the implications for the shipping industry. For most items, especially in the 1920s, the three mainland eastern states predominated. The bulk of the meat exported was shipped from the east, Queensland contributing most of the beef and pork. Towards the end of our period the south and west became more significant in lamb and mutton shipments with quantities approaching 20 % of the total. Dairy products tended to originate in the east and similarly, for cheese and eggs, became less concentrated during the second decade of our period. Tasmania was insignificant throughout with the notable exception of fruit, two-thirds of apple exports and a high proportion of pears originating there.

Discussion on the trade in wool and refrigerated cargo may appropriately be followed by a brief mention of the trade in sugar and in dried and preserved fruits (Table 13) for both, especially fruits, were commonly carried by liners as berth parcel cargo. It is appropriate also to link them together in this context for both owed much of their early expansion in the inter-war years to the guarantees of tariff preference given at the Imperial Economic Conference of 1923.[1] The Conference chairman, mak-

[1] The initial post-war growth of the sugar industry, however, flowed from government assistance. The Commonwealth government sought independence from imported supplies and to populate the vulnerable north. (See the Reports of the Sugar Inquiry Committee in *C.P.P.* 1929/31, III, 37–154).

Table 12. *Exports of refrigerated products, 1920/1–1938/9* ('000 cubic feet)

	Eggs in shell	Butter	Cheese	Beef, frozen and chilled	Pork	Mutton and lamb	Fresh fruit	Total
1920/1	32·1	7,501·7	280·8	7,217·7	6·5	2,573·1	2,343·5	19,955·4
1921/2	62·9	10,355·0	373·3	4,988·6	6·1	4,299·1	4,345·7	24,430·7
1922/3	96·1	6,456·9	160·6	6,145·3	5·8	7,856·8	4,839·2	25,560·7
1923/4	51·0	5,355·8	112·8	4,225·3	2·1	1,865·8	3,522·3	15,135·1
1924/5	53·8	11,792·3	307·2	11,395·4	2·4	2,356·4	4,522·3	30,429·8
1925/6	119·1	7,946·4	202·8	8,602·1	3·6	4,016·3	6,683·0	27,573·3
1926/7	245·2	6,231·0	107·9	4,507·9	19·3	4,383·7	3,383·9	18,878·9
1927/8	85·8	8,049·1	204·3	6,794·1	5·6	2,173·2	8,330·3	25,642·4
1928/9	226·8	8,315·1	245·5	7,597·3	8·0	3,981·0	3,691·9	24,065·6
1929/30	277·6	8,738·9	111·6	6,297·9	37·5	4,706·7	8,745·5	28,915·7
1930/1	464·4	13,245·1	253·2	6,253·0	346·7	5,121·2	7,499·9	33,183·5
1931/2	771·6	16,368·3	214·1	6,664·5	296·6	7,747·5	10,066·9	42,129·5
1932/3	1,301·1	18,370·0	347·6	6,200·0	676·7	7,818·6	12,276·7	46,990·7
1933/4	1,525·8	19,829·5	274·4	7,070·0	788·1	8,020·6	10,727·6	48,236·0
1934/5	1,689·2	21,308·3	492·8	9,677·4	872·6	9,196·5	10,200·8	53,437·6
1935/6	1,350·6	17,260·2	382·2	9,149·6	947·3	8,344·0	11,236·6	48,670·5
1936/7	1,281·3	14,148·4	410·2	11,638·8	1,077·4	9,771·4	11,129·4	49,456·9
1937/8	877·9	16,018·3	802·3	14,948·7	1,364·4	9,459·4	11,406·2	54,877·2
1938/9	789·0	18,631·7	1,058·4	14,163·3	1,234·1	7,421·8	12,285·7	55,584·0

ing the U.K.'s proposals, expressed his sympathy with the producer's dilemma in deciding whether to embark upon large-scale sugar production. To ensure the security which the sugar growers wanted he gave a ten-year guarantee of preferential entry to Britain and also a non-terminable preferential entry for dried fruits. Three years later the 1926 Imperial Conference stressed the advantages of 'the combined value of preference and security' which empire sugar producers enjoyed in the U.K. market.[1] A contributor to the history of the Colonial Sugar Refining Company in Australia, which markets all Australian sugar exported, notes that during the 1930s 'the economic aid given by tariff preferences on Empire sugar entering the U.K. and Canada...enabled...Australia...to sell the whole of [her] output' at a much higher price than that obtained by non-empire producers who, moreover, often failed to market the whole of their crop. He goes on to draw attention to the relatively low price obtained for export sugar as compared with the higher price realised on domestic sales.[2]

Evidence given before the Sugar Inquiry Committee was united in its conclusion that sugar exports were uneconomic. It suggested also, however, that domestic sugar prices had never been increased in order to subsidise losses incurred on exports.[3]

For all three items, sugar, dried fruits, and preserved fruits, the U.K., Canada, and New Zealand formed virtually the only market, Britain taking at least two-thirds and often more than 80 % of each commodity shipped. Except in the first of our sample years (when Queensland sugar apparently was shipped from N.S.W. ports) the export trade in sugar was dominated by shipments from Queensland ports. The states of shipment for dried and preserved fruits show greater diversity. On the basis of aggregate weight, Victoria predominated with between two-thirds and three-quarters of the total, her closest rival being South Australia. Individual items, however, tended to be shipped from different states. The greatest proportion of dried apples, for example, came from Tasmania. Canned pineapples

[1] *U.K.P.P.* Cmd. 2009, pp. 176–8. Cmd. 2769, p. 38.

[2] J. M. Dixon, 'The Structure of Sugar Markets' in A. G. Lowndes, ed. *South Pacific Enterprise* (Sydney, 1956), p. 57.

[3] *C.P.P.* 1929/31, III, 65.

Table 13. *Exports of sugar and dried and preserved fruits, 1920/1–1938/9 ('000 tons)*

	Sugar	Dried and preserved fruits
1920/1	4·1	8·7
1921/2	1·9	11·5
1922/3	5·1	16·0
1923/4	15·5	19·4
1924/5	82·7	42·9
1925/6	208·8	32·3
1926/7	66·5	32·9
1927/8	154·6	38·0
1928/9	199·4	57·2
1929/30	181·7	65·2
1930/1	199·1	71·3
1931/2	287·9	59·1
1932/3	187·0	65·0
1933/4	307·9	91·7
1934/5	311·5	84·8
1935/6	300·6	71·9
1936/7	406·3	82·7
1937/8	428·1	103·7
1938/9	443·0	111·4

came from Queensland, apricots and pears from Victoria whence also were shipped the bulk of the currants and sultanas.

The least significant of the liner cargoes selected for analysis is the trade in hides and skins. It consisted chiefly of the trade in cattle hides and in sheepskins, usually with the pelt wool still attached. Minor items (from the shipping point of view) in the trade included calf skins and horse hides, rabbit and other furred skins. Usually exports are recorded in terms of the numbers of skins or hides shipped. Except with the residual entry 'all other furred skins' it is possible to estimate total tonnages by assuming an average weight per skin or hide; this type of calculation has been made to obtain the figures shown in the table below. As will be seen, the maximum weight shipped amounted to about 70,000 tons, usually it was between 60,000 and 70,000 tons. About three-quarters of exported hides and skins were consigned to Europe and almost all the remainder to the U.S.A. Individual

Table 14. *Exports of hides and skins, 1920/1–1938/9 ('000 tons)*

	Hides and calf skins	Sheepskins	Furred skins	Total
1920/1	6·6	17·3	3·1	27·2
1921/2	11·3	24·7	4·2	40·3
1922/3	16·4	36·0	7·0	59·5
1923/4	24·0	25·6	4·9	54·6
1924/5	29·7	21·2	6·5	57·3
1925/6	23·6	29·0	7·4	60·0
1926/7	22·9	31·3	7·2	61·5
1927/8	26·1	38·1	6·7	70·9
1928/9	21·8	37·4	5·7	64·9
1929/30	19·7	40·6	4·8	65·2
1930/1	19·9	38·3	4·4	62·8
1931/2	7·6	29·7	3·5	40·8
1932/3	11·5	32·2	3·9	47·7
1933/4	12·6	32·2	4·9	49·8
1934/5	18·3	32·2	4·2	54·8
1935/6	21·5	38·2	4·5	64·3
1936/7	28·4	37·8	3·3	69·6
1937/8	28·6	37·8	2·2	68·7
1938/9	32·2	36·5	1·9	70·7

items tended to be linked with different markets. France was the largest buyer of sheepskins with wool; the U.S.A. predominated in sheepskins without wool; most of the cattle hides shipped were to the U.K., but towards the end of the 1930s Japan also became an important buyer. The trade in furred skins, rabbit, opossum, kangaroo and the like was divided unequally between the U.K. and the U.S.A., the latter taking the major share. The states of final shipment on the whole were Victoria and N.S.W. which together contributed about three-quarters, the remainder being drawn in fairly equal proportions from the other mainland states.

Contrary to popular belief, the tramp did not dominate Australia's oversea shipping services. The items of trade already discussed represent demand for liner vessels. In the carriage of cargoes in bulk, however, the tramp found its normal employment. From Australia this meant the carriage of grain, timber, and minerals. The grain trade makes an appropriate point at which to begin our discussion of these items, it was here that the tramp found its major area of employment. This is not to suggest that tramps carried all, or even the bulk of Australia's grain exports. As discussion in chapter 2 suggests, the liner was often as important as the tramp in grain carrying. But it is in the carriage of such bulk cargoes that the tramp was, and is, most closely and regularly engaged. The Australian grain trade between the wars meant (as it means today) the export trade in wheat. Other grains were also shipped but in far smaller quantities, in occasional years Australia was indeed an importer of oats, maize and barley. The relative importance of the trade in wheat and in other grains is illustrated in the export data. During the whole of our period about 50 million tons of wheat were exported as contrasted with a total of only a million tons for all other grains. As well as its importance to the shipping industry, the export trade in wheat was significant also in the balance of payments. After wool it was the largest single contributor to export earnings with between 10 % and 30 % of the total.

The wheat-growing industry in Australia in contrast with the wool industry was not concentrated into the eastern states. (In Queensland and Tasmania indeed production was barely sufficient for local needs.) It was an industry important in South and Western Australia also which together accounted for about 40 % of total production during our period. Unlike wool, a higher proportion of wheat output was retained locally for animal feed and for human consumption. In the more populous, pastoral east, a relatively smaller surplus was thus available for export than in the south and west. Productivity moreover tended to be higher in the west than in the east. If the eastern states clothed Europe, the granary of Europe in Australia was located more in the south and west than in the east. The proportion of the total contributed by the exporting states varied considerably from year to year according to local conditions. N.S.W., for example, contributed as little as 2 % (in 1929/30) and as much as 25 % in five years of our period. Generally, however, South and Western Australia together contributed more than 35 % in each of the 19 years of our period, in 14 of the years their joint contribution exceeded 50 %, and in 7 years 60 %. In every year the balance was drawn fairly equally from N.S.W. and

Victoria. With flour, on the other hand, the two eastern states were the major exporters. In every year of our period more than 60 % of flour exports came from the two eastern states, in 15 of the years the proportion exceeded 65 % and in 10 years 70 %.

The export trade in wheat differed from the trade in wool in other ways, some of which help to explain its fluctuating fortunes. In contrast with wool, both the production and especially the oversea trade in wheat are characterised by marked instability during the inter-war years. In the early 1930s, when peak production was achieved, output was 50 % up on the 1920/1 total. Yet at the end of our period production was only 6 % higher than it had been in 1920/1. The swings in export figures were more violent. Exports in the early 1930s show an increase of about 70 % over the 1920/1 total. In 1938/9, however, a gain of only some 10 % had been achieved compared with the beginning of our period.

The expansion of the Australian wheat industry after the First World War derived in large measure from the revived imperialism which is to be traced during the inter-war years. A by-product or extension of war-time collaboration (the 'economics of seige', Sir Keith Hancock describes it), the 1920s and 1930s are years when renewed imperialist thinking sought greater empire self-sufficiency. Notwithstanding the economic diversification experienced in Australia during and after the First World War, a major role assumed in Australia was the increase of its rural sector. An expanding agricultural industry, in addition, harmonized both with the policy of closer settlement adopted in Australia and with the wider aspirations of the Empire Settlement Act.[1] As is well known, the overall achievements of the Act were disappointing and within Australia itself the policy of closer settlement had only limited success. Although the labour force employed in the rural sector increased during the period, the rise in wheat production was also accompanied by rising labour productivity and by depopulation of the wheat area.[2]

The more dramatic expansion of wheat production during the early 1930s, however, had different origins. Long before 1930

[1] For a survey of imperial sentiments along these lines see the Proceedings of the Imperial Economic Conference of 1923, *U.K.P.P.* Cmd. 2009, p. 86 ff.

[2] E. Dunsdorfs, *The Australian Wheat-Growing Industry, 1788–1948* (Melbourne, 1956), part 2, chapters II and IV.

Australia had become a firmly established member of the international wheat economy. Producing only 3 % or 4 % of the world's wheat in the 1920s, Australia nevertheless contributed 8 % to 15 % of the world's trade in wheat. From the Australian balance of payments point of view the export trade in wheat, as already noted, was also very important. It was indeed considerations of export income which led to the impressive increase in

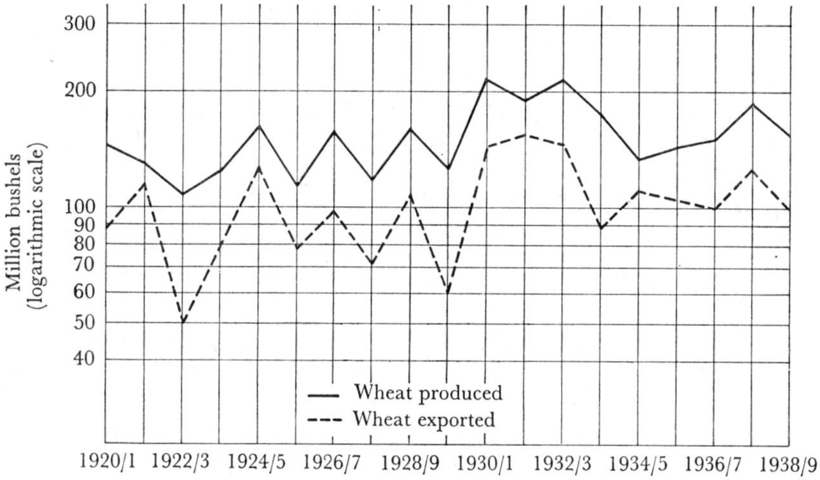

Fig. 3. Production and Export of Wheat. (Source: Bureau of Agricultural Economics, *The Australian Wheat Growing Industry* (Canberra, 1964); *Year Books*.)

wheat production and export in the early 1930s. The onset of world-wide depression in 1929, accompanied by a sharp fall in commodity prices, was at once reflected in Australia in balance of payments difficulties. Part of the remedy adopted was to restrict imports and reduce oversea borrowings. Another was the inauguration of the tragic 'grow more wheat' campaign by the Scullin government in early 1930. In a world beset with falling food prices and excess agricultural capacity, farmers throughout Australia were exhorted to grow more wheat. In N.S.W. the 1930/1 target figure for wheat production was double that of the preceding year. Everywhere in Australia more wheat was grown; the acreage under wheat rose by about 20 %. The rise in production was accompanied by an expansion in exports, illustrated in Figure 3. It was accompanied also by widespread rural distress, by an increase in the incidence of rural bankruptcy until partial mororatoria were introduced, and by the passing of the Wheat Bounty Act in November 1931. It was followed in January 1934 by the setting up of the royal commission on the wheat, flour and bread industries upon whose reports much of this discussion is based.[1]

After 1933/4 output in Australia was reduced. Elsewhere, notably in the U.S.A., production fell even more sharply throughout the 1930s. During the decade Australia's share of the reduced world trade in wheat fluctuated between 15 % and 24 %. Hence, although there were local problems, peculiar to Australia, others were common to all the wheat-exporting nations. In the international context two major problems may be identified. The first was to achieve some equitable all-round trimming of wheat production and to establish national wheat-export quotas. The second was connected with the adversity suffered by the world's shipping industry. The problem of excess wheat production was the subject of a number of international conferences which ultimately produced the International Wheat Agreement of 1933.[2] International cooperation broke down almost immediately, partly because Argentina would not, or could not fulfil the conditions of the agreement, partly because the international demand for wheat had been overestimated. During the remaining inter-war years, world trade in wheat ran at a level much lower than in the 1920s. The effect on Australia was to bring wheat production back almost to the level of the early 1920s and to reduce exports from their peak annual average of 150 million bushels between 1930 and 1933 to about 100 million bushels.

The expansion of wheat exports in the early thirties was also encouraged by lower ocean freights; these helped to compensate the exporter for the lower wheat prices obtained. In 1928 the charter rate for wheat (Australia to the U.K.) ranged between 39*s*. and 41*s*. per ton; in the early thirties it was less than 20*s*. Liner rates registered a comparable fall. Declining ocean

[1] A number of reports were made; see especially: *C.P.P.* 1932/4, IV, 2,425; 1934/7, IV, 1, 17, 283, 481, 621.

[2] See P. de Hevesy, *World Wheat Planning and Economic Planning in General* (1940).

freights, however, created considerable difficulty for the world's shipping industry. Uneconomic voyages resulted in the laying-up of tonnage. The quick-run solution adopted by many countries was a shipping subsidy. Britain was among the last of the maritime nations to follow this course. It is thus not altogether surprising that many U.K. tramps temporarily disappeared from the Australian grain trade.

The direction and volume of the combined trade in wheat and wheat flour is illustrated in Table 15 below for selected major trading areas. If the two components are shown separately, as in Tables 16*a* and *b*, certain features are at once obvious. On the whole the two items go to different destinations. Although Europe was a heavy buyer of Australian wheat, only the U.K. was a significant market for flour. During the decade of the thirties, moreover, the U.K.'s share of the rising total of exported flour tended to fall. After Europe, Japan was a large buyer of Australian wheat, especially during the early 1930s before trade between the two countries was interrupted. The market for flour, generally speaking, was found in the less-developed countries, initially Egypt, later in the far east and Pacific islands where, presumably, milling capacity in port areas was inadequate to handle large quantities of imported wheat.

The export performance of the two items also shows contrast. The quantities of wheat and flour shipped vary from year to year. The fluctuations in wheat were more violent, however. Taking the period as a whole, the long-term increase was less significant with wheat where, as already noted, a gain of only 5% or 6% was achieved by 1938/9 as compared with the 1920s. Flour exports were steadier and growth over the whole period is relatively even, the total approximately doubling between the beginning and end of our period.

The growth in the export trade in flour is in part a reflection of expansion in the flour-milling industry in Australia. Between the early 1920s and 1939 the total horse-power of flour mills increased by about 40%.[1] According to the royal commission on the wheat, flour and bread industries, indeed, milling capacity was vastly in excess of local requirements, especially in

[1] *Production Bulletin.*

Table 15. *Exports of wheat and flour, 1920/1–1938/9 ('000 tons)*

	U.K.	Europe incl. U.K.	Egypt	Japan	Eastern countries incl. Japan	South Africa	Total
1920/1	1,110	1,698	335	—	22	68	2,262·0
1921/2	1,188	1,950	184	206	281	57	2,998·3
1922/3	363	730	114	100	189	103	1,196·2
1923/4	699	1,044	199	363	470	133	2,061·1
1924/5	1,146	2,349	204	188	276	121	3,173·4
1925/6	660	931	191	291	423	103	1,899·8
1926/7	778	1,551	289	115	232	70	2,420·7
1927/8	612	982	237	86	209	205	1,808·0
1928/9	602	969	349	151	299	132	2,697·0
1929/30	651	780	144	75	218	57	1,497·7
1930/1	1,191	1,672	214	474	605	33	3,661·5
1931/2	1,489	1,866	139	576	765	13	3,957·9
1932/3	1,473	1,626	52	482	795	—	3,766·1
1933/4	1,341	1,481	30	211	444	1	2,134·3
1934/5	1,192	1,279	66	417	826	—	2,657·8
1935/6	1,369	1,702	21	304	586	9	2,613·2
1936/7	1,343	1,913	32	67	258	—	2,426·8
1937/8	1,815	2,253	29	76	321	25	3,094·2
1938/9	969	1,111	25	1	383	45	2,338·3

the principal flour-exporting states, N.S.W. and Victoria (which contributed between two-thirds and three-quarters of the total shipped) and South and Western Australia. In its fourth report in the early 1930s the royal commission estimates that existing milling capacity fully employed was enough after supplying local needs to yield an exportable surplus almost double the quantity then being shipped.[1]

In part also the growth experience in flour is related to the rise in importance of the eastern market in the 1930s. To a greater extent than elsewhere, shipments to the east (other than to Japan) were restricted by considerations of price. The sag in food prices which characterises the depression of the 1930s made possible increased shipments to these poorer markets. As noted above, the ability to exploit this latent potential market

[1] *C.P.P.* 1934/7, IV, 582.

Table 16*a*. *Exports of wheat, 1920/1–1938/9* (*% distribution*)

	Total ('000 tons)	% shipped to U.K.	Europe incl. U.K.	Egypt	Japan	South Africa
1920/1	2,056	50·4	79·0	13·6	—	1·5
1921/2	2,677	40·9	69·2	3·3	7·5	1·3
1922/3	844	34·2	77·6	—	11·8	8·1
1923/4	1,604	38·4	59·0	2·2	21·8	6·2
1924/5	2,773	38·0	81·2	1·8	6·8	3·5
1925/6	1,452	41·2	59·7	1·2	20·0	5·7
1926/7	1,980	35·9	74·9	6·3	5·8	2·7
1927/8	1,420	38·6	64·6	7·2	6·0	13·1
1928/9	2,193	25·1	41·8	6·0	6·9	5·1
1929/30	1,081	53·2	65·0	2·9	7·0	3·8
1930/1	3,193	33·5	48·5	2·6	14·8	0·8
1931/2	3,412	38·6	49·6	1·3	16·8	0·4
1932/3	3,202	42·6	47·3	0·9	15·0	—
1933/4	1,649	74·0	82·2	0·3	12·6	—
1934/5	2,034	54·2	58·5	0·2	20·4	—
1935/6	2,062	60·8	76·6	—	14·3	0·4
1936/7	1,922	61·6	91·1	—	3·5	—
1937/8	2,531	65·1	82·1	0·5	3·0	1·0
1938/9	1,690	51·1	59·2	0·6	—	2·7

helped to cushion Australia during the depression's early difficult years.

Another large area of demand for tramps derived from the trade in coal, metals, and ores (other than precious metals). About one million tons of minerals were shipped each year, at times this figure was exceeded, and in 1923/4 a total of 1¾ million was reached. For a number of reasons it is useful to make a broad distinction between the trade in coal and the trade in other minerals. First, their export record is exactly opposite. During our period the coal industry watched its export trade dwindle from about 2 million tons to about 400,000 tons a year. With other minerals, however, in aggregate, if not always by individual components, the trade almost exactly doubled. Secondly, whereas the oversea coal trade was carried on almost exclusively from Newcastle, N.S.W., the production of, and hence the trade in, other minerals was less concentrated. From

Table 16*b*. *Exports of flour, 1920/1–1938/9* (*% distribution*)

	Total ('000 tons)	% shipped to					
		U.K.	Europe incl. U.K.	Egypt	Japan	Eastern countries incl. Japan	South Africa
1920/1	205	35·7	36·2	26·8	0·2	11·1	18·0
1921/2	321	28·8	28·9	30·2	1·8	25·1	6·9
1922/3	352	21·2	21·4	32·3	0·4	25·7	9·9
1923/4	456	18·1	21·4	35·8	3·0	26·4	7·4
1924/5	400	23·2	24·2	38·5	—	22·2	5·7
1925/6	447	14·1	14·3	38·9	—	29·7	4·5
1926/7	440	15·4	15·7	37·6	—	26·7	3·8
1927/8	387	16·6	16·8	34·8	—	32·0	5·1
1928/9	503	10·3	10·4	43·2	—	29·5	4·4
1929/30	415	18·3	18·7	27·0	—	34·5	3·9
1930/1	468	25·7	26·4	27·8	—	28·3	1·7
1931/2	545	31·4	31·6	17·4	2·7	34·9	2·0
1932/3	563	19·3	19·6	4·5	0·6	56·0	—
1933/4	484	25·2	26·5	5·1	1·1	49·1	—
1934/5	623	14·2	14·4	3·8	0·2	65·8	—
1935/6	550	21·2	22·2	3·8	1·5	52·8	—
1936/7	504	31·4	32·3	6·2	—	38·0	—
1937/8	562	29·8	31·3	3·0	—	43·5	—
1938/9	647	16·4	17·1	2·4	—	59·1	—

South Australia, for example, came almost all the zinc concentrates, about one-half of the silver/lead concentrates, the whole of the iron ore, and a high proportion of the lead pig and copper matte exports. Tasmania vied with the south, especially in the 1930s, in the shipment of silver/lead concentrates and it shipped almost the whole of Australian exports of part-processed zinc. Queensland was prominent in the export trade in lead matte and to a lesser extent also in lead pig. N.S.W. exported a little of each mineral, and was prominent in lead pig and copper ingot. Finally, although the total amount of shipping space required for the combined trade in coal and other minerals remained fairly steady, the trade routes differed. More than one-half of the coal exported at the beginning of our period was shipped to New Zealand, the bulk of the remainder was consigned to the

Pacific islands and to the Pacific-coast countries of South America. Metals and ores, however, were consigned to quite different destinations. Throughout the 1920s about 80% of exports went to European countries. In the 1930s although the proportion was lower it remained high at about two-thirds. Almost the whole of the remainder was consigned to the U.S.A. or to Japan.

Before 1914 a flourishing and expanding oversea trade in N.S.W. coal had been developed on the basis of low freight rates offered by the U.K. shipping industry.[1] Developments in oversea coal markets, the increasing use of oil, and the disappearance of the special features which had made low freight rates possible, led to the rapid decline of coal exports. By the end of the twenties (see Table 17), once the immediate post-war recovery had come to an end, coal exports sagged. The decline from the pre-war export total of around 2 million tons to less than 400,000 tons a year caused serious hardship on the N.S.W. coalfields as well as leading to a sharp re-deployment of shipping.

The export trade in other minerals offers brighter contrast. Shipping freed from the coal trade found employment in this developing area in which between 1920 and 1939 the average annual tonnage exported almost doubled. It was a varied trade and included the export of ores, of concentrates, and of part-processed or smelted metals in the form of ingots, matte, or cast pigs. Generally speaking Europe was the principal destination for concentrates and smelted metals whereas iron ore exports were consigned to the U.S.A. and to Japan, especially to the latter. Variations in the composition of the trade are shown in Table 18. In the 1920s ore exports were relatively unimportant, the trade, in roughly equal proportions, consisting of concentrates, especially zinc, and of part-processed lead, copper and zinc. The 1930s are characterized by steady growth in the export of smelted lead, a more uneven growth in the trade in zinc bars, and by a decline in the trade in copper. The decline in copper exports reflects in part the low prices obtainable in world markets and also reduced copper production in Australia which the low oversea prices induced.

[1] For a discussion on the relationship between U.K. shipping and the oversea trade in N.S.W. coal see articles by the present author in *Economic Record* vols. 36 (393–413) and 37 (371–81).

Table 17. *Exports of coal, 1920/1–1938/9 ('000 tons)*

	Total	New Zealand	Americas and Pacific Islands	Eastern countries
1920/1	2,161·3	737·8	456·8	685·7
1921/2	1,028·7	427·2	240·9	331·9
1922/3	1,114·1	394·7	477·0	229·2
1923/4	1,336·4	731·3	394·2	182·9
1924/5	978·0	580·3	206·3	143·4
1925/6	794·3	459·2	230·1	76·0
1926/7	807·0	413·8	260·4	100·0
1927/8	556·0	313·0	144·3	79·8
1928/9	346·6	164·4	139·4	20·1
1929/30	294·5	180·8	75·0	22·3
1930/1	387·8	198·0	111·5	50·3
1931/2	344·0	110·7	122·8	68·3
1932/3	282·9	100·0	115·7	43·6
1933/4	292·4	99·2	126·0	53·1
1934/5	305·1	105·2	51·9	124·3
1935/6	307·5	99·8	131·4	55·2
1936/7	340·3	111·2	131·2	66·2
1937/8	392·8	119·7	135·3	100·8
1938/9	382·0	112·9	178·1	33·3

The important development in the trade in minerals in the 1930s, however, took place in iron-ore exports. The dramatic rise in the quantity in 1929/30 when more than a half million tons were shipped was in part due to the N.S.W. coal strike and to a fall in the domestic production of pig-iron. The unsteadiness of iron-ore exports thereafter and their tapering down by 1939 reflects on the one hand the fluctuating optimism about the size of ore deposits available and, on the other, hostility towards Japan. During the 1920s and early 1930s extravagant hopes of unlimited iron-ore resources in the various Australian states had been severely shaken. By the end of the 1930s they were being replaced by views which were unduly pessimistic.[1] Uncertainty about reserves of ore coincided with growing hostility towards Japan. Since Japan was a major market for

[1] H. Hughes, *The Australian Iron and Steel Industry, 1848–1962* (Melbourne, 1964), p. 121.

Table 18. *Exports of ores, metals and concentrates other than precious metals, 1920/1–1938/9 ('000 tons)*

	Total	Ores	Concentrates	Lead	Copper	Zinc	All metals
1920/1	113·9	5·9	47·2	20·9	23·5	3·3	60·8
1921/2	221·1	0·7	128·2	73·3	9·3	8·2	92·2
1922/3	508·2	9·0	363·4	99·4	9·0	24·7	135·7
1923/4	461·5	8·6	301·9	109·9	6·9	31·9	151·0
1924/5	407·9	9·6	242·5	117·7	3·7	32·3	155·6
1925/6	470·6	10·4	293·9	130·4	4·7	29·0	166·2
1926/7	289·5	7·2	124·9	124·5	4·1	26·8	157·4
1927/8	551·6	15·8	320·9	163·8	7·3	24·8	214·8
1928/9	434·8	52·6	196·8	144·6	6·5	32·6	185·3
1929/30	996·9	587·0	203·9	161·1	10·9	32·9	206·0
1930/1	523·4	133·5	177·3	154·6	12·0	45·4	212·6
1931/2	351·9	36·1	62·2	195·3	12·0	45·5	253·6
1932/3	318·8	15·1	77·5	181·6	8·4	34·9	226·1
1933/4	425·7	70·1	132·5	184·3	5·2	32·3	223·1
1934/5	721·8	398·2	110·6	183·6	0·5	27·4	212·9
1935/6	905·5	437·8	219·2	194·1	1·0	42·3	248·4
1936/7	683·8	275·2	182·4	174·0	3·4	47·7	226·1
1937/8	705·6	189·3	269·9	212·7	1·9	30·9	246·4
1938/9	736·6	138·5	295·8	204·4	1·0	44·6	302·3

iron ore it thus was easier for the government to prohibit from 1 July 1938 the export of iron ore. It was in part this hostility towards the export of war material to Japan, apparently, which earned for the then Mr Menzies his 'pig iron' sobriquet.

The remaining export commodity to be examined, the trade in timber, need not long detain us; it was not a heavy user of shipping. Generally speaking timber exports amounted to between 200,000 and 250,000 measured tons, in eleven of the inter-war years indeed the total was well below 200,000 tons. As a user of shipping, it may be noted in passing, it was the timber *import* trade rather than timber exports which offered employment to shipping. Imports of timber usually exceeded 500,000 measured tons and in eight of our years more than 750,000. Timber exports in the main consisted of the hardwoods of Western Australia whence were shipped about three-quarters of the total, the remainder as a rule coming from N.S.W. In contrast with most other branches of Australia's export trade,

Table 19. *Exports of timber, 1920/1–1938/9 (% distribution)*

	Total ('000 tons measured)	% shipped to: Europe incl. U.K.	Eastern countries	South Africa	New Zealand
1920/1	225·9	19·1	13·9	32·3	26·5
1921/2	201·2	10·9	9·1	38·7	24·8
1922/3	184·7	7·1	6·4	47·9	28·1
1923/4	223·1	14·1	6·6	23·1	34·0
1924/5	271·3	15·3	4·7	39·9	35·6
1925/6	236·2	9·6	15·9	41·6	27·8
1926/7	260·2	7·7	25·2	40·3	22·9
1927/8	206·6	7·9	22·9	41·9	18·2
1928/9	193·3	11·8	14·5	27·0	24·4
1929/30	171·9	15·7	17·1	21·2	29·0
1930/1	132·1	20·5	18·0	9·2	35·8
1931/2	98·9	30·4	23·9	19·0	16·7
1932/3	56·1	29·8	21·3	12·6	7·0
1933/4	95·8	18·3	22·1	15·4	21·1
1934/5	156·1	17·5	27·4	13·0	25·4
1935/6	158·5	18·3	10·1	17·0	29·5
1936/7	157·6	22·3	19·0	13·1	30·3
1937/8	212·0	19·9	14·0	13·4	23·1
1938/9	163·6	19·2	8·0	15·4	43·4

Europe was not the major market for Australian timber exports. In only three of the inter-war years did Europe's share exceed 20 %. The chief importers of Australian timber were South Africa and New Zealand, especially in the decade of the 1920s when their combined share exceeded 50 % of the total. Their share in the 1930s tended to be rather lower at about one-third. The distribution of the trade as a whole is shown in Table 19.

The impact during the inter-war years of Australian economic development upon ocean shipping has been illustrated from the recorded experiences of eight major export groups. The tonnage of exports tended to exceed imports which, along with the migrant trade, served as back-haul cargoes for the shipping industry with one notable exception—the oil trade, mentioned below. But export data give a lopsided picture of the country's economic growth as a whole. Except negatively, the record of exports gives no clue to the industrialisation of Australia between the wars. Exports remained unchanged. Economic diversification had little effect on the export profile. Apart from minor modifications in markets or in the widening range of meat exports and so on, the eight groups dominated the scene throughout the inter-war years, just as they do today. But the demand for shipping was also affected by changes in the economy not brought out in the export data. The two aspects of importance are the trade in oil and industrial growth in Australia. With industrial growth, the failure of Australian industry between the wars to develop an oversea market is less relevant than its originally intended role in import replacement. With both oil and industrial change, that is to say, interest centres on their effect upon the import sector.

The rapidly growing trade in fuel-oil (including motor spirit) in the inter-war years is a characteristic shared by all advanced societies at this time. To secure handling economies specialised shipping was introduced for the transport of oils. Because specialised for the carriage of liquids in bulk, tankers were not, at that time, used in other trades. This resulted in one-way shipping utilisation and a rise in the tonnage of shipping cleared in ballast. Table 20 shows the tonnage and source of Australian oil and petrol imports. The impressive rise in the quantity imported needs little explanation. Above all it reflects the growing domestic use of petrol in motor-vehicles, as elsewhere in the world. Motor-vehicle registrations in 1920/1 totalled about 100,000 or about 20 per 1,000 of population, by 1938/9 the total was almost 900,000 or about 125 per 1,000 of population. To a much lesser extent also the growth in oil imports reflects its increased use in secondary industry and at sea. By 1938/9 factories were using 50 million gallons a year. At sea, oil tended increasingly to supersede coal during the inter-war years. The switch to oil was conspicuous in both the Australian oversea fleet and also the coastal fleet. The dual attraction of reduced labour charges in the engine room and independence of N.S.W. coal strikes as already noted made motor vessels attractive to Australian ship-owners. In the oversea sector the shift to oil-burners was especially rapid in the 1930s. Entries to the port of Sydney, for example, as early as 1929 included $2\frac{1}{2}$ million net registered tons of oil-burning ships, ten years later the total had

Table 20. *Imports of oil, 1920/1–1938/9 (quantity and source)*

	'000 tons	% from		
		N.E.I.	U.S.A.	Iran
1920/1	221·0	38·4	60·9	—
1921/2	182·5	37·7	57·3	—
1922/3	283·6	47·0	53·0	—
1923/4	424·1	44·9	47·4	4·1
1924/5	574·7	49·7	43·7	6·3
1925/6	727·7	45·4	45·0	8·9
1926/7	941·8	43·9	41·4	10·2
1927/8	1,314·4	33·3	35·9	3·5
1928/9	1,255·0	55·7	38·0	5·2
1929/30	1,439·8	50·8	39·5	6·3
1930/1	1,071·8	49·4	38·7	6·0
1931/2	820·0	37·9	49·7	8·3
1932/3	983·8	38·8	44·3	9·3
1933/4	1,053·1	46·4	39·2	8·3
1934/5	1,067·9	58·2	26·1	10·1
1935/6	1,263·5	54·7	25·5	9·0
1936/7	1,357·2	58·4	22·3	7·8
1937/8	1,632·8	57·7	20·4	9·6
1938/9	1,575·5	58·3	14·4	7·0

doubled. Over the same period entries of coal-fired ships had fallen from about $3\frac{1}{2}$ to $2\frac{1}{4}$ million net registered tons.[1]

The diversification of Australia's industrial structure between the wars covered a wide range. It included among many others: textiles; the electrical sector; iron and steel production; and also, if more tardily, metal-using industries. The development of import replacement industries had an uneven effect upon the demand for shipping. The incidence on shipping varied. Some items, such as 'knocked-down' motor chassis, occupy less space in this state than in final form. Other items imported in the semi-finished state may have required not less but more space. Some local developments probably passed unnoticed by the shipping industry. The local textile industry, for example, was impressive chiefly for the employment it offered. The number of employees in woollen and cotton mills rose five-fold and the

[1] *Maritime Services Board of N.S.W., Fourth Report*, p. 33.

production of woollen fabrics was also multiplied five times during the period.

Far more significant for shipping was the growth of the Australian iron and steel industry, which had emerged from its chrysalis at the beginning of the First World War. Nevertheless not even the stimulus of war had been sufficient to eliminate oversea supplies by the early 1920s when about 400,000 tons of iron and steel were imported. Local production increased as tariff protection was stepped up. Where an item was produced locally it virtually disappeared from inbound cargoes. Imports of iron, plate and sheet steel, structural steel and rails, for example, fell from more than 330,000 tons in the early 1920s to about 20,000 tons in 1939. On the eve of the Second World War, imports had fallen to about 100,000 tons, the bulk of which was tinplate, the one area in the iron and steel industry where local production had failed to meet demand. In this one sector, therefore, shipping space amounting to about 300,000 tons a year was freed. The real saving was in fact considerably more if the rise in domestic demand is taken into account. Between 1920/1 and 1938/9 the indigenous output of pig iron rose from about 360,000 tons to more than one million, ingot steel output similarly went up from about one-quarter of a million to more than one million tons. Increased local demand derived from a stepping up of diversification with metal-using industries. The motor-car assembly industry, for example, was based upon the import of motor chassis with engine, to which were fitted locally made bodies. As the country recovered from depression the industry revived, production of motor bodies increased six-fold. Its revival was accompanied by the increasing production of the enclosed motor car, requiring more sheet steel, and by increasing reliance upon sheet steel of Australian origin. At the peak in the 1920s about 200,000 tons of sheet steel had been imported, in 1938/9 the amount was less than 9,000 tons.

The tonnage record, however, shows that whatever shipping space may have been freed by the development of import replacement industry no fall is to be detected in cargo tonnages, these rose rather than fell. But if the process be examined in the round and the effect upon outbound tonnage is also taken into account, a different conclusion is reached. Excluding oil imports, by making appropriate allowance, the tonnage of inbound cargo is seen to have increased by about 30 %. But the failure of dry-cargo import tonnages to rise more steeply perpetuated the imbalance between inbound and outbound tonnages. Freight rates are in part determined, and are largely justified, by reference to both inbound and outbound earning capacity. It may thus not always serve long-term ends to eliminate or seriously reduce traffic in one direction if commodities moving in the opposite direction rely upon low freight rates to meet international competition.

Chapter 5

PORT CHARGES AND THE OVERSEA SHIPOWNER

An economy involved in ocean-borne external trade is compelled to direct attention and resources to its port facilities. Failure to provide terminals appropriate to the shipping services required, hampers growth by unnecessarily inflating transport charges. In the later nineteenth century a large proportion of Australian capital formation was required for the provision of harbours. During the inter-war years, as we have already shown, Australian ports were called upon to adapt themselves to significant changes in the demand for the complex of services they provided. Further investment became necessary. The ports were required to accommodate a greater aggregate tonnage of shipping, to cater for larger ships, and to handle an increased volume of cargo. In the early 1920s the total shipping tonnage entered at ports in the Australian states, including both interstate shipping and the coastal movement of oversea vessels was about 15 million net tons; by the end of the 1930s it had risen to a little more than 29 million. The tonnage of oversea and interstate cargo shipped and discharged rose from about 20 to about 30 million tons.

The expansion of trade and shipping activity outlined in earlier chapters had a considerable effect on port development. The new trade in oil and motor spirit, for example, required the construction of appropriate discharging equipment and storage usually segregated from other traffic. The growth of the wheat trade drew attention to, if not always the provision of, modern bulk-handling appliances. New or improved road and rail links to give greater flexibility in access became indispensable if congestion in or around the harbours were to be avoided. Bigger ships meant the creation of deeper access channels in some ports and deeper water at mooring berths. Response to the changing demands of the shipping industry involved further sustained investment. In certain Australian ports the main investment was in the improvement of existing berths rather than the massive provision of additional space. Many ports at the beginning of our period had large areas of under-used quay space which lent themselves to adaptation. Increased aggregate tonnage of shipping entered at Australian ports reflected the increased size, not number, of vessels. The largest number of vessels in port in any single day was the same, or even less, at the end as at the beginning of the period. The basic problem was the modernisation of existing berths.

The port of Melbourne is a good example. It consists of piers in the bay and wharf areas on the River Yarra and in Victoria Dock. The port has largely been created by dredging. During the inter-war period the total tonnage of oversea vessels entered was doubled, inter-state tonnage rose by a quarter, the actual number of vessels entered, however, fell from 4,700 to 3,500. The total lineal footage of berth space rose by no more than 5 or 6 %. Rather was the investment concentrated on channel deepening and upon increasing the number of berths suitable for large vessels. In 1920 less than 3 % of berth space had a depth alongside greater than 30 ft., by 1939 almost 20 % had been brought up to this standard.

It is not intended here, however, to undertake a detailed survey of Australian port development as such, vital though it was for the country's external trade during the period. Instead we are concerned only with those aspects of Australian port-development which impinged upon the costs of oversea shipping. The aim of the present chapter is to determine whether Australian ports were appropriately equipped to service and handle the oversea shipping upon which the sustained development of the economy depended; whether they endeavoured to maximise their advantages to attract shipping; and whether they charged rationally for the services provided. Expressed in another way, our aim is to examine those components of port expense considered significant by an oversea shipowner; to relate them to rates of freight; and to compare where possible with ports elsewhere, especially those consigning to Europe items competing with Australian commodities. A feature of the inter-war years, the 1920s particularly, is the recurring complaint that Australian port charges were 'high'. Discussion which follows largely supports the complaint but suggests that to some extent the oversea shipowner himself may have been in part responsible.

The item usually labelled 'port charges' in voyage accounts includes port taxes and cargo charges. Taxes are levied in all ports everywhere and are designed to cover expenditure incurred by port administrations in the provision of navigational aids and wharf facilities. Cargo charges cover stevedoring costs and the like. There is a third, less concise but much more publicised element: port turn-round. International preoccupation with the speed of vessel turn-round is perennial and attests to its importance. It reflects a number of factors: the degree of sophistication in cargo-handling appliances; the organisation of port labour; the efficiency of port administration in smoothing the flow of shipping and of cargo; and, not least, the efficiency of inland transport undertakings in preventing port congestion. The rapid clearance of inbound, and the punctual supply to the wharves of outbound cargo often serves as the key constraint to turn-round. Its inclusion here follows logically from the cost element involved in port delays, its examination forms an indispensable part of our enquiry into costs.[1]

(*a*) THE PORTS OF AUSTRALIA

The relative importance of each state and of principal ports in cargo handling is illustrated in Figures 4, 5 and 6. Ports differ in many ways and for many reasons. Their physical properties may have been determined by geography or by man. Their development is the result of numerous well-known stimuli, trade, development of their hinterland and so on. Satisfactory definitions of an efficient port are wanting. Nor are the attributes of a 'good' port unchanging, given constant adaptation to the changing needs of the shipping industry. The contemporary innovation of cargo 'containerisation', for example, and the

[1] The main sources used for this chapter are: *The Annual Reports* of the Sydney, Melbourne and Fremantle harbour authorities (whose cooperation is here gratefully acknowledged); A. G. Whitlam, 'Australian Port charges', *Economic Record*, vol. VI, Supplement; and the report made by Sir George Buchanan on 'Transport in Australia' published in *C.P.P.* 1926/8, v, 81 and 241.

argument for inland container assembly 'ports' is a good illustration. The recent Rochdale Report on ports in Britain draws attention to the far-reaching changes which might follow in the design of docks and quays if container handling should become widely adopted. During and immediately before our period the

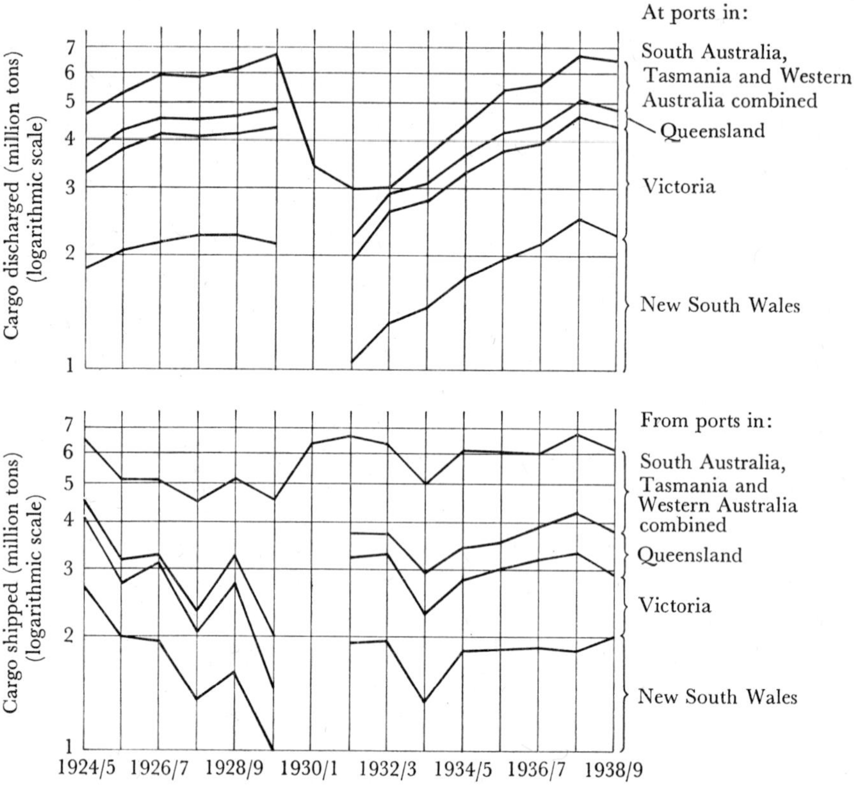

Fig. 4. Oversea Cargo discharged and Shipped 1924/5–1938/9. (Source: *Transport and Communication Bulletin*. No data published for 1930/1.)

major consideration was harbour depth and the tendency for vessel size and draught to increase. In 1917 the Dominions royal commission grappled with the problem of definition and, taking access waterways into account, stated the minimum requirements of a first-class port in terms of the depth of water available. For Australia it concluded that provision should be made for vessels of up to 38 ft. draught. At this time only Hobart and Sydney were of this standard; they alone are of this standard today. As we have shown, innovation in marine engineering has made larger vessels possible without a proportionate increase in draught.

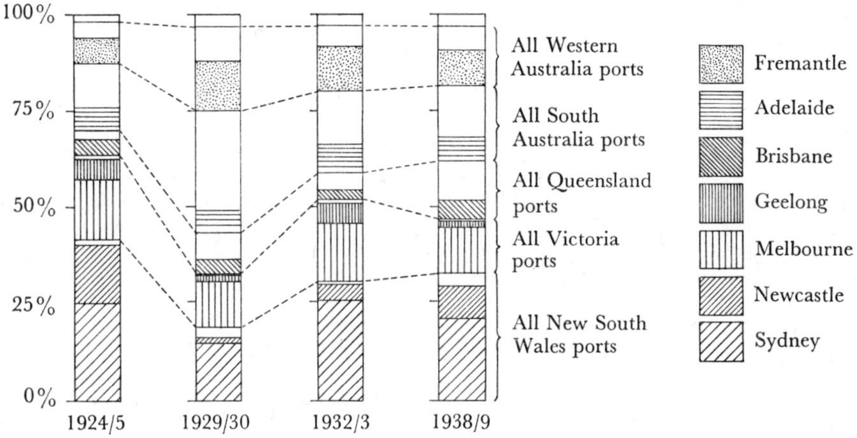

Fig. 5. Oversea cargo discharged in Australian States (percentage distribution). (Source: *Year Book* and *Transport and Communication Bulletin.*)

The Australian coastline is some 12,000 miles long. It is indented by a number of safe natural harbours and by other inlets which have facilitated the construction of harbours and docks. In the 1920s and 1930s some 5,000 miles of the total coastline were drawn into the oversea trade. The dispersal along the coastline of a small population has brought with it a number of problems for the shipping industry. They reveal a striking contrast with the export problems of countries with a larger occupied area per linear mile of coastline. In the North American mid-west or the central plains of India exports have a long overland haul and concentrate at its conclusion at a relatively small number of large ports. In both areas the supply of rolling stock and of rural loading facilities exercised the major constraint. It is significant that in North America the chief stream of complaint was directed against deficiencies in the rail haul.

Each Australian state, other than the Capital Territory developed initially around, and clung to, the port from which it was first settled. Subsequent population movement and the expansion of settlement in the main has remained on, or close to the coastline. As a consequence, wherever possible, minor ports sprang up along the coast giving a relative short rail haul and a

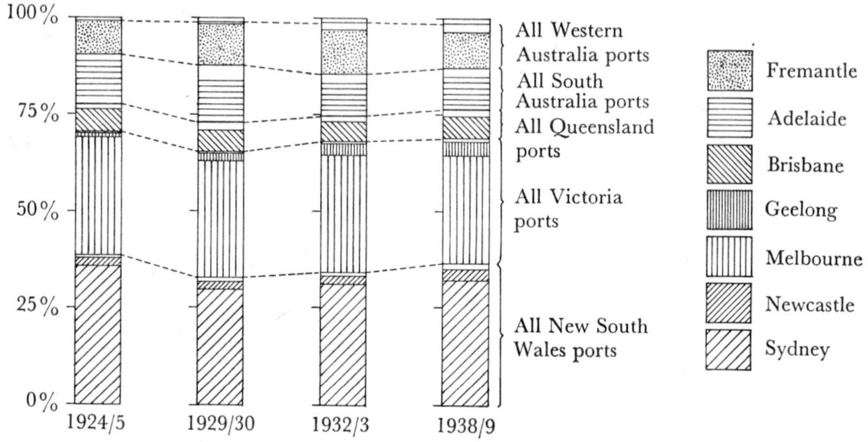

Fig. 6. Oversea cargo shipped from Australian States (percentage distribution). (Source: *Year Book* and *Transport and Communication Bulletin.*)

multiplication of ports. Nevertheless, most of the oversea trade of each state during our period was carried on through the capital port. In aggregate, through the six principal ports, flowed 85–90 % of the total tonnage of inbound cargo into Australia. Exports were drawn more widely, in the early 1920s about 75 % of Australia's export cargo tonnage was shipped through these ports. By the end of the 1930s the proportion had fallen to about 55 %. In contrast with North America, the Australian oversea trade is dispersed through many outlets. An important consequence in the inter-war period is that full cargoes to or from any single port were extremely rare except for tramp bulk cargoes. Liners, especially those engaged on the European route, spent a week or more after reaching Fremantle in circling the continent from west to east, discharging cargo *en route*. On reaching the east and completing discharge they began loading once more. They retraced their route, loading at each port before clearing the Commonwealth at Fremantle.

Calls at state capitals to distribute and collect part cargoes did not exhaust the itineraries of oversea vessels. Although the oversea trade of each state is largely channelled through its capital many other ports were also involved. During the inter-war years as many as forty ports had some connection with the oversea trade. The total included not only secondary ports but also a host of minor ones of varying importance. The early appearance of such ports and their rapid multiplication as noted above reflects the spread of population, the initial lack of land-transport facilities, and the nearness of settlement to the sea. Where areas with access to minor ports became involved in the oversea trade, their demands for direct oversea shipping links were hard to resist. In some instances no more than the occasional visit of a tramp was needed. But for many relatively small ports regular visits became increasingly necessary and increasingly common during the inter-war years.

Reference has already been made to the decentralisation of wool sales and its effect upon oversea shipping. More significant to the shipowner was the tendency, also mentioned in chapter 4, for the export trade in refrigerated meat to expand. It was an expansion which witnessed not only greater activity at existing ports but also the spread of additional meat-preserving works at Queensland ports. Before the First World War, refrigerated vessels called at only a few ports to obtain cargoes. During the 1920s the number of ports they visited tended to increase. No refrigerated ship in 1913 called at more than 6 ports, but calls at 7, 8, 9 and even 10 ports were not uncommon by the late 1920s. Details of shipping movement in 1913 by 5 leading companies engaged in the Australian trade show that only 14 % of the total number of refrigerated ships loaded at more than 5 ports on a voyage. In 1924 about 22 % of the refrigerated ships of 15 companies loaded at more than 5 ports; by the end of the 1920s the proportion had risen to 37 %. The actual number of ports loading refrigerated items doubled during the 1920s. A comparable multiplication of calls was also true, though to a lesser extent, with non-refrigerated vessels.

The cost burden of providing extensive shipping services did not pass unremarked in the U.K. nor unnoticed in Australia. The important 1929 Oversea Shipping Conference (discussed on pp. 239–45) adopted a recommendation urging the reduction of the number of ports of call. But where the cost of land transport was high, local reluctance was strong. As an editorial in the *S.M.H.* pointed out: 'were inland and coastal transport cheaper, it might pay shippers through having more economical oversea transport, to have fewer ports of call for overseas steamers, though the economy would have to be very real to overcome the efforts of each port to attract all oversea ships possible'. Almost a decade later much the same arguments were being put forward. 'The reduction of the number of loading and discharge ports for individual ships would result in considerable benefit' to both owners and shippers, noted the same newspaper.[1] During our period the use of secondary ports in fact increased. The early and mid-1930s saw further service extensions. In 1935, for example, the Aberdeen and Commonwealth and the new entrant, the Blue Star Line, added North Queensland ports to itineraries.[2] By the end of the 1930s about 25 % of export cargo tonnage was being shipped through the minor ports as compared with only 15 % in the early 1920s.

For many of the minor ports involvement in the oversea trade meant almost exclusively the handling of export cargoes. They were rarely used for the discharge of oversea imports. The proportion of imports discharged at the minor ports moreover tended to fall, from about 6 to about 3 %. In 1938/9 about thirty minor ports handled between them approximately 1·7 million tons of exports but less than 200,000 tons of imports. Imbalance in utilisation was most conspicuous in the minor ports. It was also present elsewhere. Ports of secondary rank such as Newcastle in N.S.W., Geelong in Victoria, Port Pirie in South Australia, and so on, invariably handled a far bigger outbound than inbound oversea tonnage. Imports from overseas tended overwhelmingly to be discharged in the east, especially at Sydney and Melbourne (see Figure 4). Between them these two ports regularly accounted for 60–66 % of the total throughout the inter-war years. Exports on the other hand were not so closely a reflection of population distribution. Sydney and

[1] *S.M.H.* 15 April 1929, 14 June 1937.
[2] *S.M.H.* 5 December 1935.

Melbourne rarely shipped more than 40%, often only one-third, of the total tonnage of oversea cargo. The diffusion of the oversea trade and the servicing of a large number of under-utilised ports was a complaint frequently made by the oversea shipowner in explanation and part justification of freight levels. He complained not only of the operating expenditure involved in making a series of port calls, he resented the duplication of port taxation which followed.

(*b*) PORT TAXES

Complaint concerning port taxes levied by Australian harbour authorities was never completely absent between 1920 and 1939; it was most conspicuous in the 1920s. *The Times* included a number of references to Australian port taxes, especially during 1923 when comparable charges in British ports were being lowered from their war-time peaks towards pre-war levels. The Sydney Harbour Trust commissioners in their report for the year ended the 30 June 1923 revealed an unusual sensitivity to criticism in London and in Australia 'regarding the alleged excessive port charges levied in Australia'. They pointed out that increased port taxes in Sydney derived not from war causes but from the higher cost of servicing the harbour's capital debt. They also claimed that port taxes in Sydney were lower than elsewhere in Australia. In the following year the question was discussed at the Fourth Conference of Australian Interstate Harbour Authorities. It was resolved: 'after giving full consideration to the correspondence between the Prime Minister and the State Governments, and the requests to this conference from the Sydney and Melbourne Chamber of Commerce in respect to port charges...' that no reductions are possible. The question was aired also at the Imperial Economic Conference in 1923 and again at the 1929 Oversea Shipping Conference. Apart from minor variations, the level of port taxes remained unchanged throughout the period. Harbour revenues, however, tended to rise as the tonnage of shipping increased. Shipowners' complaints persisted.

Their complaint was based partly on fact, partly on incorrect assumption. As we shall show, they were correct in asserting that the various harbour authorities in Australia failed to adhere rigorously to the non-profit principle of port administration. They were correct also in two further assertions: that the major Australian ports showed large operating surpluses and that these were used not only to offset operating losses on minor ports but also for other state expenditure. But the oversea shipowners also assumed that they inevitably contributed the bulk of port taxes and on these grounds justified decisions to increase rates of freight. In fact, as we shall show, they were not the major contributors of port taxes and it is far from easy to establish the effect of port taxes on individual freight rates.

In Australia during the inter-war years the Commonwealth government controlled ocean lights while the states retained control of harbours including pilotage and the like. State control facilitated the pursuit of ends judged socially desirable even at heavy cost. One objective, as we have seen, was to provide a large number of small ports. On the grounds of the costs involved, many observers considered this aim to have been overemphasised. Many of the ports were suitable only for the smallest of coasting vessels and were costly to maintain. The tiny N.S.W. port of Nambucca, for example, handled only a few tons of cargo each year. It was a particularly costly port to maintain. By the later 1930s revenue per ton of all cargo handled amounted to less than 1 % of expenditure per ton of cargo. But the principle adopted in N.S.W. and elsewhere in Australia was to subsidise the uneconomic ports from the revenue of major ports. The principle was extended, moreover, to use revenue from the major ports to meet expenditure in no way connected with ports.

Oversea shipowners protested against the use of major port revenue to maintain the smaller ports and even more bitterly against the use of ports as state revenue raisers. They invoked the well-established and widely accepted principle that port revenues should be adequate only to cover operating costs, interest charges, and an allocation to reserves but not to earn profit. The principle was publicly adopted in Australia at the 1923 Conference of Commonwealth Government and State Premiers. It was enunciated by Prime Minister Bruce at the 1923 Imperial Economic Conference in London. All the states, he said, 'have subscribed to the proposition that revenue should not be derived from this particular source [*sc.* port charges], and the charges in our ports should be limited to the pure costs of providing the services which are required by shipping entering into our different harbours'.[1] Five years later the British Economic Mission referred in its report to the complaints it had received about port charges: 'that in many cases the sums levied are in excess of the amounts necessary to provide the services, the balance being used as Commonwealth or State revenue'.[2] Comparable comment is contained in the report made around the same time by the Commonwealth Committee on the Co-ordination of Transport in Australia.[3]

Some ambiguity in interpretation existed, however. It is not clear if the non-profit principle applied to the aggregate experience of *all* port administrations in Australia, or of individual states, or of the major ports only. If it were intended for all administrations then a rough equivalence was in fact achieved. If state administrations were regarded separately, N.S.W. repeatedly showed a heavy loss. Other states showed a surplus, paid into consolidated state revenue. But if, as oversea shipowners clearly intended, the revenue of major ports should be used only to meet expenditure incurred at major ports, the non-profit principle was never pursued during the inter-war years. The years 1924 to 1928 were singled out for examination at the 1929 Overseas Shipping Conference. The details published show that during these four years a surplus of almost £4 million had arisen from major port operations. During the 1920s as a whole the contribution made by major ports to state revenue was considerable. Melbourne alone contributed £1·2 million to Victoria, Sydney about the same to N.S.W. The N.S.W. public-works department undertook in return certain port repairs; their value fell far short of the payments made by the port to consolidated state revenue.

Although condemned at the 1929 Overseas Shipping Conference little change took place in the 1930s. In Sydney the finances of the trust were separated from state revenue and a reserve fund created for the surplus. After deficits in the first few years of the depression the fund grew steadily to almost

[1] *U.K.P.P.* Cmd. 2009, p. 315. See also *The Economist* 11 August 1923.
[2] *C.P.P.* 1929, II, 1,258. [3] *C.P.P.* 1929/31, III, 339–46.

£1 million by 1939. Elsewhere the practices of the 1920s continued. By 1938 Melbourne's payments to the state treasury totalled £4·1 million; harbour loans at that time were rather less at £3·2 million. Fremantle Harbour Trust also continued to make payments to state revenue. Only in N.S.W. were the finances of the main port separated from those of the state, in line with the recommendations of the Commonwealth Committee on the Co-ordination of Transport in Australia. Another recommendation of this committee, that certain minor ports should be closed and oversea trade concentrated at the larger ports, was ignored. In 1938/9, for example, the excess of operating expenditure over revenue in the minor ports of N.S.W. amounted to about £140,000 on a combined revenue of less than £50,000.

Throughout the inter-war years, taxes levied at the major ports continued to exceed expenditure. To what extent is it justified to regard the excess revenue collected as a burden to the shipping industry and passed on to shippers in higher rates of freight? Oversea shipowners in fact contributed rather less to port taxes than they appear to have imagined or apparently were prepared to admit. Port taxes were of two kinds: dues levied on ships and dues levied on cargo, the latter being paid not by the shipowner but by the shipper. Taxes levied on ships included Commonwealth light dues and charges made by state harbour authorities for pilotage, and in respect of navigation and wharf facilities. The bulk of the taxes collected by each state derived not from ship dues but from the cargo rate. This was not uniformly applied. In all states some differentiation in the cargo rate was to be found favouring exports at the expense of imports. In Victoria no cargo rate was levied on exports; in Western Australia exports of local origin were exempt. Whatever its application it was paid by the shipper, however, not by the shipowner. It dominated port tax collections. In Melbourne, for example, cargo rates represented about 70 % and dues on shipping only 20 % of total port tax collected. It is nevertheless valid to suggest that cargo dues would have produced a higher total had the rate on imports been applied equally to exports. A reduction of ship dues would thus have been possible.

The impact of port taxes paid by shipowners upon rates of freight is difficult to evaluate, partly because each state levied tax, not all ships visited every state; partly also because rates of freight varied according to commodity. For individual voyages it is not difficult to calculate the total tax paid and its relationship to freights charged. Details of aggregate experience are more difficult to manipulate. Two estimates are available, one relating to a single port, the other to a single year. The first relates to Sydney in 1923 when the trust commissioners were especially sensitive to criticism. They claimed that port and tonnage dues levied in Sydney on oversea shipping represented no more than 1*s*. per ton of oversea cargo shipped and discharged. It is not difficult to agree when they continue: 'it is not easy to see how any possible reduction in the charge made by the trust could appreciably assist in lowering the present high freights between Great Britain and Australia'. This, however, is to look at one set of port taxes in isolation; we know that many oversea vessels in fact paid port taxes in each state. The second estimate relates to the year 1928. Calculations made of taxes levied in the ports of Sydney, Melbourne, Adelaide and Fremantle in this year together with Commonwealth light dues and pilotage suggest that the total represented about 2*s*. per ton of oversea cargo shipped and discharged. The Buchanan report also calculates port taxes levied on a vessel of about 6,000 net tons which loaded at the five mainland capital ports staying 72 hours in each; the total port tax similarly represented 2*s*. per ton on cargo. Could the taxes have been reduced? Did they affect rates of freight? It is possible to argue that some of the compulsory pilotage was no longer essential. During the Seamen's Union Strike in 1925 oversea shipping docked without pilot assistance. It is also possible to argue that other dues were pitched high. But how high was debatable. No one advocated the total abolition of port taxes. An equitable level was assumed to lie somewhere between zero charge and the charge actually made. If we make the quite arbitrary assumption, for purposes of illustration only, that it was possible to halve port taxes, the total saving per ton of oversea cargo would have been 1*s*. If allowance is then made for the varying rates of freight charged, a saving of 1*s*. per ton in port tax if passed intact to the shipper would have produced a freight rate reduction ranging between ½ % and 5 %, depending upon the item carried. Although freight rates declined in the 1930s, the maximum rate reduction derived from tax savings of this magnitude would have remained relatively small for most items. In total, however, the sum was large and involved a payment overseas.

If, moreover, it can be shown that Australian port taxes were indeed higher than elsewhere in the world it lends additional point to the shipowners' complaint. In 1931 the Sydney Harbour Trust commissioners attempted some comparison of port taxes in Sydney and Melbourne with those in Wellington (New Zealand), London and Liverpool. In the later 1930s the official Commonwealth *Year Book* also published detail for the same two Australian and two British ports in order to refute 'the ill-informed criticism of the port charges levied upon shipping in Australian ports'. The figures cited show that charges in the British ports mentioned were twice to three times as high as those in Sydney or Melbourne (or in Wellington). Oversea vessels, however, as we have already shown, normally visited not one, but a number of Australian ports, paying port taxes in each state. The sum of port taxes inevitably tended to be much higher than taxes in a single British port. It is, of course, equally true that British vessels, cargo liners especially, discharged cargo at more than a single British port. A feature of the inter-war years discussed in the previous chapter was in fact the diffusion of oversea trade among British ports other than London. But the appropriate comparison to make is with the port taxes charged in countries competing with Australia in European markets. Where ships loaded at a single port, rather than many, and where port taxes were significantly below those in Australia an immediate marketing advantage was thus obtained. Details are difficult to obtain, however, because of the wide variety in methods of tax application. The Buchanan report includes a reference to port taxes in comparing tramps loaded at Portland (Victoria) with others loaded in two Indian and three North American ports in the early 1920s:

Port tax per ton of wheat loaded at					
Portland (Victoria)	New York	New Orleans	Montreal	Karachi	Bombay
8*d.*	1*s.* 1*d.*	1*s.* 1*d.*	11*d.*	8*d.*	4*d.*

Only Bombay proves to have been less expensive than Portland (which never balanced its expenditure and revenue). Portland on the other hand was considerably less costly in port tax than the North American ports. But a tramp which loaded a similar total quantity of wheat at *two* Australian ports found itself required to meet port taxes equal to almost 2*s*. per ton of cargo loaded. It seems unmistakably clear that repeated port calls undoubtedly inflated this element in voyage overheads. The aggregate effect passed on in higher freight rates inevitably affected the economy.

Australians were slow, or unwilling, to concede the accuracy of the shipowners' view. If the economy of the country required a multiplicity of port calls it is shortsighted not to have devised a more appropriate form of port taxation. In 1933 the *Annual Report* of the Sydney Harbour Trust explicitly, and for the first time, acknowledged the cost effect upon shipping of repeated port calls in Australia. The relevant passage is worth quoting extensively:

> the difficulty which confronts oversea shipowners...in Australia... is the number of ports at which it is necessary for their vessels to call, and, while investigation by different authorities has shown that the charges at the individual ports are not unduly high for the services rendered to shipping, it is admitted that when the charges payable at four or more ports for similar and unavoidable services such as pilotage, towage, etc.; are totalled the aggregate is a very high figure.

The report, despite this, goes on to divert attention by suggesting that Suez Canal charges 'constitute a much more serious hindrance to oversea shipping visiting Australia than do the charges levied at the ports in the Commonwealth'.

(*c*) CARGO HANDLING, LOADING CHARGES AND PORT TURN-ROUND

The importance of quick turn-round needs little elaboration. It affects both the shipowner and the economy involved in ocean trade, if with differing degrees of immediacy. The numerous official and semi-official investigations which have been made into turn-round have their origin generally in the crises from time to time reached in port congestion. In Britain, in the years immediately after the Second World War, the rapid revival of trade in the bomb-damaged ports led to congestion, the delay of exports, and to the setting up of a working party of investigation. In January 1950 the Sydney Chamber of Commerce published the report of their 'Enquiry into the slow turn-round of ships in the port of Sydney'. A year and a half later similar considerations of export delays persuaded the prime minister to institute an enquiry into the 'Turn-round of ships in Australian ports'.

To the shipowners, vessel turn-round is an ever present theme of interest. Time spent in port represents lost earnings. Each unnecessary day in port adds to the possibility of a voyage resulting in loss rather than profit. But the shipowner is also concerned with the costs he incurs in cargo loading and discharge. It may well be true, as Australian coastal shipping companies have sometimes complained, that the oversea shipowner is less willing to resist rising Australian stevedore charges because they represent only a relatively small proportion, not the whole, of his port cargo charges. The oversea shipowner nevertheless cannot completely disregard them. He is interested in speed, and also in the cost of cargo shipping and discharge. He is thus preoccupied simultaneously with a number of related factors: the efficiency of cargo-handling equipment, the price and organisation of waterside labour, and also the avoidable time spent in port. The last factor tends to dominate official enquiries. It includes not only the more obvious features, time spent waiting for a pilot, or in waiting for a berth and so on; it also involves cargo flow. Failure to ensure availability of export cargoes at the ship side, or the rapid removal from the quay of discharged cargo adds unnecessary delay. Inland transport facilities often prove a major constraint. A record harvest in N.S.W. and the simultaneous arrival of additional ships all clamouring for cargo threw a strain on the railways. Insufficient rolling stock to deal with the abnormal demand inevitably meant delay to the shipping in Sydney. In August 1928 reported wheat prospects created some uneasiness in Australia. The *Daily Commercial News and Shipping List* voiced a number of doubts. What chance had the

State Railway departments: 'of coping with the mammoth rush that all the indications suggest is about to crash down upon us?' In the previous season Australia did not have an outstanding harvest: 'nevertheless, steamers were kept waiting in Australian ports for periods ranging from six to seven weeks because they had not the rolling stock to cope with the rush of grain and give our wheat growers the advantage of early delivery on board'.[1]

Evidence supplied to the 1929 Overseas Shipping Conference shows that cargo-handling charges formed a higher proportion of port expenses than port taxation. The detail also suggests that the proportion of operating expenses represented by cargo handling charges was tending to rise in the later 1920s. In the following pages vessel turn-round is examined under the twin headings of innovation in cargo handling appliances and the role of waterfront labour. A concluding section attempts to determine the speed and cost of port turn-round and to compare Australian cargo charges with ports elsewhere in the world.

The modern port with its various mechanical aids for cargo handling is a development of the years since 1945. During the inter-war years human labour did most of the work nowadays performed or assisted mechanically. Nevertheless, even by the contemporary standards of the time, Australian ports were relatively ill-equipped in the two appliances most commonly found: wharf lifting gear and bulk-loading equipment. It mirrors in part the under-utilisation of individual Australian ports during these years and the unwillingness of harbour administrations to incur expense. The supply of wharf cranes for the handling of oversea cargo in marked contrast with Britain and elsewhere in Europe was not, except at Fremantle, normally undertaken by Australian harbour authorities. In the two busiest ports, Melbourne and Sydney, cranes were rarely to be found. In 1920 along Melbourne's 11 miles of quays and wharves occupying an area of about 70 acres only 10 wharf cranes were to be found. At the end of the period, when the port was handling more than 6 million tons of cargo, its quays had only 15 cranes. The absence of such aids forcibly struck the oversea

[1] Quoted *Fairplay* vol. 109, pp. 217–18.

observer. The Buchanan report commenting on Sydney notes that 'as a port it does not conform to modern standards, and the wharf equipment leaves much to be desired'. The harbour commissioners in their annual statement for 1928 defended the port. Wharf cranes are not essential in Sydney, they argued, because the port is a terminal. Ships spend a long time in the port and are well equipped with their own lifting gear to handle cargo. In further justification they claimed that the cranes supplied some years previously had been little used. It is ironic that their *Annual Report* three years earlier had included observations made by the trust's chief engineer following his tour of ports overseas. Among his recommendations was one urging that more wharf cranes should be provided by the trust at Sydney.

As a rule, therefore, ships relied on their own deck gear for loading and discharge. In the minor ports of the world, even today, ships' gear is often used for this purpose. It is surprising that it continued to be necessary in most major Australian ports down to 1939. Shipowners prefer to use shore gear and ship gear together or separately as need arises to speed economic despatch. U.K. shipowners complained at the time of the 1929 Overseas Shipping Conference that most Australian ports were defective in this respect. But they also admitted that they were reluctant to press for wharf cranes lest, at high cost, they be compelled to use them at all times regardless of loading considerations. Even today the bulk of the general cargo handled at Sydney is dealt with by ship loading gear.

The second contemporary wharf appliance of interest is bulk storage and loading equipment for grain. Here also Australian ports fell behind. In part their failure to introduce bulk handling extensively, unlike the North American grain terminals, reflects the smaller volume of grain consigned through individual Australian ports. As noted above, in contrast with the marked concentration of the North American grain trade wheat exports from Australia were spread more thinly through a greater number of ports. About one-third of wheat exports were shipped in Western Australia, a third in South Australia, and the remaining third from Victoria and N.S.W. jointly. Sydney, the largest single wheat-exporting centre, shipped on average about a half million tons of grain a year during the later 1930s. The eastern grain elevators in Canada shipped 4 million tons or more and handled in all a total approaching 5 millions in a year.

Only at Sydney had consideration been given to the provision of bulk wheat-loading facilities before our period opens.[1] At no other wheat-exporting centres before the First World War had the quantity exported justified the installation of this important aid to vessel despatch. War-time shipping scarcity and inability to dispose readily of export surpluses, among other expedients, witnessed the setting up of a Commonwealth wheat-marketing system. The persistence of carry-over led to the offer of federal advances to states to assist in the construction of wheat-storage centres. Unlike North America, the possibility of frost damage to grain is negligible in Australia. Storage facilities prior to 1914 had been relatively rare. But only in N.S.W. was any serious attempt made during the war to establish rural storage centres. It was accompanied by the development of a bulk-wheat terminal at Sydney. Work on the elaborate port loading appliance based upon concrete silos was not complete until the 1920/1 wheat season.

The switch to bulk loading was accomplished only gradually. In 1923/4 only 20 % of the wheat exported was shipped in bulk. The initial teething troubles would seem to have made bulk loading somewhat more costly than the shipment of bagged wheat.[2] But once under way the change gathered momentum. The introduction of appropriate railway wagons for the land haul and the growing popularity among shipowners of the Glebe Island wheat terminal encouraged both the use of bulk loading and the expansion of storage facilities. By the later thirties bulk storage capacity amounted to about 7 million bushels. (Licensed grain storage capacity in Canada at the St Lawrence and Maritime ports at this time amounted to about 30 millions.) Bulk loading became more common in the later 1920s and especially during the 1930s. By 1932/3 two-thirds of the wheat exported was in bulk, thereafter the proportion frequently exceeded 80 % and even 90 % in three of the years. By the later 1930s about one-half or a little more of the total N.S.W.

[1] Information has been drawn from the *Annual Reports* of the harbour authorities and from the 'Second Report of the Royal Commission on the Wheat, Flour and Bread Industries', *C.P.P.* 1934/7, IV, 17 ff.

[2] See *Fairplay* vol. 79, p. 960.

wheat crop was regularly handled at the elevators. The concentration of all Sydney's wheat shipment at Glebe Island was complete by 1937. The wheat terminal had been designed with vessel turn-round requirements in mind. The facilities provided made it unnecessary to move a vessel once docked. General cargo could be discharged, bulk wheat shipped, and bag wheat loaded for the 'topping up' of cargo from the same point. A bulk-loading rate of 1,400 tons per *hour* was achieved by 1930. Ironically, wheat charters were still specifying a minimum bulk-loading rate of 1,000 tons per *day*. Loading times for bagged wheat were much longer. In the later 1930s a record for loading bagged wheat was established at a mere 340 tons an hour. Given cargoes of up to 9,000 tons the time saved clearly was considerable. It was an aid to turn-round for which the shipowner was prepared to pay. During the mid-1930s the homeward freight rate on bulk loaded wheat from Sydney was 2*s*. 6*d*. to 3*s*. per ton less than bagged wheat, a saving of almost 10 % on current rates.

Elsewhere in Australia advances in wheat-loading techniques were slower to be introduced and were less impressive. In Melbourne and Adelaide 'bulk' wheat loading took a primitive form. It involved slinging wheat in bags, emptying the contents into the hold, and returning the empty bags to the quayside. It offered a very small time advantage over ordinary bag loading but, more important, facilitated subsequent discharge. It represented a saving for the shippers' internal costs in bags and also secured a lower rate of freight. In Fremantle a similar form of bulk loading was introduced in 1928. In 1931/2 it was replaced by something approaching the more customary method of bulk loading. It revived the abortive attempt made at the end of the war to introduce such loading appliances.[1] In 1931 Westralian Farmers Ltd, a producers' cooperative assumed financial responsibility for the erection of bulk wheat-loading facilities at Fremantle. Although generally it was the policy of the Fremantle harbour authority to own and to work all port equipment, the trust was unwilling to bear the expense involved in bulk wheat equipment. It permitted an outside body to assume control. Co-operative Bulk Handling Ltd, set up in 1933 by the

[1] For details see *U.K. Trade Report*, 1921, p. 35.

Westralian Farmers provided the equipment with the aid of a loan floated in London.[1]

In contrast with the Sydney wheat terminal, the concrete child of the harbour commissioners and the N.S.W. department of agriculture, the Fremantle terminal was a cheaper, much less elaborate timber and roofing iron building. It was not only less costly to install, it was also portable. It had a much less impressive rate of loading. The disappointing loading capacity was commented upon in the trust's *Annual Report* for 1934: 'this system, in our opinion, at best can only be regarded as a bag eliminating method of handling wheat from trucks direct abroad [sic., presumably aboard] ship and in no way comparable at the shipping end with the orthodox method of bulk handling with its terminal, storage and rapid ship loading facilities...'. In the meantime the question of bulk wheat storage and orthodox bulk loading facilities at Fremantle was under consideration by the Commonwealth royal commission on the wheat industry and by a Western Australia royal commission. The latter recommended the building of concrete silos with a capacity of 30–40,000 tons. War reached Fremantle before the new concrete silos. Compared with Sydney, loading at Fremantle was painfully slow. The bulk loading total at Fremantle for 24 hours was about the same as could be achieved in a single hour at Sydney. Nevertheless, it probably halved the loading time for bagged wheat and between 1931/2 and 1938/9 the proportion of wheat loaded in bags at Fremantle steadily declined. At the end of the period about 90 % was loaded by bulk conveyor.

The coming of war speeded up wheat despatch in Australia. Silos were built in Victoria and only in the south did bagged shipment persist. In the country as a whole by 1941/2 about one-half of all wheat exported was being shipped by bulk loading equipment; by 1949/50 about 80 % was consigned in bulk. The post-war introduction of mechanical trimming further increased the rate of loading.[2]

[1] J. Sandford, *Walter Harper and the Farmers* (Perth, 1955) chapter 7. The Westralian Farmers Co-operative Ltd, whose role in the shipping scene is mentioned in chapter 6 below, was the central organisation and promoter of co-operation in Western Australia.

[2] Australian Stevedoring Industry Board, *First Report*, 1950, pp. 33, 64–5. Sandford, *op. cit.* p. 164 ff.

The introduction of wheat bulk loading in Australia in the early 1920s was accompanied by a decision on the part of the shipping industry to alter existing wheat charter-party arrangements. The revision secured for the shipowner a reduction in cargo-loading charges; a brief review of events and consequences is therefore merited. Changed loading methods was one of a number of contributory factors. Another was the post-war decline in freight rates without any relaxation of the conditions, often onerous to the shipowner, normally written into Australian wheat charter-parties. There was in addition the aim of the U.K. Chamber of Shipping to introduce standard forms for charters in the bulk trades of the world. Lending urgency to the need for institutional revision was the enactment in Australia in 1924 of the 'Carriage of Goods by Sea Act'. This, together with the earlier Navigation Act, dispelled uncertainty regarding liability for damage to cargo. It manifested in Australia developments comparable with those taking place in Britain at the time. It also gave to Australian shippers for the first time the right to sue oversea shipowners in Australian courts. Wheat charter-parties normally in use in immediate post-war years often stipulated conditions and routes not always the most economical to the shipowner.[1] They were not standard except in vesting control of stevedoring in the charterer, not the owner. It is the wresting away of stevedore control by the shipowner and the economy thereby achieved which forms the theme of the present brief reference.

Stevedore control by the charterer was not peculiar to Australia at this time. In origin no doubt it stemmed from administrative convenience. It had outlived whatever usefulness it once may have had. By the beginning of our period it merely perpetuated a practice by which the shipowner was required to pay for an essential service a sum greater than that actually received by the operator giving the service. To the charterer the practice represented a source of profit. A rate per ton for cargo handling was agreed between shipowner and charterer. The charterer then contracted with a stevedoring company to perform the work at a lower rate. The difference between the two, retained by the charterer, may be seen variously as a bribe, rebate, discount or

[1] For some illustrations see *Fairplay*, vol. 79, pp. 960–1.

commission, depending upon the extent of the jaundice in the eye of the observer. A letter from a London correspondent published in *Fairplay* in 1925 alleged that the 'rebate' obtained by charterers in Australia amounted to 4*d*. or 5*d*. per ton on bulk wheat and 5*d*. to 7*d*. on bagged wheat. With the current loading rate of 1*s*. 1½*d*. for bulk and 2*s*. 0½*d*. for bagged wheat the sum involved in rebate amounted to between one-fifth and one-third. In 1925 a representative of an Australian shipping company estimated that the additional cost paid by the shipowner for stevedoring in these circumstances amounted to £150 to £200 per vessel. This is an arbitrary estimate but on a 5,000 ton vessel probably equalled between one-fifth and one-quarter of stevedoring charges.[1]

The alteration of the charter-party to transfer control of stevedores to shipowners was not accomplished without resistance from Australian merchants. It required the support of the British shipping industry as a whole by way of 'club' indemnity, and involved the Chamber of Shipping of the U.K. in protracted negotiations. An important function of the Chamber of Shipping is the work of its documentary committee in the preparation and oversight of standard charter forms. The importance of the charter-party needs no elaboration. The document forms the basis of any legal investigation arising from disputes over failure to perform contract. The adoption of standard forms reduces the incidence of such disputes.

The first reference to the introduction of a standard charter form for the Australian wheat trade is in the annual report of the Chamber of Shipping in 1921/2. But not until the end of 1926 was the 'Austral' form finally adopted. It was, ultimately, introduced unilaterally by the shipping industry in the face of unyielding opposition by the principal charterers in Australia, the Australian Grain Shippers Association. Their resistance concerned the appointment of the shipowner's agent and the appointment of the shipowners' stevedores over which they wished to retain control. The Chamber issued a press release outlining the failure of the two sides to reach agreement.[2]

[1] *Fairplay* vol. 96, pp. 412–13.

[2] *Fairplay* vol. 101, pp. 222–3, 444; *S.M.H.* 4 December 1926; see also C of S *Annual Report* 1926/7, pp. 72–3. *The Times* 22, 28 January 1927.

The adoption of the form was made obligatory for all British shipowners who wished to retain the advantages of 'club' protection. At the first, when the Australian merchants declined to accept the 'Austral' form, a compensation scheme was introduced by the Chamber of Shipping to defray loss from delayed loading. Before long resistance disappeared; the form was accepted by early 1927. It did not eliminate conflict, however, it merely shifted the site of dispute. New problems arose over cost apportionment of loading operations. Ambiguity existed in the interpretation of the form and in its connection with 'the custom' of individual ports. A dispute arose over the precise point at which the shipowner became financially responsible for loading. To the onlooker it seemed 'very much as if merchants are raising this question of enhanced loading costs to owners as a *quid pro quo* for any advantages secured to shipowners under the new Austral form of charter'. A comparison of loading charges borne by the owner of a ship before and immediately after the adoption of the 'Austral' form showed that for virtually identical work the charges had risen by 60 %.[1] After prolonged negotiations agreement was reached between the Chamber of Shipping documentary committee and the Australian Grain Shippers Association in July 1928. The form was fully accepted, responsibility for loading charges established and all extra costs paid by shipowners during the 1927 wheat season were refunded by the charterers.[2] The resolution of the issue in favour of the oversea shipowner was an advantage when freights remained below the high levels of 1920 and 1921. It thus also benefited the Australian primary producer. The true losers, unless they were able to devise alternative sources of income, or could absorb the lost revenue in greater efficiency, were the Australian grain merchants. It is possible also to indicate a further repercussion which flowed from the elimination of the intermediary between oversea shipowner and stevedore company. The preponderance of the oversea shipowners on the stevedoring scene was doubtless always important. It is possible, however, that the influence exerted by the oversea shipowner was increased when direct contact between the two groups was established. It was said of the oversea shipowner in the later 1920s and early 1930s that his

[1] *Fairplay* vol. 103, p. 615.

[2] *Ibid.* vol. 108, p. 196.

preoccupation with the speed of vessel turn-round made him, and the stevedoring company he hired, less resistant to the growing demands of dock labour.

Throughout the inter-war years, cargo handling remained an area dominated by the stevedoring industry, as indeed it does today. In Australia, as elsewhere, it is an industry characterised by industrial unrest and frequent strikes. Strained industrial relations have their origins in the essentially casual nature of waterfront employment. In the past especially, perhaps less so today, the arrival date of shipping and the extent of possible labour requirements has always been a matter of some uncertainty. As a consequence, therefore, labour hirings have been on a casual basis for specific work undertakings or specific periods of time. It is an industry with a high labour turnover. In times of general unemployment labour drifts into and out of stevedoring. A full week's pay in such circumstances is rare. In Britain between the wars the average for workers regularly following dock work was about a half week's work. Only in very recent years have decasualisation schemes become more usual. The major feature of such schemes is the elimination of surplus labour on offer and the payment of attendance money where work is not available.

The Australian stevedoring industry, noted Mr Justice Foster in 1946, has 'a long record of turbulence and struggle stretching back to pre-arbitration court days, a story of evil conditions, low wages, of unsatisfactory relationships, of bitterness and unrest'. The history of the industry has yet to be written. It is unfortunate that the sources most readily available are not always satisfactory for the limited purposes of the present survey.[1] It is, for example, difficult to obtain indicators of employment and, even more difficult, measures of output over time, the chief interest of the oversea shipowners seeking quick despatch. Here

[1] The main sources, apart from inumerable newspaper references in the *S.M.H.* and, to a lesser extent, in *The Times*, are: K. F. Walker, *Industrial Relations in Australia* (Harvard, 1956); M. Perlman, *Judges in Industry* (Melbourne, 1954); Australia, *Commonwealth Arbitration Reports*, vol. 26, pp. 866–955. (Mr Justice Beeby's award on wages, etc. of waterside workers.) I have to acknowledge also the granting of access by the Commonwealth Department of Shipping and Transport to an unpublished official report: 'Conditions on the waterfront at the principal ports of the Commonwealth 1939' (C of A *Archives Office* B.P. 107/3).

we are concerned only with those features of the Australian waterfront which affected the oversea shipowner. Examination of the stevedoring industry is restricted to estimating the numbers employed and the losses resulting from strikes.

Between the wars stevedoring in Australia was everywhere in the hands of private contractors except at Fremantle where wharf (but not ship) labour was controlled by the harbour authority.[1] In general terms the development of the Australian shipping industry during our period is made up of two contrasting phases. The first, marked by excessively strained relations, lasted until 1928. It witnessed declining productivity, constant militancy and rising costs for the oversea shipowner. The second phase, the 1930s, the power of the main union broken, witnessed a reversal of this trend. The number of persons seeking dock employment fell sharply at the end of the 1920s and throughout the 1930s ran at a much lower level, militancy was reduced, and output tended to rise. To a large extent the new situation followed from the Transport Workers Act of 1928. Of the Act it was said in 1939 in the official report on conditions on the Australian waterfront that:

> it cannot be disputed that the Transport Workers Act had many beneficial results. Following its introduction there has been a period of ten years of work on the waterfront free from industrial troubles. During that time there has been continuity of essential transport service, marked acceleration in the loading and unloading of cargo ...and the adoption of constitutional methods for the settlement of disputes.[2]

The wharf labourer on the other hand may have agreed more readily with the more recent view that: 'generally the Australian waterfronts during the 1930s were dismal work places... steady employment was hard to obtain, and labour conditions were degrading'.[3]

The casual nature of wharf employment makes it difficult to

[1] The only known oversea shipping company with an interest in the Australian stevedoring industry is the Orient Line. In 1931 the company bought a third share in the Brisbane Stevedoring & Wool Co.

[2] C of A *Archives Office* B.P. 107/3, p. 25.

[3] Perlman, *op. cit.* p. 137. See also Australian Stevedoring Industry Board, *First Report*, for comments on the 1930s, pp. 15–19.

estimate the number actually employed. For the 1930s, but not for the 1920s, some indication of the number seeking employment in the industry is available in the 1939 report on conditions on the waterfront. For a single year, 1938, the report is also important in outlining the average daily number actually employed in certain ports. The investigation undertaken in early 1939 stemmed from demands made by labour for the abolition of the Transport Workers Act. The origin of the Act lay in the repudiation by the Waterside Workers Federation (W.W.F.) of Mr Justice Beeby's arbitration award for the stevedoring industry in 1928. With the primary object of protecting volunteer workers but incidentally also to eliminate job control and sectional delays, the Act was passed in September 1928. It required the formal licensing of waterside workers, licences were issued annually thereafter (except for a short break) in the ports to which the Act applied. The significant exclusion is Sydney, where workers returned to work immediately, and hence were exempt, and Fremantle which gained exemption from the Act in December 1929. The information contained in Table 21 below is thus an incomplete guide to the total labour force on offer. At Sydney, dealing with about the same quantity of cargo as Melbourne, we may safely assume that a comparable amount of labour was available. The information suggests therefore that at the capital ports of the mainland during the 1930s the amount of stevedoring labour on offer ranged between 10,000 and 15,000 with a marked tendency for the number to fall during the 1930s.

'A licence is not a guarantee of work, however, and the amount of employment is not affected by the number of licences issued.'[1] The gap between the number of licences and employment is amply illustrated in details for 1937/8. Not surprisingly, the discrepancy is widest at the larger ports. The small, purely seasonal Queensland sugar ports, for example, employed a handful of wharf labourers only in the sugar season; they worked elsewhere during the remainder of the year. At the larger ports the flow of work varied from month to month and from day to day. In Melbourne in 1937/8 the monthly quantities of cargo handled in thousands of tons were:

[1] *C.P.D.* vol. 117, p. 248.

January	469	April	575	July	582	October	450
February	507	May	553	August	412	November	598
March	628	June	500	September	476	December	571

During the year the daily average number of waterside workers actually employed was 1,948. The maximum number picked up in any one day was 2,587 and the greatest number at work on any single day (in March) was 3,862. At this time the W.W.F. argued that the port needed about 3,500 registered workers, the rival union put the figure lower at 2,700 to 3,000 and the shipowners at only 3,000. The figure needed was clearly about 3,000. Yet in December 1938 there were no fewer than 5,730 licensed workers in the port, some 200 more than the number registered in 1950. At Brisbane where 3,460 licences were issued in 1937/8 the total number employed throughout the year was only 1,163 and of these 470 were employed only intermittently because of age, limited capacity or ill health. Port Adelaide in December 1938 had 1,228 licensed waterside workers and actually employed on average about 1,000. If we assume therefore that the active labour force at Sydney compared closely with Melbourne, and Fremantle closely with Brisbane, it would seem that in 1938 the five mainland capital ports together employed on average between 6,000 and 7,000 active workers. For Australia as a whole we would be justified in assuming, on the basis of a proportionate distribution of cargo, that in 1938 the active labour force totalled between 11,000 and 12,000. It also seems probable that the labour force in 1938 was somewhat lower than it had been in 1928. Today with wharf employment largely decasualised and with the total of cargo handled up from approximately 30 to 80 million tons of oversea and interstate cargo, the total labour force is 22,000.

Output in the industry as a whole was declining during the 1920s. Mr Justice Beeby in his award concluded that in Melbourne and Fremantle there had been a noticeable reduction in output during the 1920s and 'that in some smaller ports the labour return given for the wages paid is unfairly restricted'.[1] During the second decade of our period output in the industry rose. The elimination of union control and the diminution of competition (if the decline in licences issued is an accurate

[1] *Commonwealth Arbitration Report*, vol. 26, p. 883.

Table 21. *Number of licenses issued at ports at which the Transport Workers Act applied 1928/9–1938/9*

	Melbourne	Adelaide	Fremantle	Brisbane	Total all ports
1928/9	10,880	3,456	2,882	4,649	27,503
1929/30	8,267	3,014	1,924	2,596	18,757
Feb.–June 1931	5,889	2,233	—	2,654	12,878
1931/2	5,140	1,802	—	2,311	11,444
1932/3	4,528	1,632	—	1,917	10,079
Sept. 1933	3,562	1,478	—	1,513	8,360
1933/4	4,053	1,516	—	1,722	9,318
1934/5	3,960	1,402	—	3,134	10,836
1935/6	6,422	1,342	—	3,590	13,738
1936/7	5,293	1,278	—	2,873	11,745
1937/8	7,278	1,264	—	3,460	14,390
1938/9	5,772	1,244	—	3,854	13,215

Source: C of A *Archives Office* B.P. 107/3.

Table 22. *Industrial disputes involving coastal shipping and wharf labour, 1920–38*

	No. of disputes (1)	No. of work people involved: Directly (2)	Indirectly (3)	No. of working days lost (4)	Col. (4) as % of all working days lost by strike action in Australia
1920	56	369	NA	373,329	20
1921	29	822	NA	342,649	35
1922	28	1,047	384	74,031	8
1923	16	791	87	22,217	2
1924	15	1,762	471	29,727	3
1925	24	4,437	2,261	165,139	14
1926	24	1,630	479	31,607	2
1927	29	1,218	50	2,476	1
1928	36	9,324	7,042	361,992	48
1929	1	91	—	91	1
1930	3	1,582	—	16,035	1
1931	8	536	352	10,121	4
1932	3	85	—	860	1
1933			(Not stated)		
1934	5	163	6	2,002	1
1935	19	5,040	961	99,067	2
1936	2	25	—	37	1
1937	5	350	24	2,750	1
1938	4	328	1,542	59,068	4

Source: *Year Book.*

indicator) lessened the tendency prominent in the 1920s to share out thinly the available work. Strikes, and the time lost thereby, also decreased during the 1930s. In the first decade Australian industry as a whole lost on average annually about $1\frac{1}{2}$ million working days as compared with only one-third of that figure during the 1930s. The strike record of the waterfront and coastal shipping sector is shown in Table 22 above. They are grouped together in the records and reference to contemporary newspaper sources is necessary to disentangle them. In general, it is clear, these two groups of workers were more militant in the 1920s than in the following decade. The annual average of days lost in the first decade is 400,000 but only 20,000 in the second. Waterside strikes were endemic throughout the 1920s. In 1920 and 1921 the strikers were chiefly inter-state sea personnel, in 1922 and 1923 the Commonwealth Government Line was the main target. Stevedores imposed their overtime ban and strike in 1924 and embarked upon their mammoth, self-destroying strike against the Beeby award in 1928. It involved defiance of the Arbitration Court, of federal government, the police and culminated in ugly violence and even loss of life.[1]

The vexatious and costly delays produced by strikes became increasingly an irritant to oversea shipowners during the 1920s. Omitting from consideration the 1925 strike of British seamen in Australian ports, no fewer than 119 British vessels were delayed for a total of almost 1,000 days between 1924 and 1928. In 1928 itself 68 vessels were held up for a total of 600 days. The financial effect of a strike which delays shipping is difficult to cost with any exactness. The consequential revision of sailing schedules and loss of trade cannot be estimated. The direct and measurable costs arising from Australian waterside strikes in the 1920s were considerable. In terms of individual ships, charges in respect of depreciation and interest, crew wages and other operating costs amounted to about £250 per day for a vessel of about 8,000 gross tons.

Apart from strikes which involved oversea shipowners in additional expenditures, is it possible to show that port delays

[1] Outside our main argument is the strike of British seamen in 1925 whilst their vessels were in Australian ports. In October 1925 no fewer than 35 British ships with an aggregate gross tonnage of 315,000 were tied up in Australian ports. The strike dragged on for three months.

were greater or that loading charges were higher in Australia than elsewhere? There is no lack of evidence pointing to excessive delay. In 1925 when Australian ports were heavily congested, ships on arrival waited 20 or even 30 days for a loading berth. Three years later the chairman of Sir R. Ropner & Co. Ltd, a tramp line whose ships were frequent visitors to Australia said, in a pessimistic vein, that the Australian market will remain unpopular with owners until the fear of labour troubles has been allayed. No owner, he said, could calculate to within £600 or £700 what his expenses at loading ports will be.[1] Australian ports were sensitive to such criticism. In 1931 the secretary of the Western Australia Wheat Pool rejected complaints of delays. He claimed that during the current season 62 ships had been loaded and had spent an average time at Fremantle of only 11 days 20 hours each. But the evidence if voluminous is not easily analysed, partly because the ingredients included in cargo charges do not always lend themselves to easy analysis and because they are not always uniform. The Buchanan report, which cannot be accused of partiality, compares loading charges at Portland, Victoria, with those in three North American and in two Indian ports. Although the figures were modified in the light of protests from the Portland Chamber of Commerce they nevertheless show that stevedoring and dunnage charges per ton of wheat loaded were much higher in Portland.[2] They amounted to:

Portland	3*s.*	New Orleans	3*s.*
New York	2*s.*	Montreal	2*s.*
Karachi	7*d.*	Bombay	1*s.*

A less disinterested, but not necessarily a less accurate source of evidence is the Chamber of Shipping. Its *Annual Report* for 1928/9 states that port charges, stevedoring and commission on 6 British vessels loading in Australia in 1927 amounted to 27% of gross freights earned as compared with 16½% in South African and 9¼% in Indian ports.

Covering a wider range but not lending itself to such exact comparison is the information on operating experience in the

[1] *Fairplay* vol. 95, pp. 309–10; vol. 106, p. 158.
[2] *C.P.D.* 1926/8, v, 224; see also *Fairplay* vol. 112, pp. 648, 650.

later 1920s supplied by a number of British lines. In general terms the detail shows that average wheat-loading times varied as follows:

Sydney	550 tons per day	Portland (Oregon)	1,210 tons per day
South Australia	430 tons per day	Buenos Aires	440 tons per day
Fremantle	400 tons per day	Quebec	2,370 tons per day
Karachi	700 tons per day		

Individual port performances often outshone the averages. In Fremantle in 1932, for example, a record for bagged wheat was set up at 26·06 tons per gang/hour. The average for all West Australia ports at this time was 23 tons; four years earlier a rate of only 12·53 at Fremantle had been accepted as an average.[1]

Slower loading meant a longer stay in port. True loading charges therefore take into account not only stevedoring but also the cost of extra time including depreciation charges. A series of grouped tramp voyages analysed in this way show that loading time and loading costs per ton of wheat ranged from as little as 3*s*. 8*d*. in Karachi to 11*s*. 8*d*. in Australia, the next highest charge below the Australian being one-third lower. Although representative they were not typical for all ships visiting Australia throughout the 1920s, however. The lowest Australian charge compares not unfavourably with the highest non-Australian loading charge per ton. The lowest charges at Sydney in 1926 and 1927, for example, were not very different from those of Karachi. Illustrations and qualifications to show either tendency may be multiplied. It is difficult to reach any firm conclusion based upon quantitative analysis. In general, it seems fair to say, the cargo charges and cost of turn-round were in fact higher in an Australian port than in many other ports of the world during the 1920s. It is also fair to say that, generally speaking, the gap narrowed during the 1930s.

In part it may well have been that in his overwhelming desire to secure quick turn-round the oversea shipowner frustrated his own purpose. Given that the Australian sector represented only a proportion of his total port charges he may have preferred industrial peace at any price. It is not difficult to visualise situations wherein the shipowner preached the exercise of

[1] *Fairplay* vol. 122, p. 546.

moderation rather than resistance when local stevedoring companies experienced labour disputes. As Justice Beeby dryly noted: 'employers, for reasons which it is not necessary to traverse, although always protesting, acquired the habit of gradually yielding to the conditions imposed by the [waterside workers] federation'.[1]

[1] *Commonwealth Arbitration Report*, vol. 26, p. 874.

Chapter 6

SHIPPING CONFERENCE AND COMPETITION

Perhaps the most controversial feature of the shipping industry both past and present is the ring or conference organisation as trading associations of shipowners are usually called. The conference is the product of the economics of liner management and is the response made to competition. It is a type of trading association not normally found in the tramp sector of the industry where, on the whole, the free-play of market forces receives complete expression. Except during war-time, or during the 1930s when world-wide depression led to the introduction in Britain of tramp-shipping assistance and of some measure of control, tramp ships are hired in direct and open competition. The effects of competitive supply on tramp freight rates and on rate determination are considered in the following chapter. Liner traffic, in contrast, is usually organised into rings in order to eliminate competition. The essence of the liner trade is adherence to a fixed route and fixed timetable. Tramp ships have cargoes provided by the charterer. Liner companies assume the responsibility, and financial risk, of finding cargo and passengers for the voyages which they have programmed. Tramps are usually chartered by size to take full loadings of a single, high-bulk low-value commodity, usually, though not always, from a single port of loading to a single port of discharge. Liner cargoes are drawn from a heterogeneous range of items large and small, normally described as berth parcel cargo. There may be many ports of loading and many ports of discharge. The normal London to Sydney passenger liner voyage, for example, involves short calls at Fremantle and Adelaide and a two-day halt at Melbourne before the vessel completes its journey at Sydney. The maintenance of a programme requires a liner to sail full or empty at the scheduled time. Hence the greater the amount of cargo which can be attracted within the time available the greater the profit (or the smaller the loss).

Growth in the number of competing liner companies increases the likelihood of rate reductions in the scramble for cargo. The closing years of the nineteenth century witnessed the introduction on a number of shipping routes of rigidly time-tabled subsidised mail-carriers, subject to heavy penalties for failure to maintain schedules. At the same time, the spread of maritime nationalism leading to the growth of liner fleets tended to create conditions favourable to rigorous competition. Shipping conferences began to appear around this time.

In place of competition, liner companies agree to combine. Under penalties they adopt uniform rates for the carriage of passengers and cargo and in other ways endeavour to avoid the competition described above. The uniform-rate agreement is usually restricted to the berth parcel normally carried by liners. Generally speaking, it ignores tramp cargoes which liners from time to time may carry. When such cargo is carried by liners, the tendency mentioned above receives full expression. In order to fill space which otherwise would remain unoccupied, cargo can be attracted by a low rate of freight. A feature of the 1920s, described above, was the growing practice for liners to lift in berth parcel quantities at cut rates, commodities more commonly taken in bulk by tramp vessels. It was an aspect of competition not to the liking of tramp owners.

A conference is brought into existence on a specific trade route. A company operating on many trade routes may simultaneously belong to a number of self-contained rings. It is not unusual, moreover, to have different conferences, albeit with overlapping membership, covering the outward and return directions of a single route. Generally speaking, national boundaries are ignored; shipping conferences are international in composition. Friction between national groups within a conference, if it exists, rarely receives publicity. An example of alignment on a national basis is to be traced in the 1930s with the Japan–Australia conference when differences were widely publicised. They were, however, not only the product of national rivalry in shipping but also a derivative of the trade war concurrently being waged between Australia and Japan.[1]

[1] The trade negotiations are described in chapter 3, the repercussions on shipping are referred to below.

Public dislike and suspicion of monopolies have attracted considerable attention to shipping rings. Nations dependent upon oversea shipping, whether provided nationally or by expatriate owners, have at some time looked with misgivings at the conduct of shipping organisations. In Britain at the turn of the century a Commons select committee examining shipping subsidies also looked with an unfriendly eye at rings. The best known public investigation is the 1909 royal commission on Shipping Rings. The reports of the Dominions royal commission between 1912 and 1917 and the work of the Imperial Shipping Committee during the inter-war years have also testified to continuing interest in the monopoly aspect of a vital national industry. Where the shipping industry serving an economy is owned abroad, mistrust is usually keener and easier to manipulate for political advantage. It is sometimes true, often expedient, and always nationally self-reassuring to attribute marketing difficulties in the export sector to deficiencies in expatriate-owned shipping services. National self-consciousness often goes further, hence, in part, the current emphasis upon the indigenous ownership of an oversea fleet in underdeveloped nations. To list only three: The Black Star Line of Ghana, the Nigerian National Line, and Djakarta Lloyd of Indonesia all bear witness to the political importance attached to some measure of participation in oversea carrying and independence of the 'shipping combines'. Nor is hostility dead in the older, developed economies. Both in the U.S.A. and in Australia interest in the conference system is once more alive as is shown by the recent U.S.A. Congressional hearings on 'discriminatory ocean freights' and by the 1965 examination in Sydney of shipping companies' records.

The conference system is thus well known.[1] But there are a number of reasons which justify reference to it in the present work. State intervention in the conferences found in Australia's oversea services includes features, and was productive of results, not found elsewhere. Above all, as discussion in the following chapter shows, the homeward conference rates were determined in the full glare of publicity. In Australia, moreover, the state not only permitted monopoly conditions to survive, it also

[1] The standard work is D. Marx, *International Shipping Cartels* (Princeton, 1953).

allowed its own shipping line to join the conference. It went further. It amended its statutes in such a way that, whatever its motive, the monopoly was strengthened. The object of this chapter is to outline the main conferences; to focus upon the areas of dispute to which they gave rise; to discuss the institutional devices consequently introduced; and to assess the effects of the conference system on the quality and efficiency of the services and shipping provided. References in this chapter to freight rates omit discussion on rate determination, rate levels and rate stability; these aspects are considered in the following chapter. Freight rates are referred to here only in connection with disputes concerning, or intervention in, the conference organisation.

During the inter-war years three conferences controlled liner shipping on Australia's major oversea trade routes. In order of importance they are: the two conferences on the Europe-Australia route and one on the Japan–Australia route. A conference once controlled the India–Australia route but by the later 1930s foreign competition had disappeared and the trade was virtually monopolized by the British India Line. There was also a conference on the Pacific route to North America. It appears to have had no importance during the later 1920s and in the 1930s it was competition, not cooperation which lends colour and interest to this route; as we show in a subsequent section.

(*a*) THE JAPAN–AUSTRALIA CONFERENCE

The Japan–Australia conference provides an example of the system in its more sophisticated form. It attracted notice for only a few years in the 1930s. It merits brief discussion, first to round off our description of the system in Australia's oversea services. Secondly, we need to understand the arrangements of the conference in order to assess its effects on the shipping industry. And finally some reference to it is necessary because of its connection with the Japanese–Australian trade-treaty negotiations.

As we have outlined in chapter 1, a liner service between Australia, China and Japan was begun in 1872 by the British E and A Line. In the mid-1890s it was joined by ships of the

Japanese N.Y.K. which set up a monthly service. With the more rapid growth in trade between Australia and Japan which distinguishes the 1920s additional Japanese lines appeared. In the immediate post-war years the O.S.K. began a service and five years later was joined by the Japan–Australia line, a composite of three companies. Both secured an entry into the trade when, on the threat of a rate war, the E & A and N.Y.K. lines capitulated. The older and more customary method of conference organisation, rate uniformity, was augmented in 1935 by two freight-pooling agreements. In the northbound direction (the Australian wool trade with Japan), 50 % of freight receipts were pooled, in their subsequent division the E & A Line received 20 %. In the southward direction 60 % of freights were pooled, the E & A's share being 25 %.[1]

The conference captured the headlines of the Australian press when the Japanese lines declined to renew the pooling agreement on its expiry at the end of 1935. At this time there were 12 Japanese and 3 British ships in the conference. As well as being greater in number, the Japanese ships tended to be bigger, newer, and faster. On the face of it, it is not altogether surprising that the Japanese companies were reluctant to continue arrangements which must have seemed merely to subsidise a less efficient competitor. This is probably an oversimplification. The expansion of Japanese shipping activity between Japan and Australia in the 1930s was part of a wider expansionist movement which alarmed British shipping circles. The British press reported at length on each development of Japanese shipping in oversea sectors. The Chamber of Shipping and its committee assembled large files on Japanese shipping activity. In the Australian context there may also have been local factors not immediately connected with shipping. It is likely that the Japanese action stemmed from the growing awareness that the Australian government would not for very long delay the introduction of some tariff restrictions. In 1935 price cuts of Japanese goods imported into Australia increased Japan's share of the Australian market at the expense of Great Britain. The Japanese stand over shipping may well have been in anticipation of Australian trade restrictions. The subsequent negotia-

[1] I.S.C. *38th Report*, 'British Shipping in the Orient', p. 86.

tions about shipping affected, and were affected by, the policy of trade diversion adopted in Australia in May 1936. As discussed in chapter 3, this was a weapon aimed largely at Japan. Nations adopting unilateral trade restrictions seem, on the surface at least, somewhat myopic in not always appearing to anticipate retaliation.[1] One repercussion possibly not foreseen was in shipping. A reported slogan: 'Japanese ships for Japanese goods' although denied by the Director of Japan's Bureau of Shipping caused alarm in Australia. 'There is an uneasy feeling in Australian circles that, under present conditions, with the Japanese Government purchasing wool, there may be a move to insist upon the shipment of all wool purchased by Japan in Japanese vessels.'[2]

During the latter part of 1937 and the first half of 1938, discussions on the conference took place in Tokyo. The first Japanese offer would have reduced the E & A's share by about one-quarter; it was quickly rejected. The new freight pooling system finally agreed, retained the pooling proportions, namely 50 % of northbound and 60 % of southbound, but varied the divided percentage. Henceforth, instead of 20 % of the northbound pool and 25 % of the southbound pool, the E & A line was to receive 22½ % of each. Without annual details of cargo carried, or the amount of freight earned respectively by the E & A Line and its Japanese competitors, it is difficult to estimate accurately the justice of the proportions. If, as seems likely, the line contributed about 15 % of total tonnage, its share of the pool does not seem ungenerous.

(*b*) THE GENESIS OF THE CONFERENCES ON THE U.K.–AUSTRALIA ROUTE

Important in the short term in the mid 1930s, the Japan–Australia dispute never in importance rivalled the conferences on Australia's major trade route. Until very recently Australia's oversea trade has been overwhelmingly concentrated in the direction of Europe, initially almost exclusively to the U.K.

[1] It is unfortunate that the Australian official department concerned does not yet feel able to grant even restricted access to its files.

[2] *S.M.H.* 27 January, 17 February, 4 March, 1938.

Understandably the British shipping industry has always been primarily interested in the direct route between the U.K. and Australia. Understandable also is the appearance at an early date of a conference covering the U.K. to Australia route to be quickly followed by another for the reverse direction. They dominate the discussion on the conference system between the wars. From the Australian viewpoint also, these two conferences have always been the most important. It is appropriate, therefore, to concentrate attention upon them. In the pages which follow descriptive prefixes 'outward' and 'homeward' are used. In this context outward means outward *from* the U.K. to Australia, homeward means homeward *to* the U.K. from Australia.

A conference organisation first appeared in the U.K.–Australian trade as early as 1884, according to evidence given before the 1909 royal commission on Shipping Rings. It was an outward conference only. It was unusual for two reasons. First, it covered sailing vessels as well as steamers, the nearest parallel being a conference of sailing ships operating in association with steamship lines in Germany's South America trade.[1] Secondly, in its early days, it differed from other conferences in its composition and method of operation. It was not merely an association of shipowners, and it did not restrict itself merely to the adoption of uniform rates. It was far more complex as the following description of the Australian outward conference by Sir Thomas Sutherland before the royal commission on rings suggests. It was, he said:

> a combination of owners and brokers popularly known as 'Davis'. 'Davis', I believe was the name of the house or office wherein this combination, many years ago, commenced existence, in the days when the Australian trade was principally carried on by sailing ships. The various members of this Conference hold their interest in it by means of shares, which are supposed to be allotted in proportion to their importance in the trade. The agreement, under which the trade is worked, is definite until 1st March, 1911, and thereafter until terminated by two-thirds majority, but any single signatory may retire on giving two month's notice. This combination works, on the whole, for peace, and if there were none such, shipowners would be

[1] *U.K.P.P.* Cd. 4668, pp. 12, 32.

worse off than they are now, while as regards the shippers, they would not have such fine fleets at their disposal as they have now with regular and well-understood rates of freight to work by. Shortly stated, all the cargo steam owners pay into the Association account on the basis of 12½ per cent of their freight, and there is now no chartering except an occasional sailing vessel in the event of the steam tonnage being insufficient for the requirement of the trade. The contributions to the Association are divided amongst the members according to their shares, and the cargo steamer owners have a pool among themselves. The Association has a fixed tariff of rates which applies to all cargo steamers. The mail steamers' rates are higher than this tariff (except for weight) and vary according to the demand for space. They can quote the same rates as the cargo steamers if they wish to do so, but it is understood that they will not quote less. The rates of freight are fixed by the 'Rates Committee' of 'Davis', very often after consultation with the 'Merchants' Committee' in the Australian trade. The net result of the system, so far as the P & O Company are concerned, is that last year we received back only £91. 16*s*. 6*d*. as a return on our shares, beyond what we paid in. So far, therefore, as our experience goes, our connection with 'Davis' does not hinge on its direct profit, but upon the indirect advantage accruing from friendly co-operation amongst all concerned in the shipping trade.[1]

'There is no homeward conference from Australia,' went on Sir Thomas Sutherland, 'but there are agreements in reference to the conveyance of the more valuable products, such as butter and fruit, which require refrigerated tonnage and rapid delivery.' In a trade like that to Australia 'in which a large proportion of the homeward cargo is suitable for chartering [*sc.* of tramp shipping] and in which the homeward cargo requires more tonnage than the outward, a conference is *pro tanto* less able to secure a monopoly than a conference in a trade in which these features are absent'. He perhaps felt it unnecessary to add that the composition of the outward trade to Australia with its emphasis upon liner cargoes and the absence of bulk shipments, made a conference in that direction so much the easier to institute and to maintain. Within a few years, certainly prior to the First World War, a homeward conference was in existence,[2]

[1] *U.K.P.P.* Cd. 4685, Q. 20,489.
[2] *U.K.P.P.* Cd. 4668, p. 36; Cd. 4685, Q. 14,727.

however. Its original title, the Australasian Refrigerated Tonnage Committee, might suggest that the committee was a more formal recognition of the 'agreement' referred to by Sir Thomas Sutherland. It was, in fact, the expansion of refrigerated exports which brought the conference into existence. After 1900 the range of exports widened and shipments of refrigerated items increased. Nevertheless, it is likely that from the outset the committee concerned itself with non-refrigerated cargoes as well and that then, as now, the only cargoes outside its purview were those normally regarded as tramp loadings, bulk cargoes of cereals, ores, etc.

At the first, membership may have been restricted to British lines. Soon after the ending of the First World War, however, a more international composition is to be found. In some instances, with Scandinavian lines especially, entry to the homeward conference was delayed by the existence of unexpired long-term carrying agreements. Membership of the conference, and the adoption of uniform rates, awaited the termination of such contracts. After 1922 ocean freights throughout the world tended to drift downwards, the extension of the conference was encouraged. By 1925 French, Dutch, Danish, Italian, Norwegian, Swedish, and finally German lines were brought into membership.[1]

The year 1925 also marks the substitution of the more restrictive title 'Australian' for Australasian and the omission of the word 'Refrigerated' from the title to acknowledge the wider range of cargo interests. As the Australian Tonnage Committee (A.T.C.) it survives today with its offices in the heart of the London shipping world. Membership of both outward and homeward conferences was overlapping with occasional exceptions where a line specialised in one-way voyages. The Blue Star Line, for example, admitted though not without conflict to the conference in 1933, initially was a member only of the homeward conference.

(*c*) THE OUTWARD CONFERENCE

For reasons suggested below, the outward conference, from the U.K. to Australia, on the whole was less of an irritant than the homeward conference. Public interest in the outward con-

[1] *The Times, Trade Supplement*, 17 June 1922, 276*c*; *S.M.H.* 31 February 1928; *Fairplay*, vol. 86, p. 694.

ference was concentrated into the years immediately before and immediately after the First World War. Before the war it was mentioned during hearings of the 1909 royal commission on Shipping Rings and of the Dominions royal commission. After the war it formed the subject of a special investigation carried out by the Imperial Shipping Committee. Before the war attention was focussed upon the level of freight rates. After the war, the question of deferred rebates and discriminatory treatment of 'disloyal' shippers dominated enquiry.

The commission on rings heard evidence from a number of trading associations in the U.K. using vessels associated in rings. Three representatives of such trading bodies were active in the export trade to Australia. One, a founder-member and the chairman of the Australian Merchants Association since its inception, expressed himself as particularly satisfied with the ring. In one answer he went so far as to say: 'the shipowners... in the Australian trade have been very reasonable in their freights'.[1] It would seem, from the repetition of certain questions, that the commissioners doubted their own ears. They found it difficult to believe that the witness was in fact a merchant and not a shipowner. 'This evidence you have given' runs a final question, 'if favourable to the shipowners, has all been given from the merchants' point of view?' Two further witnesses if less fulsome also expressed satisfaction with the ring. One argued that it was not in 'anybody's interests, either merchants' or shippers', that a tramp should come in and cut the rates in a regular line of steamers'.[2]

Similar questions were put a few years later to witnesses appearing before the royal commission on the Dominions. Some of the evidence struck a more critical note than that of 1909. The evidence given in London to a marked extent repeats the earlier testimony. That in Australia shows that importers were less content. Mr Berry, an importer representing the Melbourne Chamber of Commerce, was particularly critical. Nevertheless, no savage indictment comparable with that later to be used in attacking the homeward conference is contained in the Australian evidence. Published Australian comment does not appear to

[1] *U.K.P.P.* Cd. 4670, Q. 2,791, 3,065.
[2] *Ibid.* Q. 11,825 ff. and *U.K.P.P.* Cd. 4,685, Q. 13,658.

support the following statement embodied in the royal commission's final report: '...in principle it is not desirable that the operations of steamship companies should remain longer without some measure of Government supervision (although so far no action has been taken on the findings of the Royal Commission on Shipping Rings) in spite of representations made by more than one Dominion Government'.[1]

It is not, however, possible to conclude from the relative absence of complaint that outward freights were indeed as 'reasonable' as royal commission witnesses suggested. Imports into Australia from Europe consisted of a wide range of items from silks to steam engines. The very breadth of the range reduced the focus of attention upon particular rates. Nor should the existence be ignored of associations of importers whose aim of price stability gave them an interest often parallel with that of the shipping rings. Australian merchants were, it was stated in 1922, frequently in communication with shipowners through these associations.

In Britain as early as 1902 the Australasian Merchants Association was set up, the membership included British manufacturers. The association was closely involved in, and membership overlapped with, the Australian section of the London Chamber of Commerce; this section in turn included British shipowners. In Australia in 1910 was established the Australian Association of British Manufacturers and their Representatives, an offshoot of the British association mentioned above. By 1922 membership totalled 800 of whom about 500 were British manufacturers and about 300 were their Australian representatives. A few years later a separate U.K. section was created. It would seem probable that those associations on the whole tended to acquiesce in, or not to be resistant to, rate increases. In January 1929, for example, the British outward conference announced rate increases. The Australian Merchants Association met with the owners and agreed to the raising of rates, they accepted that some increase was inevitable. But Prime Minister Bruce immediately appealed to the owners to defer their proposed increases until after further consultation. The outcome of his intervention, discussed in detail below, was

[1] *U.K.P.P.* Cd. 7351, Q. 994–9; Cd. 7171, Q. 4,963–75; Cd. 8462, par. 587–8.

the Overseas Shipping Conference and the successful holding down of freight rates.[1]

Unlike exports, moreover, imports in the majority of cases had been ordered at a fixed c.i.f. price and the decision to import had been made in the light of existing freight rates. If rates had been too high importers would presumably had been forced to turn to exporting countries with access to lower freight rates. Before 1914 it was in fact suggested to the commission on rings that orders were being lost to U.S.A. manufacturers because of high freights between the U.K. and Australia but no evidence was produced.[2] It is perhaps worth adding that when in the 1920s U.K. manufacturers were experiencing marketing difficulties in Australia, attention in the U.K. press was focussed on the burden of the Australian tariff rather than upon the level of ocean freights. With exports, on the other hand, the amount paid in freights played a significant part in the disposal of Australian primary products in highly competitive markets overseas. As we shall see in our discussion of the homeward conference, preoccupation with outbound freight rates was almost obsessional.

The absence of complaint about freights from Europe thus may or may not indicate acceptable or reasonable freight rates. But there can be no doubting the existence of keen Australian hostility towards, and condemnation of, two other aspects of the outward conference during the immediate post-war years: deferred rebates and a boycott of 'disloyal' shippers. A normal feature of the conference system and a traditional source of friction between shipper and owner is the loyalty contract based on deferred rebates. In order to establish and to maintain the patronage of a shipper, the owner agrees to make a rebate on freights actually paid, after the expiry of a loyalty testing period, usually six months. Should a shipper use non-conference vessels his accumulated rebates become forfeit. The system is defended by the owner on the grounds that without some penalty the shipper will take advantage of, and make use of, rate-cutting non-conference vessels. Assured and constant support is

[1] *U.K.P.P.* Cd. 4670, pp. 100–21. Board of Trade *Journal*, various references to meetings of the associations. *The Times Trade Supplement* 20 and 27 May 1922; *The Times* 8 and 12 January 1929 and many other references throughout the period.

[2] *U.K.P.P.* Cd. 4668, p. 65.

essential if regular, adequate services are to be provided. The system is attacked by shippers on the grounds that it vests excessive power in the owners, eliminates any possibility of competition, and facilitates the introduction of artificially high freight rates. This was an old source of contention between owner and shipper. It assumed crisis proportions in the Australian outward conference in 1920 and brought the question of shipping rings again before an official committee. On this occasion moreover the investigation was aimed specifically at the deferred rebates system in the U.K. to Australia trade, unlike earlier manifestations of public interest where more general terms of reference had applied. In November 1920 a complaint from the Commonwealth government was made to the Imperial Shipping Committee. It alleged that accumulated freight rebates, amounting to £700, due to the government of Victoria had been declared forfeit because shipments had been made outside the conference on ships of the Commonwealth Shipping Line. The complaint also alleges that penalties additional to the customary rebates forfeiture were being exacted. It was claimed that shippers using the Commonwealth line had subsequently been barred from using conference vessels.

The Commonwealth Shipping Line, as already noted, was retained after the end of the First World War partly because of the state socialism of the Labour Opposition, partly because members of all three political groups thought it expedient to retain the line as a weapon to control the conference and thus hold down rates. In the Senate it was claimed: 'that we could defeat the objects of the Shipping Ring by lowering freights, because even if the Australian people had to make up the loss incurred on their boats they would be gaining by having goods delivered in Australia at a cheaper rate'.[1] No member present in federal parliament dissented when Mr Bruce asserted that: 'a majority of the members of this Chamber are prepared to go on with the Line for one reason, and for one only, and that is that they fear the machinations of the great Shipping Combine if it is left unfettered in the Australian trade. They are desirous of seeing the Commonwealth Line kept in existence for the sake of maintaining competition with that Combine.'[2] It was a time

[1] *C.P.D.* vol. 92, p. 3,263.

[2] *C.P.D.* vol. 98, p. 13,345.

when nationally owned fleets were not uncommon. The governments of the U.S.A., France and Canada, had similarly undertaken the ownership and operation of state fleets during the war. It was a form of 'state socialism' condemned by a number of institutions in many parts of the world.[1] In the U.K. it was adversely commented upon by the Chamber of Shipping and at annual meetings of shipping companies. In December 1921 the chairman's address to the Orient Company shareholders included the following mention of the Commonwealth line: 'it was unfortunate that at this rather anxious juncture the private British shipowner in the Australian trade should have to sustain the competition...of the Commonwealth Government Line. Although they are assured that damage to the shipowners is not intended, even if it did not result in driving the shipping interests of this country out of the Australian trade, it must, in any case, immediately and inevitably act as a strong deterrent to their development.' It was the allegation of stronger reactions by U.K. shipping interests, however, which focussed attention upon the outward conference in 1920.

As a matter of urgency the Imperial Shipping Committee looked first at the alleged boycott of shippers who had used the state line. Its interim report in the summer of 1921 notes that: 'the evidence which was tendered to us on behalf of the Australian Government was to the effect that firms or persons who shipped by the Commonwealth Government Line, besides incurring the loss of rebates, ran the risk of having cargo shut out by some of the Conference Lines from ships which were not full, on any occasion on which they might wish to make use of their services...certain definite instances were brought before us in evidence...(and) it is clear that some such cases have occurred.'[2] Discussing evidence given by Lord Inchcape the committee concluded 'that such cases as may have occurred are due to unauthorised action on the part of subordinate officials in certain of the Conference Lines'. To give maximum publicity to the shipowners' repudiation of any intimidatory policy, the committee published correspondence between Mackinder, chairman of the Imperial Shipping Committee and Lord

[1] S. D. Cole, 'The State and Merchant Shipping', *Brassey* 1921–2, (305–14).
[2] *U.K.P.P.* Cmd. 1486.

Inchcape. The following extract from Lord Inchcape's reply was widely quoted: 'I am authorized to say that the shipowners ... will not either directly or indirectly be parties to a policy or practice of penalizing or of threatening to penalize shippers who may not give all their shipments to the Conference Lines, by shutting out cargo where there is room for it, or by other discriminating methods beyond the forfeiture of rebates in accordance with agreement...'

The boycott had engendered much ill-will in Australia. The *S.M.H.*, normally opposed to state enterprise in general and to the Commonwealth Shipping Line in particular, and at this time not unfavourably disposed to the U.K. shipping lines, came out with a strongly worded editorial. Freight wars and the withholding of loyalty rebates may be legitimate and acceptable practices, the editorial argues, but a boycott such as that alleged is indefensible, it 'compels people to ask what are the ultimate objects of those who take such an unwarranted action'.[1]

The second complaint, on deferred rebates, was investigated in a more leisurely fashion, the report not appearing until 1923. The essence of the problem concerned the creation of equal opportunity for the state line. The existence of an Australian statute which prohibited the payment of rebates put the state line at a disadvantage. The Australian Industries Preservation Act *inter alia* made it an indictable offence to monopolize or to attempt to monopolize any part of the trade of the country. Section 7A of the Act specifically prohibited the payment or giving of any rebate, discount, refund, or concession to any person upon the express or implied condition that the recipient deals, or has dealt exclusively with the giver. The Act, it may be noted in passing, owed its origins to a domestic issue and not to any failings on the part of the oversea shipping industry nor to any desire to curb that industry. Australian legislation prevented the payment of any rebates in Australia. It also prevented the Commonwealth line from paying rebates outside Australia. But it could restrict lines owned overseas only on that part of their operations conducted *from*, not *to* Australia. Hence the advantage they enjoyed over the state line in shipments to Australia.

[1] *S.M.H.* 30 March 1921.

Hence too, in contrast with the system in many other parts of the world, the homeward conference from Australia was characterised by the absence of deferred rebates. Whether or not such rebates were widely made before being prohibited in 1909 is uncertain. Clearly the concept was known in Australia and rebates were made in the west on freights paid in Australia.[1] As discussed below, the payment of rebates was legalised in Australia in 1930. But by then the state line had ceased to exist. It is not without irony that the lifting of the prohibition was designed primarily to assist those shipping lines which the Australian government had sought to curb and discipline in 1920.

Given the rebate advantage enjoyed by the oversea lines it was unrealistic not to anticipate that the Commonwealth line would attempt to charge comparable real rates. It is difficult, however, to be confident that the Commonwealth line in fact confined its rate reductions to achieving equality. For a second disadvantage under which the state line laboured was the high cost structure imposed by pay and manning on the Australian scale. An economic rate of freight was obviously higher than that charged. Complaint in the Australian press and in addresses at annual meetings of shipping companies in the U.K. frequently asserts that the Commonwealth line was guilty of gross undercutting. Its losses borne by the Australian tax payer, the theme runs, the line irresponsibly cut the rates of freight to uneconomic levels. Influenced by these beliefs the conference lines retaliated with propaganda, by withholding accrued rebates, and, in some instances as already noted, by a boycott of those shippers who used the state line.

The object of the Commonwealth government in referring the complaint to the Imperial Shipping Committee was to reduce competition between its own line and the conference lines to a more equitable basis. The solution it envisaged was the enactment in the U.K. of legislation comparable with its own prohibiting deferred rebates. The Imperial Shipping Committee declined to make such a recommendation. It considered 'that the conference system must be accepted as a necessary concom-

[1] *Western Australia* P.P. 1905, I, paper 8 'Report of the Royal Commission on Ocean Freights Etc.' p. 9 ff.

mitant of modern commerce...and, as for a loyalty arrangement we find that it is necessary for the conference to have some assurance of some continuous support from shippers such as will constitute an effective method of preventing intermittent and irresponsible competition for berth cargo by outside ships'.[1]

The deferred rebate was not the only method by which to assure 'continuous support', however, and the Imperial Shipping Committee drew attention to the agreement or contract method. Introduced in South Africa in 1911 as a substitute for deferred rebates the agreement system also provided a tie, if a weaker tie, between shipper and owner. Freed of the illegality, in Australian terms, of the deferred rebate, the agreement was thus an alternative which the Imperial Shipping Committee pressed the Commonwealth government to accept. In so far as the agreement provided for arbitration to deal with disputed freights, it was possible to argue that association with the conference would enable the state line and hence the state to participate in rate determination. Rejecting the view that it should recommend the prohibition of deferred rebates, the Imperial Shipping Committee instead urged the adoption of the agreement in parallel with the continued use of the deferred rebate system. The committee ended its report with the suggestion that 'it is very desirable that an effort should be made to find a solution on the lines indicated'. A cauda to this solomonic solution may be found in the record of proceedings of the Imperial Economic Conference held later in 1923 wherein the following letter to the chairman of the Imperial Shipping Committee is reproduced. It is signed jointly by the chairman of the Orient Line and the London representative of the Commonwealth Shipping Line. It requires no elaboration:

In reply to the question you have addressed to us, we are glad to say that the optional system of rebate or agreement, evolved in the Australian trade as a result of the inquiry by the Imperial Shipping Committee into the rebate system, is working satisfactorily. The form of agreement as originally introduced has already been signed by over 800 firms, and now that certain amendments are about to be made to meet the wishes of the Merchants' Association, and the

[1] *U.K.P.P.* Cmd. 1802, pp. 17, 19.

document, subject to these, has been formally approved by them, it may be anticipated that the number of firms adopting the agreement alternative will be increased.[1]

By March 1923, that is within five years of the end of the war, the very instrument retained to act as a scourge had lost its sting. It had, moreover, not only openly associated with the conference, but had also accepted the principle of rate uniformity.[2] The retention of the line after 1923 moreover may, in fact, have worked to Australia's disadvantage. The line suffered from a high cost structure, some details of which are examined in chapter 8. Between March 1923 and the time when the line was sold it served as the relatively least efficient operator in the conference. In order to minimize its losses the line was much less resistant to a policy of rate increases than it might otherwise have been if its operating costs equalled, or fell short of its fellow conference members. This is to suggest that far from operating as an instrument to force rate reductions, the line may have acted as a brake to reductions or even as a spur to rate increases.

To many in federal parliament and in Australia as a whole the association of the government line with the conference was a bitter disappointment. It was regarded as a betrayal. Throughout the years between 1920 and 1923 parliament (and the country as a whole) had been keenly interested in and sharply divided on, the usefulness of the state line. Many members opposed its retention. They argued that the conference would be unable to exploit a monopoly situation because of the world's surplus shipping capacity. As Bruce pointed out, this 'will be a more effective control upon its operations than we can impose'. Others interpreted an offer by Lord Inchcape in 1921 as evidence of weakness. In 1921 he offered to recommend to the conference lines that their fleets should be sold to the Australian government or alternatively, he offered to buy the Commonwealth line. In a pungent speech the deputy leader of the opposition castigated the conference: 'they [*sc.* the conference lines] want to buy our ships in order that, as a combine, they may more effectively regulate freights and fares. Make no mistake

[1] *U.K.P.P.* Cmd. 2009, p. 302. See also *Fairplay*, vol. 86, p. 694.
[2] *S.M.H.* 27 April 1923; *Fairplay* vol. 89, pp. 174–5.

about that...if we adopt that line of reasoning we shall be playing right into the hands of the great Shipping Combine.'[1]

The collaboration of the Commonwealth line with the outward (and inevitably also with the homeward) conference was astringent medicine for Australian opponents of the conference. The sense of outrage persisted in Canberra for many years. Almost to the eve of war in 1939 questions about the Commonwealth line were being asked in the House. Hughes, the creator of the line, was no longer in office when the rate agreement was reached with the conference. But only a few months earlier, when still prime minister, he had denied the rumoured collaboration. The member for Dalley no doubt recalled with wry amusement the rebuke he had received from Hughes at the time. He had put down a question on the rumour. Hughes gave a caustic reply: 'there is no truth in the rumour. Where did the honourable member hear a yarn like that...? As a matter of fact, I believe the honourable member himself invented the rumour. Certainly there is no truth in it.'[2]

(*d*) THE HOMEWARD CONFERENCE

Comment in Australia on the homeward conference tended to be more searching, more sustained, and in contrast with the outward far more concentrated upon the level of freight rates. To some extent this may be explained by the differing importance of the two conferences. The outward conference was but a small part of the larger picture of the U.K. shipping scene; it controlled the shipping concerned with a highly important but not completely vital sector of Australian trade. The homeward conference, on the other hand, filled almost the whole canvas of Australia's oversea shipping services and involved a handful of exports crucial to the Australian economy. Differences in conditions of marketing and the keen competition encountered overseas inevitably attracted to the homeward freights a closer scrutiny than was either possible, or apparently desired with outward cargoes. There is the additional factor that in the

[1] *C.P.D.* vol. 98, pp. 13,314, 13,321, 13,347. *Fairplay* vol. 81, pp. 70–1. *S.M.H.* 30 November 1921.

[2] *C.P.D.* vol. 99, p. 841.

climate of the time increases on inbound freight rates, that is on imports, added to the protection afforded by the tariff. On outbound rates, especially homeward rates to the U.K. and continent, any reduction achieved is tantamount to an export subsidy. In connection with homeward rates therefore it is not surprising that shipping companies were sensitive to Australian comment.

Local opinion was often expressed in colourful, emotive language. (In federal parliament on one occasion the conference lines were apostrophized as 'this gang of British capitalists'.[1]) It was usually filled with hostility and prejudice. It undoubtedly mirrors the apprehensiveness of a vulnerable economy dependent upon exports of primary products in the ships of a merchant fleet owned overseas. Vocal expressions of dislike provide the backcloth of opinion against which must be seen other attempts at public control of the conference monopoly. Three possible checks to the conference may be mentioned: in general, considerations of external market limitations and, more specifically, the constraints deriving from the competition of non-conference vessels and from state intervention.

The limited range of export cargoes drawn from the primary sector explains the domestic strength of the producing interests and the jaundice-filled eye they cast upon ocean freights and oversea shipping companies. It also, in the international context, accounts for the vulnerability of the export sector of the economy. On arrival in oversea markets, Australian commodities competed not only with similar items produced within the importing country, but also with identical products from other parts of the new world. The price realised on such exports is determined not by reference to the Australian producers' cost structure alone; it depends as well, on the cost structure of the lowest cost producer. A witness before the royal commission on rings, engaged in the import trade in Australian refrigerated products, made the point long before the First World War that 'prices in London are governed by conditions absolutely unconnected with Australia'. The element in marketing costs represented by stable or rising ocean freights might thus become especially significant when commodity prices were low or falling.

[1] *C.P.D.* vol. 94, p. 5,681.

It would be unrealistic to attribute indifference to the shipowner, and unreasonable to postulate a situation in which, by excessive freights, he eliminated demand for his own fleet. In 1930, the Commonwealth prime minister, drawn from the Labour party, and hence at that time instinctively hostile to private monopoly, indeed acknowledged the realism of shipowners. 'From my discussions with them [*sc.* the conference lines] I believe that they realise that it would be unwise for them to risk killing the goose which lays the golden egg. They are aware that excessive freight rates would so seriously hamper Australian production as to injure their own trade.'[1] Commodity prices varied over time, hence the importance of the freight element in total production or marketing costs also varied. Discussion in chapter 7 on freight stability examines these aspects in greater detail.

The second possible check to the monopoly of the homeward conference lay in competition from 'outside' vessels. Vessels outside the conference included the Commonwealth line before March 1923, tramp ships, and non-conference liners. None was important with the possible exception of the temporary intervention by the Commonwealth line. At its period of peak activity the state line carried about 8 % of all outbound cargo. Assuming that the whole of its cargo was carried to Europe, it probably carried about 10 % of all Europe-bound cargo. Surplus shipping capacity was a feature of the early post-war years. In these circumstances the willingness of the state line to lower rates unilaterally before 1923 accounts for the sharp hostility shown by the conference. But the state line possessed neither sufficient tonnage nor sufficient refrigerated space to make in the short-run any very marked impact upon the homeward conference. And when it had agreed on rate uniformity it ceased to represent a threat to the conference.

Competition in the Australia–Europe trade from tramps and other non-conference liners was of no greater significance. Japanese vessels made occasional sorties into the trade in the 1920s but never apparently on a scale sufficiently large to attract much notice or reaction.[2] In the 1930s the tighter control described below made such encroachments less easy. As for

[1] *C.P.D.* vol. 123, p. 1,134. [2] *S.M.H.* 22 October 1924.

possible tramp competition, enough has been said in chapter 2 to suggest that cargo poaching was more likely by liners than by tramps. Although tramp-lifting of non-refrigerated liner cargo cannot be entirely dismissed, for the reasons already given the amount involved was likely to be small.

After 1930 the homeward conference monopoly was challenged only twice, by the U.K. Blue Star Line and by a producers' association in Western Australia which chartered its own shipping. In early 1933, following the Ottawa Conference and the reintroduction of imperial preference, the Vestey group's Blue Star Line found its South American trade in refrigerated meat handicapped. It turned to the Australian meat trade. Initially the homeward conference sought to exclude the line on the grounds that excess capacity already existed. As a result of government intervention which is discussed below, the conference by this date was able to prevent the entrance of outsiders into full participation. Exclusion from the conference would have restricted the Blue Star Line to a minute proportion of the trade. Ultimately it arranged an association with a local refrigerated meat exporting group and thus ensured adequate cargoes. Three days later it was admitted into full conference membership in order to prevent a rate war.[1] In Western Australia, as mentioned in chapter 1, a producers' co-operative set up the 'West Farmers Line' in the early 1930s. It followed and indeed sprang from state intervention in the shipping world in and after 1929. It represented a direct challenge both to the homeward conference and to the institutional changes stemming from the new role assumed by the government. Its activities are also linked closely with rate determination. Hence the significance of the 'West Farmers Line' is more appropriately assessed in discussing the effects of the conference on services and in the following chapter on freight rates.

The third check to conference activities lay in public control. Much has already been said to indicate the interest shown by the Australian government in the oversea shipping services and more especially in conference developments affecting Australia's exports. With some reason a visitor to federal parliament

[1] *S.M.H. passim* April, June, July, and 19 September 1933, 24 January and 15 June 1934. *C.P.D.* vol. 141, pp. 3,169–70.

might conclude that the oversea shipping companies were 'fair game', denied the protection of game laws or the periodic relief of a close season. At times the 'sport', in parliament boomeranged upon the heads of attackers and bystanders alike. On 14 April 1921, for example, a motion condemning homeward freights as 'excessive and crushing' was carried by two votes. Prime Minister Hughes failed to take the matter seriously and was absent from the chamber during the division. It took all Hughes' parliamentary skill next day to remedy the damage.[1] The murmuring background complaint in the 1920s culminated in a noteworthy illustration of state intervention in 1929. It is significant for a number of reasons. It determined the whole pattern of shipowner–shipper relationships during the 1930s. It produced important innovations in the shipping organisation of the oversea trade in Australian primary products. It involved the Commonwealth government in the amendment of a statute in order to legalise contractual links between shipper and the conference lines. It was unfortunate that the Bruce–Page government which had initiated state intervention in 1929 was out of office by October of that year. It was thus left to a Labour government with its background of state socialism and no friend of the conference to promote the amendment, the effect of which was to reinforce the conference monopoly. It created a new role for the Australian government in connection with freight-rate determination. It also inaugurated a new, less hostile attitude on the part of the Australian government towards the conference system. In part it reflects the inability of the short-lived Labour government to grapple with all the measures it may have considered desirable. The financial crisis into which the country was plunged itself provided enough problems to beset the Scullin Labour government. In part also, perhaps even largely, the Lyons government which replaced the Labour government contained genuine converts to the acceptance of the conference system. If not entirely persuaded of the value of the system as such, at least the government for the first time was prepared to view the problem less narrowly. In part also it is probably a reflection of a world-wide coming to terms with the whole question of monopolies and public policy. The

[1] *C.P.D.* vol. 95, p. 7,447 ff. See also Earl Page, *Truant Surgeon* (1963), p. 67.

S.M.H. expressed this thought in July 1929 in its editorial comment on the amendment of the Australian Industries Preservation Act: 'economic thought is not [*sc.* now] so afraid of agreements, combines, and trusts as when the Act was passed'.

Intervention by the state in the oversea shipping scene at the end of 1928 was sparked off by a rumour of increased freight rates. But it is also a reflection of a wider uneasiness which was growing in Australia in the later 1920s. Two years earlier Prime Minister Bruce had invited a group of economists to enquire into the economic effects of the Australian tariff. High costs, high wages and a tendency for unemployment to increase without any diminution in industrial stoppages added to the general disquiet. The N.S.W. coal industry was uneasy during the second half of 1928, the miners finally beginning their mammoth strike early in the following year. The Timber Workers Union struck in January 1929. Overall there was anxiety about public finance and the oversea borrowing necessary to finance the growth of industry and urbanisation. Both had been proceeding rapidly in the 1920s. In 1928 the government invited an Economic Mission from the U.K. to survey the economic situation in Australia. The mission's report, dated 7 January 1929, concluded that Australia had borrowed excessively and had mortgaged the future too heavily. It also reached the conclusion that oversea freight rates were indeed too high, as alleged by various groups with which the mission had made contact.[1] A few weeks before the mission reported, a news leak indicated that freights were to rise even higher in the new year. Although the rumour related only to the U.K. outward direction Prime Minister Bruce correctly anticipated a similar increase in homeward rates. He immediately cabled Lord Inchcape to delay the increases on the grounds that it would lead to the defeat of his government. Bruce's biographer considers that his subject exaggerated, possibly to make 'the shipowners' flesh creep'.[2] Whatever the reason, the intervention nevertheless secured delay and led to discussions with the shipping companies. The outcome was the Overseas Shipping Conference held in Sydney

[1] *C.P.P.* 1929, II, 1,257–8.

[2] C. Edwards, *Bruce of Melbourne* (1965), p. 147 ff. Viscount Bruce himself was kind enough in the course of a letter to the author, to confirm the accuracy of the published account.

between 4 and 6 April 1929. The term Conference is here used in its more customary sense. To prevent confusion the initial letter is capitalised in subsequent pages.

The members of the Conference 'were constituted under direct appointment by (the) Prime Minister with the duty of examining on broad lines the general position of the transport of Australia's oversea trade'. They included a shipowners' delegation from London, led by Sir Alan Anderson of the Orient Line, together with representatives of two other conference lines, and P. M. Hill, assistant general manager of the Chamber of Shipping of the U.K. In Australia, assisting the London shipowners were the members of the Oversea Shipping Representatives Association (O.S.R.A.) led by the experienced, able and much respected chairman T. S. Gordon (later Sir Thomas Gordon) of Birt & Co. of Sydney. The shippers' side included two importers and ten representatives of the major agricultural and pastoral exporting interests in the various states. The formal opening of the Conference was preceded by press publicity as the London shipowners made their leisurely way around the Australian coast from Fremantle to Melbourne and thence overland to Sydney via Canberra. Bruce met the shipowners as they passed through Canberra. He later denied that any decisions had been reached, 'indeed the subject of freights was hardly mentioned at the meeting'.[1] At each port the shipowners attempted by press statements to create an acceptable climate of opinion. In a country highly sensitive to its vulnerability in world markets and resentful of its dependence upon 'foreign' owned fleets this was not easy. It required much persuasion to convince local opinion that the shipowners might have any case.

Although convened by the government, the Conference was intended to be of a purely private nature. Bruce made this clear when he opened the proceedings at Sydney on 4 April 1929 with an address of welcome. In a lengthy speech, a compound of optimism and exhortation, he delivered his 'charge'. Enunciating the main areas of contention which he hoped the Conference would examine, he referred to the importance of oversea shipping services to the Australian economy. He stressed that: 'this is not, and I am quite determined it is not going to become a

[1] *C.P.D.* vol. 120, p. 1,291.

Government Conference...I propose it should be entirely one between importers and exporters'.[1] Notwithstanding the personal warmth which Bruce sought to inject, the meeting opened in a temperature more appropriate for refrigerated products. Tensions soon eased. 'A reading of the reports of the debates at the shipping Conference...makes it plain that all parties represented in the Conference—producers, importers, and shipowners—acknowledge the community of interest. The problem is how the different interests can be organised to work together, so as to ensure the most efficient and economic handling of produce and its transport from Australia.'[2] The Conference ended with a unanimous report urging action to effect economies in the use of shipping.

Unanimity hinged upon the credibility of the shipping lines' losses. It proved a serious initial obstacle. Once the evidence was accepted, the need to find a solution became inescapable; evasion of responsibility became difficult. Once the shipowners' figures of loss were admitted it became imperative for the Australian shippers to increase the shipowners' revenue either by agreeing higher rates, or by forcing up the real revenue from existing rates. Even less palatable for the producers and shippers, for whom hitherto a blanket condemnation of shipowners had seemed enough, was an awareness of their new responsibility. Should whatever remedies they now recommended prove to be inadequate, requests for further rate increases would be virtually impossible to withstand.

The Conference made a short, interesting report signed on 6 April and published by the government within a week.[3] 'It was the unanimous opinion of this Conference...that the figures... demonstrate that, during the last three years, the regular British cargo lines have suffered heavy losses in the Australian trade'. It goes on to make a series of recommendations. None contains any criticism, overt or implied, of the shipping companies. It would seem to reflect noteworthy success by the shipowners in convincing an audience of sceptics.

The recommendations were of two kinds: institutional innovations capable of being introduced by the signatories them-

[1] *S.M.H.* 5 April 1929. [2] *S.M.H.* 8 April 1929.
[3] *C.P.P.* 1929, II, 2,189. *S.M.H.* 12 April 1929.

selves, and changes which hinged upon government action. The report urged upon the government the desirability of reducing imposts levied in Australia upon expatriate shipping companies in respect of income tax, harbour dues, navigation charges and the like. Harbour dues were singled out. The report reminds Mr Bruce that no more than lip service so far had been paid by the states to his assurance about harbour dues given at the Imperial Economic Conference six years earlier. Changes in taxation and port charges were not immediately possible. Port charges were largely the responsibility of the states whose autonomy in this area had been retained. The taxation of shipping companies was a federal responsibility but fiscal changes are necessarily slow. Certain reliefs were ultimately granted and are mentioned in our discussion of rate determination.

With legislation, however, prompt action by the federal government was possible. It was in fact an essential preliminary to the introduction of organisational changes recommended by the Conference. The Australian Industries Preservation Act, as we have already shown, outlawed trade agreements involving the payment of rebates, discounts, and the like. Whether accurately or not, the Act was also thought to prohibit annual contracts at fixed rates of freights as recommended by the Conference. Doubt was removed in 1930 by an amending act legalising agreements:

> in relation to the carriage of goods to other countries, made and entered into between shippers and shipowners or their representatives...and approved by the Australian Oversea Transport Association, whereby, in consideration of periodical sailings to be provided by the shipowners, and the carriage of goods of the shippers at agreed rates, the shippers agree to ship exclusively by the shipowners,...nor shall...the refusal to extend the advantages of the agreement to shippers who do not offer to enter into it be deemed to be an offence.

Two features merit notice. The amendment demonstrates complete acceptance by the government of the homeward conference monopoly. The legality of permitted agreements was restricted to those 'approved' by the Australian Oversea Transport Association (A.O.T.A.). This was a body recommended by the Conference and created with official sanction; it is discussed below. Secondly, the amendment specifically allowed discrimination against shippers who declined to enter into agreement.

The Industries Preservation Act was amended in another very important way, namely to legalise the payment of rebates. The use of rebates has always been regarded by shipowners as an important linchpin in maintaining the stability of the conference system. In the U.K. outward conference, it will be recalled, the enforcement of the penal aspects of the rebate system in the early 1920s aroused discontent. It was in part responsible for the complaint made by the Australian government to the Imperial Shipping Committee. Hitherto the payment of such rebates was illegal in Australia and they were absent from the homeward conference. Now they were sanctioned in order to permit the newly created shipper–shipowner agreements to be enforced. In the light of the earlier official hostility it was too much to expect when rebates were legalised in 1930 that the *deferred* rebate should have been allowed. Instead, cash discounts were allowed, in line with the agreement system generally. They were made at the time when the freights were actually paid. In 1930, for example, when the freight rate on wool was increased by 1/16th penny per pound the new price was subject to a deduction of 1*s.* 9*d.* per bale 'loyalty rebate'. The net effect of these changes was that the rate on a bale of wool was increased by only three pence, to a 'loyal' shipper. But given the power to withhold the rebate from shippers not entering into agreement, it was in fact comparable with the deferred rebate in creating a tie between shipper and owner.[1]

The Conference was also productive of important changes in the institutional framework in marketing and shipping. It had agreed unanimously that to prevent freight increases, 'organising to economise' was imperative. 'To achieve this end, the Conference resolves that representative committees should be forthwith created in the several Australian states to define and bring about the economies which shipowners find possible.' The recommendations were promptly adopted. A committee was formed from representatives of shipping companies and shippers

[1] *C.P.D.* vol. 154, p. 342. *S.M.H.* 12 April 1937.

and the A.O.T.A. was brought into existence in June 1929. It consisted of primary producing interests and exporters, referred to in the following paragraph, formally associated as the Exporters Oversea Transport Committee (E.O.T.C.) to form the shippers' side of the A.O.T.A. Representing shipowners was the O.S.R.A., in existence since before the First World War. After the Conference the O.S.R.A. organization was extended with local branches in every major port, the headquarters remaining in Sydney. From the O.S.R.A. was drawn the Shipowners Oversea Transport Committee (S.O.T.C.) which, together with the producers representatives (the E.O.T.C.), formed the A.O.T.A. The functions of the A.O.T.A. were three: to secure economies in shipping by rationalising tonnage, where possible to have one vessel call at a port instead of several, each loading only a part cargo; to approve of freight rates; and finally to approve of agreements between shippers and owners as now required by law. The involvement of the A.O.T.A. in freight-rate determination is examined in the following chapter, its success in fulfilling the other two functions is looked at below.

Before attempting a balance sheet, however, two offshoots of the Conference may be mentioned: controlled marketing and shipowners' policy changes. In 1930 various associations already existed in the country to represent primary producers' interests. A Dairy Produce Control Board had been set up along with a Control Board for Dried Fruits in 1924, a Canned Fruits Control Board followed in 1926, and a Wine Oversea Marketing Board in 1929. All had been set up on a statutory basis in response to requests from producers for export marketing control. Other voluntary organisations had also been set up to represent pastoralists, meat shippers and so on. The legislation of 1930 setting up the A.O.T.A. was in part responsible for the extension of powers of the producers' associations. They increased in number during the 1930s, notably with the creation of the Meat Board, and they steadily expanded their role in the control of marketing. The Meat Board, for example, set up in January 1936 was given power to regulate meat shipments (a point previously noted in connection with the chilled-beef trade) to arrange contracts via A.O.T.A. for freight rates, to promote oversea sales, to appoint a London branch and so on. The Apple and Pear Board set up two years later had somewhat similar powers together with the right to determine export quotas for each state. The difficult years of the early 1930s made some control of oversea marketing essential. The various boards also became important elements in the process of rate determination discussed in the following chapter.

The improvement of relationships between the government and shipowners was referred to above. Not less important for future harmony, and not the least of Conference achievements was the impact it had upon shipowners. Their recognition of the unpopularity from which they suffered was an essential preliminary. Correctly they saw that in part it stemmed from inadequate understanding in Australia. There was a failure to see the world-wide difficulties of the shipping industry in general and of the Australian sector in particular. 'The remote cause of much of our trouble in Australia is publicity...with a good story and a clear case we had a bad press and confusion' was the dry comment of one shipowner. There can be no doubting the improved tone in press comment in Australia as discussion in Sydney in early April revealed the extent of the shipping lines' losses. For perhaps the first time Australian opinion was jolted into an acute awareness that oversea shipping services were in danger. Part of the remedy lay in a better press. Here the owners had already achieved much in the short-term during their visit to Australia. Their long-term relations with the local press were also considered. Another related problem stemmed from the non-Australian ownership of the oversea merchant fleet. The solution here was to create a more favourable background in which the shipping companies were seen to be more closely identified with Australia. One measure, not adopted, might well have been the creation of a board of local directors. The personal standing in the local scene of the more senior members of the O.S.R.A. was an obvious advantage. Australian enterprise offered many precedents for such use of local expertise and prestige. Although no local boards were created it would seem clear that the O.S.R.A., more especially the headquarters in Sydney, was given wider powers of decision. Major policy matters continued to be decided in London. But it was both desirable and administratively more convenient with the new A.O.T.A. structure, to allow and encourage the O.S.R.A. to interpret in the light of local conditions policy broadly defined in London.

(*e*) THE EFFECTS OF THE CONFERENCE SYSTEM

Two questions remain unanswered. How successful were the new arrangements introduced as a result of the 1929 Conference; what long-term contributions did they make to the shipping scene? Secondly, what were the effects of the conference system on the shipping industry? Did it produce excessive rates of freight and lead to the inefficiencies often associated with a protected industry? Rates of freight, their determination, and the effect of the conference upon rate stability are discussed in the following chapter. Here we examine the achievements of the 1929 Conference and the effects of the conference system upon shipping and services. The major innovation of the 1929 Conference was the freight agreement system and the creation of the A.O.T.A. for its administration. The A.O.T.A. was an institution formed by the coming together for two specific purposes of representatives of shippers and shipowners. It existed federally and was duplicated in each state. The dual role of the A.O.T.A. consisted of forecasting shipping-space requirements and the ratification of freight agreements. Estimating in advance the probable volume of cargo to be shipped from each port was particularly susceptible to possible error. Shipowners agreed to provide an adequate supply of tonnage for the Australia to Europe trade. But shippers were under no compulsion to provide cargoes. Although 'shipowners and shippers together are to mobilise their knowledge and resources in the common interest' there existed no obligation to guarantee the shipment of cargo.

Shipowners' reactions to the new arrangements initially were favourable. The Chamber of Shipping in 1930 at the onset of depression cited the rationalisation policy as a model for adoption elsewhere in the world: 'Rational co-operation between shippers and shipowners is needed, and the success of experiments on these lines in Australia...is significant, and has come just in time to mitigate severe losses.'[1] Judgment based on a longer trial period was more critical. On the whole, advance forecasting of the amount of shipping needed was not successful. The A.O.T.A. largely failed because the task was impossible. Given the retention of choice to ship or not to ship, given the existence of conflicting aims and interests and considerations of marketing, and given the sharp decline in import cargoes from Europe in the early 1930s, the efficient and rational use of shipping was not easy. At the first wool sale in 1930 to be served by 'rationed' shipping, at Fremantle, 'three, instead of the usual ten or twelve, vessels took the wool for the United Kingdom or Continent'. Later reports are cooler. During the remainder of 1930 and in 1931 no 'really effective rationalisation of tonnage has been possible...The Ideal aimed at was the carriage of seasonal exports by the same number of steamers which brought imports...But imports had dwindled almost to vanishing point as a result of new tariff policy and the exigencies of exchange'. Shipowners were not slow to remind the A.O.T.A. of its duty, adding that: 'as vessels were arriving practically empty of inward cargo, it was vitally necessary to be able to provide for export requirements well in advance'.[2] In the following year forecasts appear to have been slightly more successful but it was probably the revival of the volume of inbound cargo which diminished but did not completely eliminate criticism. Late in 1936 'shipowners pointed out to shippers that one of the difficulties they had to face was the poor regulation of exports'.[3]

The second major function of the A.O.T.A. was connected with both the level of freights and the approval of annual freight agreements made between shippers and owners. The introduction of the system of freight rebates via the agreement rather than by the older deferred rebate method has already been mentioned. The appearance of what to many was a less objectionable way of securing a tie between shipper and owner brought the homeward and the outward conferences closely into line. As a result of the investigation into the outward con-

[1] C of S, *Annual Report*, pp. 65, 75–6.

[2] *S.M.H. Financial and Commercial Supplement*, 16 February 1931 and 11 February 1932. *Fairplay* vol. 117, p. 273.

[3] *S.M.H.* 12 February 1937.

ference by the Imperial Shipping Committee in the early 1920s, it will be recalled, the agreement system had been introduced as an alternative to deferred rebates since 1923. In the homeward conference no formal link between shipper and owner existed until the agreement system was legalised in 1930, and then only for agreements 'approved' by the A.O.T.A.

The agreement principle was simple. An undertaking was signed by representatives of all lines in the homeward conference and by shippers. Current for a year, sometimes longer for refrigerated products, the agreement provided fixed freights from which a 10 % cash discount was allowed to signatories. Initially there were difficulties in arranging agreements, mostly in connection with wool buyers representing foreign buying groups. 'Their trouble is that they have to arrange their shipments as far as possible with ships of their own nationality.'[1] The system was successfully introduced and survived until the outbreak of war—but not without tension, disagreements, and some acrimony. The main area of contention, not surprisingly, concerned rates of freight. Shippers at times sought to repudiate rates agreed by their representatives. Failure to secure concessions often evoked strident demands to abolish the A.O.T.A. In July 1933, for example, shippers requested Prime Minister Lyons to turn back the clock to before the creation of the A.O.T.A. It was impossible, Lyons told the delegation. 'The only action open to the government was to repeal the amendment which had legalised the agreement system but, he said, this would not bring about a reduction in freights which the Government was powerless to effect.'[2] Nevertheless, the same government a short time later demonstrated that it was far from powerless in its dealings with the 'West Farmers Line', the most resistant body to the new arrangements. Government support for the A.O.T.A. involved an extension of state participation, especially in rate determination. Bruce had succeeded in restricting the state's role. His successor in office found his government brought into the arena in support of the homeward conference. The situation is not without humour when a Labour ministry berates a section of its

1 (Prime Minister Scullin) *C.P.D.* vol. 125, p. 3,646.

2 *S.M.H.* 30 December 1933; *Finance and Commerce Supplement*, 13 February 1934.

electorate for challenging and seeking to overthrow a 'capitalist' monopoly exercised by an expatriate group.

The West Farmers Line (or Wesfarmers Line) was an offshoot of the Westralian Farmers Co-operative Ltd. It was brought into existence largely to defy the homeward conference and as a protest against the A.O.T.A. With the growth in Western Australia of both the cooperative movement and of the wheat trade in the 1920s the Farmers became more and more influential in the wheat pool marketing system. At the same time they acquired experience and expertise in arranging wheat charters. The Farmers collided with the conference line owners in the early 1930s when they moved backwards from voyage charters to time charters and sideways into wool carrying. Wheat voyage charter arrangements constituted normal shipping agent–tramp activities. But time charters involved the assumption of ship-management functions; wool shipments encroached upon the conference 'monopoly' of fine cargo carrying and infringed upon the agreement. The movement into wool by the Farmers was prompted partly by dislike of the conference monopoly, partly by consideration of profitability at a time when funds were tight.[1] The Farmers move into time chartering also coincided with the fall in freight rates associated with the onset of world depression.

In retrospect, however, it was the championship of the local producer which was best remembered by the Farmers' protagonists. John Thompson, the Farmers' president, in a press statement outlined his associations' role: 'in making a strenuous fight to establish the right for a shipping business to Europe, and, by so doing, provide the only safeguard against exploitation by a powerful monopoly. By reason of its power to refuse any new line admittance to the A.O.T.A.... this monopoly had a giant's grip on...the produce of Australia...'[2] For the Western Australian producers, dislike culminated in the creation of a competing body. Official determination to maintain the new organisation it had brought into being doubtless explains the pressure brought to bear by the Commonwealth

[1] For an interesting and unsympathetic view of the shipping conference in Australia see J. Sandford, *Walter Harper and the Farmers* (Perth, 1955), chapter 9.

[2] *S.M.H.* 12 April 1937.

government on the Farmers. The historian of the Farmers reached no firm conclusion about the 'politics behind this move'.[1] It would seem from the following comments, however, that it was indeed official policy to support the conference in order to cater for Australia's shipping requirements as a whole. Speaking of the Western Farmers, Mr Thorby, minister for commerce, complained that:

> negotiations such as have been carried out in the past cannot continue with any degree of success if small groups of producers and exporters dissociate themselves from the Government's efforts and continue to act independently and charter small tramp steamers inefficiently equipped. Such ships can only cater for limited quantities of Australian goods and ultimately bring about disorganisation amongst the Australian exporters. For many years past the Commonwealth, in conjunction with producers and exporters of Australian produce, as well as shippers of such goods, have conducted continuous negotiations with a view to securing improvements in the general transport of our primary produce overseas...Since February 1936 I have been in constant contact with the exporters and ship owners, endeavouring to secure further improvements...If the Australian producers and exporters would only realise that the negotiations which have been so successful in the past have been undertaken in their interests alone, I am sure that no further hindrance will be attempted by the out-of-date methods which certain sections of the community are seeking to adopt.[2]

Many shippers on the other hand, and not only those in Western Australia, probably agreed with the Farmers' spokesman that 'it was inconceivable that Australia should allow a system whereby shipowners, sheltering behind an amendment to an Australian Act of Parliament, were permitted to dictate rates of freight, make space available in whatever ships they wished and, at the same time, decide if other shipping companies should be allowed to enter the berth trade'.[3] It was in fact an exaggeration to suggest that the shipowners alone 'dictated' freight rates; the evidence (discussed below) suggests a wider basis. Nevertheless, the conference lines disliked the precedent which the Western Australian producers were creating. The

[1] Sandford, *op. cit.* p, 195.
[2] *S.M.H.* 5 September 1936.
[3] *S.M.H.* 12 April 1937.

same press statement made it clear that to the producers: 'it appeared that shipowners were more concerned with removing competition'. At the period of maximum activity the Farmers had fifteen vessels on time charter. Since the economics of a time charter depend upon maximum ship utilisation, the Farmers were seeking outward cargoes from Europe for the return journey. In return for rate concessions the conference lines made a: 'request...that the Westralian Farmers should not take part in the shipping of berth cargo to Australia'.

After 1937, when the 'West Farmers Line' acceded to the freight agreement system, complaint about the A.O.T.A. disappears. It is probable that trade revival and increased prices rather than any sudden burst of popularity was responsible. As demand for Australia's exports picked up, so realised prices edged back towards the peaks of the 1920s. Preoccupation with the level of freights, with freight agreements, and with the controlling agency tended to lessen. It would, however, be incorrect to dismiss the A.O.T.A. as an irrelevancy. The combination of shippers and shipowners meant a sharing of responsibility and with it a lightening of the burden of dislike hitherto borne by the owners alone. More important, it permitted prior negotiation and consultation.

Our second question concerns the conference system and its effect upon the shipping industry. Opponents of the system charge it with complacency which produces inefficiency. Many justifications have been advanced in its defence. Broadly they run as follows. In creating a tie between shipper and owner mutual obligations arise. Members of a conference, in contrast with the nomadic tramp who 'pirates' the 'cream' of the trade, identify themselves closely with the economy they serve. They provide shipping both in the lean years and in the years of plenty. And because it is in their interests to do so, they make a significant contribution to economic growth by providing an adequate amount of appropriate shipping. Discussion in the next few pages seeks to test these claims. Three trade routes have been selected for brief examination because of their usefulness in illustrating differing forms of shipping organisation. First is the trans-Pacific route where the conference system was least important. Second is the Japan–Australia route where the conference in its more sophisticated form of freight pools is to be found. Finally, and by far the most important, is the homeward conference on the Australia–Europe route.

Interest in the trans-Pacific route is concentrated into the 1930s. It involved conflict between the Matson Company, a U.S.A. line, and the Union Company of New Zealand, a British line. On the whole it affected passenger traffic rather than cargo. As we have already shown, cargo movement across the Pacific from North America tended largely to be a one-way trade. Instead it was the important passenger trade where competition was most keenly felt. Prior to the early 1930s the Union Line operated successfully, without friction, and no doubt profitably. The competition experienced in the 1930s consisted of the two separate, but related branches: the trans-Pacific, and, an extension of this, the trans-Tasman trade. It witnessed, among many other requests for official intervention, one which sought to exclude U.S.A. vessels from the trans-Tasman trade. On the grounds that U.S.A. cabotage restriction banned foreign vessels from the trade between Hawaii and the American mainland, determined efforts were made to amend along similar lines the Navigation Act in Australia and New Zealand. A bill was in fact introduced into federal parliament in 1936 to protect British interests by imposing restrictions upon shipping in receipt of subsidies and in other ways enabled to compete unfairly with the British shipping industry. It never reached the statute book.

At this distance in time the actual volume of trade, and the amount of shipping involved seems scant justification for the massive attention it received in the press, and in the parliaments of Britain, Australia, Canada, and New Zealand. Between 1932 and 1938 *The Times* printed more than 100 major references to the dispute. The *S.M.H.* rarely misses a daily reference. In the House of Commons in 1936 ten questions were asked about the government's intentions. In Canberra's published debates, the repetitive question and answer on Pacific shipping becomes monotonous to read. Official interest in the Matson Line, indeed, survived the outbreak of war in 1939. Yet the dispute concerned only four or five British ships. All but one had been built before

1914. Their aggregate tonnage was no more than 50,000 gross tons.[1]

Difficulty arose on this route following the introduction of the U.S.A. Merchant Marine Jones–White Act of 1928. To encourage fresh building the Act provided for the payment of construction subsidies. The overall effect was disappointing to the U.S.A. in that it failed to achieve the rehabilitation of the American merchant marine. Nevertheless, the impact of the Act on British shipping in the trans-Pacific service with Australia caused not a little disappointment to U.K. shipping interests. The use made by the Matson Line of the construction and operating subsidies enabled it to capture a trade previously dominated by British shipping. Within the space of four years three new ships were added to the Matson fleet: the *Mariposa* in 1931, *Lurline* in 1932, and the *Monterey* also in 1932, equivalent to a total of about 69,000 gross tons. The two Union ships employed between Sydney and Vancouver, the *Niagara* and the *Aorangi* had been built in 1913 and 1924, they totalled about 31,000 gross tons. On the Sydney to San Francisco service the two or three Union ships were older and smaller. It was in fact the age, slowness, and relative lack of comfort of the Union vessels which enabled the Matson Line to capture the trade. Quality of service, giving a rate reduction in real terms, rather than a cutting of actual rates gained the trade for the line. Before 1931 the old Matson ships had carried about 20 % of the traffic, by 1935 this had risen to 60 %.

The Union Company's first reaction was to seek a captive trade for its Vancouver service by some form of association with the Canadian Pacific Railway. The product was the Canadian-Australasian Line Ltd, owned jointly by the Union and the C.P.R. companies. To it was sold the *Niagara* and *Aorangi* both of which were then re-registered in London. No ready solution presented itself for the difficulties on the Union's San Francisco trade, however. The company abandoned this service at the end of 1936 'after some years of heavy losses...and because under existing conditions of competition against a high State subsidy it was not practicable to continue the service or make a replace-

[1] The best account of the dispute and its background is contained in I.S.C. *35th Report* 'Services between Canada and Australia' (title abbreviated).

ment with more modern tonnage'.[1] Thus after 1936 only the Canadian-Australasian Line service to Vancouver and the Matson Line to San Francisco remained. The greater 'superiority of amenities and speed' of the Matson Line, moreover, began to divert to San Francisco trade previously serviced from Vancouver.

The remedies urged upon the governments concerned, as noted above, included demands for the exclusion of the American line from the trans-Tasman trade. The governments of both countries indeed contemplated such action. In the House of Representatives in October 1935 Mr Lyons confirmed that the U.K. government had waived its earlier objections to the trade 'between those two countries being treated as coasting trade for the purpose of making special provision for British owned shipping'.[2] A year earlier the P & O chairman had attempted, by agreement with the Matson Line to achieve a similar effect by a bilateral withdrawal from the trans-Tasman trade. Not surprisingly the Matson Line refused. In the event, this somewhat extreme step of extending cabotage restrictions was not pursued.

The true remedy lay in raising the quality of the British shipping service. It required new, fast, better vessels. But this was what the U.K. shipping interests were either unable, or unwilling to provide unaided. An undated memorandum, probably composed in late 1934 or early 1935 contains an assertion by the P & O chairman (who was also vice-president of the Canadian-Australasian Line) that the introduction of a 'new fast and luxurious vessel' was intended. No more was heard of this particular suggestion. The report of the Imperial Shipping Committee includes a recommendation for the building of two 23,000 ton vessels capable of a service speed of 21 knots. 'We are of the opinion that only a service of this type could compete with the Matson vessels for the high class passenger and cargo traffic which produced the greater part of the liner revenue on this route.'[3] With equal clarity, however, the Committee concluded that: 'we think it unlikely that the earnings of the proposed new ships could cover their operating and capital costs'.

[1] I.S.C. *35th Report*, p. 10.
[2] *C.P.D.* vol. 147, p. 1,125.
[3] I.S.C. *35th Report*, p. 21.

The 1937 meeting of the Imperial Conference noted only that the question of shipping in the Pacific was under consideration by the governments of the U.K., Australia, Canada, and New Zealand. Reporting in Canberra on the meeting in August 1937 Mr Lyons referred to the submission of a draft agreement to the four governments. Its aim was to assist the Canadian–Australasian Line in building the two recommended ships. Lyons anticipated an early signing of the agreement. His optimism was misplaced; nothing was achieved. The coming of war relieved all parties of the need to reach decision. The whole question of subsidy is lost in obscurity. It is probable that some form of official subsidy was proposed. But the four governments apparently could not agree either on its administration or on ways to control the company. The *S.M.H.* reported at one point that the New Zealand Government insisted that one of the two proposed ships should be registered in New Zealand. Later it stated that Canada was responsible for much of the delay. When, finally, agreement seems to have been reached, the time was considered inopportune for ship building. By then prices were too high.

It is also possible that the question of subsidising a competitor to the American merchant line became merged with, or was affected by, trade talks currently being pursued by Britain with the U.S.A.[1] Explanation given in the contemporary press was that Britain feared retaliation. She dragged her feet lest a too positive policy against the Matson Line stepped up the attacks of subsidised U.S.A. shipping on 'British ships in every sea'. Resolutions tabled in Congress in 1932 could have led to very severe restrictions on British shipping. An article on shipping subsidies commissioned by the *S.M.H.* asserts that possible reprisal as early as Ottawa led Baldwin to shelve a sub-committee report on shipping. Nevertheless, a few years later when the Matson Line issue was at its height, the Australian press quoted Runciman, then President of the Board of Trade, as saying, rather cautiously: 'if a sound case is established by the shipowners, I am ready to persuade my colleagues that, in the interest of British shipping and the Empire, we ought not to be

[1] *S.M.H.* 15, 17 September, 3 December 1937; 28 May, 25 July 1938. *The Times* 25 November 1937, 1 February 1938.

dependent on Foreign flags for the maintenance of Empire links'.[1]

It is abundantly clear that the U.K. company was unwilling to bear sole financial risk of providing more effective competition to the Matson Line. In the light of what was then known of the extent of the subsidies, this reluctance is understandable. Between 1931 and 1935 the Matson Line received in annual operating subsidies four times more than the Canadian-Australasian Line. But the competitive advantage enjoyed by the Matson derived mainly from the quality of service provided. Building costs for 2 new British ships were estimated at $10 to $12 millions. The Matson Line's vessels had been built with the aid of a 20-year loan (equal to three-quarters of the total cost) at a rate of interest below $1\frac{1}{2}\%$. Loans on a comparable scale for the U.K. line were not offered. Any retaliatory rate war initiated by the Canadian-Australasian Line would merely have accelerated decline. The existence of the conference organisation with uniform rates altered nothing. A freight pooling arrangement would have allowed some of the U.S. subsidy to rub off on to the Canadian-Australasian Line. No suggestion of such an arrangement has been traced; it is scarcely conceivable that one would have been considered by the Matson Line.

In contrast with the trans-Pacific route, the existence of a conference based upon freight-pooling arrangements in the Japan–Australia trade largely accounts for the continued survival of the one U.K. line at work. Apart from this single difference, all other ingredients are familiar—a picture of slow, small, old, British ships competing with faster, bigger, newer, subsidised Japanese ships. Only the plea, or justification, for the maintenance of 'Empire links' is missing from our second example. One British company was involved, the E & A Line. It competed with three Japanese lines, as we have already shown. The E & A ships were small and old. Vessel additions during the period were all second-hand and the age structure of the fleet worsened. The *Tanda*, built in 1914, joined the fleet in 1925; it was still in use in 1940. At three representative points in time the size and age structure of the three-vessel E & A fleet was as follows:

[1] *S.M.H.* 4 April 1936; see also issues of 30 November 1934; 9 and 17 April 1936.

	1922	1931	1939
Age in years	12	18	26
	19	19	27
	23	22	28
Total gross tonnage	13,300	18,200	21,200

The ships were coal burners fitted with low-pressure boilers. They were still propelled by the older reciprocating engines in 1939 although by this date as much as one-half of U.K. tonnage had switched to newer forms of propulsion. It is clear that the precise form of conference arrangements in existence permitted the U.K. fleet to survive in the trade. It was also an advantage to the shipping group to which the E & A Line belonged. The line was a subsidiary of the P & O; the vessels in the E & A Line were all ships which had become obsolete for service in the P & O or the BI and had been passed on, or down.

In contrast the ships of the Japanese fleets in the conference were larger, faster, and newer. In 1935 the combined fleet numbered 12, in 1937, 17 ships. All but one or two had been built after 1920, five dated from the early 1930s. In 1937 the N.Y.K. Line announced the scrapping of the two older vessels and the introduction of two 12,000 ton, 20 knot motor vessels. The growth both in trade between Australia and Japan, especially in the early 1930s, and also the rise in the supply of modern Japanese shipping, not surprisingly attracted to Japanese ships a growing proportion of the trade. A circular issued in July 1937 by the Mitsubishi Economic Research Bureau, possibly not entirely disinterested comment, claims that the proportion of trade carried by the E & A Line between Australasian ports and Japan had fallen from about 24% in April 1929 to 21% in December 1935. If the two periods chosen for comparison are in fact strictly comparable, it is understandable that the Japanese lines should have sought a larger share of the pooled freight receipts when discussions were begun to conclude a new agreement.

What effect did this conference have upon the shipping found on the route? We have already shown that notwithstanding the freight pooling arrangement, competition was not completely stifled; it remained very much alive. The Japanese lines gained, and the E & A Line lost, trade. The record of the Japanese lines, moreover, shows that the conference as such did not inhibit continuing investment in fleet modernisation. Japanese ship operating and construction subsidies doubtless played some part but the success of the Japanese shipping industry as a whole during the 1930s 'was less a consequence of subsidies than of enterprise and special advantages, for example, low labour costs.'[1]

In the particular area under examination here, Japanese success derived also from high freights they earned. Rate levels adequate for the E & A Line carrying about 25 % of the trade with an obsolete fleet gave a greater than average return to the modern Japanese fleets. The obvious question concerns the failure of the E & A Line to improve its fleet efficiency. In July 1938, when its ships were 24, 25 and 26 years old, a press announcement links failure to modernise with the conference dispute itself. 'The E & A Line could not consider the question of added tonnage until its share of the trade was guaranteed. The line had stated on several occasions, however, that it would make extra ships available as soon as trade warranted such action, provided, of course, that its share of the trade had been safeguarded, either by a satisfactory agreement with the Japanese lines or by Government action.'[2] It would be unreasonable, perhaps, as well as uncharitable, to dwell upon the failure to add a new or newer vessel in the year which remained between the conclusion of a new agreement and the outbreak of war. It is difficult, nevertheless, to resist the conclusion that so long as the freight-pooling arrangements persisted, the E & A Line could make a profit without further costly investment. The Japanese fleets, moreover, would not have discouraged the situation since they were modernising fast and were not anxious to see the British do the same. In this important sense the conference certainly stifled competition. But once embarked on reasoning along these lines the point of departure is quickly regained. State shipbuilding subsidies enabled a low cost ship operator to reduce his costs even further. It put him in an especially strong position *vis-à-vis* a competitor with a normally higher cost structure, worsened by the use of a relatively inefficient fleet, and lacking subsidies to modernise. The probability is that had war not supervened in 1939 the E & A Line would ultimately have

[1] *Sturmey*, p. 125. [2] *S.M.H.* 10 July 1937.

been ousted from the route. By 1939 its contribution to total tonnage was 15 % or even less. The report of the Imperial Shipping Committee (dated December 1938) states that the Japanese lines carried about 80 % of the wool trade. This was the figure claimed in 1935 and may well have been too low an estimate in 1937 and 1938 when the committee was making its investigation. A few months later, in the course of a general attack upon the problem of Japanese shipping competition, the editor of *Round Table* referred to the Japan–Australia trade and stated that the E & A Line's share 'is near to being extinguished altogether'.[1] In the light of developments on this route, all that is surprising at first sight is the *Round Table* editor's annoyed surprise. But this may be a superficial judgment. British shipping experience in the Japan–Australia trade was part of the wider problem of Japanese shipping competition in the 1930s. In many ways the dispute between the E & A Line and the Japanese lines served as a pointer. A Japanese newspaper in 1937 commented that the 'outcome of the Australian freight issue is being watched in all quarters with great interest and concern, because it will have a great bearing on the settlement of all shipping issues confronting Japan and Great Britain'.[2]

Finally we turn to the effects of the conference system upon the development of the shipping used on the homeward conference routes. Although no specific reference is made to the outward conference, inasmuch as membership of the two conferences overlapped, our examination in fact covers both. The homeward conference was the most significant of the Australian conferences. It controlled the shipment of fine cargo from Australia to Europe, the principal oversea market. After 1930 its hold on the trade tightened when it succeeded more completely in eliminating outside competition. Hence it is in this conference above all where the effects of the system are likely to be most conspicuous. Our analysis has a two-fold objective. First to seek an answer to questions suggested by what is known of the organisational arrangements of this conference. Secondly, it is our aim to test the validity of Professor Sturmey's conclusion for the British liner industry as a whole that the conference system

[1] *S.M.H.* 11 May 1939.

[2] Quoted *Fairplay* vol. 144, p. 275.

had an adverse effect upon the development of British liner services in the inter-war years.

The Australian homeward trade in fine (that is to say high freight-rate) cargo was divided between British and foreign continental lines, each enjoying a specific share. Although no formalised freight-pooling system existed, monetary penalties were exacted for 'over-carrying' the sums collected being used to 'compensate' lines which had carried less than their alloted share. In these circumstances it is not unreasonable to assume that there was little inducement for any line to over-carry. But all associations organised along these lines are vulnerable to the appearance of a dynamic, thrusting member who attracts a volume of trade greater than his authorised share. Persistently exceeding his quota, perhaps unintentionally because of some intangible, unforbidden advantage he offers, he is often tempted to press for a larger share. When finally his determination to enlarge his formal share meets resistance from fellow members, the outcome is often withdrawal, the shattering of the association, a trade war, eventual truce, and ultimately renewed co-operation.

In marine cargo services, the annual totals of goods on offer may not always be known in advance. It is thus virtually impossible to restrict vessel programmes to formal cargo shares. In the Australian homeward conference the records show that a not inconsiderable volume of under- and over-carrying was usual. They also show that over-carrying was often more common with some lines than with others. Nevertheless, the disruptive tactics outlined above do not seem to have plagued the conference. It is possible that conflict over the respective British and foreign shares was avoided from the first by the territory sharing agreements not uncommon at the time.[1] Among the continental lines very slight changes in shares took place. The sole variation of any size amounted to a decrease of less than 5 %. It moreover accompanied a decline in wool exports to the country wherein the line was registered. Some alteration also took place in the individual shares of British lines, largely to provide for a newcomer admitted to the trade in the 1930s. With these exceptions, the division of trade in the later 1920s and during the 1930s remained unchanged throughout.

[1] See *Sturmey*, p. 351.

The exclusion of competition is often held to be a strong disincentive to efficiency. 'During much of the inter-war period, the restrictions on competition within conferences meant that the agreed services continued to be provided by ships of traditional types, offering traditional facilities including speed.'[1] In the absence of internal friction and in the light of stability in the apportionment of trade, we might reasonably expect to find stagnation in the shipping scene. The circumstances outlined which applied to the Australian homeward conference appear to have provided the classic breeding ground in which inefficiency and obsolescence are normal. In fact this is not true of the Australian homeward conference in our period. It is the argument of the following paragraphs that the liner services provided for the Australian homeward conference by both British and foreign European companies were abreast, where not ahead, of other sectors of the world's shipping industry, given the limitations of marine technology at the time. British shipping employed in the conference did not deteriorate in terms of speed or size relative to either British or foreign shipping in general. Nor did it suffer decline among the shipping employed in the Australian homeward conference. Throughout the inter-war years the speed and size of British shipping in fact set the pace in the Australian homeward conference. As we shall subsequently outline, however, there may be more reason to believe that the age profile of the British shipping was tending to worsen.

In an earlier chapter reference was made to the sole aspect of oversea shipping services concerning which any sustained complaint was made by Australian shippers. They complained of the inadequate speed of the shipping catering for the mail services and for the chilled-beef trade. But it is incorrect to deduce from such local complaint that shipping employed on the Australian service was inferior to that employed elsewhere. The real kernel of the complaint is that Australia is geographically far distant from Europe. The most obvious feature, perhaps, which emerges from any discussion of marine speeds is the relative smallness of the increase in the *maximum* which has been achieved in the present century. Compared with other forms of transport, the margin between one maritime record and its successor is small.

[1] *Ibid.*

In the early 1920s the fastest merchant vessel bigger than 10,000 gross tons had a service speed of 27 knots; by 1939 1½ knots had been added by the *Queen Mary* and *Normandie*. To-day the maximum is still only 29 knots.[1] In the Australian service, speeds of 18 knots were achieved by Orient Line vessels before 1914. In 1938/9 ships of the line employed on the Australian mail services had added about 3 knots. Recent developments in ship building and marine engine design have in fact had a more profound effect upon Australian services than on the trans-Atlantic route. The P & O–Orient *Canberra* and *Oriana* both have a service speed of 27½ knots, a 30 % gain over the speed of pre-war flagships in the group.

Concentration upon the very fast, however, conceals the fact that only a handful of merchant ships over 10,000 gross tons were capable of speeds greater than 20 knots. In 1923/4 such ships numbered 11; in 1939 only 35 of the 30,000 powered ships registered at Lloyds were in this speed/size class. Between the wars, moreover, ships of over 10,000 tons faster than 20 or 21 knots were usually vessels larger than 24,000 tons whose dimensions excluded them from the Australian trade. One or two of these large ships entered Australian ports from time to time, chiefly whilst on world cruises. In the main, because of technical limitations and waterway depths the largest vessels normally employed in the Australian service had an upper limit of about 24,000 tons. For such vessels, and indeed for the majority of relatively fast, merchant ships of the time, the speed range of significance lay between 12 and 21 knots.[2] In 1939 the world's fleet included 46 merchant ships of 20,000 to 24,000 tons. Only 15 had speeds as high as 20 to 22 knots and 7 of them were employed in the Australian services. Generally speaking liner speeds of 16 to 18 knots were more common even at the end of our period. In the later 1930s there were about 450 ships larger than 10,000 gross tons: 45 % had service speeds of 16 to 18 knots, only 14 % were faster than 18 knots.

[1] That is to say the published maximum. Certain of the very large recently built ships are apparently *capable* of somewhat greater speeds; the *America* is a good example.

[2] For many years 12 knots was customarily taken as the lowest liner speed and that, generally, tramps had an upper limit of 8–10 knots. (See *U.K.P.P.* Cd. 9092, p. 54, and successive issues of *Lloyd's Register* for speed details.)

British fleets in the Australian homeward conference not only included 7 of the world's 15 ships of 20,000 to 24,000 tons capable of 20 to 22 knots, they also included a higher than average proportion of 16 to 18 knot vessels. As many as two-thirds of all ships of 10,000 tons or over were of 16 to 18 knots. About 10% of the ships were faster than 18 knots. Foreign European ships in the Australian homeward conference tended to be slower and smaller, few were as large as 10,000 tons, no regular visitor exceeded 18 knots. But if we confine analysis to vessels above 10,000 tons we exclude not only most foreign ships but also a large number of British liners in the 6,000 to 10,000 ton class, the cargo-liner size more usually found in the Australian services. The relative importance was as follows:

British lines in the Australian homeward conference

	No. of ships of 12 knots or more	
	10,000 tons and over	6,000 to 9,999 tons
1923/4	53	223
1938/9	93	198

The area for discussion, therefore, concerns relatively small ships with a relatively low speed range. We are concerned with ships of 6,000 to 24,000 tons, considerably bunched in the 6,000 to 10,000 gross ton class, and with speeds of between 12 and 21 knots. An obvious point to make is that all lines in the conference moved steadily upwards in the speed range out of the 12 knot or lower speed classes. By 1939 few British or foreign liners visiting Australia were travelling at such low speeds. For the foreign European ships employed in the homeward conference it is unfortunately not possible to illustrate their speed range in detail. They were drawn as a rule from a small number of large liner companies engaged simultaneously with a wide variety of ships in a number of different sectors. Detailed analysis of the large fleets would yield only misleading conclusions if used as exemplars for the Australian sector. An adequate measure of comparison, however, may be obtained by reference to the performance data of *individual* foreign ships at work. Speed details show that no foreign vessel regularly employed was capable of the speeds achieved by British vessels. The most appropriate foreign company which may be cited as an example is the Norwegian Wilh. Wilhelmsen Line (the old Norwegian-Australian Line). It was the most active and homogeneous of the foreign European fleets in the conference. In 1938/9 as many as 12 of its fleet made a total of 35 visits to Fremantle. It was also among the more modern of the foreign fleets in its extensive use of diesel propulsion; in 1939, 45 of its 53-vessel fleet (all under 10,000 tons) were motor ships. Nevertheless, only 36 ships of its fleet were capable of 12 knots or more, only 9 reached speeds of 16–18 knots. The maximum speed for the fleet, 18 knots, was indeed the maximum for all the foreign European ships regularly visiting Australia.

Details of British shipping in the homeward conference, on the other hand, are more readily analysed. In the early 1920s about 15 % of the combined tonnage of vessels over 6,000 tons travelled at less than 12 knots; by 1939 the proportion had fallen to 5 %. In general the tendency was for vessels to become faster as suggested by the speed profile illustrated below. In the early 1920s only 9 % of the vessels had a service speed of 16 knots or more, in 1939 the comparable figure was about 30 %. At the later date, moreover, 10 mail-service vessels achieved speeds of 19–21 knots. Table 23 also shows that vessel size was tending to increase, our second criterion of modernisation which we examine below.

Preceding discussion relating to speed has already referred indirectly to vessel size. We return here to the question of size in our brief examination of the adoption of the motor vessel. In chapter 2 the point was made that in many ways the diesel engine was well suited to the size range of ships normally employed in the Australian services. It was suggested that in comparison with other sectors the diesel was indeed more commonly used. The application of diesel propulsion, however, varied between fleets. The data show that on the whole the motor vessel had become much more usual on the Australian services provided by foreign European lines. All Italian and Danish ships entering Melbourne in the later 1930s, for

Table 23. *Australian homeward conference. Speed and size of British conference line ships of 12 knots and over*

	No. of ships in size range (tons)				
	20,000 and over	15,000 to 19,999	12,500 to 14,999	10,000 to 12,499	6,000 to 9,999
1923/4					
Speed (knots)					
19–21	—	—	—	—	—
16–18	2	5	5	5	8
13–15	—	—	7	29	164
12	—	—	—	—	51
1938/9					
Speed (knots)					
19–21	8	2	—	—	—
16–18	6	11	13	17	28
13–15	—	—	2	30	132
12	—	—	—	4	38

example, were motor vessels. About 75 % of Swedish tonnage and 90 % of Norwegian tonnage entered in the port was similarly diesel-engined. The foreign European lines engaged in the homeward conference had switched very decisively to diesels, the principal example, already cited, being the Norwegian Wilhelmsen Line.

The British shipping industry in contrast was more conservative. In 1939, 27 % of the world's diesel-propelled tonnage was registered in Britain, compared with only 18 % in Norway, her nearest rival. The Norwegian fleet nevertheless was more fully dieselised than the British. As much as 60 % of Norwegian tonnage in 1939 was made up of motor vessels; in the British fleet the comparable figure was less than one-quarter. In the British lines in the Australian homeward conference only a relatively small proportion of their total tonnage was diesel-propelled. For some ships, notably those of the mail service, their size precluded the economic use of the diesel, given the technical constraints at that time. For the larger P & O–Orient ships the diesel was inappropriate, the geared steam turbine continued throughout the inter-war years to be more usual. Even today, the latest

P & O–Orient vessels, the *Oriana* and *Canberra* are steam-turbined ships. Both were built before the recent pushing back of technical restraint which has made the diesel available for ships in this size and speed range.[1]

Even among British conference lines whose fleets in 1939 consisted solely or mainly of ships of a size then considered appropriate for the diesel, considerable variation is to be noticed. Some lines had firmly embraced the newer propulsion. In the Blue Star Line, 30 % of total tonnage was driven by motor, in Holt's Blue Funnel 24 % and in the Port Line as much as 50 %. More relevant to our argument is that all ships built for these three lines after 1930 were motorised. Other British lines, not in other respects conspicuous for ultra-conservative management, were seemingly reluctant to make the change. The Clan Line, for example, in 1939 numbered only one motor vessel in its 46-ship fleet; each of its 13 ships added in the 1930s was a steamer.

It is easier, however, to point to the variations than to explain them. A partial explanation may again follow from vessel size coupled with the year of building. Fleet additions to the three most progressive of the British fleets in the period were vessels larger than 7,000 to 8,000 tons. During the decade of the 1920s it would seem that 5,000 to 6,000 tons formed the usual upper limit for the application of diesel-propulsion. Hence all ships built for the lines during the 1920s were steamers, in general with the newer turbine in place of the older reciprocating engine. By the end of the 1920s, however, the normal upper limit for diesel propulsion was being extended to approximately 10,000 tons. We therefore find that the lines built with diesels for all their additions during the 1930s. On the whole it would seem probable that the British lines reached their investment decision by determining initially the desired size of the projected vessels to be built. Only then did they determine the

[1] Since 1959 the spread of the diesel to vessels of more than 15,000 tons has notably increased as the detail contained in a footnote on page 97 shows. Diesel-propelled ships of 30,000 tons and over today are becoming much more common. Britain, nevertheless, has continued to lag. Of the 50 ships of 30,000 tons and over launched in Britain since 1959, only 11 have been diesel-engined. Norway continues the lead taken many years ago. Vessels of this size built for the Norwegian fleet since 1959 number 73 of which 52 are diesel-engined. (*Lloyd's Annual Summary of merchant ships launched.*)

engine unit in order to obtain the designed service speed with the anticipated load to be propelled.[1]

The Norwegian Wilhelmsen Line on the other hand appears to have adopted a more flexible approach. Towards the end of the First World War and during the immediate post-war years the company added ships in the 7,000 to 8,000 tons range, all were steamers. But the vessels built for the line in the mid-1920s were all diesels and all were 5,000 to 6,000 tonners, a size range adopted presumably in order to make possible the fitting of diesel machinery. Unlike British lines which would not or could not, the Norwegian company was willing and able to tailor size to propulsion rather than propulsion to size. What seems clear, however, is that the shelter provided by the conference system as such does not seem to have inhibited either foreign conference lines nor certain British conference lines from adopting the diesel. Imperfect or unwise investment decisions may have been made by some British lines in the Australian homeward conference during the inter-war years. But the explanation may be no more subtle than the persistence of old-fashioned management. Reliance upon traditional types of vessel and propulsion may reflect no more than traditional management decisions. It would not seem entirely reasonable to attribute it to the conference system.

Our final criterion rests upon the age structure of the tonnage used in the Australian homeward conference. On this yardstick there can be no doubting the tendency for the British shipowner to lag in his investment in new tonnage in comparison with certain other foreign fleets engaged. The available evidence providing a basis for comparing British conference and British non-conference shipping visiting Australia is imprecise and possibly not completely representative. It nevertheless suggests that the British conference lines were content to maintain services with older vessels. The British non-conference lines providing tramp shipping seem to have had newer tonnage. In this

[1] The marrying together of load and designed service speed is an important consideration when deciding on propulsion requirements. Marine engines are designed to give speeds for stated loads. If turbines larger than actually required are fitted, or are called upon to carry less than the planned load, fuel costs rise as power is reduced. With the diesel, efficiency falls only slowly with reductions in power. (See A. C. Hardy & E. Tyrrell, *Shipbuilding* (1964).)

Table 24. *Age structure of British and selected foreign shipping, 1923/4 and 1938/9*

	% of total tonnage					
	Under 5 years	5–9 years	10–14 years	15–19 years	20–24 years	25 years and over
1923/4						
All British tonnage	29·1	20·6	17·4	13·6	11·0	8·1
British tonnage in Australian conference	25·8	17·4	26·1	14·2	10·2	6·1
World tonnage	26·9	25·2	14·4	11·5	9·5	12·5
French tonnage	32·3	16·9	18·9	11·4	9·2	11·2
German tonnage	51·9	4·2	8·8	10·0	9·8	15·2
Dutch tonnage	36·8	20·7	20·4	12·7	6·0	3·4
Italian tonnage	27·0	16·2	11·6	13·2	13·4	18·6
Japanese tonnage	21·7	34·5	7·5	8·3	9·4	18·5
Norwegian tonnage	30·3	23·2	14·8	12·0	8·1	11·6
1938/9						
All British tonnage	21·1	10·5	24·2	20·9	12·3	10·9
British tonnage in Australian conference	14·6	6·7	18·7	27·2	16·6	16·1
World tonnage	12·9	13·0	14·9	27·0	12·5	19·7
French tonnage	10·9	17·9	10·8	35·9	12·2	12·2
German tonnage	17·0	10·7	21·1	31·9	5·8	13·5
Dutch tonnage	19·1	20·1	16·7	26·4	9·7	7·9
Italian tonnage	1·0	9·9	18·2	26·4	15·6	28·9
Japanese tonnage	23·6	11·2	6·8	25·9	15·8	16·7
Norwegian tonnage	21·9	24·2	16·8	16·6	9·6	10·9

Source: *Lloyd's Register.*

respect membership of the conference may well have inhibited progress.

Comparisons with foreign tonnage are given in Table 24. It is to be noticed that the world's tonnage as a whole had become older if the beginning and end of the inter-war years are compared. This is largely explicable by reference to the initial renewal and replacement of lost tonnage after the First World War and the subsequent difficulties of the shipping industry as a whole. British tonnage similarly tended to age during the period but not to the same extent. Certain foreign fleets aged even more sharply, especially in the lower age groups. The German fleet, which surrendered much of its older tonnage in war reparations (and saddled the British fleet with obsolescent tonnage) emerged in the early 1920s with a very young fleet. Despite German government assistance, however, little significant investment was made in German shipping in the 1930s, hence the increased age of its fleet in 1939. There were exceptions, notably the Japanese fleet, which benefited from scrap-and-build schemes, and the efficient Norwegian fleet.[1] It is less easy to compare statistics of age structure of British and foreign lines in the homeward conference for reasons already outlined. For individual foreign conference ships, however, it is clear that they tended in most instances to be younger than the British tonnage used.

Fleet details of British shipping involved in the Australian services are illustrated in Table 25. Section C of the table shows that the age of all tonnage owned by the British members of the homeward conference was somewhat higher than for the British fleet as a whole. One-third of the tonnage was more than 19 years old as compared with a little over one-fifth in the whole fleet. Largely this reflects the existence within the huge B.I. fleet of a host of small, old ships, principally engaged in Indian waters. If account is taken only of British conference vessels which called at Australian ports (as reflected in the Fremantle records), the use of a much younger fleet is at once obvious. Of some interest in this context is the age structure of all British tonnage entered at Fremantle in comparison with British conference tonnage entered. In 1923/4 the tonnage proportions in the lower age classes for both groups is virtually the same. But in 1938/9 homeward conference tonnage tended to be older than the combined conference and non-conference British tonnage. If the evidence may in fact be taken as adequately representative of British tonnage in the Australian services there may be justification for believing that conference membership discouraged investment. Taking all criteria into consideration, however, the evidence as a whole does not seem sufficiently strong to support the assertion that the conference system alone, or even mainly, was responsible in the Australian homeward conference at least for the failure of British shipping to maintain its relative position in world shipping.

[1] For a discussion of 'nationalism in shipping in the inter-war years' and explanation of the success of individual fleets, see *Sturmey*, chapter v.

Table 25. *Age structure of British shipping in Australia's oversea services, 1923/4 and 1938/9*

	Under 5 years (%)	5–9 years (%)	10–14 years (%)	15–19 years (%)	20–24 years (%)	25 years and over (%)	% of total in size class
A: All British tonnage entered at Fremantle:							
1923/4	28·0	22·6	27·4	12·0	7·7	2·2	
1938/9	29·9	8·6	21·2	23·5	10·4	6·2	
B: Homeward conference line tonnage calling at Fremantle:							
1923/4	29·5	19·0	27·1	11·7	7·3	5·3	
1938/9	26·9	5·4	21·5	25·5	11·7	8·9	
C: All tonnage owned by homeward conference lines:							
1923/4	25·8	17·4	26·1	14·2	10·2	6·1	
1938/9	14·6	6·7	18·7	27·2	16·6	16·0	
D: U.K. fleet as a whole:							
1923/4	29·1	20·6	17·4	13·6	11·0	8·1	
1938/9	21·1	10·5	24·2	20·9	12·3	10·9	
E: Tonnage owned by homeward conference lines to show distribution by size and age:							
1923/4							
Under 6,000 gross tons	3·8	7·0	7·1	5·0	4·2	4·3	31·4
6,000 and under 8,000	6·4	7·1	7·9	2·9	4·8	1·5	30·5
8,000 and under 10,000	4·5	2·0	3·7	3·1	0·6	—	13·8
10,000 and under 15,000	6·2	0·9	4·8	1·6	0·6	0·3	14·3
15,000 and under 20,000	2·9	0·4	—	0·9	—	—	4·2
20,000 and over	2·0	—	2·6	0·7	—	—	5·3
1938/9							
Under 6,000 gross tons	1·0	0·3	1·2	4·9	6·2	4·0	17·6
6,000 and under 8,000	3·0	2·2	5·4	7·3	7·4	4·8	30·1
8,000 and under 10,000	1·8	0·5	2·5	5·9	2·2	3·6	16·5
10,000 and under 15,000	5·0	2·5	3·4	6·6	0·4	2·7	20·6
15,000 and under 20,000	0·4	—	4·0	1·4	0·4	0·9	7·1
20,000 and over	3·3	1·2	2·2	1·1	—	—	7·8

Source: *Lloyd's Register*.

Chapter 7

FREIGHT RATES: DETERMINATION AND STABILITY

An aspect of the shipping industry of considerable public interest postponed from the preceding chapter concerns ocean freight rates. It is a thorny, disputatious question. It lures the unwary into unrealistic assumptions and often to make inappropriate comparisons. Shipowners are given to making ton–mile comparisons of rail and ocean rates; it is not surprising that ocean freights should prove to be considerably lower. They also claim that ocean freights represent only a minute proportion of total production and marketing costs. During the 1920s (when clamour for lower rates was common) the published proceedings of annual meetings of the U.K. Chamber of Shipping often include speeches on this theme. In 1925, for example, the outgoing president of the Chamber spoke of rates to and from Australia. He claimed that freight charges from Britain to Australia on a £1,000 motor car was no more than 2·7 % of its landed value. The shipper, however, is usually less convinced than the shipowner that freight charges may be disregarded. The exporter of primary produce in particular remains unpersuaded. He knows that transport charges may in fact represent a high proportion of landed value, especially in times of unstable commodity prices. On Australian wheat shipment to Europe, to anticipate subsequent discussion, freight charges formed a widely fluctuating proportion of the realised export price. In some instances, as we show below, prices and freight rates moved in opposite directions. Big Australian harvests in times of world plenty pushed export prices down and the freight rate up.

It is the aim of the present chapter to examine this most contentious of all shipping questions. A number of aspects are relevant: the determination of rates; the level of rates; the differential between tramp and conference rates on comparable cargoes; the relationship of conference rates to commodity values; and, above all, rate stability, the keystone in the defence of the conference system. Tramp rates are included in the discussion for three reasons. To some extent they exercised a degree of restraint on conference rates. They armed the local shippers with a weapon to challenge the conference. Secondly, the total paid in tramp freight charges was not inconsiderable. Although tramp ships were of declining importance in Australia's oversea grain-carrying, they nevertheless continued to play a significant part. Finally, as we shall show, tramp rates were highly unstable and hence serve as a yardstick against which to view the greater stability to be found in liner rates.

Tramp ships are distinguished from liners by their freedom from fixed routes and time-tables. They are thus able to carry or to seek cargoes anywhere in the world. But this conveys an oversimplified picture. Although a tramp will carry any item, a score of bulk commodities virtually exhausts the list of tramp cargoes. The uses made of a tramp, moreover, and the freight rates charged are determined in the light of the charter agreement by which it is hired. The least important type of charter, and quickly dismissed, is the charter of a tramp on berth terms by a liner company to supplement an existing scheduled liner service. On berth, the tramp assumes liner characteristics and need not here command attention. The more common, and the more important, were (and are) voyage or time-charter agreements. Voyage charters may be for a single trip or voyage, for a round voyage, or for consecutive voyages on long-term contract. The distinction between a long-term consecutive voyage charter and a time charter is necessarily a fine one. Freight rates in voyage charters are usually stated in terms of a sum per ton of whichever commodity the vessel is to carry. It is customary with voyage charters for the port of shipment and port of discharge to be stated. Often a range of ports may be named. The Australian grain charter, for example, commonly specified (and specifies) shipment at 'Australian ports' for discharge within the Antwerp–Hamburg range of ports.

A time charter, as the name implies, is the hire of a ship for a fixed, stated time; it may be for months or years. Time charters differ from voyage charters in a number of important respects.

On this basis the charterer hires the whole ship at a stated monthly sum per ton of the vessel's deadweight capacity. With the voyage charter, the owner's revenue depends upon maximum utilisation of hold capacity. Brokers arranging voyage charters indeed aim at 'fixing' a ship of an appropriate size for a cargo of a given quantity. The owner of a vessel on time charter, on the other hand, is uninterested in the vessel's loading, subject to considerations of safety and so on. His interest concentrates on the receipt each month of the agreed hire sum. The advantages to the owner of a long period time charter are at once obvious. Today the conclusion of a time charter before the completion of a vessel on the stocks is not uncommon. In Norway, indeed, considerations of state maritime and fiscal policy require the signing of a long-term time-charter agreement before the building of a new vessel is even begun.

In the long-run, time-charter rates are probably the best indicators of the trend in ocean rates of freight. They more accurately reflect the demand for shipping, and they bear a close association with movements in building and running costs. In surveys of the world's shipping industry or of a national fleet as a whole, the pattern of time-charter rates forms an indispensable basis. For purposes of sectoral examination they are less immediately useful. In the first place, time-charters are defective in that they record the period of hire and the monthly rate per ton of a vessel's deadweight capacity without necessarily specifying the sector wherein the ship is to operate. Even where the operational sector is named, the flexibility normal in such arrangements does not preclude a vessel's use elsewhere. And even where both the shipping route and the type of commodity are specified for our period, as in Angier's annual freight surveys from time to time, the lack of information on the quantities carried on individual voyages makes a rate per ton calculation impossible. Nevertheless, as a yardstick against which to measure secular variations in commodity rates, time-charter fluctuations are important.

Voyage charter rates are spot rates, determined in the light of normal market considerations. Where tonnage available in any one sector is inadequate to meet demand, rates rise and attract disengaged tonnage from elsewhere. Where commissioned world tonnage as a whole proves inadequate, new building is begun and laid up vessels are recommissioned. The process continues until the additional tonnage becoming available matches requirements or the situation is reversed and changes in world trade damp down demand for shipping. Tonnage in excess of the amount required has the effect of depressing the charter rate. If the rate falls to the point where the revenue from a voyage is less than the voyage costs minus lay-up charges, vessels are laid-up. For an unfixed ship away from home, however, the homeward voyage to a lay-up berth may be undertaken at a rate below this point where the alternative is a voyage in ballast. Instead of laying-up at a time when long-term prospects are discouraging, an owner may prefer to scrap ships which are old and hence expensive to maintain or are otherwise costly to retain. The tramp freight market is world wide; it is controlled from a few major centres. Charters involving Australia at this time were arranged exclusively in London. Tramp freights in no single sector are therefore able to remain for long out of phase with world trends. An unexpected variation in demand (an abnormally large or small harvest, threat of war and so on) may have an immediate local effect. The diffusion into a world context restores equilibrium.

In the 1930s this simple pattern became obscured with the decline of world trade during the depression. By 1933 the volume of trade had fallen to about three-quarters of the level attained in 1929. In both the Australian sector, and in the world shipping industry as a whole, it was the tramp shipping branch which most suffered. Freight rates fell sharply. Using 1929 again as the base year, the Chamber of Shipping tramp freight index shows that rates were a quarter lower by 1933; thereafter they began to recover. Vessels were laid up all over the world. British tonnage laid up at ports in the U.K. amounted to almost one million net tons by 1 October 1930; it exceeded two million in 1931 and had reached 2·16 million by July 1932. From then the total fell, but not until the middle of 1935 was laid up tonnage reduced to a half million. Older vessels went to the breakers, new launchings fell. In the world's shipping industry as a whole the tonnage broken up between 1931 and 1935 was rather more than twice the total in the preceding quinquennium: new tonnage launched declined to one-half. In the British fleet, launchings between 1931 and 1935 fell to one-quarter of the previous five-year total; the tonnage broken up rose two and a half times. In part, the disposal of tonnage before 1935 reflects the 'scrap and build' assistance speedily introduced in certain countries. The world's fleet as a whole fell by only some 7% between 1930 and 1935 as contrasted with the 15% decline recorded for the U.K. fleet over the same years.

Assistance for the U.K. shipping industry was not introduced until 1935.[1] It was in two parts, a scrap-and-build scheme, and an operating subsidy. The latter was designed to assist tramps only. The conditions imposed by the government involved 'a real measure of organisation' of the tramp shipping industry. A brief digression is therefore necessary to examine the effect of the required 'organisation' on the method by which tramp rates were determined. The operating subsidy was intended for foreign going tramp ships employed on voyage charter only. Vessels other than foreign going tramps, and tramps on charters other than on a voyage basis, were excluded.[2] It was to be distributed by the shipping industry itself. The committee of tramp ship owners in setting up the Tramp Shipping Administrative Committee as the subsidy control agency stated its broad aims: to maintain and improve freights and to cooperate with other shipowner organisations. To improve freight rates the committee created a number of freight cooperation subcommittees with the dual aim of minimizing domestic competition, both between U.K. tramps and between U.K. liners and tramps; and of promoting 'the fullest possible employment of British tramp shipping'.[3]

Sub-committees controlled each of the main trades. That for the Australian trade not surprisingly included among its members directors and other representatives of the leading tramp companies whose ships were frequent visitors to Australian ports. It also included representatives of the Netherlands

[1] See *U.K.P.P.* Cmd. 4754 and the various reports subsequently made by the Tramp Shipping Administrative Committee.

[2] Except for oil tankers, and a few long-term carrying contracts such as those referred to above in connection with the Australian trade in sugar and phosphates, long-term charters in fact were not common at this time.

[3] *U.K.P.P.* Cmd. 4754, p. 9.

and Norwegian shipping industries. (A noteworthy feature of the scheme as a whole was the voluntary cooperation of foreign tramp owners.) The object of the sub-committees was to determine and to maintain minimum tramp rates. British tramp chartered voyages could be brought within control by withholding the subsidy if rates accepted undercut the published minima. British liner companies conformed voluntarily: 'liner organisations and individual liner owners have expressed keen appreciation of the value to them of the system of freight co-operation and of the Committee's work in this respect'. In the Australian trade, where 'co-operation of liners was secured from the start...during the last few months liners have obtained as much as 2*s.* 6*d.* per ton over the minimum'.[1] The attempt at rate maintenance was moreover supported by foreign tramps and liners who observed the agreed minima and, as mentioned above, were also represented on the freight co-operation sub-committees.

Two further possible sources of embarrassment seemed likely to hazard the scheme: undercutting by tramps on time charter and excess tramp tonnage on offer arising from unfixed ballast voyages. Time-charter rates, as noted above, are based on dead-weight. Normally an owner is indifferent to the safe use made of his ship, but the possibility that time-chartered tramps might be used by the charterer to carry at cut rates led to the insertion of a safeguard in the charter party. Tramps on time charter when used on trades regulated by the tramp committee were required to comply with the current minimum freight schemes.

The second danger lay in the flooding of a market by speculative tramp voyages in ballast. At the outset of the subsidy scheme, unfixed ballast voyages were declared ineligible for subsidy. But this seems not to have reduced ballast entries in the Australian sector. During the mid-1930s the arrival in Australia of U.K. tonnage in ballast tended to be higher than in the 1920s. Nevertheless, subsidies were paid in respect of only 24 U.K. tramp arrivals in ballast in Australia in 1935 and 11 in 1936. Since the subsidised ballast arrivals represented only 15 % of all U.K. ballast arrivals in the two years, it would seem probable that other U.K. tramps continued to arrive in ballast. But

[1] *U.K.P.P.* Cmd. 5084, pp. 4, 7–8.

whether they were making speculative, unsubsidised ballast voyages, or were on time charter it is impossible to say.

A chronological sequel to the introduction of assistance to British shipping was a tendency for tramp freights to rise. It is tempting to link the two causally, to attribute higher rates to the new method of rate determination. No causal connection necessarily existed. Subsidy payments to tramps on voyage charter were made only during 1935 and 1936; thereafter freight rates exceeded 1929 levels, the base year adopted for the scheme; no subsidy therefore was payable. On grain rates from Australia to the U.K. the introduction of a minimum in March 1935 lifted the rate immediately from 19*s*. 3*d*. to the agreed figure of 22*s*. 6*d*. per ton. In October 1935 the rate rose to 24*s*. 6*d*. for Western Australia and 25*s*. 6*d*. for eastern ports. But long before the end of 1935, rates actually obtainable were exceeding the minima. The spot charter rate on 31 December was 28*s*. and the average liner parcel rate during the fourth quarter was 26*s*. 3*d*. During 1936 when the minimum rate was raised to between 31*s*. and 32*s*. from July, the parcel rate was higher throughout the year and the charter rate on 31 December stood at 46*s*. 3*d*. Thereafter charter rates on Australian wheat to Europe on the whole stayed above 1929 rates. At the end of 1939 the rate was as high as the lowest quotation recorded for 1921. Rising tramp rates may have stemmed from the limitation of competition elsewhere. (Tonnage entered at Australian ports records no fall during the 1930s. In 1938/9, which was below the 1930s peak, tonnage entered was about 20 % up on the 1929/30 total.) The more probable cause is the gradual recovery of world trade and with it the rise in demand for shipping.

As we have already shown, and discuss further below, complaints concerning freight rates on Australian exports largely centred upon liner conference rates rather than on tramp rates. On the whole, shippers accepted tramp-rate elasticity associated with normal demand and supply conditions. They resented the insertion of an 'artificial' constraint, however. The introduction of minimum freight schemes in the tramp sector was specifically designed to arrest the unimpeded action of market forces. It did not appeal to shippers. The Australian Grain Shippers Association protested. The *West Australian* published the comments of the local wheat pool secretary, the essence of which was summed up as follows: 'now that the shipowners [*sc.* tramp owners] have shown their power to raise freights...one naturally wonders where they will stop'.[1] As events were to prove, market influences soon reasserted their predominance and no further similar protests about the tramp sector have been traced.

'Artificial' rather than 'natural' control characterises liner rating policy. To a large extent the differences reflect fundamental cargo distinctions. In contrast with the tramp trade, liner cargoes cover every item which it is possible to despatch by ship (except for oil, ores and similar bulk cargoes). Again unlike the tramp trade, liner companies hire out not the complete ship but an amount of space. A liner operator agrees to carry, as any common carrier, items lawfully presented for shipment. On many voyages a liner may operate below capacity. The liner owner, therefore, may hope, but cannot always be certain, to show a profit on every voyage. Accounts of individual voyages which have been examined show in itemised form income and expenditure including, for accounting purposes, the averaging out of overheads. They often reveal loss. But over time the traffic carried on fixed trade routes must meet the economic costs of the services provided. In determining his rates, therefore, a liner owner aims not only at eliminating competition (hence the conference organisation). He is also faced with the problem of maximising his return from the carriage of a wide range of items. He therefore takes into account not only the size and stowage factor of commodities, not only back-haul factors, distance, port charges etc., but also the value of the items to be carried on the trade route. He is given to arguing that his rating policy is deliberately designed to pitch rates at levels which represent only a minute fraction of the value of the items carried. A less flattering, although not necessarily a more accurate description of liner rating policy is that the liner owner charges what the traffic will bear. It is in fact the discrimination practised in liner rating which attracts hostile comment. It facilitates and indeed encourages comparisons upon a ton–mile basis. Resentment is not lessened when enquiry reveals rate differentials on an item moving in different directions along the

[1] Quoted *Fairplay* vol. 138, p. 3.

same trade route. Nor is hostility softened or suspicion dissipated by the well-known reluctance of liner owners to publish their rate schedules. Individual rates are quoted on enquiry but access to the entire book of rates is withheld. (The misinterpretation of motives whether justified or not is thus all too easy.) Once items are grouped, classified, and rated, particular or general rate revisions are not difficult to make by percentage adjustments.

Liner rating policy attracts dislike for another reason. In general, liner conferences prefer to adopt a flat rate for as many ports as possible. This was so in Australia's conferences. The range of services given, however, at individual ports may for the same rate vary in accordance with the custom of the port. Only when costs to the owner vary substantially is he likely to increase his rates to or from a particular port. Shippers often resent flat rating on the grounds that the owner is in fact discriminating against low-cost ports in favour of high-cost ports. In New Zealand in the 1920s local agitation concerning flat rating led to sustained public protest by shippers through the main ports.[1]

In the Australian sector during the inter-war years the determination of liner rates was not always accomplished as simply, nor as arbitrarily, nor as confidentially as is suggested in the preceding general outline. Local variations from the general pattern, their effect upon rate determination and rate levels, and their origins are examined in following pages. Three major markets were identified in earlier chapters: Europe, especially the U.K.; the far east; and North America. Most of the conference information available refers to the homeward route to Europe. Some rates for wool and refrigerated exports to Japan have been traced together with a few outward rates from Europe. Virtually nothing has been found for the North America route. But it is appropriate that the bulk of our information relates to the most important of Australia's trade routes—the homeward route to Europe—for it is upon this route above all where methods of rate determination are most divergent.

The organisation of, and secrecy about, rates on the outward

[1] See Wellington Harbour Board, *Report of Special Committee*...(1926) and *Protes against the flat rate system* (1928).

trade from Europe conforms most closely with the generalised pattern described above. About 2,000 items entered into the trade; only a few individual rates are known. Ignorance of actual rates in part stems from the unwillingness of shipping companies to grant access to the rate books. In part also it bears witness to the relative absence of adverse comment about outward rates of freight. As already noted, the outward conference formed the subject of a complaint lodged with the Imperial Shipping Committee in 1921. But it was the deferred rebate system and the boycott of shippers which attracted notice, not the actual level of rates nor the method of determination. And it was the Commonwealth government seeking to protect its own shipping line rather than Australian importers or U.K. shippers who had protested. The general impression conveyed by the evidence is that rate levels and rate determination as such were not disliked. *The Times* pointed out in its comment on the report of the Imperial Shipping Committee in 1923 that no evidence existed to show that the merchants themselves were dissatisfied with rates or with the deferred rebate system.[1] Nevertheless, despite the absence of complaint from shippers, the recommendations of the committee involved the shipowners after 1923 in formal recognition of ship user participation in the varying of freight rates. The agreement, introduced in parallel with and as an alternative to the deferred rebate system, specifically bound the liner companies to refrain from any general increase in the basis rates 'except after consultation with the Australasian Merchants' Association and full consideration of the shippers' views thus ascertained'.[2] The extent to which, if at all, the views of shippers may subsequently have been canvassed is not known. It may be significant that the records are as free of complaint concerning outward rates after 1923 as they were before. Not even the general rate increase discussed at the end of 1928 stirred the U.K. shippers into protest. Yet it was this which caused apprehension in Australia that homeward rates might rise and led to the 1929 Conference.

The homeward conference reveals a dramatically different pattern: the determination of rates stemmed from a wider basis and secrecy was absent. During the 1930s (though not in the

[1] *The Times* 10 March 1923. [2] *Fairplay* vol. 86, p. 694.

1920s) rates were fixed in consultation between shipowners and ship-users under the continuing watchful intervention of the federal government. The extended basis of negotiation followed, and indeed flowed from the changes accomplished by the 1929 Conference. Rate publicity in Australia, however, long antedated this important change. Throughout the 1920s as well as the 1930s details of rates were freely available, were well known and were widely quoted. Nor need we question the accuracy of the publicised rates. It is improbable that the details published in the local press were fictitious. The same rates were authoritatively quoted in parliament, often in response to searching questions, and they were recorded in the official Australian *Quarterly Summary of Statistics*. It is an unnecessary exercise of the imagination to doubt the reality of the published rate details available. The elaborate structure set up after the 1929 Overseas Shipping Conference to determine homeward freight rates and the absence of secrecy attaching to the level of rates from as early as 1922 makes nonsense of the generally accepted view of liner conference rate policy.

A number of factors explain the fundamental differences which existed in the homeward conference. In part the distinctive characteristics of rate determination and of the publicity given to the rates reflects the smaller significant number of cargo items involved. Rates for about fifty commodities are listed in the *Quarterly Summary of Statistics*, about a dozen of these relate to major export items. The close scrutiny given to the rates especially in the early 1930s manifests also the local reaction to the difficulties of world depression. There can be no questioning the association between marketing problems overseas and local preoccupation with the level of freights. Nor does press comment leave any doubt that the rates fixed for the homeward conference were arrived at after lengthy negotiation in which local views were not lightly disregarded. The Commonwealth government showed its willingness to cooperate with, and indeed to support the homeward conference, as we have already shown, in a number of ways: by the amendment of legislation to provide a financial tie between shipper and owner; by confirming its monopoly; and by bringing pressure upon the Western Australian producer cooperatives. It later went further and made financial concessions to oversea shipowners in order to obtain rate reductions.

By the creation of the A.O.T.A. the government established dual, shared responsibility for rate determination. The onus was placed jointly upon shipping companies and shippers. The government nevertheless found itself unable to withdraw from the scene; it was compelled to retain a place at the negotiating table. Basically this became necessary because of local dissatisfaction with the A.O.T.A. and because of official anxiety that cooperation might cease. The situation is full of paradox. The shippers, associated in the Exporters Oversea Transport Committee, were represented at the A.O.T.A. central council in Sydney by a small executive group. It was drawn from the committees formed in each state at the request of federal government by the local chambers of commerce. Members of the executive group represented each state and also each export industry.[1] In the negotiations undertaken by the A.O.T.A. the shipowners representatives, the O.S.R.A., encountered the combined opposition of the exporters representatives to any suggested increases and an equally combined demand for lowered rates. But the representatives of the various exporters also pursued sectional interests. They made unilateral demands for rate reductions on behalf of whichever export group they represented. On 1 March 1933, for example, the Meat Exporters Association announced its imminent withdrawal from the A.O.T.A. unless meat export rates were immediately lowered. In June, despite A.O.T.A. rate reductions achieved on the 'heavy wool bale', certain shipper representatives withdrew and returned home and the meeting was adjourned. Throughout the months of July, August, and September, rarely a week passed without some similar news item appearing in the *S.M.H.* The same paper later that year expressed the relief felt by many when the threatened collapse of the A.O.T.A. was averted. The A.O.T.A. 'has, in its four years of existence, achieved so much that a return to the old system under which shippers and shipowners were sharply divided would have been nothing short of a tragedy'.[2] The following year seems to have witnessed few dis-

[1] For a list of interests represented see *C.P.D.* vol. 123, p. 1,130.

[2] *S.M.H. Finance and Commerce Supplement*, 13 February 1934.

agreements at the A.O.T.A. meetings but by 1935 disputes were once more on the increase. During these years it is clear that the government was compelled to step up its role. In part this was because it was drawn more deeply into the sphere at the request of the shippers. In July 1933, for example, the Adelaide Wool Selling Brokers Association expressed disappointment at the smallness of the announced wool rate reduction. Bigger reductions, its secretary argued, could follow the granting of relief by state and federal governments.[1] In part also the government became more deeply involved because of the intransigence of certain shippers, above all the West Farmers. The action of this dissident group seemed likely to wreck the whole scheme of co-operation. Official attitude summed up in the terse, unambiguous statement by the minister for commerce, is quoted in the preceding chapter. Discussions involving the government, the A.O.T.A. and the West Farmers' Line dragged on for more than two years. Earl Page in the course of a speech at Moree on 5 May 1937 hinted, and the *S.M.H.* two days later reported, that agreement finally had been reached both on the level of freight rates and on long-term rate stabilisation. Negotiations had in fact ranged beyond rates. They had concentrated upon three important issues: on freight levels acceptable to shippers; on freedom of activity for the West Farmers' Line; and on an Australia-wide willingness to accept rationalisation in the supply of shipping tonnage. The *S.M.H.* in a congratulatory editorial drew attention to the part which had been played by the government. 'The Country Party representatives with Dr Page at their head, have been unremitting in their efforts to forward the progress of country interests...special credit must be extended to Mr Thorby (minister for commerce) for the energy and persistence which has at last met with its rewards...the new reductions [*sc.* in freight rates] in fact, appear to have been made possible by means of the government concessions to shipowners. The shipping freight agreement, is therefore, a distinct step forward as denoting...coordination of shipping and exporting interests.'[2] There can be no doubting the importance of the new methods of rate determination. Above all they spread

[1] *S.M.H.* 22 July 1933.

[2] *S.M.H.* 14 June 1937. See also *C.P.D.* vol. 141, pp. 3,481, 3,537.

responsibility. They brought to an end the previous pattern which to many in Australia seemed to be an arbitrary and irresponsible exercise of monopoly power by expatriates without a stake in the economy.

Widening the basis of rate determination involved the liner owner in a struggle whether he sought a rate increase, or merely to maintain a rate in the face of demands for reductions. State championship itself was not enough to eliminate completely the basic inherent conflict between owner and user. Shipowners spoke from the heart when they complained that Australian shippers wanted Atlantic liners—at tramp rates. The tramp owner in contrast encountered no such difficulty. His rates, as we shall show, oscillated wildly because of the nature of the open market within which they were determined. But they were not limited by secrecy; they were freely quoted in the contemporary shipping press. The lack of any concealment about tramp charter rates thus makes possible some comparison with tramp rates in other sectors (in succeeding pages some comparison of tramp and homeward liner rates is also made).

Available outbound Australian tramp rates are few in number. For the 1920s coal rates to the N.E.I. were often quoted but only rarely for other coal destinations. Some rates for wheat to China and Japan and a wool rate to Japan have also been traced. The one rate regularly quoted in the various sources, however, is the homeward rate for wheat; upon this single rate present discussion is centred. The daily quotations reported in *Lloyds List* or in the *Daily Freight Register* are too numerous to use for present purposes. The labour of extraction would not be justified by the end result. Most vessel 'fixtures' reported find their way into the daily shipping press; the number of vessels involved was large. In the 1932/3 season, for example, more than 300 tramps, and in 1936 about 200 U.K. tramps, were 'fixed' for the Australian grain trade. The need to aggregate and average is unavoidable. For many purposes the information collected by E. A. V. Angier and published annually in *Fairplay* is adequate. It contains the year's high and low, their mean, and the rate at the end of the year. More comprehensive are the details published in the *Annual Reports* of the Chamber of Shipping. These conveniently bring together in one place average weekly tramp quotations for 7 routes, 3 being for homeward grain including the Australian grain trade. In the same source also is published the tramp freight index compiled by the Chamber of Shipping. Begun in 1921, with 1920 as the base year, it is an unweighted index of rates on 21 (originally 27) routes. It was changed in 1937 to a weighted index based on data assembled in 1935 in the administration of assistance to British shipping. Yet another convenient source is the official Australian publication already mentioned: the *Quarterly Summary of Statistics* which includes a number of rates. All but one of the rates concern liners. The one exception is the quarterly average tramp charter rate for wheat. Unfortunately, details appear only from 1932 and hence cover too short a span. More useful, and indeed of greater interest in this source, is the published liner berth parcel rate for wheat. Unlike other liner conference rates published in the *Quarterly Summary of Statistics* the parcel rate for wheat was not the subject of conference agreement. It thus more faithfully reflects short-term as well as long-term changes in the demand for shipping.

The sources listed above highlight annual, quarterly, even weekly variations in the actual homeward grain rate from Australia. They make possible comparison of Australian with other grain rates, and with the Chamber of Shipping composite tramp freight index. The liner rates available also provide a measure of the accuracy of the assertion referred to above that liners undercut tramps in the Australian grain trade. A glance at annual variations gives perspective for more detailed examination. Table 26 shows details compiled by Angier together with comparable data abstracted from the Chamber of Shipping *Annual Reports*. Minor discrepancies are to be noticed, probably because the Angier figures were designed to pick out the extremes, in contrast with the Chamber of Shipping approach which sought representative rates. Nevertheless, their similarity is sufficient to enable us with confidence to indicate the prevailing levels. Both testify to the early collapse of high war-time rates, from 225*s*. a ton in 1919 to 82*s*. 6*d*. in 1921, and thereafter to the long-term downward trend.

It is of interest to compare pre-1914 rates with those of the inter-war years. The second decade of the century witnessed a massive price inflation. Many, but not all of the prices fell sharply after 1920. A complaint often made by shipowners was that freight rates in the inter-war period were considerably below those of pre-war years. 'Sea freight (*sic*) is...one of the very few commodities sold at pre-war prices. The case is far different with the elements forming the cost of running ships.' This comment was made in the Chamber of Shipping *Annual Report* of 1925/6. This assertion in fact is not true of the rate for wheat from Australia to the U.K./Continent. Angier's figures for the last five pre-war years of peace for this route are as follows:

	Highest	Lowest	Rate at end of year
1909	27*s*. 6*d*.	23*s*.	27*s*.
1910	27*s*.	20*s*. 6*d*.	27*s*.
1911	30*s*.	23*s*.	30*s*.
1912	43*s*. 3*d*.	28*s*. 9*d*.	43*s*. 3*d*.
1913	43*s*. 9*d*.	28*s*.	33*s*.

During the depressed years of the early 1930s, however, the 'low' rate touched a bottom never reached between 1909 and 1913. At the opposite end of the scale, the rate level during times of peak demand in Australia for tramp shipping, the 'high' of 1912 and 1913 was exceeded in only 8 of the years between 1921 and 1938. In 5 of the inter-war years the 'high' rate was between one-quarter and one-third below the corresponding figure in 1912 and 1913.

The fluctuations in the two quarterly homeward wheat rate series available offer a better measure of changes in magnitude. They are illustrated in Figure 7. It shows index numbers of the freight rates contained in the *Quarterly Summary of Statistics* and in the Chamber of Shipping *Annual Reports*. The base taken is the third quarter of 1922, the earliest liner quotation available, when the liner rate was 32*s*. 6*d*. and the tramp rate 35*s*. 9*d*. per ton. The index numbers presented illustrate the downward tendency already mentioned, the extreme instability of both rates, and a noteworthy closeness between the two.

The most striking feature perhaps is the close relationship between liner rates and tramp rates, the one an inseparable shadow of the other. They tended to move together in the same direction, the liner rate oscillating, if only very slightly, over a

Table 26. *Tramp freight rates for wheat—Australia to the U.K./Continent, 1920 to 1939*

(Shillings and pence per ton.)

	Angier				Chamber of Shipping			
	Highest	Lowest	Rate at end of year	Average	Highest	Lowest	Rate at end of year	Average
	s. d.	*s. d.*	*s. d.*	*s. d.*	*s. d.*	*s. d.*	*s. d.*	*s. d.*
1920	150 0	100 0	NA	125 0	—	—	—	140 3
1921	82 6	47 6	50 0	65 0	85 0	50 0	50 0	61 0
1922	52 6	35 0	46 3	43 9	52 6	35 0	46 3	44 3
1923	43 9	30 0	42 6	36 9	40 3	31 3	42 6	36 6
1924	49 0	30 0	48 6	39 6	47 6	31 3	46 6	40 6
1925	55 0	27 6	43 9	41 3	55 0	27 6	43 9	40 6
1926	54 0	22 6	47 6	38 3	53 9	24 0	50 0	36 6
1927	49 6	36 0	38 9	42 6	49 6	37 6	40 0	42 0
1928	45 0	31 0	43 9	38 0	45 0	32 0	43 9	38 6
1929	42 6	22 6	26 3	32 6	43 9	24 0	25 0	29 3
1930	37 6	20 0	31 3	28 9	33 9	20 0	30 0	27 0
1931	32 6	25 0	30 0	28 9	32 6	26 9	30 0	29 9
1932	31 9	20 3	29 0	26 0	31 3	20 0	29 0	26 6
1933	29 0	19 6	25 0	24 3	29 0	22 6	26 0	24 9
1934	29 6	21 0	26 0	25 3	29 6	22 6	25 6	25 3
1935	28 0	18 6	28 0	23 3	29 1	20 0	28 0	25 6
1936	46 3	24 6	46 3	35 6	45 6	28 0	45 6	30 3
1937	53 6	33 6	36 9	43 6	53 6	36 6	36 9	46 0
1938	40 0	33 0	NA	36 6	41 0	31 6	34 0	34 9
1939	80 0	33 0	100 0	58 6	—	30 0	58 6	40 3

Source: Angier from the January annual returns issue each year of *Fairplay*. Chamber of Shipping, *Annual Reports*.

wider range. This suggests, whatever tramp owners may have thought, that liner rates were never completely out of phase with tramp rates. The actual rates in the two series on the whole show that liner rates were indeed slightly lower than tramp rates throughout the 1920s and also for most of the 1930s. They do not appear ever to have undercut the minimum rate during the period of control exercised by the Tramp Shipping Advisory Committee. In this context, indeed, it was the tramp, not the liner, which made reductions by giving quantity rebates. It was done with sanction. In August 1935 tramps carrying more than 8,250 tons of grain from Australia were authorised to cut the minimum rate by 3*d.* and by 6*d.* if carrying more than 8,800 tons. The general tendency for liner rates to be lower than tramp rates undoubtedly helped to attract some grain shipments to liners. There is a second explanation, however, which tramp owners usually overlooked. A tramp was usually chartered for a voyage to one of a range of ports. The greater

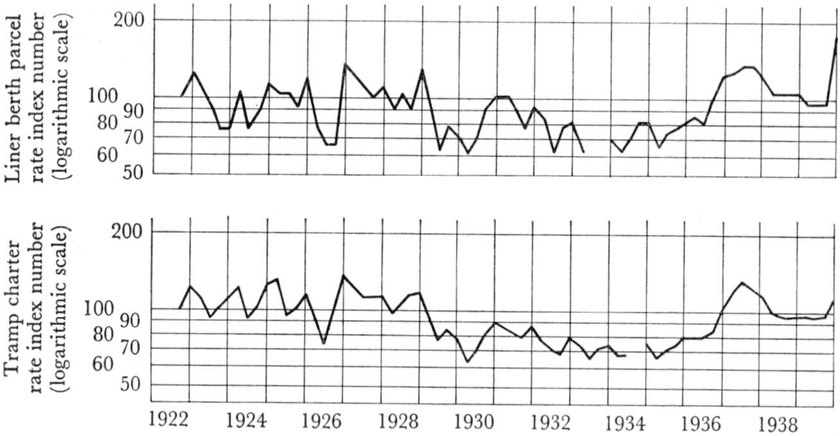

Fig. 7. Wheat freight rate index numbers Australia to U.K. (1922–39). (Source: Chamber of Shipping, *Annual Reports*; *Quarterly Summary of Statistics*.) (Third quarter of 1922 = 100.)

flexibility thus provided for the charterer justified the marginally higher rate charged by the tramp owner. As trade becomes established within fixed, narrow lines, the right to specify the discharge port at short notice becomes less essential and liner despatch often more convenient for grain shippers. By the later 1920s, moreover, liner companies in the Australian trade had extended the facilities they offered for the carriage of wheat in parcels. In the present context the significant change to note was the widening of the range of ports within which a liner would discharge parcel wheat and, as important, the right to name the discharge port *after* bills of lading had been issued.[1]

[1] See, for example, *The Times* 21 March 1927.

The second feature to notice is the extreme instability. In the 70 quarters for which the rates are plotted, the liner parcel rate is identical in 2 consecutive quarters 7 times, the tramp rate only 3 times; the liner rate remains constant once for 3 and once for 4 consecutive quarters, the tramp once for 3 quarters. The oscillations illustrated have in fact been moderated by using a log scale on the vertical axis of the figure. Each point on the curve, moreover, is the quarterly average of monthly figures, these in turn average weekly figures which themselves average daily quotations. In the real world, rates not only varied from day to day, but even during the day. Some of the hour-by-hour variations reflect little more than personality quirks of participating agents in what was then a highly personalised aspect of ship broking. The more significant variations, are those between quarters. They sprang from a variety of causes: ordinary seasonal movements, the impact of local developments, yet others illustrate the repercussion locally of international phenomena.

During the 1920s world demand for shipping remained fairly buoyant notwithstanding the general downwards trend in tramp rates of freight. On the whole it was the localised factors which played the most conspicuous part in the fluctuations to be traced. In early 1925 for example unrest on the Australian waterfront deterred British tramp owners from arranging charters which included calls at Australian ports. But the record harvest pushed up demand for shipping and the rate began to rise. During February it had risen 20 % over the beginning of the year. Charters were then accepted and the rate began to fall. By August it was 40 % below the February peak. Thereafter, the rate began to move upwards once again, partly because of ordinary seasonal movement. In part also, however, it was because the strike of British seamen paralysed certain British vessels in Australian ports. Although the strike tied up liners rather than tramps, the withdrawal from the market of such liner tonnage reacted on the rate for active tramp shipping. In 1928 another record crop swamped the Sydney grain terminals and choked the rail system because initially the quantity of tonnage on charter proved insufficient. The rate moved steadily upwards and finished 30 % higher.

A N.S.W. coal strike in the following year lasting until mid-1930 had the opposite effect. Coal imports from Britain brought additional tramps to Australia. Although two-way employment was thus given to many vessels, the additional tonnage on offer pushed down the wheat rate, from a peak of 43*s*. 9*d*. to 24*s*. It was only held at this level because an alternative source of demand arose for tramp tonnage. Production difficulties confronting the Australian iron and steel industry during the coal strike, lower domestic demand for iron ore together with the low prevailing ocean freight rates gave rise to a dramatic expansion of iron ore exports. Many of the tramps bringing coal to Australia loaded iron ore at Whyalla for Japan and Rotterdam. The quantity shipped rose ten-fold between 1928/9 and 1929/30. The tendency for the rate to recover, and for the production of pig iron to regain its earlier level caused an equally sudden fall in ore shipments.

Throughout most of the 1930s rates were considerably below the levels of the 1920s. The lower rates in general reflect the contraction of world trade and the world-wide shipping difficulties of the time. The purely local causes of rate fluctuation become overshadowed. Local influence upon rates in the 1930s moreover, centres upon liner rather than upon tramp rates. Tramp rate fluctuations of the 1930s are therefore more appropriately viewed in relation to other comparable rates. In Figure 8, tramp freight index numbers are shown for a number of rates. As well as the major yardstick, the Chamber of Shipping composite 21 route index, there are also shown rice rates and grain rates to the U.K. from Australia, Canada, the Argentine and Gulf ports. The original data have been converted to use 1922 as the base year. At once obvious is the much sharper decline which took place in grain rates in contrast with either rice rates or the composite tramp freight index. The demand for rice would seem to have been better maintained. The variety of different rates forming the basis of the composite index largely explains its relative strength in contrast with the grain index numbers. Grain rates fell sooner, faster, and farther. It was above all the overall decline in world demand for new world wheat (and hence for grain charters) which characterises the recession. Among grain rates themselves inconsistencies existed. The Argentine shows the smallest, the North American index numbers the largest proportionate decline during the first half of the 1930s. In part this probably reflects the tapering down of output in, and also of wheat exports from, North America. Exports from the Argentine, as we have already shown,

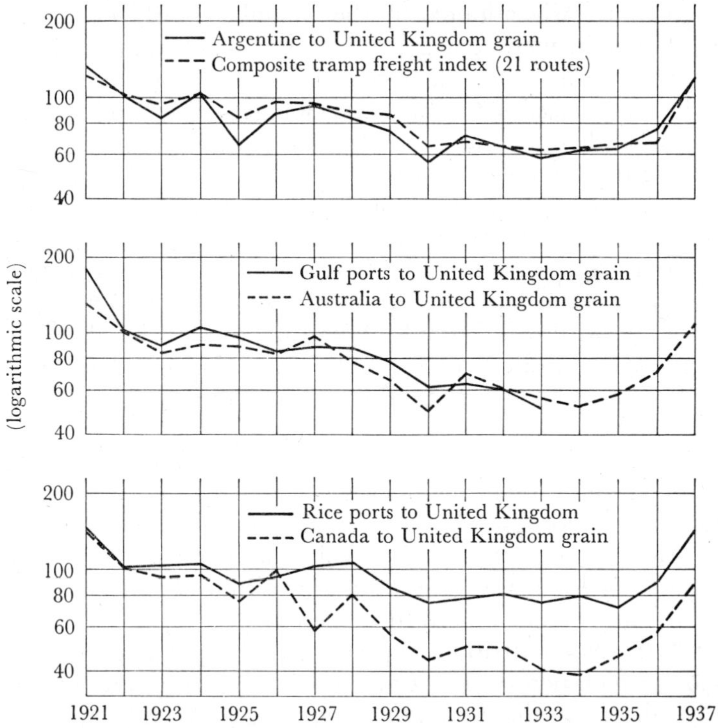

Fig. 8. Tramp freight Index Numbers (Representative Grain Routes) 1921–37. (Source: U.K. Chamber of Shipping, *Annual Reports*.)

tended to fall less. The Australian rate also held up more strongly than the North American rate and in 1935 and 1936 tended more noticeably to exceed the prescribed minimum rate. Two causes were responsible for the happier experience in the Australian sector: the overall increase in wheat production of the early 1930s (which helped to sustain the demand for shipping) and secondly the development of China and Japan as additional markets for Australian wheat. Lower wheat export prices brought China especially into the market. The tramp rates from Australia to Shanghai in the first half of the 1930s fell less relative to grain rates elsewhere.

The tramp freight index number series ends in 1937. In that year, with 1935 as the base, a new composite weighted tramp freight index was adopted by the Chamber of Shipping. With the change in methodology, differentiation of individual components was dropped. The range of actual rates included in the Chambers' *Annual Reports* was also changed. Thereafter it ceases to be possible to measure the Australian rate against those rates forming the basis of comparison for the years up to 1937. As we have already shown, the Australian tramp rate turned downwards again in 1938 and 1939 and once more passed the 1922 level only after the outbreak of war. During these two years the behaviour of the Australian grain rate would seem to have been out of line with world trends. According to the Chamber's new weighted composite grain index, the rate was almost 40 % up in 1938, and in the first 8 months of 1939 almost 30 % up on the 1935 base.

Conference liner rates for fine cargo behaved very differently. Unlike tramp rates or the liner wheat parcel rate, the hallmark and also a major justification for conference regulation of rates is the blessing of rate stability which it confers. Our sources abundantly show that rate stability was indeed a characteristic of the Australian homeward conference during the inter-war years. It was an attribute appreciated by exporters. Discussion below, which relates export price to freight rates, (and incidentally questions the overriding importance of rate stability), amply confirms that stable rates of freight do not necessarily yield constant export income. They do, nevertheless, permit a more accurate advance assessment of cost structures. As the *S.M.H.* put it: 'what representatives of the shippers asked for was not only freights as low as possible, but stable freights, so that the shipper...would know exactly the cost of transport'. A few years later, reporting the conclusion of a long-term freight agreement, the same source noted that: 'this stabilisation of freight rates for a period of years will enable those responsible for the organisation of Australian markets abroad to form accurate estimates of transport costs and exempt the man on the land from the worry of rising freights which are threatening to jeopardise the sale of goods...in the U.K.'.[1] It was mentioned also in the 1923 report of the Imperial Shipping Committee. In connection with the outward trade to Australia it was noted that: 'it enables merchants to make forward contracts with certainty, and reduces the speculative element which traders dislike. The shippers who gave evidence were nearly all in agreement that stable freights were a necessity for modern trades.'[2]

For the inter-war years, beginning in June 1922, an unbroken run of liner conference rates from Australia is available to illustrate rate stability. More than 50 separate rates are included in the source. Here discussion concentrates upon the half dozen most important. The first published rates in fact appear at the end of a period of adjustment for the shipping industry as a whole. A glance backwards is therefore a necessary preliminary. The winding-up of most war-time measures was virtually complete by the end of 1919. But during the 30 months from January 1920 to the first appearance of official Australian published rate data, the shipping industry was engaged in conversion to peacetime routines. Information on homeward liner rates from Australia in these months is abundantly available in the local press upon which we rely. The ending of the war and the freeing of merchant shipping from war-time duties was soon followed by the elimination of pent-up demand. By April 1920 the post-war shipping boom was at an end. From an acute 'shortage of tonnage the situation has been converted almost into a glut'.[3] Tramp rates, as we have seen, tumbled downwards. In the liner section of the industry impatient demands were made for lower rates by Australian shippers, themselves grappling with problems of readjustment to falling commodity prices. Rates were unchanged in 1920. To some onlookers it was 'a curious anomaly...that whilst throughout the world there has been a fall in freights, so far Australian rates with the exception of wheat freights have been unaffected'.[4] The contrary trend did not long persist. Changes were made in April,

[1] *S.M.H.* 8 April 1929, 7 May 1937.
[2] *U.K.P.P.* Cmd. 1802, p. 15.
[3] *S.M.H.* 4 January 1921.
[4] *Ibid.* 9 March 1921.

July, and again in December 1921. They helped the shippers only very little, however, if their continued complaint is to be believed. As for shipowners, 'the year 1921 will pass into history as one of the worst on record'.[1] Even at low rates of freight, excess shipping capacity and a downturn in trade meant sparse cargoes. Further rate reductions were made in September 1922. It is the rate level fixed in this month which forms the first quotation in the published official quarterly liner rate series to which reference has already been made.

Details are given in the *Quarterly Summary of Statistics* of 58 rates. They illustrate two features: the tendency for rates to move downwards until September 1939 and, above all, rate stability. Tramp freights similarly moved downwards, but in a series of convulsive jerks. Liner conference rates subsided uniformly and much more gently. In even sharper contrast with tramp rates was the steadiness of conference rates. In the 70 quarters which make up the period for which conference rates are available many rates changed only 3 times. Few changed more than 4 or 5 times, usually being those rates which had not altered immediately before official published records begin. The least stable rate was that on greasy wool for which 6 changes are recorded. One change in the wool rate, on the surface at least, involved an increase. But it was an 'Irishman's rise'. In 1932 the rate was increased by 1/16th of a penny per pound but subject to a rebate of 1*s.* 9*d.* per bale. The effect of this was to lower the actual rate by 1*d.* per 320 pound bale, with the object of encouraging shipment in bale lots and discouraging the consignment of smaller packages.

Rate details are set out in an appendix table, together with the dates when changes took place. Variations in rates were made with discrimination, not in the more customary form of overall percentage reductions. The actual reductions differed between items. Changes were nevertheless usually made over a wide range of items simultaneously, they covered most but not all commodity rates. The chronology of rate change is simply outlined. In 1922 and 1923 a number of downward adjustments were made to complete and to systematise reductions made during the immediate post-war recession. Thereafter, two

[1] *S.M.H.* 31 December 1921.

general reductions were made in almost all rates. The first took place in the second quarter of 1926. It seems not to have been in response to specific demands for reductions. The *S.M.H.* reported surprise in shipping circles when the announcement was made. *The Times* drew attention to what must have seemed an inconsistency: 'Shipping managers appear to be somewhat at a loss to give any definite explanation of the reduced rates, especially as the freight rates have long been cited as examples of the low costs of sea transport, which were emphasised by means of examples in the address this year of the President of the Chamber of Shipping.' Costs in Australia at this time, moreover, were in fact tending to rise.[1] Earlier in the year the scarcity of liner cargoes had been reported in the local press. The assertion is made in the issue of *The Times* quoted above that export prospects for Australian wool, meat and dairy produce were favourable and 'that shipowners would rather have a smaller rate on larger shipments than a higher rate on smaller shipments'. The trade promotional aspect of the reduction is referred to below.

The second wave of reductions was made in the third quarter of 1933 when rates were again varied for most, but not all commodities. Where an actual rate remained unaltered, a comparable real effect was achieved by the granting of a special rebate. The rate on apples and oranges, for example, was allowed to stand but was the subject of a 2*d.* per case rebate, equal to a reduction of 4·8 %. On both these items the rebate was subsequently increased to 5*d.* in June 1937, at the time when further changes were made in two rates only: a reduction in the wool rate and in the rate on chilled beef. Real rates of freight after the introduction of the agreement system, it will be recalled, were in fact 10 % below the quoted rates for all signatories of the agreement. It was a straight discount, applied to all items, and, so far as is known, applied to all conference liner rate shipments from Australia. Hence although it does not affect our discussion it need not be ignored completely. The causes of the general rate reductions of 1933 are of course the depressed state of world trade. We have referred to this period at a number of points already and here may omit further comment. With the excep-

[1] *The Times* 13 July 1926; *S.M.H.* 12 and 13 July 1926.

tion of the reductions in 1937 mentioned above, the rates remained unaltered until the outbreak of war.

It was, as the *S.M.H.* pointed out in its *Finance Supplement* in 1938, a remarkable accomplishment to keep the homeward conference rates stable and unchanged at a time when rates all over the world were rising sharply. On the eve of the Second World War tramp charter rates from Australia had largely made good their earlier falls; they stood only minimally below the 1922 figure. Conference liner rates in contrast were considerably lower in 1939 than in 1922. The rate for wool, butter and lamb had survived at about 70–75 % of the base figure, cheese and beef each stood at not much more than one-half of the rate in the third quarter of 1922. The rate on mutton and on most skins (along with many other less important rates) occupied a mid-way position at about two-thirds. Nevertheless, this is not necessarily to suggest that tramp rates were inordinately high. Comparison of the charges made respectively by liners and tramps may be a profitless exercise unless 'likes' are compared. The narrow differential between tramps and liners for wheat cargo established above proves only that liners charged marginally less than the tramp-determined rate on this commodity. It is not without interest therefore to note that in 1939 the homeward liner rate per ton weight for a range of high density items was more than twice the tramp charter rate per ton weight of wheat. The liner items mentioned included many with a stowage factor no more than 20 % greater than wheat. Here also some qualification is necessary. As we have already indicated, tramp charters are 'fixed' to match the ship with the cargo awaiting shipment. As a rule, therefore, we would expect a tramp to sail full. If a tramp fails to secure a cargo which yields profit the vessel is laid up. But as we have also shown, liners in Australia's shipping services sailed full or empty. It is unjustified to assume that an apparently higher liner rate necessarily ensured a higher profit.

The implications of exchange difficulties which accompanied Australia into depression have been ignored so far in this work. For most of our discussion the omission of this aspect of economic development is unimportant. In the context of freight rates and freight payments however, the course of the exchange is relevant. The interpretation of homeward rates loses its simple unity when the rate of exchange began to vary. For a short period in 1930 and for the whole of 1931, until the rate was stabilised, the problem of exchange and its effect upon freight payments held interest in Australia. It also involved the British courts in deciding which pounds, shillings and pence—sterling or Australian—were intended in freight commission agreements for Australian wheat shipments.

The loss of reserve securities and the dramatic slump in commodity prices which began in 1929 created immediate difficulties for the Commonwealth government and the banks in Australia. The Australian pound, long held at parity with sterling, moved to a discount. The premium on sterling appeared at the end of 1930 and went steadily higher; in January 1931 it reached 30%. Later in the year the Commonwealth Bank assumed responsibility for exchange rate determination and lowered the premium to 25%, £A125 to £100 sterling, at which rate it has since remained until Australia converted to the decimal system.

The repercussions of exchange fluctuations for the shipping industry derived from the not uncommon practice of paying freights in Australia in advance. Freights paid in Australia in Australian currency yielded a smaller sum in Britain when sterling was at a premium. Freights may be prepaid at the port of shipment or paid on a 'freight forward' basis at the port of discharge. For items shipped from Europe prepayment was customary; the price of imports in Australia was usually on c.i.f. basis. Tramp freights on Australian exports were similarly paid outside Australia at the port of discharge. But for liner exports from Australia freights were normally prepaid on refrigerated items and often prepaid on other commodities. It was thus the liner companies which were chiefly affected when exchange rates moved against the £A. So long as the rates notified and published in Australia were equivalent to sterling amounts, no difficulty arose. But when sterling in terms of Australian currency went to a premium,[1] British (and other European) shipowners became concerned at the cost of remitting freights

[1] The references in the *S.M.H.* in 1930 and 1931 upon which this account is based are too numerous to list individually.

prepaid in Australia. They sought to protect themselves by insisting early in 1930 on a surcharge on the rate for refrigerated items. Lacking prevision, anticipating an early ending to what was seen as a purely temporary exchange dislocation, the shipping companies agreed to share the burden of the exchange premium added to refrigerated rates. For passenger fares and for other cargoes wherever possible most of the premium was passed on in the form of a surcharge which grew as the premium itself increased. To avoid remittance charges on funds accruing within Australia, moreover, the companies made heavy purchases of ships stores locally. They thus reversed the tendency of the 1920s when the aim was to buy as few goods and services in Australia as possible because of high relative prices. The widening of the gap between sterling and Australian currency in early 1931 rammed home the point that the temporary visitor had become a permanent guest. At the May and June meetings of the A.O.T.A., shipowners declined to renew the existing freight agreements unless adequate provision were made to compensate for exchange depreciation. This was not altogether unexpected. The surcharge levied on refrigerated items was only 3 %. 'As, in the meantime, the bank rate had soared beyond 30 % even shippers were willing to admit that shipowners had made a bad bargain.'[1] The agreements were in fact renewed; on condition that all freight charges henceforth were payable in terms of sterling at the port of discharge. At the same time the surcharge on refrigerated items was raised to the appropriate level of the exchange premium. Similar arrangements were made for passenger fares. Towards the end of 1931 sterling itself became no longer acceptable to the French shipping lines. Passenger fares paid in Australia were required to be in terms of francs instead of sterling.

In one further direction exchange depreciation impinged upon the Australian shipping scene. It involved tramp rather than liner owners and was the reverse side of the coin described above. In this instance it was the British shipowner who wished to insist that the pound sterling was equal to the pound Australian. It gave rise to an action in the King's Bench Division and then, on appeal, to the Court of Appeal and

[1] *S.M.H. Financial and Commercial Supplement*, 11 February 1932.

beyond to the House of Lords.[1] It is mentioned here partly for the sake of completeness, partly because of the repercussions which might have followed. The dispute hinged upon the interpretation of certain clauses in the standard *Austral* wheat charter party form, the introduction of which was referred to in chapter 5. The *Austral* form provided for the payment of commission by tramp ship owners to the charterer or chartering agent in respect of charters they had arranged. The commission was to be paid in sterling at the time of unloading. But a further clause in the form, added at a time when the exchange favoured an Australian charterer, expressly required that the payment of sums due in Australia should be paid in Australian currency. As with the pre-payment of freights, so long as the two currencies were virtually identical, no problem arose in the payment of commission.

Uncertainty arose when parity between the two currencies disappeared. Shipowners wished to pay commissions due in Australia in Australian currency in the exact numerical equivalent of amounts payable in sterling; that is to say, if £100 were due in sterling they wished to pay the Australian charterer £A100. The charterers not unreasonably demanded payment in Australian currency after the sum due in sterling had been converted at the current rate of exchange. At a time when tramp freights were sagging, the contention of shipowners if upheld and adopted in practice would have given them a financial advantage. The payment of commission based upon sterling freights in terms of Australian currency gave an increment to the owners of about one-quarter of the commission due. Commission at 5 % on £1,000 sterling amounts to £50. If £A50 is paid as the identical equivalent, the owner saved £10 sterling on the transaction.

[1] *Lloyd's List Law Reports*, vol. 40, p. 283; vol. 41, p. 210; and vol. 43, p. 378. *Times Law Reports* vol. 47, p. 586; vol. 48, pp. 158 and 598. Questions of currency and the ambiguity often present in international contracts have given rise to a number of legal disputes in Australia and elsewhere. Twenty years after the Westralian Farmers sued the King Line for its commission, a case heard in the High Court of Australia presented the opposite side of the coin once more. In 1952 an issue brought against the National Bank of Australia Ltd. (in liquidation) by British depositors unsuccessfully sought to have their original sterling deposits repaid in pounds sterling. (*Commonwealth Law Reports*, vol. 86; G. C. Cheshire, *Private International Law*, 6th ed. (Oxford, 1961), p. 259 ff.)

A test case was taken into the King's Bench in July 1931 when Westralian Farmers Ltd, sued the King Line for the difference between what they had received, and what they considered due in commission. Judgment was given in favour of the King Line; questions of exchange did not arise, said the judge, the sum due was to be paid in Australia in Australian currency as if the two currencies were identical. The decision was subsequently reversed by the Court of Appeal and in turn was reversed once more by the House of Lords in May 1932 who found for the King Line. Before the case went to appeal, however, the exchange advantage implied in the *Austral* form, confirmed in July 1931, and reiterated in May 1932, was eliminated by amendment to the form. In October 1931 the clauses concerning commission payments were revised to provide that sums due as commission 'shall be paid (*a*) in London in British sterling, or (*b*) in Australia in the equivalent of British sterling in Australian currency at the telegraphic transfer rate of exchange for London on Australia, ruling at the end of the last day of loading'.[1]

Two closely associated factors merit brief examination to conclude our discussion: the extent to which conference rates 'promoted' trade and the relationship which freight rates bore to export prices. A common complaint about conference rates is that their rigidity inhibits rather than helps to promote trade.[2] The evidence concerning the Australian homeward conference, tenuous and imprecise though it is, nevertheless suggests that the conference itself and its members made some contribution to Australian economic growth. On the grounds of probability it is at least as reasonable to assume the existence of conference interest, as conference disinterest in the trade of the economy it serves. Conference line owners like to claim that they identify their own interests with those of the shippers they serve. This is not unconvincing on the basis of present evidence. Certain of the British lines in the Australian conference had a stake in the

[1] The amendment of October 1931 was made at the insistence of the Australian Grain Shippers' Association who were reluctant to contract for the new season's wheat on the basis of the unamended *Austral* form. (Information kindly supplied by the Chamber of Shipping.)

[2] Professor Sturmey once held the view that promotional rates are rare. (*Sturmey*, p. 334.) This view has since been modified, the present author understands.

Australian economy. The lines whose accounts are analysed in the following chapter held some of their cash reserves in Commonwealth government stock. Integration with Australian domestic enterprises was not uncommon. The Blue Star Line, for example, acquired a financial interest in the Australian meat freezing and exporting firm of W. Angliss & Co. (Pty) Ltd. The Orient Line held an interest in an Australian stevedoring company and, among other investments, had capital in the old Adelaide Airways later taken over by the Australian National Airways. In 1946 the Orient held almost one-fifth of the issued scrip in A.N.A.[1]

Conference freight rate policy clearly was influenced by considerations of Australia's oversea trade. The elimination of competition by uniform rates, however, does not in itself ensure profit for a shipping company. When demand for tonnage is brisk, and ships are full, the inefficient can survive. But for most of the 1920s and 1930s the reverse was true. Cargoes must be carried if freights are to be earned. Scullin, the Labour prime minister, testified in 1930 to the attitude of responsibility among shipowners. He recognised that they appreciated the unwisdom of killing the 'golden goose', as he put it. It is also reasonable to assume that they appreciated the greater value of a bigger 'clutch'.

The few illustrations available indeed suggest a 'broody' awareness among the owners. In early 1922, for example, when the declining price of imported frozen beef in England made exports uneconomic, a meat export bounty was introduced in Australia. Shipowners in the homeward conference on being approached immediately announced a reduction in the meat rate (of about 15%) in order to assist the meat export sector.[2] In 1926 shippers were 'surprised' by the reductions announced in the homeward Australian conference rates. Contemporary comment in *The Times* quoted above, pointed out that shipping companies have 'the satisfaction of giving practical evidence of their desire to encourage exports in every possible way'. The readiness of shipowners in 1929 to delay freight increases was accompanied also by a 20% reduction in the rate for berth

[1] 'Orient Line—Australian Annals', mimeographed notes made by the company.

[2] *S.M.H.* 12 April 1922.

parcel wheat in order to help Australian producers meet the falling world price for wheat. Tramp freights in contrast were sticky. It can also be argued that the extensive reductions announced in 1933 and the special reduction for chilled beef shipments in 1937 were also 'promotional' rate changes.

Our final point concerns the relationship between freights and commodity values and the possible constraints imposed upon trade by freight charges. Material for comparison with other sectors is not readily available. It is unfortunate, as Professor Kindleberger has pointed out, that there have been few studies of the structure of transport charges in international trade. For intercontinental movements of commodities it is conventionally assumed that freights and insurance amount to about 10% of value. Calculations made by the U.S. Tariff Commission on transport costs in 1938 for a number of leading imports into the U.S.A. show that in fact freight charges represented anything between 1% and 255% of value. A quarter of the imported items sustained freight charges in excess of 20%; freights on 17 of the items were in excess of 10%.[1] Aggregated freight charges on all imports into Australia for the three closing years of our period have been calculated from information supplied confidentially by the shipping industry to the Commonwealth Statistician. The detail shows that freight and insurance charges represented 14–15% of the f.o.b., and 12–13% of the c.i.f., value of merchandise imports during each of the three years.[2] Although these data are useful they tell us nothing about individual items, nor of changes over time either in commodity value or in rates of freight.

As we have abundantly shown, however, it was the freight charged on exports, not on imports, which acted as the focal point of local interest and contemporary complaint. In this context our discussion is concerned once again with rate stability. For a few leading export items the relationship of freights to values is examined to test the assertion made by shipowners that ocean freights formed but an insignificant proportion of commodity value. The conclusion in fact reached from

[1] Quoted in C. P. Kindleberger, *Foreign Trade and the National Economy* (New Haven, 1962), p.13.

[2] Information kindly provided by the Commonwealth Statistician.

detail set out below argues that a profitable trade for the Australian exporter of primary produce hinged directly upon freight levels. Rate stability without qualification, therefore, ought not to be elevated to a central position in discussions on freights. The shipowner is given to stating that ocean freights are so small and form so trifling an element in final costs that they may be safely ignored. In the selling price of a 4 lb. loaf in the 1930s, for example, ocean freights on the Australian wheat it contained amounted to about 10%; with Australian butter about $3\frac{1}{2}$% and so on. In the economy wherein such items are processed and the value added in processing is high this argument is valid. Freight charges form only a small fraction of the final price of an item. To the consumer, the freight element is insignificant. It is not valid, however, if used as an argument to reassure a shipper of primary produce whose commodities compete in international markets. In a high-cost economy similar to Australia's, supplying annually in the 1920s and 1930s less than one-quarter, usually less than 15%, of the world's wheat, freight charges were highly important. A 10% variation in ocean freight levels may have a considerable effect on a year's trading results. On the other hand, the conference line owner was justified in reminding querulous shippers that the extra cost to Australia of a reliable, regular shipping service was not the whole of the freight rate charged by conference lines. It was the difference between the rate they charged and an unregulated rate if, and only if, the latter in fact were lower.

For reasons similarly connected with internationally determined price levels, and their effect upon a dependent economy, stability of rates in itself may not necessarily be the panacea shipowners suggest. In times of falling commodity prices, indeed, any tendency for ocean rates to stick may be disastrous for the shipper. The emotively charged assertion that freight rates are 'high' or 'crushing' or 'excessive', is meaningless if not related to some standard. Clearly, what shippers seek is a pattern of ocean rates which shows constancy in its relationship to the realised price of the items shipped. The well-known tendency for conference rates to remain unchanged for many consecutive years and for tramp rates to fluctuate more frequently may lead us to anticipate greater constancy in the one than in the other. But there were two variables, not one. Instability in commodity prices offset the stability found in liner rates. Interestingly enough, in the two examples chosen for illustration, liner-carried wool and tramp-carried wheat, the pattern of relationship is markedly similar. For the inter-war years, ocean rates and export prices may be associated for a number of commodities at many points in time. For Australia's

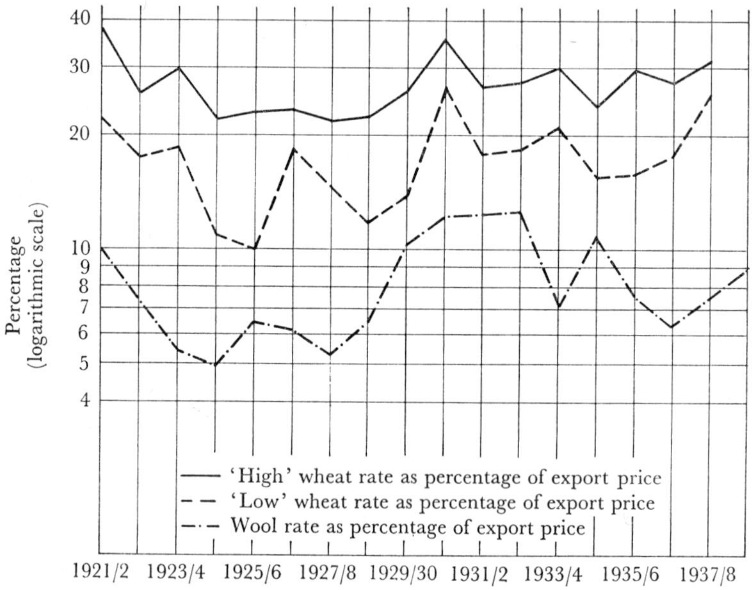

Fig. 9. Freight rates and export prices.
(Source: *Year Books* and *Quarterly Summary of Statistics*.)

two principal exports, wool and wheat, a complete set of official average prices is available in published form. Wheat export prices for the 1920s are the values 'in the principal markets of Australia'. For the 1930s the prices appear to be more representative in being the 'weighted average of shippers' limits' at the chief ports. Wool prices for the years before 1925 are 'average values' constructed from export data. Thereafter they are the average prices reported by the National Council for Wool Selling Brokers. Wool and wheat freight rates have been plotted in

Figure 9 as a percentage of the recorded export prices. Two curves illustrate the wheat price-rate nexus, both high and low rates being used to delimit the area.

Both curves follow a similar path, notwithstanding the steadiness of the freight rate for wool and the instability of the freight rate for wheat. With wheat, both rates and prices moved in the same direction. On the whole, however, the higher the export price the lower the proportion represented by ocean rates and vice versa. With wool, the rate fall in 1926 was accompanied by a price fall; in 1933 as the rate fell the price temporarily regained its plateau of the 1920s. With both items the 1920s proved the happier of the two decades. A conspicuous feature also revealed by Figure 9 is the much smaller proportion of export price represented by the freight rate on wool. In only 5 of the years shown did the proportion exceed 10%. Wheat rates were higher; in only one of the years illustrated did the bottom rate sink to 10%; in only 4 years did it fall below 15%. Similar calculations made during the 1930s for refrigerated meat exports suggest that these items also were subject to freights representing between 15% and 25% of the export price.

Chapter 8

THE ECONOMICS OF SHIPPING MANAGEMENT

The object of the concluding chapter is to discuss certain aspects of the economics of British shipping enterprises engaged in the Australian trade. It omits those aspects examined by Professor Sturmey in his wider study of British shipping. It therefore ignores considerations of the relative position of the British shipping industry within the domestic economy. Nor is it concerned primarily or even closely with international cost comparisons. References made to fleets of other nations, here as in chapter 6, are limited. Our main intention is to analyse major cost components identified in the voyage accounts of a few representative British services between Britain and Australia. In particular, we are concerned with changes over time in the operating experience of these services. As well as analysing the cost structure an attempt is also made to assess 'profitability' by comparing revenue and costs in voyage accounts.[1] The relative importance of the Australian sector and its contribution to the overall earnings of the British shipping industry are unfortunately not easily established. Nor indeed is much information available for the earnings of British shipping as a whole between the wars. Nevertheless, it is possible to obtain some impression of the order of magnitude of the sums involved. For one year, in the mid-1930s, it is also possible to suggest that the earnings of British shipping in the Australian sector contributed about 9 % to the total. Estimates of shipping earnings were made by the Board of Trade for most of the inter-war years and by the Chamber of Shipping from 1931; details are shown below. Board of Trade totals for earlier years are apparently not entirely free from un-

[1] Their desire to remain anonymous does not lessen my debt to the companies which granted access to operating records. In this traditionally 'close' industry, any relaxation of reticence is welcome. Many shipowners today are conscious that secretiveness in the past may not have served the best interests of the industry.

certainties; for the 1930s they are in agreement with estimates made independently by the Chamber of Shipping. They are higher in every instance than the Chamber's figures because of their inclusion of expenditures of foreign shipping in British ports. Otherwise they coincide closely both in rates of change and in absolute totals. Both show the sharp fall in earnings between 1931 and 1936, a reflection partly of the contraction of the British fleet actively engaged during the world depression, partly of the serious fall in freight rates which took place. In the Australian sector during the depression years, as already mentioned, the dramatic fall in import tonnages largely meant one-way employment with a consequent reduction in freight earnings.

	Board of Trade estimates (£m.)	Chamber of Shipping estimates (£m.)
1922	110	—
1923	133	—
1924	140	—
1925	124	—
1926	120	—
1927	140	—
1928	130	—
1929	130	—
1930	105	—
1931	80	73
1932	70	62
1933	65	59
1934	70	64
1935	70	65
1936	85	75
1937	130	115
1938	100	90

Source: C of S 'British Shipping Policy', Statement of General Principles, 1944.

Acting on a suggestion of the then President of the Board of Trade, the Chamber of Shipping in 1932 also undertook a detailed survey of British shipping earnings for 1931 and repeated the survey in 1936. Some details were published by the Chamber's statistician in 1938.[1] The information thus assembled

[1] *Isserlis.*

represents a considerable advance on previously published data. It nevertheless is presented within too broad a framework. Partly for reasons of space, partly no doubt to avoid the appearance of divulging confidential information, Dr Isserlis aggregates the detail under the 5 main divisions shown below. They are political not geographical divisions and hence the information is of limited usefulness; it does not by itself make possible any conclusions about individual sectors.

Source of Earnings of British Shipping Industry

	1931 Receipts %		1936 Receipts %	
	Gross	Net	Gross	Net
Trade between:				
U.K. and Empire countries	38·2	41·9	38·8	42·1
Empire countries excluding U.K.	10·5	7·0	7·7	4·6
U.K. and foreign countries	29·0	33·6	25·2	29·6
Foreign countries	10·7	9·0	14·7	13·0
Empire countries and foreign countries	11·6	8·5	13·6	10·7

Information specifically on the British tramp shipping industry was also collected for two years in the thirties, 1935 and 1936. Returns made to the Tramp Shipping Administrative Committee during the tramp shipping subsidy scheme provided certain interesting information on the nature of tramp shipping operations. An analysis of the returns for 1935 was later published by Dr Isserlis. He followed his original framework and the material as a consequence is subject to the same limitations mentioned above. Through the courtesy of the Chamber of Shipping however, it has been possible to reach behind the aggregates. The records have been analysed for both years to establish the activities of all British tramp shipping engaged in the Australian trade. A few entries in the records have been ignored because earnings are omitted or because the detail given is inadequate.[1] Apart from such omissions, however, the sum shown below represents the earnings of British tramps in

[1] In constructing his card index Dr Isserlis himself may have ignored the incomplete entries, or, more probably, was able to amplify them at the time.

the various branches of the Australian trade for the years 1935 and 1936.

Certain features revealed in the records merit brief notice for the illustration they provide of tramp employment and tramp earnings. At once obvious is the overwhelming importance of outbound carrying as the major source of earnings in the Australian trade. In both years analysed outbound carrying contributed about 80 % of total earnings. In part, but only in small part, the pattern of earnings reflects the higher incidence of inbound ballast voyages, 35 as compared with only 3 clearances in ballast. Inbound 'earnings' voyages clearly earned proportionately much less than the outbound. The higher earnings in 1936, it should be noted, derived less from increased tonnage carried than from higher rates of freight. The information provides a telling illustration of the recovery of rates between January 1935 and 1936. The quantity of wheat shipped in 1936 was only 76,000 tons more than in the preceding year, yet freight earnings on wheat were £400,000 higher.[1] On six leading cargoes, freights increased by £700,000 but tonnage by only 134,000 tons. On all tramp cargoes, inbound and outbound together, the net increase in cargo tonnage was only 125,000 tons or a gain of 5 %. Freights earned in 1936, however, were two-thirds up on the 1935 figure. The point may be noted in passing that the Australian trade did not offer a very important area of employment for British tramps. In 1935 tramp freights in the Australian sector represented no more than 5·7 % of all British tramp freights and 6·6 % of freights earned by tramps larger than 3,000 gross tons.

Tramp freights would appear to have contributed between 20 % and 25 % to the gross total of British shipping earnings in 1935.[2] For 1936, but not for 1935, it is the conclusion of our discussion in following paragraphs that British tramps in the Australian trade accounted for a similar proportion of British

[1] But the quantity of wheat shipped to Britain was higher in 1936 by about 300,000 tons. The rate to the U.K. recovered more fully and more quickly than other wheat rates from Australia during 1935 and 1936. In contrast with the rate to eastern ports, moreover, the rate to the U.K. was also higher, hence earnings rose faster.

[2] This estimate is based upon the assumption that oversea disbursements by British shipping in 1935 were proportionately the same as shown in the detail published for 1936 by Dr Isserlis.

Freights earned by British tramps in the Australian trade, 1935 and 1936

	1935 (£'000)	1936 (£'000)
Trade between:		
Australia and Britain	1,034	1,717
Australia and other Empire countries	45	406
Australia and foreign countries	444	392
Coastal ports	5	31
Totals	1,528	2,546
All inbound	120	484
All outbound	1,404	2,032
Totals	1,524	2,516
(Excluding coastal engagements.)		

(Apparent errors in totals due to rounding.)

earnings in the sector. Our discussion of necessity is based upon a number of assumptions. The basic assumption, and the furthest from the truth, is that freight rates are homogeneous, that ton for ton the rate on all commodities is identical. This has already been shown to be untrue. Nevertheless, in calculating the sum earned by British shipping in the Australian sector the unsophisticated use of simple uniform percentages has been adopted throughout for the sake of simplicity.

Official estimates of expenditures on freight are available only from 1936/7 for imports. Only one estimate of total outbound freights has been traced, also towards the end of our period.[1] Freight charges on imports were officially estimated for the years 1936/7 to 1938/9. The stated sums represent about 13 % of the total value of merchandise imports. This constitutes a higher proportion than the figure of 10 % conventionally adopted for intercontinental freights. It also differs sharply from the very low figures claimed by shipowners to represent the customary

[1] Information on import freights kindly supplied by the Commonwealth Statistician (letter dated 23 July 1965) who confirms that information for earlier periods is not available. For export freights see *C.P.D.* vol. 155, p. 1,123. For a discussion of the relevant calculations to be made in determining the contribution of shipping earnings to the balance of payments see *Sturmey*, pp. 185–7.

level of freights on the landed value of manufactured items. Not forgetting these reservations, the following totals are obtained by applying the ratio of 13 % to import values for earlier years. Extending the calculations we obtain an approximate figure for the earnings of British shipping in the import trade:

	Imports (£Am.)	Freight paid (£Am.)	% of cargo carried by British ships	Assumed earnings of British ships (£ (sterling) m.)
1938/9	109·4	15·2	64·8	7·9
1937/8	127·2	18·6	60·7	9·4
1936/7	103·0	13·8	58·9	6·5
1935/6	108·2	13·1	52·5	5·6
1934/5	93·7	12·1	51·2	5·0

Freight charges on exports are harder still to estimate. The one official figure which has been traced, given in a parliamentary answer in May 1938, mentions the amount of £A10·5 million a year. The estimate is unsupported by stated evidence or by other comment. Calculations made for freights on wheat, wool, and the major refrigerated items yield a figure of more than £A9 million for these items which represented no more than 65 % of the total value of exports. Rejecting the figure of £A10·5 million as too low, we adopt instead as a basis for calculation a figure of 13 % of export values. Previous discussion in chapter 7 noted the wide variation in export freights as a proportion of export prices. For convenience nevertheless, and because the margin of error in the *total* of British shipping earnings is likely to be small, the 13 % has been used to estimate freight earnings for the three years 1934/5 to 1936/7. The detail suggests that British shipping in the Australian trade in the mid-1930s earned about £6 million on outbound cargo; £11 million to £12 million on outbound and inbound combined. Earnings of this magnitude constituted about 9 % of the gross earnings of the British shipping industry at this time.

In our discussion of the economics of shipping management we concentrate upon the operating experience of liner services. In part this is to acknowledge the greater importance of the liner in the Australian trade between the wars (as today), in part because only liner records have been made available, and in part also because of the unspecialised nature of tramping. The voyage accounts to which the author has been given access all relate to liner operations. Records of tramp companies whose vessels called at Australian ports have not been traced. Such records, even if available would not, however, necessarily shed light on the economics of shipping in the single sector under review. As noted above, tramps making frequent consecutive voyages to Australia in a given trade are likely to have been engaged on time charter. The owner's accounting records with such engagements are limited to details of wages, crew victualling, marine stores and insurance. Other relevant expenditures are normally met by the charterer. The analytical problem with accounts relating to tramps engaged on voyage charter stems from the difficulty of associating cost components with individual sectors. A voyage which involved the carriage of Australian inbound or outbound cargo would normally span a number of different sectors in the course of a year. A typical case-history of employment for a tramp engaged in a series of voyage charters in a year might well be:

Britain to North America
North America to Australia with motor vehicles
Australia to China with flour
China to Vancouver in ballast
Vancouver to Australia with lumber
Australia homewards with wheat

No attempt would normally be made in the voyage account analyses to apportion the various disbursements between sectors. A disgruntled tramp owner might and frequently did complain of the relatively high charges his vessels had to meet on Australian voyages. But his criticism was often based upon the evidence of *ad hoc* calculations rather than on detailed systematic analytical comparison. Voyage charges on the whole were aggregated and not split into the various component legs.

Analysis in the following pages consists partly of an outline of the theoretical framework of costs and revenue. Partly also it includes a detailed examination of voyage accounts of passenger liner services and of cargo liner services between Britain and Australia. Our main object is to determine the proportion of the total represented by each main cost item, to identify changes in their proportions over time, and to discuss the relationship of certain cost items to operating experience. Some attempt is also made to relate costs and earnings.

Liner voyage account analyses consists of four elements: (1) administrative overheads; (2) running costs; (3) revenue from fares, freights, and bar and shop profits; and (4) the charges visibly and directly made against revenue. Organisation overheads include advertising, other administrative expenses, and depreciation. Running costs include the expenditures made for fuel, stores and repairs, charges for crew, canal and port dues, and hull insurance. Revenue included gross earnings of bar and shop (no account was taken of wages involved), passage money, and freight earnings. Charges against revenue consisted of passenger victualling, stevedoring charges, and the various commissions and rebates paid. From the point of view of final balance it would represent a simplification if charges against revenue were deducted at an earlier stage and a figure for net revenue only brought into the account analyses. The effect, however, would be to exclude from consideration important variables which make possible a comparison between individual voyages and for the whole fleet between different years. They provide useful indicators of cost variation and offer a measure of relative efficiency.

The outline of cost appropriations shown below differs from the more general outline constructed by Professor Sturmey for a completely specialized passenger ship. Apart from the inclusion of a head for cargo handling and minor variations in terminology, the chief difference is in the apportionment of agency charges. Sturmey includes the item with organisational overheads, it is here shown as a variable. Such charges could fall within either section. Where a shipping company opens a permanent establishment overseas the costs are usually borne under the appropriation for administration overheads. Where it preferred to make use of an agent to undertake identical work, payment was usually made on an *ad valorem* commission basis. It formed a variable figure and was charged directly against revenue. The second of these two methods has been adopted in the accounts analysed and the original allocation of costs has been followed here. Not all the items shown in the voyage accounts are itemised below. Entries representing less than $\frac{1}{2}$%, such as 'cinema' or 'library' charges, have been aggregated under general miscellaneous headings. The cost item for 'wireless', relating to the hire of both equipment and operator, has been added to wages. Nor is there always uniformity between companies in the accounting appropriations. One company recorded 'towage and pilotage' separately, others presumably added the amounts to canal and port dues. Companies were not always systematic in their own allocation of costs. One company made no distinction between fixed running costs and variable charges. In no accounts examined has any indication been given concerning the payment of canal dues in respect of passengers. It is possible that passenger dues for the Suez Canal (payable throughout the inter-war years) were included with other direct charges against revenue; or that they were summed with the fixed dues based upon a ship's 'Suez tonnage'. With these reservations in mind, the make-up of the cost structure for passenger and cargo liners in the Australian trade was as follows:

Overheads

- Administration
- Advertising
- Depreciation

Running costs

- Fuel
- Wages
- Crew victualling (including ship's laundry)
- Stores (ship and engine room)
- Repairs and maintenance
- Canal dues
- Port dues
- Insurance of hull
- Other running charges

Charges against revenue

- Passage money expenses:
  - Commission and rebates
  - Other charges
  - Victualling
- Freight expenses:
  - Cargo charges (stevedoring)
  - Damages
  - Charges on freight
  - Agency commission

Details taken from voyage account analyses and shown in an appendix table give an itemised distribution of costs for certain passenger services and cargo services between Britain and Australia in representative years. The accounts relating to service 'C', differ from the remainder in three important respects. First, they aggregate all victualling charges and combine the cost of provisions for crew and passengers. Secondly, and an extension of the first, they do not differentiate between running costs and general charges made directly against items of revenue. Thirdly, they make no allocation for administrative expenses; instead they record the payment of a fixed percentage commission to managing agents. To facilitate comparison the commission paid to managing agents is here regarded as an administration charge. Together with depreciation charges it gives a composite figure for administrative overheads. Further comparison is possible with other services in respect of fuel and wages, all else is hidden in the aggregations. Information available for the two cargo services relates respectively to the two decades; service E's accounts not being available before 1937, it is not possible therefore to be confident that it is fully representative for the whole of our period. Passenger service accounts analysed cover the whole period for services A and C, and for most of the period in the case of service B, they are thus more truly reflective of long-term operating experience. Interestingly enough, the passenger services show marked similarity for the three main appropriations. Points of similarity and contrast are taken up in our detailed discussion of individual cost items. A summary outline compiled from the appendix table is given below.

In general, charges for administration over time formed a fairly constant proportion of total costs within individual services. For service A the figure ranged between 4 and 6 % throughout the period; for service B between 2 and 3 %, and for service C usually about 8 %. Except with the last, where the sum represented a fixed percentage of gross charges, the accounting method adopted was to share out *pro rata* between the voyages the total sum of office expenses, charges for advertising and so on. The largest single company overhead was the sum allocated for fleet depreciation. It also tended to vary more and, during our period, moved upwards more significantly than office overheads. Depreciation charges were usually based on the straight-line historic cost principle and was customarily at the rate of 5 % per annum. In times of rising prices the amount accumulated in depreciation reserves is rarely sufficient to permit fleet renewal without some supplementation. Tax provision, which in

Shipping cost appropriations in Australian oversea services, 1923/4–1938/9

Services		Overhead charges (%)	Running costs (%)	Charges against revenue (%)
I. Passenger				
Service A	1923/4	20·1	58·3	20·0
	1932/3	24·5	51·4	23·9
	1938/9	23·4	50·7	25·2
Service B	1923/4	19·1	59·4	19·7
	1932/3	29·8	46·3	23·3
Service C	1923/4	15·5	83·3	
	1932/3	23·4	76·4	
	1938/9	21·7	77·2	
II. Cargo				
Service D	1923/4	16·3	60·7	22·5
Service E	1938/9	17·0	44·7	37·2

this context is ignored, may by its initial allowances for the rapid writing-off of new investment speed the process of rebuilding reserves. There is an additional factor that the life of a modern ship is often as much as 30 years. Depreciation at 4 or 5 %, even ignoring investment allowances, may thus provide a margin for increased capital costs. In a successful year, moreover, a company might prefer to charge the entire cost of a vessel's modernisation against the year's revenue, rather than to draw on reserves. Such an instance was traced in the accounts analysed on the conversion of a vessel from coal to oil burning in the early 1920s.

The inter-war years witnessed a tendency for capital costs, and hence depreciation charges, to rise. In part this reflected higher shipbuilding prices. In the immediate post-war years shipbuilding prices fell sharply from their high war-time levels. The price of second-hand ships, always a more striking guide to the demand for shipping, also tumbled. *Fairplay* published bi-annually shipbuilding prices per ton deadweight and also the 'ready' price of a 7,500 deadweight ton dry cargo carrier. The trough in both prices was reached in 1932/3 after which a revival is to be traced. The lowest inter-war year price was, nevertheless, about 25 % above pre-war levels. Not only were unit building costs higher. The changing nature of shipping requirements in the Australian sector between the wars also added to building costs. Passenger ships increased in size, they also embodied new marine features and higher standards of passenger comfort. The Orient Line's *Orama II*, built in 1924, was a marked advance on older ships in the line. She served as a model for her four sister ships. Her design incorporated gravity davits for lifeboats, and space for 1,700 passengers and almost 10,000 tons of cargo. She was fitted for the large-scale conveyance of refrigerated cargo. Her design illustrates in part the response made by the British shipping industry to the growth in Australian demand for fast, refrigerated food carriers. Ten years later the supply of shipping for the chilled beef trade also involved heavy costs, both in new building and in conversion. In addition, as we have already described, the ships in use were tending to increase in size.

There is still a further cost factor, one which it is difficult to quantify: the cost implications of improvements made in crew accommodation. As the area of a ship given up to crew space is enlarged, either as a result of legislative or of trade union action, two results follow: higher first costs (which add to annual charges for depreciation), and possibly also a reduction in a ship's revenue-earning capacity. Between the wars the number of seamen employed in foreign-going British ships was tending to fall in relation to the tonnage of shipping in use. In 1920, for example, 2·0 seamen were employed per 100 net tons of shipping, by 1939 the figure had fallen to 1·83 men per 100 net tons.[1] Nevertheless, improvements in crew quarters offset any economies in crew space which derived from higher productivity at sea. So far as is known, no broadly based quantitative assessment of the cost implications of enlarged crew space has ever been made. The naval architect divisions of certain companies engaged in the Australian trade are of the opinion that the first costs of improved crew accommodation on inter-war shipping formed a significant item for the owner. About the effect on revenue earning space they were much less certain and far less unanimous, however. Through the courtesy and help of the Registrar-General of Shipping a crude attempt has been made to

[1] *U.K.P.P.* Cmd. 5096 (Report on deck manning, etc.). The report deals with vessels over 200 ft. long and 750 gross tons.

measure the changing volume of crew space provided on ships built for the Australian service in the 1910s, again in the early 1920s and again in the late 1930s. The evidence points unmistakably to an enlarged amount of ship space per crew member. This is to say that although the ratio of crew numbers to ship's tonnage was falling, the amount of space given up to crew use was tending, proportionately, to rise. We cannot, however, deduce that a reduction in revenue-earning space necessarily followed. So far as it is possible to tell from registration detail, vessel plans, and other vessel data, much if not most of the crew accommodation provided was in the form of superstructure housing—deck houses, round houses, poop accommodation and so on. This is to suggest that better, enlarged crew space was provided in areas not previously or normally used for cargo carrying. In such circumstances the revenue effect on a ship's carrying performance was likely to be slight. The additional steel plating used in building deck-housing would affect the loadline, and thus the deadweight capacity; but the effect on carrying is likely to have been negligible. Since 1945 the effect of improved accommodation where sited below the main deck is likely to have been more noticeable; the problem awaits detailed examination.

The British fleets in service in 1938/9 in the Australian sector tended to be older than their counterparts 20 years earlier. Their total tonnage was higher, much of it built after the First World War. Depreciation charges therefore were greater, both in absolute terms and as a proportion of costs. Service C diverted $5\frac{1}{2}$% of its disbursements in 1923/4 and $10\frac{1}{2}$% in 1938/9 to depreciation reserves, the actual sum was also twice as high in 1938/9. The first costs of the fleet at the close of the period were about three times higher than in 1920/1. The published balance sheets of the P & O show the depreciated value of its fleet in 1913/14 as £$3\frac{1}{2}$ million as compared with £$7\frac{3}{4}$ million in 1938/9 when the fleet in service was much older.[1]

Few of the British lines engaged in the Australian trade added significantly to their fleets in the immediate post-war

[1] Although the companies normally adopted a straight-line historic cost basis for depreciation some profits in a successful year might well be used to speed up the writing-off of capital.

years at the time of peak building prices. The Commonwealth Government Line, in contrast, was created with vessels bought in 1916 when the price inflation was at its height. Fleet additions were built in the years 1919 to 1922, during the worst years of inflation, and were, moreover, built locally at high cost.[1] In part the heavy depreciation charges with which the line was faced accounts for the acute difficulties it experienced when the freight market collapsed in the early 1920s. Requests by the line's general manager for a writing down of book values went unheeded until the Bruce–Page government took office.[2] When Prime Minister Bruce created the Commonwealth Shipping Board in order to take over the Commonwealth Government Line, the value of the fleet was written down to about £4¼ million. In first costs plus additional capital expenditures the line had originally cost £12·8 million of which only £2·2 million had been recovered in depreciation charges.

Running costs on the whole are fixed charges—voyage overheads, Sturmey labels them. In the short-term, individual charges vary only slightly. Some economy may be possible in the wages of catering staff or on their overtime payments for individual voyages depending on the number of passages booked. When demand for passages switched from first to one-class in the early depression years, for example, the lower standard of dining saloon accommodation required relatively fewer waiters. But the overall effect on costs is minimal. In some instances the same charge may be a fixed running cost or a variable. Canal transit dues, for example, are a fixed and forseeable item for passenger lines, especially for mail vessels maintaining a fixed, regular itinerary via one or both canals. But for a non-scheduled cargo liner or for a tramp the same item may be either a fixed charge or a variable charge, depending upon the regularity of a vessel's route. In the Australian trade some P & O vessels in the 1920s, for example (but rarely in the 1930s), took

[1] See *C.P.P.* 1926/8, IV: 'Report on the Commonwealth Government Shipping Activities' and *C.P.D.* vol. 103, p. 641 ff. For an account of the foundation of the war-time shipbuilding industry in Australia see the article by the one-time Chief Executive Officer of Commonwealth Shipping in *Fairplay* vol. 78, pp. 74, 243, 334.

[2] For an interesting discussion on the adoption of new accounting methods see: R. L. Wettenhall, 'Aspects of Political Control in Selected Public Transport Corporations' (Unpublished Ph.D. thesis Australian National University, 1961), p. 187 ff.

the Cape route outwards and the Suez route home. In the 1930s, conference line despatches homeward via the Cape always represented a minute fraction of all homeward sailings. The actual route to be taken by vessels was rarely known long in advance for a non-scheduled despatch. The use or avoidance of a route involving a canal transit at times was often the result of *ad hoc* decision in the light of cargo liftings. In 1930 and 1931 a number of sailings homeward and to the eastern seaboard of North America were made via the two Capes in order to avoid canal dues.

Although they were fixed charges, some running costs altered considerably during the inter-war period, both in absolute terms and as a proportion of the total. The largest single running cost on the Australian route between the wars was for fuel.[1] But it was a charge nevertheless which fell sharply between 1920 and 1939, on service C its place in the lead was lost by 1939. On service A, average actual fuel charges per round voyage fell 30 %, on service C 45 % between the two years. With other charges tending to rise, not surprisingly the percentage of the total represented by fuel fell, from 21 to 16 % for service A and from 23 to 15 % for service C.[2] Three factors were responsible; first, the decline in the price of bunker coal from the abnormal 'high' of the immediate post-war years. Secondly, the adoption of oil in place of coal (which remained relatively more costly) produced fuel economies whether used for diesels or for steam raising. By 1939 about 55 % of all British tonnage used oil. In the Australian sector, as noted in chapter 2, where the liner predominates, the switch to oil was even more impressive. Thirdly, innovations in marine technology meant a more economic use of fuel whether coal or oil, that is to say more power from less fuel. On service A, oil consumption fell by about 200 pounds per mile between 1923/4 and 1938/9.[3]

After fuel, crew costs were the most significant item of operating expenditure. The accounts here examined include only

[1] Cf. *Sturmey*, p. 245 however, for details of U.S.A. ship running costs where crew charges head the list.

[2] It would seem that the cost structure for tramp ships was not as dramatically transformed. In 1938 it was stated that fuel costs for tramps amounted to nearly one-half of running costs. (C of S, *Annual Report* 1937/8, p. 90.)

[3] See also *Svendsen*, p. 33.

three items of crew costs: wages, victualling, and ship's laundry. The last item was of only marginal importance. The most important component was the sum paid in wages. On one service wages accounted for 70 % of crew costs throughout the period. On another service where a high non-British crew element was carried, wages represented only 57 % in 1923/4 but had reached the more customary 71 % in 1938/9. Wages seem to have formed a higher proportion of all crew costs on the cargo services examined where they were as high as 83 %. This does not, however, necessarily testify to a sybaritic standard of crew living on the passenger services.

The account entry for wages presumably was inclusive of allowances, whatever overtime was paid, and employers' superannuation contributions after the inception of the Merchant Navy Officers Pension Fund in 1938. Overtime payments, in contrast with the post-Second World War scene, were unlikely to have been large because of the length of the normal working day at sea, a 12-hour day then being customary. The three-watch system was not introduced until 1936 and even then its introduction was phased in order to spread the effect of reducing hours from 84 to 56 hours per week. Not until 1943 did the 56-hour week at sea become usual. During the inter-war years (as in 1966 with the British seamen's strike over hours and wages), the shipowner was extremely sensitive to any possibility of wage increase. In 1930/1 the International Labour Office examined the question of seamen's hours and more especially a suggestion that all crew except firemen should work an 8-hour day, 48-hour week, and that firemen's hours should be 6 a day over a 36-hour week. The prospect alarmed the British shipowner. It was referred to in the presidential address at the Chamber of Shipping in 1931. If the hours at sea were reduced as was being suggested, the President stated, it would add drastically to costs. For a passenger fleet of 230,000 gross tons the annual additional wage costs of an 8-hour day, 48-hour week (ignoring any further reduction for firemen), would be £244,000, an increase of 80 % on existing wage costs. For a cargo-liner fleet of 80,000 tons the comparable figure would be £52,000. At this time the industry was beginning to move into the acute phase of the depression.

Crew costs, unlike fuel charges, were higher in 1939 than in 1920. The increase took place solely in the total amount paid in wages. The cost of victualling in all the accounts examined was lower both absolutely and relatively at the close of the period than in the early 1920s. In most of the accounts examined the total wages paid per voyage were higher in 1938/9 than in 1923/4. The rate of increase seems to have been lower on services not employing Asian crews. Services where the Asian element was high show a sharp increase in wage payments to the European officers. Increased charges in respect of wages were not due alone to higher wage rates. Depending upon one's choice of dates indeed, it can be shown that rates of wages were lower in 1938/9 than in the early 1920s. The movement of wage rates was as follows: in May 1920 war-time bonuses were incorporated into ordinary wages and an increase was recorded; thereafter falls took place in 1921, 1922 and 1923. In May 1924 rates rose to regain the 1922 level but were reduced again in August 1925. The wage cut in 1925 was responsible for touching off the seamen's strike of that year. (The strike, mentioned briefly below, was most vigorously pursued in Australia.) Between 1925 and 1931 rates remained steady.[1] With the onset of the depression a 10 % cut in wages was made selectively in 1931 and extended to all ranks in January 1932. Beginning in March 1935 the cut was gradually restored. By January 1939 rates of pay had regained a level below the peak attained in May 1920 and, as a rule, midway between the rates of May 1921 and May 1922. The level in 1939 was a trifle higher than the rate reached in April 1923, the applicable figure in our analysis of accounts for the year 1923/4. It was the use of bigger ships and hence of enlarged crew complements per 'average' voyage in 1938/9 which chiefly explains the significant increase of wages as a running cost, not the introduction of higher rates of pay. In 1923/4, for example, the 'average' net shipping tonnage employed per P & O voyage amounted to about 9,000 tons compared with more than 12,000

[1] It has been argued that only the existence of the National Maritime Board during the 1920s prevented further deterioration. Created during the First World War and divorced from government control in 1920, the N.M.B. is the joint negotiating body for the industry and also controls the supply of labour. A noteworthy achievement of the Board was the establishment virtually at the outset of a national wage level.

in 1938/9; increases of a similar order of magnitude are to be traced in the fleets whose accounts are examined here. Not forgetting that rising productivity between the wars had decreased the ratio of crew numbers to ship's tonnage, the number of 'engagements' per average P & O voyage increased by about 30 % over the period.

International cost comparison, as already noted, is not a major objective of the present chapter. In dealing with a single sector the pitfalls of such an attempt are too numerous. For crew charges, however, some consideration must be given to international variations. The significance of crew charges in running costs is well attested in the literature; it is amply demonstrated in the accounts analysed. International competition is frequently defined solely in the terms of crew charges. Often it is accepted as an adequate explanation of the loss of a trade that the wages paid by a competitor are 'low'. Satisfactory comparisons of crew charges for the inter-war years are all too hard to obtain; the availability of some information concerning the Australian sector is therefore an additional reason for a brief reference.[1] The information available all relates to the 1920s, before the problem becomes complicated by currency devaluation.

Crew costs, as we have noted, are dominated by wage payments. An examination based upon wage rates alone is not sufficient, however, because of the differences which existed in manning scales. Ships of the same size may carry a differently constituted crew depending on a number of factors, the chief of which are the area and nature of employment of a ship and the requirements of the country in which it is registered. Manning differences under different registrations derive primarily from tradition, industrial agreement, or government legislation. In the simplest terms it is reflected in the size of a crew complement. In part national variations in manning may reflect varying degrees in skill. Asian labour charges and victualling costs, for example, are low per head. Where use is made of Asian labour,

[1] Mr B. Mogridge, author of the chapter in *Sturmey* on 'Labour Relations and Labour Costs', gives illustrations of crew costs for 12 of the years between 1901 and 1960, only 5 of the inter-war years are mentioned, in only 3 instances are comparisons made between more than 3 national fleets.

however, the number employed is often higher than if the ships were fully manned by Europeans. In part also, manning variations based upon considerations of skill dictate the choice of vessel employed. International comparisons which ignore ship type are thus often meaningless. A partial explanation of the rapid adoption of the marine diesel engine in certain countries in the early 1920s, for example, is that it enabled an owner to employ marine engineers and other engine room labour of lower levels of skill than were required for a steam-turbined vessel. Higher skills presumably carried higher rates of pay. Here such complexities are avoided and discussion is confined to simple aggregates of the number of hands employed.

The most useful comparison to make is between crew charges on ships of identical size and type under different registrations. Information relating to three years is available. It was assembled and published at the time in order to illustrate the handicap suffered by ships employed in the Australian sector and manned on the Australian scale. The actual financial effect of such handicaps on the operating experience of the Commonwealth Government Line was estimated in 1926/7. The additional cost of running the line's seven steamships manned on Australian instead of British articles was £220,000 a year. The loss of £189,905 anticipated for the year 1926/7 would thus have been converted into a profit of £30,000 had the vessels been registered in the U.K. For the year ended 31 March 1926 the actual crew costs incurred for the 5 *Bay* ships compared with the comparable figure for the ships manned on British articles were as follows:

	Australian articles	British articles
Crew numbers	170	154
Year's wages	£204,987	£87,229
Additional victualling costs	£9,510	—

Data for other vessels converted to index numbers are shown below. In all four examples it will be seen that the Australian index number is considerably higher than the figure for British and other fleets, it confirms in quantitative terms the spate of contemporary complaint about the high-cost operation of Australian vessels. Protected by the Commonwealth Navigation Act and associated together in a shipping conference, Australian owners engaged in the coasting trade could ensure that freight charges were 'adequate'. In the oversea services freight rate agreements also existed. They were of small benefit to the Commonwealth Government Line, however, which experienced mounting financial loss. It posed to the Australian government the problem which confronts all high-cost economies seeking to maintain oversea shipping lines. In the absence of other cost-reducing innovations the alternatives were: a translation of the ships to the British registry; a deterioration of wages or manning conditions; pressure on the homeward conference to raise the rates of freight; or continued subsidy. The first two were politically unthinkable, the third would scarcely have helped the Australian primary producer; and the last was what the Bruce–Page government was not prepared to do.[1] The index numbers for the Japanese and U.S.A. fleets are of interest. They provide a grain of evidence to challenge two expressions of opinion concerning these fleets: first, that U.S.A. wage costs in the early 1920s may have been as low as those in the British fleet, and secondly that Japanese wage costs were doubtless far below British in the 1920s.[2]

In the mid-1930s, on the other hand, wage rates on the trans-Pacific route by the U.S.A. Matson Line and the British Canadian-Australasian Line were virtually identical.[3] This is, however, a special case. Although the two vessels of the Canadian-Australasian Line were registered in Britain, the crews were largely recruited in Sydney and were paid at rates more akin to Australian than to British articles.

Waterfront labour disputes in Australia which affected oversea shipping have been referred to in previous discussion on wharf labour. With a single exception, strike action within the British shipping industry itself had little or no effect on the Australian scene. Shipping strikes were endemic between 1920 and 1926, when the break-away seamen's union collapsed. But they were short, they tended to be localized, and they were without far-reaching consequences. The single exception, which

[1] For the steps taken by the Bruce–Page government to dispose of the line see Wettenhall, *op. cit.* p. 384.

[2] *Sturmey*, p. 316.

[3] I.S.C. *35th Report*, pp. 24, 25.

Table 27. *Comparative crew costs, 1923–1929*

	U.K.	Australia	Norway	Denmark	Sweden	France	Netherlands	Japan	U.S.A.
1923: 6,000 ton vessel									
(i) Crew numbers	100	114	—	—	—	—	—	—	—
(ii) Monthly wage	100	184	—	—	—	—	—	—	—
(iii) Overtime rate	100	220	—	—	—	—	—	—	—
(iv) Monthly overtime	100	300	—	—	—	—	—	—	—
1924: 5,800 ton vessel									
(i) Crew numbers	100	132	108	—	103	113	97	160	105
(ii) Wages	100	212	62	—	102	74	91	106	200
1926/7: 6,000 ton vessel									
(i) Wages	100	308	—	48	75	—	—	—	130
1929: 5,250 ton vessel on transfer from Australian to British articles									
(i) Crew numbers	100	149	—	—	—	—	—	—	—
(ii) Wages	100	231	—	—	—	—	—	—	—

Sources: *S.M.H.* 7 May 1923 and 20 September 1924. *C.P.P.* 1926/8, IV, 15. *Fairplay* vol. 111, p. 60.

affected Australia above all, was the strike of the second half of 1925.[1] The strike was touched off by the wage cut of 1 August 1925. Beginning in the middle of the month an attempt was made to tie up British shipping everywhere. The strike was a failure in the U.K. from the start, where it scarcely survived to the end of the month. It collapsed in South Africa at an early date. But in New Zealand and more especially in Australia the strike dragged on for many weeks.

The strike of British seamen in Australian ports became entwined with the industrial actions of the local, far more militant waterside workers' union and Australian seamen's union, both of which had engaged in strikes during the first half of 1925. Perhaps partly for this reason the British seamen's strike in Australian ports persisted long after it had ended elsewhere. The climate of militancy and unrest was infectious. Where British crews might have wavered and expressed reservation they were 'helped' on by local militants. In terms of their engagements and of the nowadays much publicised Merchant Shipping Act of 1894, the crews were in fact not striking but breaking their articles. In consequence the shipping companies through the O.S.R.A. in early September swore out warrants. Many seamen were convicted and imprisoned in a ruthless attempt to break the 'strike'. By early September also the Union itself was issuing exhortations from London to the seamen in Australia to rejoin their ships. When exports began to pile up Prime Minister Bruce intervened. He was reported as threatening the strikers with deportation. He warned them against being used by local extremists.

Assistance given locally to the striking British crews was no doubt an expression of genuine sympathy for a closely associated group of workers. It was also the tactical exploitation of a local situation. Any reluctance by British crews to join their striking comrades (or to 'blackleg', according to one's point of view) produced a violent reaction from Australian dockers and seamen. The Orient Line's *Orvieto*, for example, on which the crew

[1] The main source used is the *S.M.H.* which contains no fewer than eighty comments or reports on the strike and many other, uncounted, less important references between August and December 1925. See also: *Fairplay* vol. 97, pp. 2, 107, 266. *The Economist* 21 November, 12 and 19 December 1925. *The Times* 8, 10, 17 and 24 October, 6 and 14 November and 1 December 1925.

remained 'loyal', was prevented from sailing by the action of the dockers' union in withholding supplies. Two men, notorious in the local scene, appear frequently on the stage and served to act as a rallying point for the more militant left. Walsh, born in Britain, leader of the Australian seamen's union, and a naturalized Dutchman, Johannsen (or Johnson), became the targets for official reaction. Strenuous attempts were made in 1925 to deport them. Amending legislation was rushed through both houses (time limits being applied to the debate on the grounds of urgency) which provided *inter alia* authority to deport persons, other than those born in Australia, 'who have been concerned in Australia in acts directed towards hindering or obstructing to the prejudice of the public, the transport or the conveyance of passengers or the provision of necessary services...' The measure was violently and bitterly, but unsuccessfully opposed in the House. An opposition spokesman quoted, with relish, an extract from the *Manchester Guardian* accusing Bruce of using the shipping strike as an excuse for a concerted attack on labour. Earle Page of the Bruce–Page coalition government, recalls in his autobiography that he and Bruce went to the country in November 1925 'on the issue of a mandate to enforce constitutional law against mob rules and strikes'. Their government was overwhelmingly returned.[1] The cost of the 1925 strike is referred to below.

The charges in the accounts against revenue require little comment. They consist of the costs arising directly and visibly from the conveyance of passengers and cargo. Most of the voyage accounts examined have three major cost appropriations for charges against revenue: commissions paid to agents and rebates made in respect of freight and passenger traffic; the victualling of passengers; and the charges incurred in cargo handling (stevedoring, crane hire, lighterage etc.). These were charges which varied with the number of passengers or amount of cargo carried. Victualling charges per voyage tended to fall between 1923/4 and 1938/9. Cargo-handling charges, in con-

[1] Earle Page, *Truant Surgeon* (Sydney, 1963), p. 172. See also: *C.P.D.* vol. 110, pp. 931, 964; vol. 111, pp. 1,840–50, 2,708, 2,714; vol. 112, pp. 177–80. Parliament rose on 24 September 1925 and was dissolved on 3 October 1925. Sittings were not resumed until 13 January 1926 by which time the strike was over.

trast, rose by more than 20% on Service A between the two outside dates. In general they tended to represent a higher proportionate charge against freight revenue in 1939 than in the early 1920s.

Our final point concerning operating expenditures relates to lay-up costs. After a series of unprofitable voyages the question arises of continued operations. If a ship is old and its repair bill is mounting and if the current trend in freight rate seems to be downwards, a shipowner may prefer to dispose of the ship. The alternative to selling, or running at a loss is to lay-up; this also involves certain charges for the shipowner. Apart from insurance, depreciation and charges in respect of administration, there are also the 'operating' costs of lay-up to be met. These are sizeable. Hence the decision to lay-up is taken only when voyage results suggest that the losses from continued operation will exceed laying-up charges. This point was frequently reached during the inter-war years. In the accounts analysed lay-up charges are given for a number of ships during many of the years. In 1938/9 detail for 17 vessels laid up for a total of 600 days has been analysed. Charges were in respect of wages and victualling, fuel, water, stores, repairs, hire of wireless equipment, port dues and insurance. Any administrative expenses incurred were debited to those vessels which remained in commission. No depreciation charges were made against the older, coal-burning ships, the first cost of which by this date had been completely written off. The charges, exclusive of depreciation amounted to as much as £130 per 'ship-day'. For the oil steamers and diesels the total daily 'ship-day' charge inclusive of depreciation was about £210. For one line whose accounts have been examined the charges incurred in vessel lay-up amounted to 8% of operating profit in that year.

Before turning to a glance at 'profits', a brief discussion of taxation is necessary because of the handicap suffered by expatriate shipowners in the Australian sector. The tax disability in Australia was common to all oversea shipowners. No attempt is made at comparison with other national groups also at work in Australia's oversea services, however. Tax comparison for national fleets as a whole is difficult enough, any narrower approach is scarcely possible without disproportionate labour.

Nor are we concerned here with the taxation of British shipping in Britain. We assume that U.K. shipping companies were no more disadvantaged by domestic tax levels than other industrial enterprises.

Between the wars Australia was one of the few major participants in international trade which declined to exempt from local income tax, oversea shipping companies owned abroad. Generally speaking, most countries involved adopted some system of relief during the 1920s. The problem of taxation was one which came into prominence towards the close of the First World War. It began when the U.K. in 1916 as part of a general tax increase in both the level and incidence, introduced the taxation of foreign shipping using British ports. Following the retaliatory wave which was thus provoked, considerable effort was directed to closing the lid of the box which Britain had opened.

The early post-war years witnessed a number of attempts to achieve some form of relief. It was a subject claiming both imperial and international attention. It was discussed at meetings of the Imperial Economic Conference and, as discussed below, was investigated by the I.S.C. Successive meetings of the International Chamber of Commerce and of the International Shipping Conference adopted resolutions criticising double taxation and urging its abolition, at least on a reciprocal basis. The League of Nations recommended that tax should be levied only in the country in which the real centre of management is situated. Many bilateral arrangements followed. By the mid-1920s double taxation agreements, at least concerning shipping, had been made between Britain and the U.S.A., Norway, Sweden, Denmark and so on. In 1929/30, the Chamber of Shipping was able to report that the only large maritime nations with which Great Britain had *not* arranged reciprocal exemption were France and Italy. By the following year the total number of such bilateral agreements had reached a total of forty-two.

Countries lacking an ocean-going fleet had little to gain from such agreements. Conspicuous among such countries were members of the Empire. At the International Shipping Conference in June 1928 complaints were made by a number of members that Dominion countries had not followed Britain in the abandonment of such double taxation. It was, however, a topic which impinged upon questions of competence and jurisdiction. It was for this reason that in 1923 the I.S.C. was reluctant to recommend the adoption of any of the alternatives included in its report on the taxation of shipping within the Empire.[1] The Committee agreed that the complaints concerning taxation were justified. 'The difficulties may not appear very great in connection with any one jurisdiction but in the aggregate of the whole Empire they amount to an impediment to commerce.' Nevertheless, the members felt that the question of political competence and state revenues passed beyond their terms of reference.

The Imperial Economic Conference met in the same year. A sub-committee studied both the taxation of shipping and the relevant I.S.C. report. It was attracted by the tax exemption agreement on shipping currently being concluded between Britain and the U.S.A. It similarly turned away from any solution which might seem to 'impair the right of any country of the Empire to tax income arising within the sphere of its jurisdiction'.[2] It contented itself with recommendations that the normal basis of assessment to income tax of non-resident British shipowners should be the actual trading results, not a statutory percentage of freights and passage money. By 1926 the conference recommendations had been implemented in India and most of the Crown Colonies; by 1928 in South Africa and elsewhere.

In Australia, however, fiscal and political considerations tended to perpetuate the taxation of oversea shipping companies. The basis of assessment moreover remained unchanged. Taxation everywhere is disliked. It was especially resented by expatriate shipowners operating in Australian waters because the arbitrary method of assessment, as already noted, ignored the more customary basis of taxing profits. Income tax levied on shipping companies owned overseas was on the basis not of profit but of gross earnings, the method condemned by the Imperial Economic Conference. At Commonwealth level, income tax was charged on '10 % (later reduced to $7\frac{1}{2}$ %) of the

[1] *U.K.P.P.* Cmd. 1979. [2] *U.K.P.P.* Cmd. 2009, p. 348.

amount received for freight, passengers and mails shipped at Australian ports for carriage overseas'.[1] State income tax similarly calculated was at the lower rate of 5 %. Fiscal provisions covered both inward and outward gross earnings, in practice only outward freights were taxed. The states, generally, followed the Commonwealth in similarly basing tax on gross earnings. Queensland and N.S.W. tax law gave shipowners the option of proving profits but in practice the states were not always willing to accept accountants' certificates. In part, no doubt, as the Commonwealth royal commission on taxation noted in the early 1930s, there were many difficulties in determining not only profits, but also the ratio properly attributable to a given part of a voyage.[2] Nevertheless no attempt seems to have been made during the inter-war years in Australia to achieve a more equitable basis for the taxing of oversea shipping companies.

Taxation based not on profits but on earnings yields curious anomalies. Evidence supplied to the I.S.C. in 1923 showed that one line on six consecutive voyages between Britain and Australia incurred losses totalling £102,000. It nevertheless paid about £18,000 in federal and state income tax in Australia in respect of these voyages. For a number of other vessels in the same year the average 'taxation was 8·68 per cent of the port charges and other expenses'. Stating the obvious, to ensure its inclusion in the I.S.C. report on the taxing of shipping companies, the President of the Chamber of Shipping reminded his hearers that 'shipowners...took these charges (*sc.* for income tax) into account when estimating the expenses of a forthcoming voyage, and that they therefore entered into the freight which was charged'.[3] Taxation figured prominently as a topic of discussion at the 1929 Overseas Shipping Conference in Sydney. Shipowners complained of the high costs involved in voyages to Australia and of the burden of Australian tax. The report of the Conference drew attention:

To the general recognition by a large number of countries of the principle that, when shipping profits are made, they should be taxed once, and once only, namely in the country of residence of the ship-

[1] *U.K.P.P.* Cmd. 1979, p. 8.
[2] *C.P.P.* 1934/7, III, 2,018.
[3] *U.K.P.P.* Cmd. 1979, pp. 24, 31.

ping company, in harmony with the general principles evolved by Governments and the League of Nations for relieving international commerce from the friction and waste of double taxation. We believe that it would be in the ultimate interest of Australia, as a large exporter, to adhere to this principle...pending the adoption of this principle...Australia should give immediate effect to the attached scheme for relieving overseas shipping from the incidental injustice of double taxation...

It was not a suggestion likely to meet with much support since Australia owned little oversea shipping for which reciprocal benefit could be claimed. It was unlikely to gain wide support in default of some alternative advantage accruing to the country; as the leader writer in the *S.M.H.* was quick to point out: 'a proposal to abolish income tax on the proceeds of oversea shipping owned overseas would command attention were it made plain that the abolition would be fully reflected in lower freights and fares'.[1]

The taxation of oversea shipping companies, on the original arbitrary basis of gross earnings persisted until 1939. Complaint also continued. The size of the total contribution made by oversea owned shipping companies, however, is impossible to establish. The most likely source of information, the archives of the Commonwealth Commissioner of Taxation, contain only the aggregated tax collection of *all* resident and *all* oversea shipping companies.[2] As a proportion of total Commonwealth tax revenue, the amount paid by shipping companies, resident and overseas, was always small, usually less than $\frac{1}{2}$ %.[3] The argument that the Commonwealth could easily forego that part of the annual $\frac{1}{2}$ % which derived from oversea shipping companies is hard to refute.

At a time of falling freight rates, declining trade and disappearing profits, any additional financial burden for the operator is clearly undesirable. When the overall operating

[1] *S.M.H.* 15 April 1929. It is ironic that prior to 1927 the Commonwealth Government Line escaped taxation in Britain at the same time that its British competitors were being taxed in Australia. It 'ruffled' the editor of *Fairplay*, see vol. 104, p. 607.

[2] Information from Commonwealth Archives Office, reference P. 311/60.

[3] See 8th and 12th to 23rd Reports of the Commissioner of Taxation published in *C.P.P.* Tax paid by tramp ships is aggregated with other 'casual tax payers'.

experience shows a loss, the payment of tax exacerbates even further. The records of a company made available to the author contain some information on taxation in a readily usable form. It is *not* a company renowned for inefficient management. In 1923/4 Australian tax paid by the company represented 18 % of the surplus of operating revenue over operating expenditure after allowing for depreciation but before paying tax. During the 1930s the company's trading operations invariably witnessed a loss, that is to say a surplus of operating expenditure over operating revenue, usually even before taking depreciation into account. It nevertheless paid tax each year in Australia. In 1932/3 and 1938/9 the amount paid in tax was about the same as that which it had paid in 1923/4.

We turn in conclusion to that thorniest of questions: shipping profits. It is a subject shrouded in discreet commercial silence and usually discussed in the doubtful terms of annual dividends paid on capital. No published work known to the author examines a shipping company's performance in recent years in the light of *actual* voyage accounts. Studies of the industry concentrate on the colourful aspects rather than on the industry's economic performance. Where profits are mentioned, recourse is usually had to published balance sheets. For most liner companies, balance sheets published before 1932 moreover are not very informative; since that date the amount of detail revealed has increased. Professor Sturmey's recent work on British shipping, in the context of profits also based upon published balance sheets, has thrown much light on the profitability of shipping management. If the present author disagrees with his basic conclusion it does not diminish the debt due to him for his valuable pioneer work. Such disagreement as there is, moreover, relates to his view of the 1930s and does not question the validity of his assessment for the post-1945 period. He has used a sample of published balance sheets in order to compute 'voyage profits as percentages of real capital for liner companies'. Real capital values have been calculated on the basis of building costs and the market price of second-hand vessels adjusted for age. This leads him to the conclusion that between 1932 and 1939 apart from 1932 and 1935 'the liner companies in the sample earned more than enough to cover current interest on the capital employed after allowing proper depreciation', based upon current asset values.[1]

Definitions of real capital differ widely. Not every economist or accountant would necessarily agree on the precise label which should be attached to sums representing accrued depreciation and other reserves held in suspense accounts. Most long-established shipping companies by 1920 had amassed large reserves from the profits of successful war-time trading and from the accumulation of sums allocated for fleet renewals. Many liner companies' balance sheets even after 1932 did not specify in the profit and loss account the precise source of the profit shown. A not uncommon description used is: operating profit *and* income from investment. In some instances profits included returns from business enterprises not connected with shipping. But the inter-war years are less associated with economic diversification than are the years since the Second World War. In the accounts examined here some such sources of profit have been noted but the sums involved have been relatively minor. The two significant sums brought into account were the profit (or loss) on actual shipping operations and the interest earned on reserves, usually held in fixed-interest-bearing securities, often including Commonwealth of Australia stocks.

For the services discussed here it is clear that the actual conduct of shipping operations in many of the inter-war years, especially in the 1930s, resulted not in a surplus but in a deficit. Only the interest receipts from reserve funds enabled the companies to pay modest dividends and to continue to operate ships. We examine the chronology below. Initially, however, we attempt to answer the question: is it correct to regard interest on reserve funds as 'voyage profits', and to consider as operating profitably a company which only survives on such interest? The fact that the interest enabled a liner company in the 1930s both to allot a sum for depreciation (adequate on the basis of historic

[1] *Sturmey*, p. 248. The percentages after depreciation range from 3 to 4% in 1932 and 1935 and from 5 to 15% variously in the remaining years. The Chamber of Shipping's view of liner profits was very different, based as it was upon historic cost principles. For the 7 years 1932–8 'profits from voyages of liner companies... represented $6\frac{3}{4}$ per cent on the total capital at risk (including reserves) or only $1\frac{3}{4}$ per cent after providing for normal depreciation'. *Annual Report* 1939/40, p. 70.

cost) and also to declare a dividend should not be allowed to obscure the failure of that company's shipping operations to produce a surplus of revenue over operating expenditure. The sums in reserve along with the company's fleet and other physical assets form shareholders' capital.[1] Interest earned upon reserves thus represents a return on shareholders' capital. But in the long-term, if a shipping company's operating activities result in a deficit, the prognosis is unfavourable. Its dissolution is surely a matter of time. The continued use of obsolescent vessels without costly modernisation and conversion does nothing to increase operating profitability. On the other hand, depreciation charges are lower on older vessels. Fleet renewal or expensive modernisation eats into depreciation reserves. Annual depreciation charges thereafter are greater; and interest earned from depleted reserves smaller. Bigger fleet units and higher building prices characterise the inter-war years. On both counts therefore the probability is that sole dependence on reserves is ultimately a self-liquidating process. (The Cunard company revelations in 1966 point the moral.)

It is clear from voyage account analyses that the 1930s were years of special difficulty. Only the existence of large reserves enabled the services to survive until the new demands of war transformed the complexion of voyage accounts. For the services here examined (perhaps also for the liner companies forming part of Professor Sturmey's sample) it is questionable that higher dividends would have solved the difficulties confronting liner companies in the 1930s. 'At almost any time during the whole period (i.e. 1932 to 1960) the liner companies as a whole earned sufficient to justify new issues of capital for purposes of expansion and their alleged inability to raise new capital was a consequence of attempts to rely entirely on self-financing by limiting dividends not of any inability to earn profits.'[2] A more generous dividend policy may have facilitated the raising of outside capital as Sturmey suggests. Additional finance would have permitted fleet modernisation. But, inescapably, the fact is that the new vessels built for services A and C in the middle and

[1] It should perhaps be explicitly noted that the practice of the shipping companies themselves has been followed here in using accounting concepts of capital.

[2] *Sturmey*, pp. 248–9.

late 1930s were no more profitable than their sister ships built in the early or mid-1920s. After a decade of failure to match shipping expenditures with falling revenue (if the experience of the services analysed is typical) it is not altogether surprising to find the British liner industry in early 1939 seeking a 'liner defence fund' or subsidy. A number of foreign fleets had benefited from subsidies from the early 1930s, both in 'scrap and build' renewal programmes and in straight operating assistance. The British and Norwegian fleets were significant exceptions. One would like to have access to Norwegian companies' voyage accounts to be certain that they were not similarly living 'off their fat'.

In our discussion of the services described we rely upon their actual trading experience as revealed in their voyage accounts. From them it is abundantly clear that the years 1932–9 were not years of profit but of continuing loss. From reserve funds charges for depreciation and dividend payments were met. For much of the period operating revenue failed to meet expenditure even before depreciation. It is a reflection both of falling revenue and rising costs. As we have noted already, the movement of freight rates was steadily downwards, they were accompanied by passage rates. Revenue data converted to index numbers per average voyage are given in Table 28. At once obvious is the sharp fall in passage money receipts in 1932/3, a faithful reflection of the overall downturn in demand for passenger accommodation in the depression years. The same years also witnessed a decline in imports into Australia and hence decline in outward freight earnings. The expansionist export policy deliberately adopted to grapple with the depression on the other hand forced homeward freight earnings upward. In subsequent years homeward freights contracted for service A among others but nevertheless remained above the figure for 1923/4. Taking all earnings together, however, it is to be seen that the level of 1923/4 was not regained. Bearing in mind that the 'average' voyage in 1938/9 employed considerably more tonnage than in 1923/4, and that most costs had risen, it is clear that the shipping companies were not enjoying the luxury of whatever is the marine equivalent of feather bedding.

The difficulties experienced were most severe after 1930. But failure to match revenue receipts and the sum of running costs, overheads and voyage variables can also be traced well before 1930. The 1925 strike, for example, was costly and disruptive, its repercussions persisted well into 1926. The companies chiefly concerned were the Orient, the P & O branch service (which employed an all-British crew unlike the P & O main services), the Aberdeen, and the Commonwealth and Dominion lines and so on. In all, 71 British ships were involved. They were held up in Australian ports for a total of more than 4,000 days. They incurred excess expenditures directly attributable to the strike amounting to no less than £¾ million. The accounts of one of the services here analysed registers a fall of 80 % in the surplus of revenue over total operating expenditure from 1924/5 to the financial year 1925/6 covering the strike. With another of the services a modest profit in 1924/5 was followed the year after by a loss equal to 4 % of gross revenue.

The year of the strike, 1925, in fact seems to have marked the true beginning of difficulties for the shipping industry as a whole. Post-war reaction was finally complete. Perhaps more important, shipowners at last were viewing their difficulties as long-term rather than ephemeral set-backs. From 1925 onwards, that is to say well before the onset of the 'great depression' of the thirties, shipowners began to talk gloomily about a 'shipping depression'. From then on the tone of comment assumed a sombre note. At each annual general meeting of the Chamber of Shipping, uneasiness was expressed about the continued inverse movement of shipping costs and earnings. The term 'excess shipping capacity' gained currency. Towards the end of the 1920s the Chamber's *Annual Report* could point to freight levels below those of 1914 and to shipping costs at least 70 % higher. World trade had increased 10 % over 1914 but shipping tonnage available had gone up 40 %.

The Australian sector, although defensively organised, could not entirely escape the malaise. Service C achieved an operating surplus throughout the 1920s. For service A, operating experience was more in line with the general trend complained of by chamber members and by shipping companies in other parts of the world. With service B, operating deficits were avoided until 1928. Other lines in the Australian trade, foreign as well as

Table 28. *Liner revenue index numbers 1923/4–1938/9*

(Average per voyage, 1923/4 = 100.)

	Passage money			Freight receipts			
	Out-ward	Home-ward	Total	Out-ward	Home-ward	Total	All receipts
Service A							
1923/4	100	100	100	100	100	100	100
1928/9	86	79	83	85	113	98	90
1932/3	69	77	73	55	154	101	87
1938/9	104	108	106	71	117	93	99
Service C							
1923/4	100	100	100	100	100	100	100
1928/9	89	100	89	84	87	85	91
1932/3	35	55	41	38	102	71	52
1938/9	71	85	73	72	101	87	80

British members of the homeward conference, suffered heavy operating deficits in the three years 1926 to 1928, as they were able to prove to the satisfaction of the 1929 Overseas Shipping Conference at Sydney. Their losses, certified by accountants, were accepted by the traditionally suspicious and not entirely friendly members of the Australian delegation. In attempting to establish a fair rate of return the Conference decided that the oversea shipowner had a right to expect 10% on the capital employed. (Here again it is the accountants concept of capital which is intended.) To achieve such a result in 1926 required an increase in freight earnings of about 48% and in 1928 an increase of about 36%. But as already noted, at about the time the Conference was held in Sydney, the Chamber of Shipping in London was noting that freights had fallen to a level below that of 1914.

Almost before the delegates to the Conference had returned home the world-wide depression in shipping and trade had begun. For many sectors and branches of the British shipping industry the financial position deteriorated. In the Australian sector, liner service A saw its annual deficit increase to a peak in one year when it was equal to close on 10% of total revenue. Service C, which had survived the 1920s, similarly failed to meet operating expenses out of revenue for each year until 1938/9. Only service E showed a surplus, and that minute, and for only one of the two years examined. The coming of war in 1939 immediately translated the companies back to the threshold of 1914 when reserves once more began to be accumulated on a large scale.

POSTSCRIPT

Analysis in preceding chapters has sought wherever possible to point the appropriate conclusions from the changes traced in the relationships between British shipping and the Australian economy. We have obviated the need for a lengthy summary of our conclusions by focussing attention throughout on the implications for each side of the partnership of the topics examined. It is, nevertheless, not unnecessarily repetitive to underline the dilemma which existed in the partnership by seeking a short answer to the question implicit, where not explicitly stated, throughout the work: was the Australian economy adequately supplied with oversea shipping services between the wars? Or, put more subjectively, were Australian shippers satisfied with the services they received? The answer to the question in the second form is, clearly, no. They remain dissatisfied to this day.

The argument in this book has concerned itself with two themes simultaneously. On the one hand our discussion has outlined the changing oversea shipping needs of the Australian economy. On the other we have examined the operating requirements and experience of the British shipping industry which during our period supplied most of Australia's oversea shipping services. The two themes were intimately related and were always inter-dependent. Nevertheless, they were also in conflict. In many ways the objectives of each side of the partnership were mutually antagonistic and impossible of achievement at one and the same time. Profitable shipping operations at a time when international trading conditions were unfavourable often required freight rates higher than the Australian shipper was prepared to pay. From the shipowners' viewpoint the peculiar handicaps of the Australian route, the longest in the world, plus the relative smallness of the economy, gave rise to serious problems of under utilisation.

Nevertheless, the relationships between British shipping and the Australian economy were not without advantages. The placement of services by the British shipping industry in the

Australian sector was one of a number of similar such inputs. But for British shipping it was a sector of especial importance, an importance not accurately portrayed in terms either of the total tonnage employed nor of the contribution made by the sector to British shipping earnings as a whole. In many ways the inter-war years form a highly unusual period. It was happy fortune for British shipping that economic developments during the inter-war years brought Australia and Britain closer together.

The post-war boom of the 1920s gave way to a depression more truly meriting the adjective 'great' than did the economic experience of Western Europe a half century earlier. Contracting trade in the 1930s, moreover, was more noticeably accompanied by growing economic nationalism including the sphere of ocean transport. In a world of maritime chauvinism, where some form of shipping subsidy was fairly common, the British shipping industry struggled for survival. In some ways its reactions and unwillingness to initiate change suggest the decline of an outdated, ossifying form of entrepreneurial activity. Often its methods were inept. In the Australian sector the experience of British shipping presents a brighter picture, however. Not only was it relatively more successful, but it was also willing to experiment in a number of ways in order to satisfy the demands of the Australian shipper. Above all it was prepared to experiment in the creation of a wider basis for freight rate determination, the tallest hurdle faced by an expatriate shipowner. The result was the A.O.T.A., the joint negotiating and consultative body described in chapter 6. Not forgetting the dissatisfaction in Australia with the A.O.T.A. (which often is as clamorous today as it was in the thirties), there can be no denying the usefulness of the institution. The deliberate attempt to widen the basis of rate determination was a novel departure at that time; it is rare even today.

As an area of employment for British shipping the Australian sector was particularly important at a time of contracting world demand for tonnage. As noted above (pp. 42–8), British tonnage entering Australian ports during the 1930s not only survived at the high level of the late 1920s, the total tonnage figure was in fact raised by 1939. Elsewhere in the world British shipping activity declined. Much British tonnage was taken out of commission and laid up or broken up. It required the Second World War to revive the fortunes of much of the British shipping industry.

In the Australian oversea services, as discussion in chapter 8 has shown, the British shipping industry during the 1930s on the testimony of the accounts examined failed to achieve a profit. But there are reasons for believing that the Australian sector offered relatively more profitable employment for British shipping than elsewhere in the world. In large part the achievements of British shipping in the Australian trade derived from and reflects the successful working out of the agreements reached at Ottawa. In order to offset some of the effects of declining world trade an important objective of the Ottawa Conference was the 'lowering or removal of barriers' to trade between British Commonwealth countries. As a result it was hoped that: 'the flow of trade between the various countries of the Empire will be facilitated, and that by the consequent increase of purchasing power of their peoples, the trade of the world will also be stimulated and increased'.[1]

The outcome of Ottawa for Australia was a marked concentration on extending and of maximising her role in the supply of the British food market. The effect of this on British shipping was to maintain its employment for the direct carrying trade between Australia and Britain. We are not here concerned with the 'ifs' of historical alternatives. However, it is not without interest to point out that if adverse international trade developments had not induced Australia (among other British Commonwealth countries) to concentrate on the British market, British shipping in Australia's oversea services might well have had a less happy experience. If the Australian trade drive had been more widely diffused and differently motivated the conclusions of this book might well have been vastly different. If, for example, Australia had not deliberately sought for so long to exclude Japan from the Australian market, the failure of British shipping in the Australian sector might not have been confined to the E & A and the Canadian-Australasian lines.

[1] *U.K.P.P.* Cmd. 4174, p. 10. For a critical examination of the aims of the Conference see W. K. Hancock, *Survey of British Commonwealth Affairs*, vol. II, *Problems of Economic Policy 1918–1939*, part I (1940).

The advantages of the partnership for the Australian economy are less obvious because of the difficulty of measuring or determining how successful the alternative might have been. If the complaints of the shippers are to be taken at face value, the economy suffered. It was a judgment stemming largely from concern over freight rates. The major preoccupation of the Australian shipper at this time was with freight rates (more especially with outbound rates), with the shipping requirements of the export sector, and with those institutional factors which influenced, controlled, or fashioned those rates. Contemporary comment and interest in Australia thus tended to concentrate on the homeward rate to the U.K.; on the shipping needs of this route; and on the homeward conference.

The needs of the export sector overshadowed other local interests. But this excessive concentration resulted in some myopia. Freight rate discussions, for example, as we have noted in previous chapters were lopsided. They caused Australians to overlook the elementary fact that outbound rates are not calculated in isolation. They reflect and are compounded of an amalgam of charges including, above all, the two-way employment of the shipping at work. Fiscal measures, or the development of import-replacement industry which results in any imbalance in the demand for shipping creates new problems at the same time that they are solving the old. Where the aim of an economy is to diversify and broaden its industrial base, high inbound freights impinge upon planned diversification. High inbound rates may raise the import price of intermediate and semi-processed items required by the new, expanding industrial structure. At the same time the availability of high inbound rates permits a low or lower outbound rate. The deflection of interest to the export sector at a time when diversification is being pursued may thus run counter to policy intentions. On the reverse side of the coin, if inbound rates are pitched low they not only weaken tariff protection against finished imported goods, they are also productive of proportionately higher outbound rates. This inevitably acts as a disincentive to the export sector in its efforts to compete successfully in oversea markets supplied on an international basis.

Rates of freight apart, Australia's shipping needs also had two conflicting ends. The importer required regular all-the-year round arrivals, the exporter a more seasonal provision of tonnage. As well as for the relatively short concentrated period of peak wheat shipment, the Australian exporter wanted specialised refrigerated vessels for the normal three or four month meat-shipping period. He required fast ships, to give short transit times, and frequent sailings of vessels substantially equipped with refrigerating plant. To the British shipping industry, however, the failure of the Australian economy to provide full cargoes regularly from a small number of large, well-equipped ports often involved one of two solutions, neither acceptable to the Australian exporter. It often meant the provision either of services not considered entirely suited to Australia's needs or the provision of adequate services at a price the Australian exporter could not pay or was unwilling to pay. It also meant the substantial provision of dual-purpose passenger-mail services on which the carriage of high-quality (that is to say, high-freight) cargo formed an essential, indispensable part of the economics of shipping management. It meant also, to choose a second example, a conspicuous lag in the development of the highly specialised chilled beef trade which relied upon an especially short transit time.

The difficulty of reconciling the problems confronting each side of the partnership seem as intractable now as during the inter-war years. Many of the measures currently reported in the press or discussed in Commonwealth parliament have an all-too familiar appearance. The repetitive nature of local comment and complaint extends even to the 'baneful' effect on coastal shipping of the Navigation Act. In recent years the Act has been criticised in terms identical with those used in the 1920s. In the oversea sector local criticism still revolves around the three related aspects of freight rates, tonnage rationalization, and the conference system.

In an attempt to hold down or check rising costs confronting the shipowner (and thus to avoid rate increases) a 'new programme of rationalization of shipping services between Australia and Europe is being worked out by a committee operating under the direction of British and continental lines in Sydney'. So ran a news item in *The Times*.[1] Only the dating of

[1] *The Times* 8 July 1966.

this item has changed. The words used, the object of the programme, and the looked-for results, could all have been transcribed from sources of the 1930s.

Hostility towards the conference system today is as keen as ever. The 'Heine' case in 1964 concerning the admission of Heine Bros. (Australasia) Ltd, to the Japan–Australia conference and the rumoured hints of renewing the teeth of the Australian Industries Preservation Act illustrate the point.[1] In March 1965 the Commonwealth Attorney-General 'denied an allegation that he had ordered the seizure of papers from overseas shipping offices in Australia'. What had happened, he is reported as saying, is that a 'Commonwealth police officer requested certain papers from the Sydney offices of an overseas shipping conference...he was given them'.[2] As this is being written, it is understood that Commonwealth legislation on the conference system is imminent.

Local interest is still to be traced also in the use of the state line for oversea carrying as some check for the conference. Public debate today, moreover, perpetuates the division of opinion on this issue along the same party lines. As noted in the introduction, the present-day successor of the Commonwealth Government Line of Steamers is little used in the oversea sector. Its wider use is sought by the Labour party. During the course of a visit to New Zealand in January 1965 Mr Whitlam, deputy leader of the federal opposition, urged upon his New Zealand audience the desirability of a joint Australian–New Zealand shipping line. That neither country should have a nationally-owned shipping line was 'farcical', he said. A nation's trade was not secure when carried by the fleets of other countries. Mr Whitlam also seized an opportunity in March 1966 to urge the use of the state line in the oversea sector. Mr Whitlam spoke during the second reading debate on the bill to extend the financial powers of the Australian Coastal Shipping Commission, the authority responsible for the management of the Australian National Line. Although the bill was designed merely to increase the commission's borrowing powers the opposition used the debate as an occasion to contrast their own policy, with that of the government, concerning the use of state shipping.

[1] Reported in *Fairplay* 14 May 1964.

[2] *S.M.H.* 4 March 1965.

The government's policy, Mr Whitlam asserted was to limit federal maritime participation to coastal shipping. 'My Party', he continued, 'takes a much broader view of the...Commonwealth Government's obligations with respect to shipping. We state that the Commonwealth should progressively construct, charter and operate sufficient ships to carry an equitable share of Australia's exports and imports.'[1] It is, no doubt, not surprising that a dependent economy should evince a keen interest in its oversea shipping services. In many ways perhaps it serves as a safety valve for producer discontent. But the explanation offered by Viscount Bruce in 1923 about his countrymen seems as true today as it was between the wars:

It is very difficult to make the people of Australia understand that cheap freights are dependent to a great extent upon the possibility of running ship services on a profitable basis, but it is also very difficult to make them understand that an arrangement between shipping companies may possibly have the result of giving them an improved service and cheaper freights.[2]

[1] *C.P.D.* 23 March 1966 (p. 505). [2] *U.K.P.P.* Cmd. 2009, p. 314.

Appendix I

THE 'TON'

The word 'ton' is used in connection with ships and marine cargo in many ways. The following brief description omits much of the detail which a marine surveyor or freight department would consider essential. Any of the standard works on naval architecture, shipbuilding or on cargo stowage will give considerable space to each of the aspects cursorily dismissed in the following paragraphs.

Ships' tons

The *displacement* ton is chiefly quoted for warships. It is the volume of water displaced by a ship and is expressed in cubic feet or in the weight of the water displaced, expressed in tons of 20 cwt. The *deadweight* ton is similarly the weight of a ship; *deadweight capacity* is the tonnage of cargo (in tons of 20 cwt.) which a ship can carry. It is the difference between the displacement of a vessel on her light draught and her loaded draught. The deadweight capacity is chiefly used in connection with tankers, dry-cargo carriers and specialised bulk-carriers. Charter-parties are usually based on deadweight tonnages.

There are two further 'tons', the *gross* and the *net* registered ton. These are the 'measurements' of a ship registered by one of the international classification societies—Lloyd's, Bureau Veritas, American Bureau of Shipping and so on. Measurement tons are measurements of volume expressed in tons of 100 cubic feet. They refer to the internal volume of all enclosed spaces. The *gross* registered tonnage is the total volume. The *net* registered tonnage is the gross minus the non-revenue earning space—engine room, crew accommodation, chart room and so on. The gross registered tonnage figure is normally used to describe passenger liners and in *Lloyd's Register of Shipping* for all vessels. Many official collections of shipping statistics are compiled in terms of net tons, a better yardstick of earning or carrying capacity.

Of less general importance are the two tonnages used as a basis for Suez and Panama Canal dues. These tend to be higher than the registered tonnages in that they include shelter-deck space and other areas normally ignored. Neither canal authority accepts national registration tonnage figures. Instead they issue a tonnage certificate in respect of each ship and thus obviate the need for subsequent 'measuring'. Once cargo has been carried in a particular space on a canal transit this area ever afterwards (until change of ownership) is liable for canal dues.

The three 'tons' chiefly used with merchant shipping, deadweight, gross and net registered, bear no constant relationship to each other. They vary considerably between vessel type and often from vessel to vessel. As an approximation it is generally considered that 160 tons gross equals 100 tons net. The ratio of deadweight to registered varies even more. A passenger liner's net tonnage to deadweight capacity tonnage ratio is often as high as 100:50. With an oil tanker the ratio is as low as 100:250, the relationship usually considered fairly typical with cargo carriers. An example will illustrate the point:

Tonnage	Passenger liner *Orcades*	Oil tanker *Velutina*
Gross	28,164	18,666
Net	15,839	11,391
Deadweight	12,010	28,220
Ratio	177:100:63	164:100:250

Cargo tons are of two kinds: a weight ton of 20 cwt. and a measurement ton of 40 cubic feet. Many items shipped are dense in character with a low bulk-to-weight ratio. Others have a high bulk-to-weight ratio and thus require more hold space than the denser items. A consignment of cigars requires about 180 cubic feet of stowage space in which to load 2,240 lb.: a ton of lead or iron ore on the other hand will stow in 12 to 14 cubic feet. Differences in density have given rise to the convention that cargo which occupies more than about 40 cubic feet per ton of 2,240 lb. is treated, that is to say, charged as 'measurement cargo'. Cargo which occupies 40 cubic feet or less per ton weight is charged as 'deadweight' or 'close' cargo. The importance of these distinctions has encouraged the publication of a number of works devoted to stowage, to the calculation of 'stowage factors' and to the inclusion in various annual marine publications of stowage factors for the commoner cargoes carried. The stowage factor of any commodity is 'the figure which expresses the number of cubic feet which a ton (of 2,240 lb). will occupy in stowage—*not the actual cubic measurement of a ton*'. Stowage factors include an appropriate allowance for stowage and dunnage (materials, permanent or temporary, used to facilitate efficient stowage and to protect cargo). They are based upon the principle of economy of cargo space. (For a full discussion on this aspect see R. E. and O. O. Thomas, *Stowage*, the edition used here is the fourth edition published in 1957.)

Appendix II

The tables listed below are set out in following pages in amplification of summary outlines given in preceding chapters.

1. Vessel size and voyage frequency of oversea arrivals at Fremantle.
2. Exports of refrigerated items.
3. Liner freight rates.
4. Liner voyage account analyses.

Table 1. (*a*) *Vessel size and frequency of oversea entries 1923/4 and 1938/9, tonnage*

	Vessels making each year					
	One voyage		3/4 voyages		5 or more voyages	
Tonnage range	No. of vessels	Gross tonnage	No. of* vessels and voyages	Total tonnage entered by all voyage entries	No. of* vessels and voyages	Total tonnage entered by all voyage entries
			1923/4			
100– 2,999	3	503	—	—	—	—
3,000– 4,999	50	215,461	1 (3)	13,257	—	—
5,000– 7,499	72	415,301	12 (37)	234,513	—	—
7,500– 9,999	28	223,007	4 (12)	104,763	—	—
10,000–12,999	6	67,695	1 (3)	33,543	—	—
13,000–15,999	1	13,144	3 (11)	143,399	7 (40)	595,376
16,000 and over	2	71,500	1 (2)	41,674	3 (17)	276,949
Totals	162	1,016,611	22 (68)	571,149	10 (57)	872,325
			1938/9			
100– 2,999	6	12,393	—	—	—	—
3,000– 4,999	31	145,160	3 (11)	48,923	—	—
5,000– 7,499	71	431,043	12 (41)	264,371	3 (19)	136,143
7,500– 9,999	45	377,058	9 (28)	237,512	5 (32)	283,396
10,000–12,999	12	132,069	4 (14)	150,072	2 (10)	106,155
13,000–15,999	1	15,241	2 (8)	119,488	1 (6)	189,892
16,000 and over	—	—	5 (20)	457,256	7 (35)	843,429
Totals	166	1,112,964	35 (122)	1,277,622	18 (102)	1,459,015

* Total number of voyages shown in brackets.

Table 1. (*b*) *Vessel size and frequency of oversea entries, 1923/4 and 1938/9, percentage*

	% Tonnage of		
		Vessels making	
Tonnage range	All entries	One voyage	More than one voyage
	1923/4		
100– 2,999	0·14	0·05	0·28
3,000– 4,999	14·77	21·19	5·57
5,000– 7,499	38·19	40·85	34·38
7,500– 9,999	23·27	22·92	23·78
10,000–12,999	6·51	6·66	6·30
13,000–15,999	7·86	1·29	17·26
16,000 and over	9·25	7·03	12·42
	100·00	100·00	100·00
	1938/9		
100– 2,999	1·15	1·11	—
3,000– 4,999	7·75	13·04	2·48
5,000– 7,499	27·00	38·72	17·25
7,500– 9,999	26·10	33·88	18·31
10,000–12,999	15·10	11·87	18·43
13,000–15,999	5·90	1·38	10·48
16,000 and over	17·00	—	33·05
	100·00	100·00	100·00

Source: Fremantle Harbour Trust, *Annual Reports.*

Table 2. *Exports of refrigerated items (a) State of shipment*

Commodity and year	% Shipped from N.S.W.	Victoria	Queensland	S.A.	W.A.	Tasmania
Butter						
1922/3	16·7	52·0	25·9	4·4	—	—
1927/8	21·0	32·7	45·7	5·9	—	—
1932/3	18·8	42·2	33·8	4·2	1·0	—
1938/9	10·4	28·5	55·6	3·2	1·8	—
Cheese						
1922/3	3·2	10·1	80·4	6·3	—	—
1927/8	1·1	2·2	96·7	—	—	
1932/3	3·3	28·0	55·3	13·4	—	
1938/9	0·6	37·1	26·4	35·9	—	
Beef						
1922/3	4·9	2·1	85·6	0·7	6·5	
1927/8	2·1	1·2	90·2	—	6·5	
1932/3	4·9	4·5	81·1	—	9·3	
1938/9	5·9	4·6	81·5	—	7·8	
Chilled beef						
1938/9	—	—	98·5	1·5	—	—
Lamb and mutton						
1922/3	37·6	56·1	—	3·7	0·5	—
1927/8	38·1	60·3	—	0·7	0·4	—
1932/3	35·8	56·5	6·2	—	—	—
1938/9	24·1	54·4	2·3	11·9	6·3	—
Apples						
1922/3	1·5	16·0	—	0·6	15·8	66·1
1927/8	1·2	20·4	—	11·7	3·9	62·7
1932/3	6·6	25·4	—	4·5	8·8	54·2
1938/9	0·8	5·3	—	6·0	23·9	63·3

Table 2. *Exports of refrigerated items*
(*b*) *Principal oversea destinations*

Commodity and year	% Shipped to U.K.	Europe excl. U.K.	Eastern countries	Pacific islands
Butter				
1922/3	87·7	—	10·3	—
1927/8	83·6	—	10·5	—
1932/3	92·7	—	5·3	—
1938/9	94·5	—	3·7	—
Cheese				
1922/3	94·8	—	3·4	—
1927/8	95·8	—	2·7	—
1932/3	95·5	—	2·1	—
1938/9	96·9	—	1·9	—
Beef				
1922/3	73·4	15·5	2·6	3·4
1927/8	55·5	29·2	4·7	5·9
1932/3	80·6	7·6	3·5	4·1
1938/9	88·7	1·8	3·0	0·7
Chilled beef				
1938/9	99·9	—	—	—
Lamb and mutton				
1922/3	97·0	0·2	1·1	0·4
1927/8	87·2	2·9	4·4	1·6
1932/3	96·8	1·0	1·2	0·3
1938/9	97·1	0·3	1·4	0·3
Apples				
1922/3	96·4	—	—	—
1927/8	76·3	21·3	—	—
1932/3	77·2	19·7	—	—
1938/9	81·6	15·1	—	—

APPENDIX II

Table 3. *Liner freight rates*

For each commodity listed below the opening rate in the third quarter of 1922 is given followed by the variations subsequently recorded. Variations are shown by index numbers (third quarter of 1922 = 100) for the first month of the quarter wherein the variation took place. The normal 10% cash discount allowed to shippers within the A.O.T.A. agreement has been ignored as also are the special discounts occasionally given and mentioned in our discussion above on freight variations.

Wool greasy, per pound

July 1922 $1\frac{1}{4}$*d.* + 5%	100
October 1925	90
April 1926	81
April 1932	86
July 1933	81
July 1937	72
October 1939	114

Butter, per box of 56 pounds

July 1922 5*s.*	100
October 1924	90
April 1926	80
July 1933	74
October 1939	100

Cheese, per pound

July 1922 $1\frac{1}{2}$*d.*	100
January 1923	75
October 1924	66
April 1926	59
July 1933	54
October 1939	91

Beef, per pound

July 1922 $1\frac{1}{8}$*d.*	100
April 1923	88
October 1925	75
April 1926	66
July 1933	55
October 1939	89

Lamb, per pound

July 1922 $1\frac{1}{2}$*d.*	100
October 1924	92
April 1926	84
July 1933	75
October 1939	108

Mutton, per pound

July 1922 $1\frac{3}{8}$*d.*	100
October 1922	91
October 1923	82
April 1926	73
July 1933	66
October 1939	118

Apples, per bushel case

July 1922 6*s.*	100
October 1922	84
January 1923	75
October 1923	66
April 1926	59
October 1939	84

Source: *Quarterly Summary of Statistics* and *S.M.H.* to correct occasional errors in the *Summary*.

Table 4. *Liner voyage account analyses (% distribution of disbursements)*

	1923/4 (%)	1932/3 (%)	1938/9 (%)
SERVICE A			
Overheads			
Administration	4·19	3·72	6·20
Depreciation	15·31	18·00	15·34
Miscellaneous	1·47	2·79	1·90
Running costs			
Fuel	21·40	17·17	16·43
Wages	7·31	7·42	9·47
Other crew costs	5·87	4·62	3·80
Stores and repairs	7·64	6·52	6·81
Canal dues	5·55	8·24	7·29
Port charges	4·19	6·35	5·57
Insurance	8·36	1·16	1·41
Charges against revenue			
Commissions	4·78	5·72	7·10
Victualling	4·72	4·13	6·51
Stevedoring	6·40	6·82	7·04
Other cargo charges	4·13	7·26	5·58
SERVICE B			
Overheads			
Administration	2·07	3·15	—
Depreciation	16·77	24·33	—
Miscellaneous	0·28	2·35	—
Running costs			
Fuel	18·83	15·24	—
Wages	13·18	7·22	—
Other crew costs	3·97	2·64	—
Stores and repairs	10·56	6·18	—
Canal dues	—	8·53	—
Port charges	6·12	5·54	—
Insurance	6·81	0·96	—
Charges against revenue			
Commissions	2·57	3·88	—
Victualling	4·69	2·17	—
Stevedoring	8·21	10·28	—
Other cargo charges	4·23	7·03	—

Table 4 (*cont.*)

	1923/4 (%)	1932/3 (%)	1938/9 (%)
SERVICE C			
Overheads			
Administration	8·72	8·58	8·82
Depreciation	5·46	11·34	10·68
Miscellaneous	1·33	3·52	2·21
Running costs			
Fuel	23·30	15·85	15·05
Wages	15·58	16·15	18·47
Provisions	9·85	8·67	9·69
Stores and repairs	15·14	9·46	11·25
Dues	7·98	12·27	10·47
Towage	1·21	1·63	1·20
Insurance	2·92	3·82	2·83
Charges on cargo			
Port and general	2·86	4·36	3·60
Cargo	4·52	4·25	5·31

	1923/4 (%)	1938/9 (%)
	SERVICE D	SERVICE E
Overheads		
Administration	7·14	4·44
Depreciation	6·70	15·68
Miscellaneous	2·51	0·32
Running costs		
Fuel	23·08	14·24
Wages	8·59	6·73
Other crew costs	6·03	1·78
Stores and repairs	9·56	7·96
Canal dues	3·30	0·56
Port charges	8·17	9·68
Insurance	2·01	3·74
Charges against revenue		
Commissions	5·36	6·67
Stevedoring	14·25	19·72
Other cargo charges	2·94	7·52

BIBLIOGRAPHY

OFFICIAL SOURCES

The complete references given to official sources in individual footnotes make it superfluous to list them here. I have pleasure in acknowledging separately, however, the grant of access by the Commonwealth of Australia Department of Shipping and Transport to the unpublished 'Report on Conditions on the Waterfront' (C of A *Archives Office*, BP 107/3).

SERIAL PUBLICATIONS

(Official publications omitted)

Serial publications most frequently consulted or cited are:

Campbell, F. S. (ed.). *Ports, Dues, Charges and Accommodation* (annual publication).

Chamber of Shipping of the United Kingdom. *Annual Reports; The Economist; Fairplay.*

Freemantle Harbour Trust. *Annual Reports; Lloyd's Register.*

Melbourne Harbour Trust. *Annual Reports; Motorship.*

Port of London Authority. *Annual Reports.*

Sydney Harbour Trust. *Annual Reports; Sydney Morning Herald; The Times.*

BOOKS AND ARTICLES

The following list includes some works consulted but not cited in footnote references. The place of publication for books is London unless otherwise stated.

Barnard, A. (ed.). *The Simple Fleece* (Melbourne, 1962).

Bes, J. *Chartering & Shipping Terms* (1951).

Boxer, B. *Israeli Shipping and Foreign Trade* (Chicago, 1957).

Branch, A. E. *The Elements of Shipping* (1964).

Brigden, J. B. *et al. The Australian Tariff—An Economic Enquiry* (The 'Bruce' committee) (Melbourne, 1929).

Burley, K. H. 'The Overseas Trade in New South Wales Coal and the British Shipping Industry, 1860–1914', *Economic Record* vol. 36, pp. 393–413. 'The Organization of the overseas trade in New South Wales Coal, 1860–1914', *Economic Record* vol. 37, pp. 371–81.

Butlin, N. G. *Australian Domestic Product, Investment and Foreign Borrowing, 1861–1938/39* (1962).

Chalmers, H. *World Trade Policies* (Berkeley, 1953).
Chamber of Shipping of the United Kingdom. *Port Facilities of Great Britain* (1930).
Copland, D. B. *Australia in the World Crisis, 1929–1933* (1934).
Copland, D. B. and Janes, C. V. *Australian Trade Policy—A book of documents 1932–1937* (Sydney, 1937).
Dunsdorfs, E. *The Australian Wheat-Growing Industry, 1788–1948* (Melbourne, 1956).
Edwards, C. *Bruce of Melbourne* (1965).
Fayle, C. E. *The War and the Shipping Industry* (1927).
Field, F. V. (ed.). *Economic Handbook of the Pacific Area* (New York, 1934).
Fisher, A. G. B. 'The Balance of Trade between South Africa and Australia', *The South African Journal of Economics* vol. 5, 1–10.
Fitzharding, L. F. *William Morris Hughes* (1964).
Forster, C. *Industrial Development in Australia, 1920–1930* (Canberra, 1964).
Gorter, W. *United States Shipping Policy* (New York, 1956).
Gorter, W. and Hildebrand, G. H. *Pacific Coast Maritime Shipping Industry, 1930–1948* 2 vols. (Berkeley, 1952–4).
Hall, N. F. 'Trade Diversion—An Australian Interlude', *Economica* new series v, 1–11.
Hancock, W. K. *Survey of British Commonwealth Affairs*, vol. II, *Problems of Economic Policy 1918–1939* part I (1940).
Hardy, A. C. & Tyrell, E. *Shipbuilding* (1964).
Hevesy, P. de. *World Wheat Planning and Economic Planning in General* (1940).
Hughes, H. *The Australian Iron and Steel Industry, 1848–1962* (1964).
Hughes, W. M. *Policies and Potentates* (1950).
Hunter, A. *The Economics of Australian Industry* (Melbourne, 1963).
Isserlis, L. 'Tramp Shipping, Cargoes and Freights', *Journal of the Royal Statistical Society*, vol. 101, pp. 53–146.
Johnson, E. R. and Huebner, G. G. *Principles of Ocean Transportation* (New York, 1920).
Kindleberger, C. P. *Foreign Trade and the National Economy* (New Haven, 1962).
King, G. A. B. *Tanker Practice* (1965).
Knowles, K. G. J. C. *Strikes—A Study in Industrial Conflict* (Oxford, 1952).
Kreider, C. J. *The Anglo American Trade Agreement* (Princetown, 1943).
League of Nations *Commercial Policy in the Interwar Period* (Geneva, 1942).

—— *The Course and Phases of the World Economic Depression* (Geneva, 1931).
—— *Europe's Trade* (Geneva, 1941).
—— *Industrialization and Foreign Trade* (Geneva, 1945).
—— *International Trade in Certain Raw materials and Foodstuffs* (Geneva, 1939).
—— *The Network of World Trade* (Geneva, 1942).
Lowndes, A. G. (ed.). *South Pacific Enterprise* (Sydney, 1956).
Mance, H. O. and Wheeler, J. E. *International Sea Transport* (1945).
Marx, D. *International Shipping Cartels* (Princeton, 1953).
Meyer, F. V. *Britain's Colonies in World Trade* (1948).
Milner, I. F. G. *New Zealand's Interests and Policies in the Far East* (Institute of Pacific Relations, New York, 1940).
Mountfield, S. *Western Gateway* (Liverpool, 1965).
Nicholson, D. F. *Australia's Trade Relations*, (Melbourne, 1955).
Oram, R. B. *Cargo Handling and the Modern Port* (Oxford, 1965).
Otterson, J. E. *Foreign Trade and Shipping* (1945).
Page, Earle, *Truant Surgeon* (1963).
Perkins, J. O. N. *Britain and Australia Economic Relationships in the 1950's* (Melbourne, 1962).
Perlman, M. *Judges in Industry* (Melbourne, 1954).
Purbrick, A. B. and Needham, W. R. *Reed's Tables of Distances* (1953).
Quin-Harkin, A. J. 'Imperial airways, 1924–40' *Journal of Transport History* vol. 1, pp. 197–215.
Radius, W. A. *United States Shipping in Transpacific Trade 1922–1938* (Palo Alto, 1944).
Ross, I. C. *Australia and the Far East* (Sydney, 1935).
Sandford, J. *Walter Harper and the Farmers* (Perth, 1955).
Sargent, A. J. *Seaways of the Empire* (1918).
Schedvin, C. B. 'Economic Policy in Depression and Recovery in Australia 1927–1935' (Unpublished Ph.D. thesis, University of Sydney, 1963).
Schonfield, H. J. *The Suez Canal in World Affairs* (1952).
Shepherd, J. *Australia's Interests and Policies in the Far East* (Institute of Pacific Relations, New York, 1940).
Stevens, E. F. *Shipping Practice* (1932).
Sturmey, S. G. *British Shipping and World Competition* (1962).
Svendsen, A. S. *Seeverkehr und Schiffahrtswirtschaft* (Bremen, 1958). [Transl: *Sea Transport and Shipping Economics*]
Thomas, R. E. and O. O. *Stowage: The Properties and Stowage of Cargoes* (4th edition, 1957).
Thorbecke, Erik. *The Tendency Towards Regionalisation in International Trade, 1928–1956* (The Hague, 1960).

Walker, E. R. *Australia in the World Depression* (1933).

Walker, K. F. *Industrial Relations in Australia* (Cambridge, Mass. 1956).

Wellington Harbour Board. *Report of Special Committee on the Flat-Rate System* (Wellington, 1926).

——*Protest Against the Flat-Rate System* (Wellington, 1928).

Wettenhall, R. L. 'Aspects of political control in selected public transport corporations' (Unpublished Ph.D. thesis, Australian National University, 1961).

Woodruff, W. and McGregor, L. *The Suez Canal and the Australian Economy* (Melbourne, 1957).

Worshipful Company of Shipwrights. *Shipbuilding and Ships*(Papers read at the Company's Exhibition 1947).

INDEX